Russian Irrationalism from Pushkin to Brodsky

Russian Irrationalism from Pushkin to Brodsky

Seven Essays in Literature and Thought

Olga Tabachnikova

Bloomsbury Academic
An imprint of Bloomsbury Publishing Inc

B L O O M S B U R Y
NEW YORK · LONDON · NEW DELHI · SYDNEY

Bloomsbury Academic

An imprint of Bloomsbury Publishing Inc

1385 Broadway	50 Bedford Square
New York	London
NY 10018	WC1B 3DP
USA	UK

www.bloomsbury.com

BLOOMSBURY and the Diana logo are trademarks of Bloomsbury Publishing Plc

First published 2015

Library of Congress Cataloging-in-Publication Data
Tabachnikova, Olga, 1967- author.
Russian irrationalism from Pushkin to Brodsky : seven essays in literature and thought /
Olga Tabachnikova.
pages ; cm
Includes index.
ISBN 978-1-4411-7120-7 (hb : alk. paper) 1. Russian literature–Philosophy. 2. Irrationalism
(Philosophy) in literature. 3. Russian literature–History and criticism. I. Title.
PG2944.T33   2015
891.709–dc23
2014040081

ISBN: HB: 978-1-4411-7120-7
ePub: 978-1-4411-0258-4
ePDF: 978-1-4411-0995-8

Typeset by Newgen Knowledge Works (P) Ltd., Chennai, India
Printed and bound in the United States of America

To the memory of my father Mark Tabachnikov, a man of great wisdom and joy, without whom the world is so much smaller.

Тьмы низких истин мне дороже нас возвышающий обман . . .
*[The lofty illusion which elevates us is dearer to me than the darkness of
low truths . . .]*

Aleksandr Sergeevich Pushkin

Contents

Acknowledgements

Personal

I am especially grateful to my colleagues Aleksandr Medvedev of Tiumen, Natalia Vinokurova and Olga Stukalova of Moscow and Jörg Schulte of Köln for their help and support – in their valuable comments, insights and discussions as well as technical matters.

Institutional acknowledgements

The author gratefully acknowledges the financial support of the Leverhulme Trust and the University of Bristol (Russian Department) during the years 2009–11 (Leverhulme Early Career Fellowship).

Great literature walks on the edge of the irrational

V. Nabokov

There is no doubt – I have to justify myself. The only question is – what to begin with: the form or content . . .

Lev Shestov, *Apotheosis of Groundlessness*

A Word of Caution

When my 10-year-old daughter complained about the emotional hardship of life, I asked her – do you think it would have been better if man had only intellect, and no feelings? She thought for a second and replied – it would have been easier, but then you would not even be able to appreciate that it is easier . . .

By the same token, when my 5-year-old son asked me about the biggest number, I reminded him that he knew very well that there was no such thing, as he could always add one to obtain a bigger number still. So he exclaimed: 'But if there is no end, then there is infinity!' I nodded and he cried out bitterly: 'Oh, how much I dislike this!'

I see no better way to precede this discussion on irrationalism than to quote these sentiments of my children. Because intuitively, arguable as it may be, one often feels that irrationalism, whether Russian or not, stems from the restricted nature of our reason, and is conceived in that unbridgeable gap between 'mind' and 'soul', in that darkness of our being where reasoning logic wrestles with our emotional strivings, where finite is confronting the infinite – life meets death, joy meets tragedy . . .

This book is an attempt to peep into the abyss. Any such attempt is risky and – one might say – irrational, since 'it is impossible to embrace the un-embraceable', as ironically pointed out by Koz'ma Prutkov[1] – an invented persona, a phantom, a mockery of excessive rationalism – so typically Russian, one might exclaim. And this exclamation takes us even further to the edge: not only is this topic so vast that it would take longer than a life-time – not to complete the task, but at least to saddle up the horse – but even more seriously, it is potentially a dangerous topic ('I wouldn't want to be in your shoes' has been – quite sensibly – a reaction of many people to this scholarly endeavour). For it encroaches upon the murky waters of national character, mentality,

---

[1] Kozma Prutkov (Козьма Прутков) was a fictional character invented by Aleksei Tolstoi and his cousins: Aleksandr, Aleksei and Vladimir Zhemchuzhnikov. As explained in Chapter 7, using Prutkov as an imaginary author they produced a highly satirical account of the bureaucratic and authoritarian Russian regime of the 1850s and 1860s.

cultural identity, etc. – the stereotypes simultaneously deceptive and revealing, the creatures able to blow up the fragile system of political correctness. Moreover, the concept of irrationalism itself is so blurred and ill-defined that approaching it with any kind of rigour is bound to cause caustic laughter and contempt in many quarters. Yet, it is as ever tempting to wake up the dragon. Because only little steps, only successive approximations can bring us closer to the unattainable. Of course there is, as ever, no victory for Don Quixote's ridiculous crusade. Still, others may be tempted to follow in his footsteps, whatever they may think of his doomed struggle. Walking on an obscure and dangerous path is always an unrewarding, but fascinating task.

Thus: you have been warned . . .

Introduction

There is, in the air, a striving towards extremism, towards the irrational. Maybe it is because the 'rational' appears so pathetic . . . 'If the light within you is darkness . . .'

Father Alexander Shmeman

Russia, once compared to a giant sphinx, has been traditionally considered in the Anglophone world, as a culturally alien, often threatening, and enigmatic entity. While being recognizably European, Russian culture at the same time displays some distinctly Oriental and mystical features, one of the most idiosyncratic of which is Russian irrationalism. It revealed itself in philosophy, theology and the arts (most notably literature) taking shape in the protopope Avvakum's autobiography in the seventeenth century and the teachings of Grigorii Skovoroda a century later; developing into Fedor Dostoevsky's messianic irrationalism, Lev Shestov's critique of speculative philosophy and, through various modernist and post-modernist intellectual and cultural movements, to the present day. The history of Russian irrationalism and its socio-cultural impact on the life of the country and the outside world are still to be comprehensively studied. This is essential, in particular, for understanding contemporary Russian society and its development, with all the implications of this for the West.[1]

While the subject is treated to a greater or lesser degree in author-specific works, for example on Dostoevsky,[2] there is an absence even of monographs devoted specifically to irrationalism in any particular author.[3] Cultural histories of Russia likewise treat

---

[1] While being extremely fruitful in the last 200 years in the fields of philosophy, theology and the arts, Russian irrationalism can also be regarded as having given rise to such ugly extremes as militant nationalism on the one hand, and backward anti-scientific beliefs on the other. In contemporary Russia both reached a level where urgent measures were required. Thus, for example, the First Sceptics' Congress (an international symposium) took place in Moscow in October 2001, organized by the Russian Academy of Sciences, Moscow State University and Russian Humanist Society 'against anti-science, charlatanism, and irrationalism in Russia'; similarly a conference 'Future of Russia under the Threat of Fascism' gathered in Moscow in May 2006 with more than 150 representatives of different NGOs, youth associations, democratic political parties, independent anti-fascist groups, ethnic associations, experts, journalists and cultural figures taking part.

[2] Recent examples include Malcolm Jones, *Dostoevsky and the Dynamics of Religious Experience*, London: Anthem Press, 2005, and Pattison and Thompson (eds), *Dostoevsky and the Christian Tradition*, Cambridge: Cambridge University Press, 2001.

[3] A rare exception is T. R. N. Edwards, *Three Russian Writers and the Irrational: Zamyatin, Pil'nyak, and Bulgakov*, Cambridge: Cambridge University Press, 1982.

irrationalism as a theme rather than the dominant.[4] Thus our understanding of Russia's socio-cultural history is missing a vital key which may be able to unlock various stereotypes, including the famous enigma of the 'Russian soul'. Hence this book – as an attempt to mark the path.[5] At first ambitiously conceived as an integral whole, it was eventually defeated by the enormous vastness of the task, and rendered itself into a collection of essays, being stepping stones towards the horizon of a comprehensive picture. Our primary interest in this book is to study the ways in which irrationalism manifests itself in Russian literature and thought, especially that, in Russia, literature lies at the heart of culture; it is 'a magic mirror that speaks back', and, as part of Russian art, it 'has more power over life than life has over art'.[6]

Our chronological focus is on the last two centuries, as implied by the title of the book, although it is hardly possible to study modernity without taking a look back at the roots concealed in the past. Moreover, whether our focus is on a national culture or on an individual mind, a place within those for both rationalist and irrationalist modes of perception and existence is, most likely, not a discrete combination, but an inseparable blend.

Our aim thus is to distil and analyse manifestations of the irrational in Russian literature and thought, bearing in mind the elusive nature of our understanding of the concept as such. It is indeed clearly multifaceted, and one can talk about it in a variety of terms, including philosophical, cultural, social and religious, and ranging to such manifestations of irrationalism as a semiotics of individual behaviour, and, generally, a particular mind-set.

On top of that, there are two separate issues at stake here: irrationalism per se, common to all humans, and its Russian branch. Although the branch of the same tree, it is often coloured differently, and gives different blossoms and different fruits; and thus deserves a special study. Below I will try to explain why. But first, we must clarify the concept of irrationalism per se.

*   *   *

I want to say that vanity is in fact a very touching human feature. And this is true about each and every one of us. Because even the name that we gave ourselves some time ago: homo sapiens, a Wise Man [in Russian: 'A Man of Reason' – Человек Разумный] – is, in fact, such an exaggeration, that even in it alone there is plenty of comic and unjustified vanity. And if we look closely into what actually is the subject of pride (open or hidden) of each of us, then a wave of tenderness and compassion for humanity becomes simply overwhelming.

Igor Guberman, *Kniga stranstvii* (*The Book of Wanderings*)

---

4   For example, James P. Scanlan (ed.), *Russian Thought After Communism: The Recovery of a Philosophical Heritage*, Armonk, NY: M. E. Sharpe, 1994; although James Billington's classic cultural history, *The Icon and the Axe*, does give the irrational full presence in its treatment of 1,000 years of Russian culture and politics.

5   See also Olga Tabachnikova (ed.), *Mystery Inside Enigma: Facets of Russian Irrationalism between Art and Life*, Amsterdam-New York: Rodopi, forthcoming in 2015.

6   Richard Peace, *Russian Literature and the Fictionalisation of Life*, Hull: The University of Hull, 1976, p. 16.

Concept of (Russian) irrationalism: Methodological problems

The difficulty begins right at the beginning: with definition, and soon involves a whole range of further questions. When we use the term of irrationalism or its derivatives, we do not feel the need to nail down our meaning, as we obviously presume some commonly shared understanding of it. Thus the literary critic Efim Etkind in his essay on Tolstoy writes about Pierre Bezukhov's agonizing thoughts on the prospect of marrying or not marrying Helen, that his final decision seems to be negative, but 'the final phrase contains an instinctive refutation, *which is so strong precisely because it is irrational*' (italics mine). My students too characterized Bezukhov as 'more irrational than Bolkonsky', because 'his actions are often spontaneous'. They deemed Pechorin also irrational because he was 'contradictory', with his actions conflicting with his words. Spontaneous, contradictory, based on instinct rather than thought, defying logic . . . But is instinct necessarily separated from reason and opposed to it? And whose logic are we talking about? There are, in fact, many more questions on the way to formulating our understanding of the irrational and irrationalism. Indeed, rather irrationally, the need to be rigorous, to take a rational, conceptual approach to irrationalism poses more questions than it answers.

A formal definition pertaining to philosophy states that irrationalism is 'a fundamental approach to the world where any attempt at a conceptual understanding of the universe is ignored or deemed futile, and is replaced by the intuitive and unconscious'.[7] In other words, it is a stance which stresses 'the dimensions of instinct, feeling, and will as over and against reason'.[8] This is problematic in more than one way. First, some important instances of what appears to be irrationalism in Russian culture are left overboard – for example, early Slavophiles, who, while displaying irrationalism in various ways, such as their romantic cult of the feeling and deep affiliation with the Russian patristic teachings, at the same time respected reason, and especially religious thought. If, on the other hand, we define irrationalism by constructing a formal logical negation of the concept of rationalism (much better understood, in comparison), we arrive at a less radical formula, but equally of little help: irrationalism then must be 'a philosophical position which denies reason its supreme and sole role in acquiring knowledge and testing the truth'. This lands us at a 'normal' human vision which combines reasoning with intuition. To accommodate the above, irrationalism must be a stance which denies or restricts the role of reason in cognition in favour of the intuitive appreciation of the universe; and the extent of the role which reason plays can be (apparently at our discretion) scaled up or down, to avoid the result becoming all-inclusive or too restrictive. Also, akin to amoralism and immoralism – where the former simply ignores or denies morality, while the latter actively opposes it – we can talk of irrationalism which ignores or denies reason, as well as of anti-rationalism

---

[7] The following dictionaries and encyclopaedias have been consulted: Encyclopedic Dictionary by F. A. Brockhaus and I. A. Efron, Modern Explanatory Dictionary of the Russian language by Efremova, Small Academic Dictionary, New Philosophical Dictionary, Great Soviet Encyclopedia, Ushakov's Explanatory Dictionary, Great Encyclopedic Dictionary, Modern Encyclopedia, Wikipedia.

[8] Britannica Online Encyclopedia. See <http://www.britannica.com/EBchecked/topic/294716/irrationalism> [accessed 31 July 2012].

which militantly opposes it and fights against it. These are hardly ever delineated, and philosophers like Lev Shestov, who struggled against reason and rationalism, are still labelled irrationalist rather than anti-rationalist. But even more significantly, as was mentioned above, it is not clear what is meant by reason as opposed to intuition, and – as we shall discuss shortly – whether such an opposition is justified.

There is also a challenging problem of accommodating both perspectives on Russian irrationalism – from within Russia and from the outside. This reveals an interesting, but deceptive paradigm. Yurii Lotman stresses the need to treat foreign impressions of another culture as coded texts. It is only the appropriate decoding which can reveal to us the truth as well as errors inherent in such outsiders' observations, and moreover to draw valuable data from the very character of the misunderstandings: 'While observing the same reality a foreigner and a native create different texts at least because of opposite directions of their interests. A native notices deviations from the norm, but not the norm itself, as the latter is obvious for him and not worthy of attention. By contrast, a foreigner perceives the norm itself as strange and worthy of notice, whereas when he encounters an excess his inclination is to perceive and describe it as a custom'.[9] Not to mention a lack of appreciation of multi-layered complexity of another's culture, with its hidden irony, ambivalence and figurative meanings which an outsider can easily take literally.

This prompts yet another key question: is there such a thing as Russian irrationalism at all, or is this concept simply a result of a foreign misinterpretation of Russian culture? Or perhaps, then, it is an invention of Russians themselves for whatever self-fashioning or defensive reasons? After all Russia is seen from the West as suffering from the complex of exceptionalism (исключительность), manifested in numerous messianic sentiments of the country's unique way and a role of saviour for Western Europe and beyond, the ideas of the third Rome, Tiutchev's famous and by now hackneyed 'Russia cannot be understood with the mind alone' ('Умом Россию не понять'), Blok's 'Skythians', and many more similar instances, with phrases asserting national uniqueness (scattered through classical Russian literature and grating on the taste of the Other, be it Western Europe or Russia's immediate neighbours): 'it is only we Russians who . . ', 'it is only here in Russia that . . ', up to the self-mocking lines about the Soviet period: 'on top of everything else, we also make space rockets, dam the river Enisei, and are ahead of the whole planet in ballet'.[10]

Does this suggest that the concept of irrationalism is culturally dependent? The point is that even if we were to restrict ourselves to just one culture, and use our intuitive understanding of irrationalism, which at least gives an illusion of being commonly shared, it soon becomes clear that we are still nowhere near a firm ground. Indeed, what we encounter is essentially an intrinsic relativity (or subjectivity) of the concept. As Andrei Stepanov, a Chekhov scholar from St Petersburg, notes about the

---

[9] Yurii Lotman, 'K voprosu ob istochnikovedcheskom znachenii vyskazyvanii inostrantsev o Rossii', in *Izbrannye statii v 3-kh tomakh*, vol. 3, Tallinn: Aleksandra, 1993, p. 138. Translation of this and of all the other quotations in this book is mine, unless otherwise stated.

[10] An excerpt from a version of the song by Yuri Vizbor 'Rasskaz tekhnologa Petukhova'. In Russian: 'ещё мы делаем ракеты, перекрываем Енисей, а также в области балета мы впереди планеты всей!'

writer, 'Chekhov [has] [. . .] an understanding of the reciprocal relationship between the rational and irrational. Chekhov's characters, when they act rationally from their own point of view, continually perform deeds which are completely irrational from other people's viewpoints'.[11] And further on Stepanov talks of '. . . mutual transitions of the meaningful into meaningless and back again . . .', when 'initially rational intentions' lead to an irrational outcome.[12]

Thus, speaking more generally, our understanding of meaningful and meaningless – as well as of rational and irrational – depends crucially on our vantage point. In Neil Cornwell's book on the absurd in literature the very first epigraph says, 'We are overwhelmed by a flood of words, by polemics, by the assault of the virtual, which today can create a kind of opaque zone . . . The question of sin has been displaced from the centre by a question that is perhaps more serious – the question of meaning and meaninglessness, of the absurd' (Paul Ricoeur).[13] Clearly this displacement of essentially the question of ethics by the question of meaning and absurd is characteristic of the modern era, and already at the turn of the nineteenth century Lev Shestov wrote: 'there ends for man the thousand-year reign of "reason and conscience"; a new era begins – that of "psychology"'.[14] According to Lidia Ginzburg, it is paradoxes of human psyche (and/or the acute realization of them) that determine this new 'era of psychology' – that is to say, when the predictable linearity of emotions – within which a hero of Karamzin, for instance, would rejoice in marrying his beloved and grieve upon the death of his relatives – got reversed (when everything started to happen against the accepted common sense), the 'psychology began'.[15]

Furthermore, the same clashing encounter of meaningful and meaningless is what Yurii Lotman distinguishes as the main plot-creating aspect of Turgenev's prose. For him Turgenev's novels play in Russian literature of the nineteenth century a demythologizing, sobering up role (what was often said about Chekhov!). 'For Turgenev it is precisely heroism which asserts the inevitability of a senseless denouement', whereas 'a mythological plot is constructed on the events being non-accidental and meaningful', for 'the meaning of a myth is to ascend the chaotic accidentality of empirical life to a logical and meaningful model'.[16] Those characters of Turgenev whose life loses its meaning continue to live, while those for whom it has gained a high meaning – die. 'Although the meaninglessness and purposelessness of an exploit not only does not diminish, but even increases for Turgenev its value – still the value of the exploit does not invest it with meaning'.[17] 'The effect of meaninglessness – Lotman continues – is

[11] Andrei Stepanov, 'Lev Shestov on Chekhov', in Olga Tabachnikova (ed.), *Anton Chekhov Through The Eyes Of Russian Thinkers: Vasilii Rozanov, Dmitrii Merezhkovskii and Lev Shestov*, London-New York-Delhi: Anthem Press, 2010, p. 171.

[12] Ibid., p. 172.

[13] See Neil Cornwell, *The Absurd in Literature*, Manchester: Manchester University Press, 2006.

[14] Lev Shestov, 'Dostoevsky i Nitzshe', in *Sochineniia v 2 tomakh*, Tomsk: Vodolei, 1996, p. 352. In translation (by Spencer Roberts), <http://www.angelfire.com/nb/shestov/dtn/dn_7.html> [accessed 12 February 2014].

[15] See Lidia Ginzburg, *Literatura v poiskakh realnosti*, Leningrad, 1987, p. 177.

[16] Yurii Lotman, 'Siuzhetnoe prostranstvo russkogo romana XIX stoletiia', in *Izbrannye statii*, op. cit., vol. 3, p. 105.

[17] Ibid.

created by the look from outside, from a different world, from the position of an observer who does not understand or does not accept the motivation, aims and logic of that world into which he bursts or which he observes. For Pavel Petrovich Kirsanov [from "Fathers and Sons"] an infusoria, swallowing a particle of dust under the microscope is meaningless.[18] Similarly, for Bazarov the 'old men Kirsanovs' are meaningless and, by the same token, the frogs which he dissects and infusoria which he observes have meaning only in the perspective of his own goals – to see 'what's going on inside it'. What are the frog's own goals and whether they include the prospect of being dissected is of no consequence to him, in the same way as the inner meaning of nature is equally of no consequence. He ignores it when declaring nature a workshop rather than a temple. 'Nature, in its turn, ignores his goals, rendering his plans meaningless. At the same time Bazarov's behaviour is meaningless from the point of view of a peasant who perceives Bazarov as a jester or fool'.[19]

Thus both within the Absurd and within the Irrational (of which Absurd seems to be the 'logical' end) the relativity principle plays a crucial role, because it is precisely the system of coordinates, the vantage point, the side we are coming from that determines our conclusions. This difficulty can, in fact, be at the same time methodologically inspiring, for it suggests that irrationalism arises from the inability (or unwillingness) of its observer to construct a model of the observed, to explain it by the means of an algorithm, from the position of the logic available to him, or, in other words, to find a suitable coordinate system from which the irrational phenomenon would make a rational sense.

This implies that rather than defying or ignoring the voice of reason, irrationalism encompasses those actions and phenomena whose logic we, as observers (and sometimes even as perpetrators! – when our own (re-)actions, as it were, are beyond our comprehension), cannot grasp. It emerges out of discrepancy, out of conflict which exposes the limitations of a purely rationalist enquiry – be it a tragic conflict of human finiteness and divine infinity or of a fantasy genre delivered through the incompatible with it rationalist discourse, causing the viewer to hesitate 'with which key, – mystical or positivistic, he must unlock the narrative'.[20] This also means that irrationalism occurs in the situations where our – either as individuals, or as mankind – rational faculties seem of no help.

Given the relative nature of the concept of irrationalism, it appears that insisting on a rigorous formal definition of it would be counter-productive. The way forward therefore is to be selective, but also virtually to succumb to subjectivity and to work on individual cases (like medicine or art do), while keeping in view the broader framework (like science does). This broader framework tells us of some general features of the concept of irrationalism, based in particular on its evolution and helps to draw a distinction between Western and Russian cases.

[18]   Ibid.
[19]   Ibid., p. 106.
[20]   See Oleg Kovalov (explaining the theory of Tsvetan Todorov), 'The Irrational in Russian Cinema', in Olga Tabachnikova (ed.), *Mystery Inside Enigma: Facets of Russian Irrationalism between Art and Life*, op. cit.

On faith and reason in Russia and in the West

. . . That victory, when faith defeats reason, involves an immense battle.

Nikolai Kuzansky

. . . following exclusively the irrational way is dangerous, for it can lead to the illusoriness and unreliability. By the same token, the rational is not always negative. It can be fiery, it can have Sophian wisdom within it, and transmit some all-understanding, all-embracing element.

Valentin Silvestrov

A Russian person is stupid not because he is stupid, but because he does not respect reason.

Fazil Iskander, 'Poet'

Although the principal rise of the irrationalist trend in world history can be measured from the time of the Enlightenment, as a radical reaction against it, the origins of the irrationalist approach to the world in the form of mysticism, intuition, instinct and so forth are evident from the time of antiquity, together with a continuous wrestling of two opposing traditions. As demonstrated in the volume under my editorship,[21] whether we talk, along the lines of Nietzsche, of the elemental and passionate Dionysian tradition as opposed to the Apollonian principle of classical ordered beauty, or, following Erich Auerbach, divide culture into two fundamental branches – arising either from the symbolism of the Old Testament or the ratio-based ancient Greek philosophy; or, like Lev Shestov, radically confront reason and faith, as epitomized by Athens and Jerusalem respectively, or consider Aristotelian versus Platonic philosophical heritages, or any further variations of a rationalist and irrationalist variety, there is little doubt that both constitute an intrinsic part of human history and human nature itself.

Using the words of Joseph Brodsky, 'here, on Earth, all forms of life, from tenderness to frenzy, are just conformism',[22] and principal human striving can be perceived as a perpetual attempt to find protection (or escape) from the surrounding chaos, to invest it with meaning, that is to find law and order within it, which one might also call the Truth. And one could perhaps regard both science and religion as a result of this human struggle against chaos and accidentality. As it were, the goal is the same, but the means are different. However, it would be a misleading simplification to regard science as resulting from a rational outlook, and religion – from the irrational, and, along the same lines, to oppose reason and faith. Yet, despite it being too crude a model of reality,

---

[21] For further discussions of these ideas see the chapters by Odesskaia, Ivashkin, Olaszek and McCabe in Olga Tabachnikova (ed.), *Mystery Inside Enigma: Facets of Russian Irrationalism between Art and Life*, op. cit.

[22] Iosif Brodsky, 'Razgovor s nebozhitelem', in *Forma vremeni. Stikhotvoreniia, esse, piesy*, in 2 vols, Minsk: Eridan, 1992, vol. 1, p. 223. In Russian: '. . . Здесь, на земле, от нежности до умоисступленья все формы жизни есть приспособленье . . .'.

it is precisely this fundamental opposition around which the question of irrationalism traditionally revolves.

Also, there are some important differences in the interplay between faith and reason in Russia and in the West. Looking at them reinforces singling out Russian irrationalism as opposed to its Western equivalent, which emerged largely in opposition to predominantly rationalistic development of Western culture. At the same time it reveals some anthropological constants, common to Russian and Western cultures alike.

Thus, as Svetlana Pogorelaia explains,[23] Ancient Greek philosophy was based on the primacy of reason and rationality, and its principal purpose was to discover the inner logic of their development. The influence of this philosophy on Christianity was rapid, with the question of faith and reason remaining painful throughout. This was manifested in the attempts of Clement of Alexandria and Justin the martyr to merge faith with reason already in the first centuries of Christianity. Later, via St Augustine, this unity became part of Western scholastic thought, and in the Middle Ages the problem of faith and reason stood among the principal ones for scholastic theology and philosophy. Based on this tradition growing from the first centuries of Christian Church, St Thomas Aquinas created his theoretical system (Thomism, later evolving into neo-Thomism) which aimed to resolve this theoretical problem for Catholicism by finding harmony between faith and reason. Yet the dispute on the relationship between these two entities has remained both principal and uneasy in Western Christianity. Starting from the post-medieval times, associated with the names of Descartes, Spinoza and Leibnitz, and especially from the Enlightenment era, classical philosophy began most decisively to identify the world with rationality per se, cleansing mind from any irrational elements. This tendency was met with opposition. However, these opposing voices in a sense only continued Aquinas's striving for harmonization by their reconciliatory attempts, even if they (like, say, Rousseau, Goethe and Schlegel) wished to oppose to reason the forces of life itself. Thus they essentially remained in the framework of the classical (i.e. rationalistic) type of philosophizing.

However, starting from antiquity, there developed the Dionysian (an instinct-based tendency) in the rationalist culture of Ancient Greece, which can be viewed as an early form of irrationalism. Philosophically irrationalism emerged in the form of Scepticism as a kind of heresy against the rationalist constructions of ancient philosophy. In the medieval times it was Scholasticism, mentioned above, which showed resistance to the concept of rational understanding of God inherited from antiquity, and promoted instead a mystical observation of the Divine. Scholasticism thus provided a philosophical foundation for Mysticism (conceptions of Bernard de Clairvaux and Meister Eckhart) which served, like Scepticism in philosophy, as a heretical diversion within orthodox Christianity with its respect to Divine Reason.

With the growth of secularism, irrationalism gained various functions of mysticism and became a secular form of heresy directed against fundamental principles of Western culture – intellectual, moral and aesthetic. This explains in sociological terms

---

[23] See Svetlana Pogorelaia's doctoral dissertation, 'Zapadnoevropeiskii irratsionalizm kak factor dukhovnoi zhizni Rossii' (subject: philosophy), Moscow, 2003.

the strengthening of the irrationalist stance in the eighteenth century and its gradual evolution into the nineteenth century as a separate philosophical school which gained momentum and reached its peak in the twentieth century. Generally, after the Middle Ages, the irrationalist tendency has taken shape in a number of conceptions and schools which emerged as a reaction against the rationalism of the Enlightenment, against the positivist cult of scientific knowledge.

From a theological perspective the source of the opposition between faith and reason can be traced to Original Sin, viewed as a tragic split within a human being, when the primordial (Divine) wholeness broke up into mind and soul, ethics and aesthetics, spirit and body, leading to further oppositions such as the one above – between faith and reason, and its derivatives such as between art and science and so on. As Lev Shestov believed, the Fall was 'a choice of an inferior faculty with its passion for a distinguo and for general ideas, with pairs of opposites: good, evil; true, untrue; possible, impossible. [. . .] the fruits of the forbidden tree could just as well be called synthetic judgments a priori'.[24] Thus, in Biblical terms, if one adopts the above perspective, it is possible to view irrationalism and rationalism as coined at the very beginning of humanity, at the tragic Fall.

According to the Russian Orthodox tradition, which understands the soul as a sum-total of all spiritual activity, Original Sin resulted in a division within human nature, whereby human soul, which was designed to be simple and holistic, split into three abilities perceived by man as independent: mind, emotions and free will, and it became human task to reunite them into one Divine whole. The soul in its wholeness does not know a contradiction between the above three faculties, and it is the ability of the soul to be holistic which is called faith. This unique position that faith occupies in Russian Orthodoxy in relation to other human abilities eliminates the potential conflict between faith and reason. This is best summarized in the words of Saint Maxim the Confessor (Maksim Ispovednik): 'Faith is the highest kind of cognition – it exceeds the mind, but does not contradict it'. By the same token, as Tatiana Chumakova points out, there is a specific ontological epistemology, characteristic not only of Old Russian thought, but also of Russian religious philosophy, which results in the concept of the 'suffering reason' – reason involved with the heart ('the heart with thought') – clearly demonstrated in the works of Tsar Ivan IV (Ivan the Terrible). Hence, Russian striving to 'animate' reason, to deal with it only in the context of 'living life', to reject abstractions, has deep roots.

In other words, in the Russian case we may be dealing with a different kind of reason, one which is inseparable from feelings and which craves the heavenly truth, the ideal, but within the shell of the 'living life'. Kireevsky, for instance, argued that a Russian Orthodox believer can arrive at atheism, but not (in contrast to a Western Christian) through a natural evolution of mind.[25]

---

[24] Czeslaw Milosz on Lev Shestov from 'Shestov, or the Purity of Despair', in Czeslaw Milosz, *Emperor of the Earth. Modes of Eccentric Vision*, Berkeley–Los Angeles–London: University of California Press, 1977, pp. 99–119, p. 107.

[25] See I. Kireevsky, 'O neobkhodimosti i vozmozhnosti novykh nachal dlia filosofii' (1856) in I. V. Kireevsky, *Polnoe sobranie sochinenii v dvukh tomakh*, ed. by M. Gershenzon, Moscow, 1911, reprinted by Gregg International, Hampshire, 1970, p. 250.

Along the same lines, Oliver Smith noted that 'the spirit that lives in much Russian thought is not a fixed pattern (an "ethos" that is passed on through a given canon) but a pathos that perpetually treads water between the unordered irrationality of individual experience and the concordant rationality of absolute comprehension. And the history of Russian thought is one not of ideas but of persons'. Even the attempts, especially wide-spread in the nineteenth century, to borrow Western European rationalism and transplant it onto Russian soil, were marked by a distinctly Russian pathos. Thus Dmitrii Galkovsky speaks of the intrinsic irrationalism inherent in the very rationalism of Russians: 'In all probability, somewhere in the subconscious of every Russian there is a barbaric aspiration to Western learning, rationality. Moreover, rationality itself is perceived by Russians as something extremely irrational, not grasped by the mind, that provides secret knowledge. Amongst the schismatics there was a superstition that he who reads the whole Bible and understands it completely, would go mad. Stankiewicz read Schelling, Kant and Hegel with the same feeling'.[26] At the same time, Semen Frank argued that 'The Russian way of thinking is absolutely anti-rationalist. This anti-rationalism, however, is not identical with irrationalism, that is some kind of romantic and lyrical vagueness, a logical disorder of spiritual life. It does not involve either a tendency to deny science or inability to carry out a scientific research'.[27]

At the same time, one has to recognize that any discussions of reason, and, by extension, the problem of the opposition between reason and faith, rest heavily on the definitions of these concepts. And while, as was discussed above, irrationalism gives an impression of being universally understood more or less uniformly, the concept of reason seems, strangely, to be much more ambiguous. In fact, we are dealing here with a terminological minefield resulting from a broad range of interpretations.

A narrow interpretation of reason, which increasingly came to be used as the dominant one, views it as an intellectual instrument detached from other human faculties. Isaiah Berlin, who names Johann Georg Hamann (1730–88) as 'the father of modern European irrationalism, and a crucial forerunner of romanticism and existentialism',[28] describes Hamann's understanding of 'the human faculty of reason' as 'a lamentable, poor, blind, naked thing',[29] an arbitrary theoretical fancy;[30] it is a 'cold reason, arid, hard, with lust for domination, mad pride, ambitious, violent, hating, brutally and implacably egoistic, perverted, avid'.[31] Similarly, the worldly rootless

---

[26] Dmitrii Galkovsky, 'Beskonechnyi tupik', List 3 at <http://fictionbook.ru/author/galkovskiyi_ dmitriyi_evgenevich/beskonechniyyi_tupik/read_online.html?page=3> [accessed 22 January 2012].

[27] Semen Frank, *Russkoe mirovozzrenie*, St Petersburg: Nauka, 1996, p. 165.

[28] See the editorial text by Henry Hardy, in Isaiah Berlin, *The Magus of the North. J.G. Hamann and the Origins of Modern Irrationalism*, Fontana Press: London, 1994, p. 40. This quotation as well as the others in this and the next paragraph are given in Olga Tabachnikova, 'Patterns of European Irrationalism, from Source to Estuary: Johann Georg Hamann, Lev Shestov and Anton Chekhov – on Both Sides of Reason', in Olga Tabachnikova (ed.), *Mystery Inside Enigma: Facets of Russian Irrationalism between Art and Life*, op. cit.

[29] Ibid.

[30] Ibid.

[31] Ibid., 63.

intellect is the arch-deceiver,[32] as it can only dissect, 'disrupt and fragment',[33] and forces a fatal disintegration of a human being into disconnected, lifeless fragments; and abstraction only captivates a living being, forcing man to exist in a straitjacket of invented entities.[34]

By the same token, Lev Shestov, an equally radical and uncompromising opponent of rationalism (only in Russia, at the dawn of modernism), cherished the words of Shatov addressed to Stavrogin in Dostoevsky's *The Possessed* as revealing the helpless nature of human reason in the moral sphere: 'Reason has never been powerful enough to define good and evil or to demarcate good from evil, even approximately; on the contrary, it's always confused them shamefully and pitifully; science has always provided solutions by brute force'.[35] The same charge against reason is expressed by Hamann who claims that 'God is a poet, not a geometer',[36] thereby denying scientific reasoning any creative, imaginative qualities.

Such, rather one-dimensional, understanding of human reason as a purely rationalist faculty was characteristic also of the early Slavophiles, who identified shallow rationalism with Western-European thought. This misconception, as the Russian religious-philosophical historian Vasilii Zenkovsky remarks, was borrowed, ironically, from Western Europe. Indeed, the (derogatory) association of Western culture with rationalism originated in the 'pre-Romantic' period of the eighteenth century in the West itself, and only then was taken for granted by Russian thinkers. 'The fundamental epistemological distinction between reason and mind (рассудок/разум, *Verstand/Vernunft*) of Kant, Fichte, Hegel, Schelling and others got distorted on Russian soil resulting in the identification of rationalism as a phenomenon of general-cultural character with reasoned cognition'.[37] Zenkovsky points to the crucial role of Kant's epistemology in this process, whereby *Verstand* was a function of purely logical operations, while *Vernunft* was a source of ideas.[38]

Olga Sedakova, rising in defence of human reason in all its fullness, warns precisely against such a shallow interpretation of it which treats it merely as 'a function of purely logical operations'. She argues that this aspect of human mind – a critical, analytical, technical reason – 'comprises only a part of what deserves to be called mind; and moreover, it is a lower, marginal, or secondary part. If an intellect of this sort is mistaken for the *whole* mind, this can lead to a real disaster. The space of mind is much greater and deeper, and its central part, its core consists of perception of the *whole*, an interaction with the whole. This precedes any dismantling of the whole

---

[32] Ibid., 43.

[33] Ibid., 41.

[34] Ibid., 83.

[35] F. M. Dostoevsky, 'Besy', in *Polnoe sobranie sochinenii v 30 tomakh*, Leningrad: Nauka, 1982, vol. 10, p. 199. Cited in Lev Shestov, 'O "pererozhdenii ubezhdenii" u Dostoevskogo', in *Umozrenie i otkrovenie*, Paris: YMCA-Press, 1964, p. 193. English version of the text: Fedor Dostoevsky, *Devils*, transl. by M. Katz, Oxford: Oxford University Press, 1992, p. 264.

[36] See Isaiah Berlin, *The Magus of the North. J.G. Hamann and the Origins of Modern Irrationalism*, op. cit., p. 40.

[37] Vasilii Zenkovsky, *Istoriia russkoi filosofii*, Rostov-on-Don: Fenix, 2004, vol. 1, p. 226.

[38] Ibid.

into details and components, any "destruction" and disassembly of it, as if it was a mechanical unit. [. . .] An intellectual activity is diverse, it includes in particular our ability to imagine, to guess without any discussion or analysis, and to observe . . . and many other things'.[39]

Contemplating the same questions, Fazil Iskander elucidates the roots of this conventional one-sided understanding of reason as cold and egotistic. He observes that 'in the whole of world literature, the most piercing, most startling depictions of people with beautiful soul are necessarily linked to these people being mentally handicapped. Of this type is Don Quixote by Servantes, prince Myshkin from Dostoevsky's "The Idiot", "The Old-World Landowners" of Gogol, "A simple soul" by Flaubert, Gerasim in Turgenev's "Mumu" and Matrena in Solzhenitsyn's "Matryona's home"'. This is, apparently, because 'a normal, developed mind [. . .] develops above all for self-defense. Furthermore, by the multitude of questions that emerge in it, it inadvertently distracts the soul from its main task'; while these intellectually disarmed, and thus vulnerable individuals, unequivocally create good. They are destined for perdition, while giving the rest of us a lofty lesson. 'But if this is so, then it is precisely they who were the most intelligent people – through the intelligence of the heart'.[40]

Thus Iskander distinguishes a different type of reason – the 'reason of the heart', which has in it a distinct echo of the aforementioned concept of 'suffering reason'. This is apparently what Dostoevsky's Aglaia Epanchina from 'The Idiot' refers to as the 'primary intelligence' ['главный ум'], and what Frank Seeley regards as one of the three vital ingredients of Christian love in Dostoevsky (the other two being true compassion and the absence of egoism).[41] In the same (essentially Christian) vein, Father Alexandr Shmeman talks, on the one hand, about reason understood in a conventional way – as intellect, as an instrument for analysis, and, on the other hand, about stupidity, – as being two sides of the same coin – that of vanity, of false pride. 'In the fallen world, intelligence is a tremendous and [. . .] demonic operation of masking the main and "essential" stupidity – that is vanity – whose gist is in the fact that while being stupidity, blindness, self-deception, meanness, it "cunningly" pretends to be intelligence. This means that it is not intelligence and stupidity that oppose each other in the world (they "together" presuppose each other, are rooted in each other), but instead intelligence-stupidity – i.e. vanity – and humility are opposed. Humility is Divine, and therefore it alone overcomes and defeats both intelligence-vanity and stupidity-vanity'.[42]

Similarly, for Iskander, reason – if it is understood broadly (rather than narrowly and scholastically as reduced rationalism) – is opposed to lies, as good to evil, and this opposition is insoluble and mystical. 'A rationalist does not understand a mystical connection between reason and lie. He does not realise that reason can never fully defeat

---

[39]   Olga Sedakova, 'V zashchitu razuma', *Continent* 2010, No. 144, <http://magazines.russ.ru/continent/2010/144/se13.html> [accessed 30 January 2014].

[40]   Fazil Iskander, *Esse i publitsistika*, <http://www.kulichki.com/moshkow/FISKANDER/isk_publ.txt> [accessed 15 January 2014].

[41]   See Frank F. Seeley, *Saviour or Superman?: Old and New Essays on Tolstoy and Dostoevsky*, Nottingham, England: Astra Press, 1999, p. 91.

[42]   Alexandr Shmeman, *Dnevniki. 1973–1983*, Moscow: Russkii Put, 2007, pp. 549–50.

lie. It can only restrict it. Reason, as well as lie, is a product of life itself. To exterminate lie entirely would mean to exterminate life as such. Hence a sad cautiousness of reason. In its struggle against lie, reason is intuitively inclined to go easy rather than to apply excessive force and thus to destroy the balance of life. Similarly, lie, according to its internal nature, and being an embodiment of evil and madness, strives to the complete extermination of reason, not realising that this would mean the extermination of life itself, including the end of lie too. And this is reason's tragedy.'[43] Yet, Iskander implies further, the fact that good is still not defeated by evil, or reason by lies, points to a supernatural (irrational, divine) origin of good (and hence of reason).

The same broad and, if you like, wise understanding of reason was typical for Pushkin. In this respect, a parallel can be drawn between Pushkin and Sergei Averintsev. As Olga Sedakova argues, they share a 'broad, light, supple, animated and inspired' mind, a 'positive mind which is located in the "heart" and "feeling", co-operates with conscience and will, and is connected to the perception of the wisely created Whole.'[44] In this vein, Pushkin's stance was expressed by him as always concisely: 'What constitutes grandeur of man if not his thought? Let human thought be free in the same way as man must be free.'[45] Sedakova points out an unconventional way in which 'heart' and 'mind' were wrestling in Pushkin's case – faith, or, at any rate, existence of God, was craved by his mind rather than his heart: 'Mind is searching for the Divine, but heart cannot find it.'[46] Thus, within, or rather instead, the traditional opposition of *fides et ratio*, 'it is precisely *mind* that can be the first reason and the main argument for faith'. The same idea is documented in Pushkin's diary: '*mon coeur est matérialiste, mais ma raison s'y refuse*'.[47] The cause of the poet's 'recoil from atheism, was not a calling of the heart or a torment of conscience, but a need of the mind. Atheism appeared to him unsatisfactory in intellectual terms: "Not to allow the assumption of the existence of God means to be more stupid than those peoples who think that the world rests on a rhynosorus"'.[48] Here it is significant that Pushkin talks of the assumption rather than of faith as such. This is somewhat reminiscent of Chekhov's famous contemplation of the same topic, where the writer sees wisdom as being a necessary basis for human relationship with God: 'between "there is God" and "there is no God" there lies an enormous field, which a true wizard walks with great difficulty. A Russian knows only one of these two extremes, and is not interested in the middle ground. That is why he usually knows nothing, or very little'.[49]

---

[43] Fazil Iskander, *Esse i publitsistika*, <http://lib.ru/FISKANDER/isk_publ.txt> [accessed 15 January 2014].

[44] Olga Sedakova, 'Sergei Sergeevich Averintsev. Apologiia ratsionalnogo', *Kontinent*, No. 135, 2008,<http://magazines.russ.ru/continent/2008/135/se24.html> [accessed 15 January 2014].

[45] Aleksandr Pushkin, 'Puteshestvie iz Moskvy v Peterburg', in *Sobranie sochinenii v 10 tomakh*, Moscow: Khudozhestvennaia literatura, vol. 6, 1962, p. 403.

[46] Pushkin's poem 'Bezverie' (1817), in A. S. Pushkin, *Sobranie sochinenii v 10 tomakh*, op. cit., vol. 1, 1959, p. 423. In Russian: 'Ум ищет Божества, а сердце не находит'.

[47] 'My heart is a materialist, but my mind objects to this' (1821) from 'Iz kishinevskogo dnevnika', in A. S. Pushkin, *Sobranie sochinenii v 10 tomakh*, op. cit., vol. 7, 1962, p. 304.

[48] Olga Sedakova, 'Sergei Sergeevich Averintsev. Apologiia ratsionalnogo', op. cit.; Pushkin's quotation is from his manuscript of 1827–8.

[49] A note in Chekhov's Notebooks, which he transferred to his Diary in the early February of 1897.

In this respect both Pushkin and Chekhov were distant from the conventional archetypical Russianness with its 'recklessness, "Asiatic" wildness, anarchy and absurdity; its "cursed questions", famous Dostoevsky-type scandals, moral "breadth" bordering on unscrupulousness, special suspicion towards the adequacy of verbal mode of expression, notorious soul-pouring, barbaric desire to be loved for your sins, flair for ideologies, "everything or nothing" maximalist tendencies and characteristic disdain of the mundane, of materialistic world [. . .] and much more' which 'constitutes the conventional "Russian" myth'.[50] It is a different Russianness that they represent – 'the other, aristocratic Russianness'.[51] Andrei Bitov describes it as a quality of being civilized;[52] while Semen Frank talks of suffering transgressed by thought, a quiet sorrow reconciled with tragedy, an enlightened spirit of reconciliation with the inevitable, with Necessity (rather than struggle, denial and revolt).[53] Contrary to the paradigm of Russian spirit being epitomized by 'perpetual rebellion, mutiny or hopeless, melancholic yearning', what is more typically Russian is 'precisely that combination, characteristic for Pushkin, of the tragic with spiritual calm, with wise humility and lucidity'. The tragic in Pushkin 'is not a rebellion, not spitefulness against life, but a quiet reconciled sorrow, light sadness'.[54]

Within this profound (Pushkinian) understanding of reason, no contradiction between reason and faith follows, because it is in fact reason which craves faith. Reason also opposes lies (as Iskander observes) as well as vanity/false pride (as Shmeman argues), rather than faith. Moreover, as Shmeman notes further, 'Christianity and Gospel begin with metanoia, a "conversion", a "transposition" of the mind, with growing wiser in the literal sense. That is why it is so terrifying when "religion" redeemed by Christ, filled again with the "light of reason", keeps opting for stupidity'.[55] Religion 'agrees with delight to the opposition of faith and reason, gets intoxicated by its own "irrationality", feels good anywhere except within reason. [. . .] As a result, inside the world and over the world the "prince of this world" reigns, who is, putting it more simply, a Fool, Lier and Cheater. Isn't it high time to say it to him openly and to stop believing in what he does *not* have – in his intelligence? (*ум*)'.[56]

However, a vulgarized interpretation of the concept of reason, connected to its distractively egotistic rather than constructively multifaceted potential, as discussed above, proves to be very resilient and long-lived, sealed in particular by Nietzsche with his opting for the irrational, understood as an opposition to rationality. In particular, this misconception entails various, rather naively outdated, juxtapositions, such as that between art and science, and leads to an exaltation of the irrationalist outlook. Indeed, one can see the temptation to declare art an intrinsically, par excellence, irrational

[50] Olga Sedakova, '*Mysl* Aleksandra Pushkina', <http://www.pravmir.ru/mysl-aleksandra-pushkina/> [accessed 20 January 2014].

[51] Ibid.

[52] Andrei Bitov, 'Moi dedushka Chekhov i pradedushka Pushkin', <http://2004.novayagazeta.ru/nomer/2004/49n/n49n-s34.shtml> [accessed 20 January 2014].

[53] Semen Frank, 'Etiudy o Pushkine', <http://www.pushkinskijdom.ru/LinkClick.aspx?fileticket=Rc1rHDWfRhE%3D&tabid=10183> [accessed 15 January 2014].

[54] Ibid.

[55] Alexandr Shmeman, *Dnevniki. 1973–1983*, op. cit., pp. 298–9.

[56] Ibid.

activity, as it 'frequently involves the suspension of the cerebral and engages instead with superstition, faith, emotion and illusion'.[57] In the same vein, as Isaiah Berlin observes about Georg Hamann and William Blake, artistic or religious imagination for them is part of a creative power, while scientific investigation, in their eyes, is clearly denied creative impulse.[58] This is supported by Hume, who claimed that 'reason taken by itself is impotent, and when it dictates it is an usurper and an impostor'.[59] At the same time, as is clear to true scientists, the inspirations behind scientific discoveries are as genuinely poetic and 'divine' as those of true artists. That is why David Hilbert famously compared the power of poetic and mathematical imagination in favour of the latter.[60] On the other hand, the interpretations of the nature of artistic activity are, in fact, similarly multi-dimensional. Not only the strict principles of Classicism, but also quite a calculated character of Russian Symbolism, testify to this. Furthermore, emotion-driven Romanticism in contrast to order-based Classicism does not necessarily represent irrationalism in its 'pure form' and is distinct from idealism, just as realism can be disjointed from rationalism, as we often see, for instance, in Chekhov. Faith and reason, art and science, mind and soul, ethics and aesthetics do not inevitably mean a rationalist-irrationalist dichotomy, yet it is at their border that the painful conflict seems to live, hence continuous strivings to polarize them. Moreover, such a dichotomy is in itself problematic. Thus Sergei Averintsev, a disciple of the Aristotelian common sense, and an adherent of the 'golden mean' of Aristotelian ethics, dismissed such oppositions as examples of bad rationality.[61] His thought resisted both 'bad irrationalism as well as shallow, bad rationalism'.[62] Hence, in particular, his core theme is 'the intense points of synthesis of the traditions of "Athens" and "Jerusalem"', with their convergence in the artistic, supple wisdom, capable of amazement.[63]

A stance opposite to the above was upheld by Lev Shestov with his irreconcilable opposition of 'Athens' and 'Jerusalem', and uncompromising, Quixotic crusade against Reason. Accusing Shestov of such misleading, unambiguous polarization of reason and faith, the contemporary Russian philosopher A. V. Akhutin writes, 'There is a disturbing boundary which separates an ultimate knowledge from infinite ignorance, does not delineate between Hellenistic Reason and Biblical Faith, but goes instead to the very heart of that Reason. It is at this boundary – in the midst of the mythologized metaphysics which Shestov has in mind when he talks of the kingdom of Reason – that philosophy is born. [. . .] Philosophy takes thought to nothingness of thought

57 Jeremy Howard, 'Viewing Askance: Irrationalist Aspects in Russian Art from Fedotov to Malevich and into the Beyond', in Olga Tabachnikova (ed.), *Mystery Inside Enigma: Facets of Russian Irrationalism between Art and Life*, op. cit.

58 See Isaiah Berlin, *The Magus of the North*, op. cit., pp. 62–3. For a further discussion on this, see Olga Tabachnikova, 'Patterns of European Irrationalism, from Source to Estuary: Johann Georg Hamann, Lev Shestov and Anton Chekhov – on Both Sides of Reason', op. cit.

59 See Ibid., p. 105.

60 Apparently, Hilbert said about one of his former students who dropped mathematics to study poetry: 'Good. He did not have enough imagination to become a mathematician'. See, for example, <http://en.wikipedia.org/wiki/David_Hilbert> [accessed 01 July 2012].

61 See Olga Sedakova, 'Sergei Sergeevich Averintsev. Apologiia ratsionalnogo', op. cit., <http://magazines.russ.ru/continent/2008/135/se24.html> [accessed 17 January 2014].

62 Ibid.

63 Ibid.

and of being, where what may happen does not yet exist. Philosophy deals not with eternal truths, but with how they are possible – with assumptions of eternal existence. Shestov himself is sometimes close to such an understanding of the "second dimension of thought", but all this intense paradoxality of philosophical thinking is immediately lost when it is split into two quite unambiguous poles – of reason and of faith'.[64]

More on the ethical dimension of reason.
Three types of irrationalism

Mind without morality is not intelligent, but morality is intelligent even without the mind.

Fazil Iskander

From the ethical perspective, in the post-medieval times a perception of reason as essentially demonic was to a large extent a disillusioned response to the Enlightenment ideas which, as Averintsev aptly observed, in their radical striving to be all-encompassing, aimed to remove suffering from human life. This, in his view, was their fatal mistake, as suffering constitutes an intrinsic and crucially meaningful part of existence.[65] By the same token, Iskander exclaims that, 'a formula of good does not exist and is not possible. If one could imagine theoretically that science has found such a formula, this would mean that conscience (совесть) becomes redundant. But it is clear that only conscience moves together with the individual through all the inscrutable turns of life. Sure, conscience is tiresome; but having spurned conscience, man becomes merely a tireless animal'.[66]

A complex dialectics between human conscience as an internal ethical regulator and legal system as an external one will be discussed in Chapter 2. The resulting behaviour of man as an ethical being can be rationalized, according to Max Weber, as belonging to a particular type of rationalism: either purpose-oriented, or values-oriented. That is, when man behaves rationally (i.e. logically) from the point of view of striving to his goal or from the point of view of his underlying values, respectively. It seems that renaming Weber's notation, may render the meaning of his terminology more transparent. Namely, let us refer to his purpose-oriented rationalism as vulgar rationalism, and to his means-oriented rationalism as moral rationalism. Otherwise one can easily re-formulate Weber's classification turning purpose into values and vice versa (for the same reason, it seems, Russian Orthodox morality warns against any

---

[64] A. V. Akhutin, 'Antichnost v filosofii Lva Shestova'– an Introduction to Lev Shestov, *Lektsii po istorii grecheskoi filosofii*, Moscow-Paris: Russky Put'-YMCA-Press, 2001, pp. 13 and 17–18.

[65] See Olga Sedakova, 'Sergei Sergeevich Averintsev. Apologiia ratsionalnogo', op. cit., <http://magazines.russ.ru/continent/2008/135/se24.html> [accessed 17 January 2014]. As Sedakova writes, 'Averintsev accused the Reason of the Enlightenment, in particular, of the following fatal error: it ceased to understand the meaning of suffering, the meaningfulness of suffering, perceiving it as an unfortunate obstacle, an imbreachment of the world order, which can – and should – be corrected by the means of reason'.

[66] Fazil Iskander, *Esse i publitsistika*, <http://www.kulichki.com/moshkow/FISKANDER/isk_publ.txt> [accessed 15 January 2014].

division between goal and means, saying that good achieved by no good means is not good).[67] Thus, vulgar rationalism is resonant with Jesuits' logic, while moral rationalism is driven by the higher considerations, of the type: 'if I don't do this now, how am I going to live with myself later?'. For example, risking your life to rescue a child follows precisely the above logic and is the case of 'moral rationalism'. Interestingly, in the eyes of one type of rationalism, the other type may easily look irrational. Moreover, there appears to be a certain duality here which will be discussed in more detail in Chapter 6.

Departing from Weber's notation of rationalism, we suggest distinguishing three types of irrationalism which will be encountered throughout this book. The first type is the one which has been predominantly referred to above – an anti-rationalist stance as a rebellious reaction against radical rationalist ideas, such as, for instance, those of the Enlightenment. The second type is connected to this in that it also grows from rationalism as its logical end, as rationalism which lost the sense of measure – it is irrationalism born of excessive rationalism as its extreme version. The behaviour of Pushkin's Herman ('*Pikovaia Dama*') or Chekhov's clerk Cherviakov ('*Smert chinovnika*') exemplify this type, as will be shown. There is, however, the third type of irrationalism which seems to be the purest and most Russian form of it. Its best illustrations seem to be present in Vasilii Shukshin's stories about his 'chudiki' – strange, slightly inadequate, but touchingly attractive heroes. This irrationalism arises from the inability to adjust to evil, from the intuitive feeling of the existence of some higher reality in conjunction with the acutely felt human impotence to change the tragic world-order. This type, which is unable to transgress into a clear understanding, cannot be any type of rationalism in Weber's sense, and thus remains pure irrationalism.

A human temptation to overcome the tragedy of existence is overwhelming. It has driven revolutions and inspired great utopian ideas, in particular those behind the Enlightenment. The results of this striving can be seen in the social order of Western civilization which has come up with very practical rational solutions, referred to by Lev Shestov as the 'ideal of settled mankind'.[68] It has erected multiple, more or less stable and solid constructions over and above the abyss, in the form of well-ordered and rationally orzganised religion, art and science.

By contrast, Russia brought about in the course of history 'very much in order to aid understanding the world, but very little that helps us live in it'.[69] But in return, trailing behind in practical terms, with its anthropocentric literature preoccupied above all by human soul, by moral problematics, Russian culture, as it were, got suspended above the abyss, unable to avert its looks. It is peering intently into the bottomless pit of existential horrors, almost charging towards them deliberately. And its notorious alcoholic haze – is it not of the same root? As Iskander once said, 'the whole of Russia is like Hamlet who is on the bottle'.[70] This, however, is a portrait of Russian culture

---

[67] Further on this, see patristic works, for instance, by the elder Siluan Afonsky.

[68] See Lev Shestov, 'Dostoevsky i Nitzshe (filosofiia tragedii)', op. cit., p. 326.

[69] These are the words of a character from Zakhar Prilepin's novel 'San'kia' (2006) in Chapter 8. See <http://sankya.ru/chapters/8.html> [accessed 4 November 2013].

[70] Fazil Iskander, 'Ponemnogu o mnogom. Sluchainye zapiski', *Novyi Mir*, No. 10, 2000. See <http://magazines.russ.ru:81/novyi_mi/2000/10/iskan.html> [accessed 20 May 2013].

before globalization, before the era of capitalism and consumerism. How much of the old ways will survive, is yet to be seen. But the fact remains, that classical Russian literature, with its distinct resonance in the subsequent periods, manifested amazing existential boldness. Lev Shestov thus described this phenomenon: 'We allow ourselves the greatest luxury that man can dream of – sincerity, truthfulness [. . .]. Other people's experience is not ours. [. . .] Any attempt to deprive us of our belief meets with the most energetic resistance. The most skeptical Russian hides a hope at the bottom of his soul. Hence our fearlessness of the truth [. . .], which so stunned European critics. [. . .] Our courage is drawn from our quite uncultured confidence in our own powers'.[71]

This reckless boldness is opposed to the pragmatically cautious wisdom of the West which hides from existential horrors in various rounded up, escapist theories: 'Realism was invented in the West, established there as a theory. But in the West, to counteract it, were invented numberless other palliating theories whose business it was to soften down the disconsolate conclusions of Realism. [. . .] A European uses all his powers of intellect and talent, all his knowledge and his art for the purpose of concealing his real self and all that really affects him – for that the natural is ugly and repulsive [. . .]. In philosophy there reigns theodicy, in science – the law of sequence'.[72] Thus, Shestov concludes provocatively, 'there lies before us the choice between the artistic and accomplished lie of old, cultured Europe, a lie which is the outcome of a thousand years of hard and bitter effort, and the artless, sincere simplicity of young, uncultured Russia'.[73]

At the same time, Russian culture too offers consolation in the face of the perpetual trauma of living, to the extent that the 'consoling pathos' of Russian literature has become a cliché. Yet, arguably, there seems to be a difference between Russian and Western European way of consolation in that the latter shows how to recoil and hide from the tragedy of existence, to remain as much as possible outside it, while the former tries to offer some moral refuge and relief within that very tragedy. Perhaps a metaphorical model can be drawn from the following abstract description of two possible ways for an individual to deal with tragedy: 'the first reaction of a human being in the face of a tragedy is roughly as follows: where has a mistake been made? What can be done to gain control over the situation; to prevent it from happening again? But there exists [. . .] another way of behaviour as well: to allow the tragedy to overwhelm you, to let it crush you; as Poles say, "to put yourself under". And if you manage to get back to your feet afterwards – you will be a different person'.[74] Russian culture, it seems, follows the second route – it prostrates under the tragedy, allowing itself to be crushed by it. That is, instead of drawing practical lessons and protecting itself by the theoretical 'anti-tragic' fence, it delves into a different metaphysical universe, sado-masochistically irrational in the eyes of some, where extreme suffering borders with profound joy (for one can truly laugh only if one can truly weep).

---

[71] Lev Shestov, 'All Things Are Possible' ('Apotheosis of Groundlessness'), <http://www.angelfire.com/nb/shestov/all/all_23.html> [accessed 2 August 2013].
[72] Ibid.
[73] Ibid.
[74] This description is given in the book by Solomon Volkov, *Dialogi s Iosifom Brodskim* and was by Brodsky's own admission offered to him by Susan Sontag. See Solomon Volkov, *Dialogi s Iosifom Brodskim*, Moscow: Nezavisimaia Gazeta, 1998, p. 49.

Cultural differences in historical perspective

Overestiming the meaning of constants [. . .] is an epistemological error. Russian life, just as any other, is subject to profound changes, which bring a concealed distinction even into things which appear similar on the outside. That is why, when embarking on an exploration of Russian consciousness, I would not want to instill either in myself, nor in others an exaggerated idea of the role of such constants . . .

Sergei Averintsev

Thus, behind the question of reason and faith, and their ethical underpinning, in Russia and in the West, there looms a more general issue of their markedly different approaches to culture. Indeed, while in Western Europe culture (including philosophy, theology and especially the arts) was respectively an academic discipline and an intellectual game, for Russians it became a substitute for life itself, with all the seriousness (almost fatefulness) that this implied. That is to say that although Russians borrowed culture (such as literature and philosophy in the early nineteenth century on a large scale) from the West, they substantially 'amended' it, enriched with their own meaning and approach, which has often regarded art as being larger than life. Russians thus, as it were, deconstructed Western syntactical order to reassemble it in a more impressionist fashion, turning it into a personal confession.[75] The resulting product would then be consumed in the West, where it was both admired and feared.[76]

Perhaps, one of the historical reasons for these diverging attitudes to culture is a different locus of cultural production – traditionally in the West universities were places for arts and literature, whereas in Russia these were monasteries. As Dmitrii Likhachev writes, 'if the culture of Western Europe predominantly was a university culture – with all the specific features of university tolerance of other cultures past and present, Russian culture, from the fourteenth century and up to the beginning of the eighteenth, was one of monastic literacy and a monastic type of economic structure'.[77] Autocratic regimes of varying ferocity also played a major role restricting life to its artistic image and forcing the latter underground. A distinct example of this is literature, which in the Russian case absorbed all other discourses including philosophy, politics and religion, and became in a sense more real than the actual reality.

Starting from Peter the Great's reforms, the life of the Russian educated society got split into two unevenly developing strands: an intellectual, philosophical development was apace with that in Western Europe, while the dynamics of the socio-political

[75] See on this, for instance, Aleksandr Ivashkin, 'The Paradox of Russian Non-Liberty', *The Musical Quarterly*, 76(4), 1992, pp. 543–56.
[76] For example, André Gide's impression of Dostoevsky's reception in the West was that he is feared for his 'chaotic', 'Slavic' element, and yet Gide himself was a great admirer of the Russian novelist seeing in him an author so 'Russian in the strictest sense of the word and withal so universally European' (André Gide, *Dostoevsky*, London: Penguin Books, 1967, p. 171).
[77] Dmitrii Likhachev, 'Religion: Russian Orthodoxy', in Nicholas Rzhevsky (ed.), *The Cambridge Companion to Modern Russian Culture*, Cambridge: Cambridge University Press, 1998, p. 43.

foundation of Russian society was delayed and differently oriented. This led to the increase in the role of random factors in Russian historical development.[78] Talking about the role of the state more generally, it is clear that in the Russian case it is not the system, but personalities that prevailed, as the system has been predominantly flawed. A lack of the lawful space created a random and unpredictable element in life, its irrationalism, and hence the irrationalism of all the agents. A very laconic summary of a high distribution of personal irrationalism in the Russian case is given in the book *Zamechatelnye chudaki i originaly* (*Wonderfully weird and original persons*) by M. I. Pyliaev, written in the first half of the nineteenth century and published by Aleksei Suvorin in 1898: 'Being personally weird is a consequence of randomness of life, and the more such randomness reigns in a society which is still inhomogeneous, the more weird personalities it produces'.[79] This is reminiscent of the following contemporary literary quotation: 'Why is it that in Russia at all times "good personal relations" play such a vital role for success of any enterprise? This is probably because any Russian perceives law as an annoying convention invented by some hostile force in its own interests. The name of this hostile force is "state"'.[80]

Manifestations of irrationalism in Russian culture have been manifold and diverse. In the arts it resulted in regarding an artist as a secular saint, and artistic craft itself as martyrdom. In social life it revealed itself in a 'victim mentality' and fatalism, in a special semiotics of behaviour marked by existential anxiety, holy foolishness and associated ironic discourse. Moreover, looking at the Russian semiotics of behaviour what immediately springs to mind is irrationalism in the economic sphere, which grows largely from the Russian saying 'Не в деньгах счастье' ('Money cannot bring happiness'). Although the saying itself is rather universal, its imprint on the Russian 'national psyche' is extremely profound. Manifestations of this include the famous extravagant scandalous behaviour of Russian merchants with smashing mirrors in expensive hotels out of the feeling of angst, emptiness and meaninglessness of existence; generally shameful and embarrassed attitude to money; desire to repent and to redeem, to cleanse yourself from the demonic and dirty impact of wealth through generous donations to charitable causes, etc.[81] In religious beliefs irrationalism manifested itself in incorporating pre-Christian, pagan elements as well as apophatic theology and mysticism, in a belief in the supernatural, and in a tendency towards religious sectarianism. Philosophy witnessed a rebellion against Western rationalist philosophical structures, methods and conclusions. There was defiance of reason and a critique of the whole history of Western speculative philosophy and autonomous ethics. This has evolved into our age, and is being exported (with the opening of Russian borders) to the wider world to such an extent that 'cultural warnings' have

[78] Yurii Lotman, '"Pikovaia dama" i tema kart i kartochnoi igry v russkoi literature nachala XIX veka', in *Izbrannye statii v 3-h tomakh*, op. cit., vol. II, p. 396.

[79] M. I. Pyliaev, *Zamechatelnye chudakii i originaly*, Moscow: Zakharov, 2001, p. 5.

[80] A. Brusnikin, *Deviatnyi Spas*, Moscow: ACT, 2007.

[81] See more on this theme in Natalia Vinokurova, 'Russian Semiotics of Behaviour, Or Can a Russian Person be Regarded as Homo Economicus?', in Olga Tabachnikova (ed.), *Mystery Inside Enigma: Facets of Russian Irrationalism between Art and Life*, op. cit. Some further discussion follows in Chapter 7 of the current monograph.

been issued.[82] Not all of these features are exclusively Russian, but in the Russian soil they had grown a peculiar national character.

The aforementioned cultural and religious differences between Russia and Western Europe can be inscribed into the broader framework of Russian and Western ways of developments, without understanding of which it is hardly possible to single out the roots and nature of Russian irrationalism.[83]

Vasilii Zenkovsky in his *History of Russian Philosophy*, gives the following cultural-historical overview, most useful for our purposes.[84] Its apparent bias, if one views it with Western European eyes, is useful too, in as much as stereotypes may serve as indicators of the painful points of cultural divergence.

On the one hand, the West, carefully guarded by Rome, was a direct heir of ancient philosophy and enjoyed a linguistic unity, of Latin, being the Church language, which provided for a readymade philosophical terminology. Russia, on the other hand, adopted its religion from an alien country – Byzantium, whose language, Greek, had never taken roots on the Russian soil. While being politically separated from Byzantium, Russia was dependant on it in terms of the Church. Yet, as Pushkin wrote to Chaadaev, 'From the Greeks we have borrowed the Gospel and legends, but not the spirit of childish pettiness and logomachy. The mores of Byzantium have never been the mores of Kiev. Our clergy, before Theophane, were worthy of respect. They had never stained themselves with the meanness of popery, and surely would not have caused reformation at the moment when mankind most of all needed unity'.[85] At the same time, unlike Western Europe, Russia did not have any direct links to antiquity and generally adopted a suspicious attitude towards the West which tried to subjugate it to Rome. This, together with the historical conditions, such as the three centuries-long Mongol rule (XIII–XV centuries) and The Time of Troubles of the early XVII century, facilitated certain tardiness in the development of Russia's intellectual history. The proximity of the West played a double and ambiguous role: on the one hand it was a teacher, on the other – an oppressor, a combination which forced Russia to combine apprenticeship with creativity.

Generally, Christianity for Russia meant the whole world outlook rather than merely a religion. In this vein Russian philosophical thought developed, up until the eighteenth century, in the framework of exclusively religious sensibility, and secularization happened in Russia much later than in the West. This religious sensibility

---

[82] Thus the aforementioned article by A. Ivashkin 'The Paradox of Russian Non-Liberty' warns against 'a huge invasion of Russian irrationalism in all the arts' of the West. An example of a study into Russian influence to the outside world is Steven G. Marks, *How Russia Shaped the Modern World: From Art to Anti-Semitism, Ballet to Bolshevism* (Princeton University Press, 2003), although it is too broad thematically to be an in-depth study. It pays little attention to Russian irrationalism as such (save for Dostoevsky) and is preoccupied mostly with Russian specifically anti-Western tendencies and influences.

[83] For more details on these historical sources see the aforementioned Vasilii Zenkovsky, *History of Russian Philosophy (in two volumes)*, Rostov-on-Don: Fenix, 1999 – reprint of the first edition: (Paris: YMCA Press, 1948).

[84] See Zenkovsky, op. cit., especially pp. 35–40, the summary of which is incorporated into a brief historical background, given here.

[85] Aleksandr Pushkin, Letter to Petr Chaadaev of 19.10.1836, <http://rvb.ru/pushkin/01text/10letters /1831_37/01text/1836/1928_740.htm> [accessed 10 December 2013].

had its own roots, its own nature which was propelled by the freedom of religious mind, for traditionally in Russia, unlike in the West, it was the state rather than the Church which served as a censor. At the same time, the adoption of Christianity was accompanied, via Byzantium and Slavic lands, by various non-Christian, apocryphal elements in the forms of myths, legends and (this time akin to the Western case) occult practices. Interestingly, religious *logos* in Russia expressed itself initially not through literature or philosophical thought, but through visual art in the form of icon-painting (иконопись) (which Ye. Trubetskoy labelled as 'speculation in colours' ['умозрение в красках']).[86] This curious fact points to the general dominance in the Russian case of the aesthetic aspect of perception, with a particularly marked, almost disproportionate, appreciation of beauty.

However, although other cultural forms such as literature and philosophy were basically belated in Russia, their incredible blossoming throughout the nineteenth century suggests that there had been, in fact, a vast potential accumulated, even if it was in some sense dormant (like in the Russian folk-story of Ilia Muromets who laid on the stove until the age of 33 and then suddenly sprang to life and went for his exploits). Curiously though, in the Russian case despite aesthetics as it were taking precedence over ethics, with the concept of beauty being dominant in Russian cultural consciousness, it is moral problematics that prevailed in Russian thought. Thus Russian philosophy revolved around a human being, and even Dostoevsky's religious search is, arguably, first of all ethically oriented. As Czeslaw Milosz put it about Russia: 'no centuries of scholastic theology and philosophy in the past, no university philosophy to speak of – but on the other hand a lot of people philosophizing, and passionately at that, on their own'.[87]

Maybe a certain reconciliation of ethical importance and aesthetic precedence is reflected in the fact that Russian philosophical thought found expression first and foremost through Russian literature, which has been always preoccupied by the so-called cursed questions, the 'ultimate' questions of existence, with its persistent 'refusal to submit to the world in which the latest discoveries (or theories) of science took precedence over the age-old injunctions of Christian morality'.[88] Furthermore, in a rather unique and characteristic way Russian literature displayed 'the struggle with the source of that morality itself, the Christian faith'.[89] And thus a marked distinction of Russian literature, and the reasons 'why could Flaubert's Emma Bovary in some sense not be imagined by the great realist who created Anna Karenina' and why 'is Dostoevsky's Marmeladov [. . .] unlike Dickens's Micawber'[90] are by no means accidental.

---

[86] See Yevgenii Trubetskoy, *Umozrenie v kraskakh. Vopros o smysle zhizni v drevnerusskoi religioznoi zhivopisi*, Moscow: Tipografiia tovarishchestva I. D. Sytina, 1916.

[87] Milosz, 'Shestov, or the Purity of Despair', op. cit., p. 101.

[88] Joseph Frank, *Between Religion and Rationality: Essays in Russian Literature and Culture*, Princeton: Princeton University Press, 2010, p. 2.

[89] Ibid., p. 3.

[90] These questions are posed by David M. Bethea in his attempts to identify the contours of specifically Russian literature as opposed to other national literatures. See David M. Bethea, 'Literature' in Rzhevsky (ed.), op. cit., p. 161.

Another way in which ethics merged with aesthetics in Russian culture is perhaps to be found in the fact that beauty for Russians had to be historically concrete rather than abstract and ideal. Moreover, Russian way of perception has been traditionally synthetic rather than analytic (or rational), which is likely to have had far-reaching consequences. Joseph Brodsky thus described this in metaphoric terms: 'Suppose you cut open an apple and take off its skin. Now you know what's inside it, but you have lost sight of its two convexities, these two cheeks of the apple. Russian culture is interested, instead, in the apple per se, it gets delighted by the apple's colour, by the smoothness of its skin and so on. It does not necessarily know what's inside it'.[91] This holistic approach, the tendency to unite (rather than to divide), to absorb phenomena in their entirety, and yet in concreteness, stood in sharp contrast to Western abstractness which, as we saw, was viewed by the Slavophile movement at least as having eventually degenerated into shallow rationalism. Alongside the immutability of the general questions there was an interest instead in the questions of concrete Christianity, in its personal as well as historical manifestations.

At the same time this desire to address the world (and in particular, man) as a whole, in its (or his) entirety, and to avoid a middle ground is part of the general radicalism of Christianity, shared by both Russia and Western Europe. Yet, in the Russian case it served only as an aggravating factor to what had already developed as Russian maximalism. Indeed, it is now a commonplace to say that Russia's special position between East and West determined its original way of development which absorbed influences from both sides. It is hard to be sure of the causal connection here, but it is believed that the geopolitical conditions themselves, including natural ones, such as vastness of space and absence of high mountains, facilitated certain maximalism in the national character. The antithesis 'everything or nothing', not supported by a common sense cautiousness, acquired a special force in Russia. At the same time it was compensated, as Zenkovsky puts it, by a certain spiritual tactfulness of religious sobriety. That is to say that Russians distanced the power of imagination from the spiritual sphere, and in this they differed from the West with its mystical cults and stigmas. This principle, where aesthetics again plays a central role, was based on the Russian desire not to give a head-start to the material side, not to roughen spiritual reality, not to mix the two spheres: spiritual and material. At least this is a perspective of Russians themselves.[92]

It is then natural to suspect that the roots of Russian irrationalism lay in this maximalism of Russian mentality, as well as in the dominance of the aesthetic aspect in it. Generally, a non-utilitarian, aesthetic approach to existence is inherent if not in the Russian cultural history per se, then at least in its (Russian) perception. Thus, the history of adoption of Christianity in Kievan Rus' by Prince Vladimir is described by the Russian academician Dmitrii Likhachev as being determined predominantly by aesthetic criteria: 'When Vladimir began choosing a faith in 986 he received

---

[91] Volkov, op. cit., p. 198.
[92] See on this, Russian philosophical histories, for instance, the aforementioned *History of Russian Philosophy* by Vasilii Zenkovsky (pp. 44–6), on which the large proportion of this historical recounting is based.

representatives from Islam, Judaism, and Rome; he heard them out but responded immediately to his own ambassadors, who had returned from Constantinople after attending a service in St. Sophia and who recounted their amazement at the grandeur of the church and the beauty of the service. Vladimir made his choice on the basis of their testimony, and that act shaped a cultural leitmotif – the idea that Russian religion was determined by aesthetic qualities (of Byzantine ritual and St. Sophia itself). Beauty determined the nature of Orthodoxy in Russia'.[93]

Significantly, the same historical event is portrayed in a somewhat different light by a Western scholar, Dean S. Worth, who lists a number of reasons for Vladimir's ultimate choice and adds pragmatic considerations to aesthetic ones: 'according to the one [motivation], he promised to be baptized if he won at Chersonese; the other, more elaborate, has him sending envoys to investigate several faiths and settling on the Greek Orthodox because of the beauty of the Byzantine church service. [. . .] one suspects that politics and diplomacy played more of a role than a beautiful church'.[94] Such a drastic contrast as in the above case, of Western and Russian approaches, is instructive, and will be adopted again in the sequel.

Another, possibly related, feature which might be responsible for the phenomenon of Russian irrationalism and which may distinguish Russia from the West is *mystical realism* inherent in the character of Russian thought. The essence of it is in the hierarchical difference of both realities – empirical and mystical. Both are acknowledged, but empirical reality survives only because of its attachment to the higher – mystical, Divine – sphere. As can be seen, for instance, from the interpretation of love by Russian thinkers of the Silver Age,[95] this premise can be understood not only (or even not so much) in the sense that the metaphysical provides a foundation for the physical reality, but rather that the metaphysical itself has a tangible, 'physical' dimension, an existence of its own – it is itself a reality.

As the Russian scholars Argunova and Tiapkov argue,[96] the distinction between Russian Orthodoxy and Western Christianity can be described in terms of religious sensibilities, responsible for exalting respectively the spiritual and material side of life, heavenly and earthly, ideal and real, disproportionately focusing either on the sublime ideas or on their practical implications, and ultimately resulting in two tangibly different archetypes of culture. Thus for Western Christians, 'expiation is interpreted as due justice which is more appropriate for the secular world', while 'in Russian culture an individual is connected to the perishable world by special transcendental relationships' and 'the genuine world is the world of spiritual grace, the kingdom of genuine freedom and equality'.[97]

Similarly, Tatiana Chumakova speaks of convergence, characteristic of the Eastern Christian tradition, rather than the divergence of two levels of consciousness which

[93] Likhachev, 'Religion: Russian Orthodoxy', in Rzhevsky (ed.), op. cit., p. 40.
[94] Dean S. Worth, 'Language', in Rzhevsky (ed.), op. cit., p. 24.
[95] See Chapter 4, especially Boris Vysheslavtsev's arguments against Freudean theories.
[96] A more detailed explanation of their argument is given in Chapter 2.
[97] V. N. Argunova and S. N. Tiapkov, *Innovatsionnoe razvitie regiona: potentsial, instituty, mekhanizmy*, Ivanovo: IGU, 2011.

represented the medieval dichotomy of 'earthly and heavenly', as the sacralization of everyday phenomena.[98] Earthly human life should be lit up, sanctified, by the action of this higher reality. This passionate search for the sanctifying light to the everyday existence, as captured in Tsvetaeva's 'the voice of the heavenly truth against the earthly truth',[99] has always been at the core of Russian religiosity and facilitated Russian acute inner intolerance of injustice, profoundly reflected in old religious verses (духовные стихи). By the same token, as previously mentioned, the primacy of moral and social aspects has been a marked characteristic of Russian thought and determined its anthropocentric character.

The above principle of subjugating earthly to the heavenly, of the supremacy of spiritual truth, lays at the core of Russian ascetics as well as such phenomena (combining pagan and Christian elements) as holy foolishness and monasticism (иночество), which can be viewed as the first culturally significant manifestations of Russian irrationalism. These should be taken not as disdain of flesh per se, but rather as means and ways towards transformation and sanctification of the world by the virtue of Divine light. Interestingly, as Gogol noticed, Easter celebrations are nowhere so full of light as in Russia. This reveals also the motif of cosmology in the Russian patristic teachings in their tendency to see the world as steeped in Divine light.[100]

Similarly, the movements of Russian schismatics (раскольники), of old Believers, while exemplifying the first dissidents, at the same time is an example of irrationalists with their utopian search and fanaticism which defies common sense. Yet, these movements reflect above all an intense ideological search of religious consciousness – its striving to protect the purity of the Russian Orthodox truth. As Florovsky stated, in contrast to existing explanations of the Schism by purely external reasons of preserving rituals, 'it is not the ritual, but the Anti-Christ which is the theme and mystery of the Russian Schism'.[101] By the same token, 'the fear of blasphemous secularization of the Church which would mean the end of utopia, the collapse of a dream, was behind the long-lasting movement of Old Believers. Utopia, so strong in Russian religious consciousness, can be taken perhaps as the extension (and the other side) of the mystical realism in the historiosophic sphere. Indeed, a search for the sacred meaning of the Tsarist power, of the history itself, the myths of Moscow being the third and last Rome expressed a profound Russian need to combine earthly with heavenly in a concrete reality. In contrast to the West with its primacy of clerical power over secular, in Russia the state (as well as the whole nation) was ascribed a sacred mission, and Tsarist power was, as it were, absorbed by the Church in that it became a fact of the clerical order'.[102]

---

[98] Tatiana Chumakova, 'Irrationalism in Ancient Russia', in Olga Tabachnikova (ed.), *Mystery Inside Enigma: Facets of Russian Irrationalism between Art and Life*, op. cit.

[99] Marina Tsvetaeva, 'Zavodskie' (1922), <http://www.goldpoetry.ru/cvetaeva/index.php?p=133> [accessed 7 February 2014]. In Russian: 'голос правды небесной против правды земной'.

[100] Zenkovsky, op. cit., pp. 42–3.

[101] Georgii Florovsky, *Puti russkogo bogosloviia*, Paris, 1937, pp. 57–8.

[102] Zenkovsky, op. cit., p. 54.

For a variety of historical reasons, Russian cultural development was latent, brewing through a long period of silence which then gave way to an explosion of literary art, with such names as Derzhavin, Zhukovsky and Pushkin at the fore, followed in sequence by theatre, painting, music and finally philosophy. The history of Russian (and for that matter Western) irrationalism also gained momentum from the beginning of the nineteenth century onwards, when irrationalist elements were stirred up by socio-political upheavals and accompanying cultural changes. Two well-studied schools of thoughts which emerged in Russia in the early nineteenth century, Westernizers and Slavophiles, respectively promoted Western rationalistic tradition, or argued for the special, almost messianic, Russian way of development based on the Russian patristic teachings. Paradoxically, both were marked by distinctly Russian features. A more reactionary Slavophiles' movement at the same time fostered and developed the typically Russian attitudes which inspired artistic masterpieces and new philosophical ideas. But, curiously, even the Westernizers school acquired some distinctly Russian colouring. With a perceptive irony Lev Shestov thus described Russia's complex relationship with the West in the country's attempts to follow in the footsteps of European progress, which were overturned by Russia's own in many ways irrationalist stance:

> Civilization came to us in Russia suddenly, when we were still barbarians, and immediately assumed the role of animal tamer [. . .] We succumbed quickly and in a short time swallowed huge doses of the things that Europeans acquired over centuries, gradually becoming used to even the strongest poisons. [. . .] All a Russian had to do was breathe the air of Europe for his head to start spinning. He interpreted everything in his own particular way, as a barbarian would. People talked to him about railroads, agricultural machinery, schools, self-government, and in his imagination these became miracles: universal happiness, limitless freedom, paradise, wings, etc. And the more unrealizable his dreams became, the more willingly he accepted them as reality.[103]

This distortion, or if you like, specifically Russian interpretation of Western achievements points to the fact that even the same concepts were differently understood in Russia and in Western Europe. As we saw above, perception of Western Europe as overwhelmingly and shamefully rationalist was widespread among the Slavophiles from early on. This can be illustrated by Kireevsky's characteristic and heavily biased protesting manifesto:

> Western person divides his life into separate strivings: in one corner there lives a religious sensibility [. . .] in another – separately, forces of the mind [. . .] in the third corner there is a striving for sensual pleasures; and so on. Cleverness thus turns easily into a cunningness, heart feeling – into a blind passion, beauty – into a dream, truth – into opinion, substance – into an excuse for imagination, virtue – into self-assurance, and theatricality becomes an integral existential companion

---

[103] Lev Shestov, 'Apofeoz bespochvennosti' (excerpt transl. by Edith W. Clowes), *Izbrannye sochineniia*, Moscow: Renessans, 1993, p. 355.

[. . .] propensity to day-dreaming serves as an inner mask for it. Duality and rational calculations are the last expression of Western culture . . .[104]

The undying and forever timely discussion of Russia vis-à-vis Western Europe in cultural terms will be continued in the second chapter of the book. Here, however, we will finish off by quoting Sergei Averintsev, who, almost 200 years later than Kireevsky and almost a century after Shestov, singled out a number of invariants of the traditional Russian consciousness. Among the important distinguishing factors, he names Russian ascetic tradition – a seemingly fruitless, weird striving for a spiritual tour-de-force, virtually for sainthood, but without using such lofty rhetoric. From any materialistic, positivist, pragmatic point of view such a striving certainly looks irrational and enigmatic. Averintsev refers to the memoirs of the well-known Russian liturgist N. D. Uspensky[105] who recalls the events of his youth when his famous teacher 'Aleksei Afanasievich Dmitrievsky, deprived during the Soviet times of any means for existence and basically starving to death, was spending his last strength and last days of his life for passing on his knowledge, completely selflessly, to the then youngster Uspensky, and was touchingly and almost comically angry if there happened to be even the slightest break in their lessons – for there was so much to teach in so little time'.[106] This is, Averintsev exclaims, what our scholarly continuity, our teaching and apprenticeship are like. 'It's not only that the teacher is performing his exploit (подвиг), giving it the efforts which could be used for his own survival. It is also the fact that the student, who is still very much a child, is fully aware that the difficult hours spent next to his stern teacher do not promise anything in terms of his practical life, except the threat of persecution. However, knowing this, he still goes to the lessons. And Russian culture, the culture of Saint Stephen of Perm, continues through him its stubborn life, resisting the institutional order, as a blade of grass, growing through asphalt'.[107]

To this individual voluntary martyrdom Averintsev cautiously (recoiling from sweeping generalizations) juxtaposes an institutional order more characteristic of the cultural history of Western Europe. He sees the essence of Russian culture as concealed in a certain degree of prevalence of a personal exploit, as in the example above, over all the corporate and institutional. Acknowledging an obvious presence of both modes of cultural organization in both Russia and the West, Averintsev stresses a relative unevenness of this presence, its differing measure. He concludes that, by contrast to the cultures of the West, in Russia 'the role of a personal, that is to a certain extent solitary, "isolated", enthusiastic striving, which does not fit into any given institutional-corporate context, is obviously large'.[108]

---

[104] Ivan Kireevsky, 'O kharaktere prosveshcheniia Evropy i o ego otnoshenii k prosveshcheniiu v Rossii' (1852) in *Sochineniia*, Moscow, 1911, vol. 1, p. 210.

[105] See Nikolai Uspensky, 'Iz lichnykh vospominanii ob A. A. Dmitrievskom', in *Bogoslovskie trudy*, vol. 4, Moscow, 1968, pp. 85–9 (quoted in Sergei Averintsev, *Sviaz vremen*, <http://www.fedy-diary.ru/html/042011/11042011–05a.html> [accessed 17 October 2013]).

[106] Sergei Averintsev, *Sviaz vremen*, op. cit.

[107] Ibid.

[108] Ibid.

The end of rationalist utopia

. . . a formula of good does not exist and is not possible. If one could imagine theoretically that science has found such a formula, this would mean that conscience becomes redundant . . .

Fazil Iskander

By comprising various intuitive, instinctive, emotional ways of cognition, irrationalism naturally borders on the problem of the power of reason and its limits. The spirit of Enlightenment, the idea of universal intellect, rapid technological advances of the second half of the nineteenth century inspired many, but also frightened some. Dostoevsky's anxious premonitions of the dangerous encroachment of science, in its technocratic sense, in the domain of human feelings encompassed concerns of various similarly minded artists and philosophers. Mitia Karamazov basically mocks scientific attempts to solve spiritual problems when he sarcastically tells Alesha about the discovery made by the physiologist Claude Bernard – that little tails of nerves in the brain are the cause of man's ability to think, and not his living soul and the fact that he is created in the divine image and likeness. Similar bitter anger is expressed in various ways by the Underground Man rebelling against 'mathematics', against the immutable world order indifferent to a single human life, and is repeated by Ippolit Terentiev in 'The Idiot'. In many ways these warnings against doomed and dangerous attempts to resolve the irrational by rational means proved prophetic, and the revolt – forever timely. Yet, it is clear today that the nature of radical rationalism is in a sense even more utopian than that of irrationalism. In fact, paradoxically, proving that radical rationalism at least (such as that of Chernyshevsky, Marx, Hegel et al.) which believed in reason alone, had essentially collapsed, was due precisely to scientific achievements.

Indeed, for a long time science was hoping that our universe could be described by a finite set of postulates. That is to say, that a finite number of equations (the derivation of which was considered to be only a question of time) could then predict the behaviour of natural phenomena, when supplied with the relevant initial data. However, an Austrian-American mathematician Kurt Gödel put an end to such hopes, for he proved that any system which is sufficiently non-trivial is essentially unknowable.

To be knowable in this context means that a certain set of axioms and rules for manipulating them describes the system fully, that is any statement about this system can be deduced from the axioms, using the rules. According to Gödel, however, there always exists a statement that can be added to the axioms determining the given system without changing anything. This simply means that there is always a statement such that neither it itself, nor its negation can be deduced from the given set of axioms using the given rules. Thus the system is unknowable – and this is true of any system which is not completely trivial. On the other hand, even such a relatively straightforward theory as the formal theory of arithmetic is already an example of such a non-trivial system! Furthermore, the systems in the centre of scientific investigations are already incredibly simplified (in order to be made into an object of study possible to handle by the means available to human beings) and represent only a crude approximation to the real life systems. But if even such simplified (deliberately idealized) constructions are unknowable, then (one can ask rhetorically) what can be said about such immensely complicated systems as human psyche, emotions and behaviour patterns? Although the connection between a technical mathematical problem and general philosophical one is not necessarily straightforward and entails a danger of vulgarization, it is nevertheless of high significance.

Thus the potential prospects of 'rationalizing' the cosmos of human relationships, of inventing 'algorithms' to describe human feelings (in a sense of algorithmically deducing if a statement pertaining to the 'system of emotions' is true or untrue), are doomed, and in this sense our universe is irrational (i.e. not amenable to algorithmization). In the above words of Iskander, 'a formula of good does not exist and never will exist'. Irrationalist aspects of human psyche will forever defeat strictly rationalist attempts to understand and classify them in rational terms. In other words, human soul, as acutely felt Dostoevsky, will remain inexhaustible. Hence his famous words, 'Man is a mystery: if you spend your entire life trying to puzzle it out, then do not say that you have wasted your time. I occupy myself with this mystery, because I want to be a man'.[109] Hence also a persistent theme in his novels – of man with a demonic rational idea, brought to his demise by encountering the irrationality of his human nature.

Moreover, as Lev Shestov once wrote in the understandable, purely human desperation: 'What we obtain through *thought*, is found to be [. . .] incommensurable [. . .] with the external world into which we have been plunged since our birth. [. . .] no matter how enigmatic may be the mysteries which surround being, what is most enigmatic and disturbing is that mystery in general exists and that we are somehow definitely and forever cut off from the sources and beginnings of life. [. . .] reality here shows us only an eternal, impenetrable mystery – as if, even before the creation of the world, someone had once and for all forbidden man to attain that which is most necessary and most important to him'.[110]

However, this is not to propagate a primitive opposition of rationalist and irrationalist modes of thought, but rather to emphasize the integral role of both in human life and cognition. If you like, this is to suggest that Russian irrationalism exists not outside, but within that profound 'suffering reason' which can be understood as equally intellectual and spiritual activity, and which penetrates into the meaning of life, thus crowned by Pushkin's famous formula: 'I want to live in order to think and to suffer'.[111]

* * *

The book is structured as a collection of seven essays of varying length, each dedicated to a specific field or theme where Russian irrationalism can manifest itself most meaningfully. These include such major areas as language, love and humour as well

[109] F. M. Dostoevsky, *Polnoe sobranie sochinenii v 30 tomakh*, vol. 28 (I), Leningrad: Nauka, 1985, p. 63.
[110] Lev Shestov, *Athens and Jerusalem,* <http://www.angelfire.com/nb/shestov/aaj/aj1_1.html> [accessed 10 January 2014].
[111] Aleksandr Pushkin, 'Elegy', in *Sobranie Sochinenii v 10 tomakh*, vol. 2, Moscow: Khudozhestvennaia literatura, 1959, p. 299. In Russian: 'Я жить хочу, чтоб мыслить и страдать'.

as related topics such as Russia's relationship with its Western Other, a literary history of Russian dreamers, impact of nature and culture on mentality, and some cases of subversion within the irrationalist theme.

Given the daunting nature of the task and a broad range of possible understandings of the very concept of irrationalism, it seemed constructive to be guided by Nils Bohr's vision – that opposite to a correct statement there stands a false statement, whereas what stands opposite to a profound truth is another truth, no less profound. By the same token, as Olga Sedakova writes, 'If the light of intellect is too flat and merciless, then the muffled darkness of the irrational is no better place for dwelling. One has to oppose not reason and its absence, but reason and reason; or, as Father Aleksandr Shmeman writes, "the clever reason and the stupid reason".[112]

It is hoped that this endeavour, while paving the way for future studies, will also help to bridge the still existing, and often painful, gap between Russian and Western European mentalities, or, in other words, will advance the (always challenging) intercultural dialogue.

---

[112] See Shmeman, *Dnevniki. 1973–1983*, op. cit., cited in Olga Sedakova, 'V zashchitu razuma', *Kontinent*, No. 144, 2010, <http://magazines.russ.ru/continent/2010/144/se13.html> [accessed 9 December 2013].

1

The Language of Irrationalism?

. . . Platonov speaks of a nation which in a sense has become the victim of its own language; or, to put it more accurately, he tells a story about this very language, which turns out to be capable of generating a fictitious world, and then falls into grammatical dependence on it. Because of all this, Platonov seems to be quite untranslatable, and, in one sense, that's a good thing: for the language into which he cannot be translated.[1]

Joseph Brodsky

Language versus culture and reality: The chicken and egg enigma

The claim that language and the underlying culture are intimately connected will hardly be met with opposition. Their mutual influence and intrinsic dialectical relationship seem undeniable. However, the degree and the nature of this inter-dependence are subtle and elusive, and remain a mysterious subject of every particular nation. In the Russian case this connection can be regarded as particularly striking, and appears crucial for understanding the phenomenon of Russian irrationalism. For, as we shall see argued in this chapter, in many ways it is the language which determines Russian national identity, way of thinking and ultimately Russian culture as a whole as well as Russian reality. In other words, Russian irrationalism starts with language.

* * *

Keis Verheil characterizes Russian culture as a culture of speaking. 'When a person is silent, the reality ceases to exist'[2] is his description of it (as opposed to his native, Dutch, culture, where 'when a person speaks the reality ceases to exist'). At the same time Vasilii Zenkovsky, like many other philosophers and historians of the Silver

---

[1] Joseph Brodsky, 'Catastrophes in the Air' in *Less Than One. Selected Essays*, Harmondsworth, Middlesex, England: Penguin Books, 1986, p. 290.
[2] Keis Verheil, 'Tishina u Akhmatovoi', in *Tsarstvennoe slovo*, N. V. Koroleva and S. A. Kovalenko (eds), Akhmatovskie chteniia, vol. 1, Moscow: Nasledie, 1992, p. 14.

Age, talks with a tinge of sadness of the Russian silence that preceded this culture of excessive speaking. He tries to defend the hidden potential of the modest and humble Pre-Petrine Russia which accumulated spirituality through icon-painting and monastic asceticism and only then exploded into Russian literature.[3] These two traditions – the silent (Russian hesychasm) and the verbal (logo-centric) – form the overall landscape of Russian culture and are usually considered synchronically. Mikhail Epstein in his elegant article on 'Word and silence in Russian culture' views them diachronically and discerns a dialectical relationship between them: 'Two features of Russian culture – silence and excessive speaking – are interconnected. And this is not a mere antinomy, where both of the opposite theses are correct. The very silence grows and strengthens as the speaking advances, and the propensity to speaking results from the intensity and inexpressibility of silence. [. . .] Russian letters are striking by the very property of displaying their profound wordlessness, they remain loudly and stubbornly silent, hiding this silence behind a multiplicity of words'.[4]

For Keis Verheil in the Russian case 'logos gives rise to reality, and not the other way around'.[5] This is expressed more strongly by Ilja Kabakov, 'in the mind, nerves and memory of each one of us there is a neurosis of endless speaking, of realisation of yourself predominantly in words, there is a continuous, ceaselessly storming sea of words, which overwhelms everything';[6] and even more strongly by the academician Ivan Pavlov with his theory of language as a second signalling system, 'The second signalling system of a Russian is developed to such a degree that objective reality is nothing for him. Word is everything'. Mikhail Epstein summarizes this in his main thesis that Russian language 'does not tell us about existence, but is itself existence'.[7]

Verheil considers Russian to be a direct heir of the Byzantium tradition, as he conjectures that 'European cultures could be divided according to their origins being either from Rome or from Byzantium into those based on Word – Logos, and those based on the idea of action, object, reality – in Latin: Res'.[8] Interestingly, those who view Russian language as Being itself, who claim its primacy over reality, in a way invest Russian culture with the idea of *Res* too, only the action is performed through language, through Logos itself. Osip Mandelshtam by-passes the above two roots by deriving Russian language from Hellenism, but supports the idea of its formative (as opposed to informative) role:

> Russian is a Hellenistic language. Due to a number of historical reasons, the living forces of Hellenistic culture, having given the West up to the Latin influences and not lingering in the childless Byzantium, rushed to the river-bed of Russian speech . . . as a result Russian language turned precisely into a sounding and speaking flesh.

---

[3]   See Zenkovsky, *History of Russian Philosophy*, op. cit., pp. 35–60.
[4]   Mikhail Epstein, 'Slovo i molchanie v russkoi kulture', *Zvezda*, 2005, No. 10, <http://magazines.russ.ru/zvezda/2005/10/ep12.html> [accessed 2 February 2014].
[5]   Keis Verheil, op. cit.
[6]   Ilya Kabakov, *Zhizn mukh* (teksty na russkom, nemetskom i angliiskom). Kolnischer Kunstverein. Edition Cantz, 1992, p. 112. Cited in M. Epstein, op. cit.
[7]   M. Epstein, op. cit.
[8]   Keis Verheil, op. cit.

<. . .> The life of language in the Russian historical reality outweighs all the other facts by the fullness of phenomena, the fullness of being which represents only an unattainable extreme for all the other phenomena of Russian life. The Hellenistic nature of the Russian language can be identified with its existentiality. A word in Hellenistic understanding is an active flesh which resolves itself in an event. <. . .> No other language resists a nominating and applied function more than Russian does. Russian nominalism, i.e. the perception of word as reality, nourishes the spirit of our language.[9]

Historically, Russian language in its written form emerged as the language for translation of the Bible. The wealth of Russian 'was acquired most of all together with the Greek Christian law, when church literature was translated from Greek into Slavic for praising God'.[10] Thus, Epstein writes, 'Perhaps this primary connection with the Greek language (and not a spoken language, but the language of the Holy Writ) explains at least in part the "intrinsic" tendency of the Russian language towards sacred practices: it is destined for "praising the Lord"', for 'as it were, imitating God'.[11]

This perception of language, as invested with creative powers with respect to reality, brings to mind a metaphor suggested by British literary scholar Richard Peace – that Russian literature is a mirror of Russian reality, but, unlike a simple mirror, it magically speaks back and shapes that reality.[12] By analogy, Epstein's claim, grounded in the premonitions of many Russian thinkers, is in fact stronger – effectively it means that Russian language is even more than a magic mirror – it is a magic wand which, by shaping the mentality and mode of thought of the nation, shapes its reality. While Herzen rests the case of Russian logo-centrism on socio-political reality, stating that in Russia 'literature is the only podium from which the nation can speak about its pain',[13] Epstein offers a more radical – almost metaphysical – explanation. He argues that Russian language is 'the only dense, tangible reality which in Russia is surrounded by the ocean of less real things'. It is this, according to Epstein, which explains why literature lays at the foundation of Russian history. Furthermore, 'Despite Chaadaev's opinion that Russia does not belong to the historical realm of nations, Mandelshtam claims that "so highly organised, such an organic language is not only a gateway to history, but it is history itself." In Russia only its language is historical, while all the other phenomena do not have a real existence, or only half-exist, they form an illusory medium of language and have it as their unattainable limit', 'real life happens not outside it, [. . .] but within it',[14] is Epstein's conclusion.

[9] Osip Mandelshtam, 'O prirode slova', in *Sobranie sochinenii v 3 tomakh*, vol. 2, New York: Mezhdunarodnoe Literaturnoe Soobshchestvo, 1971, pp. 245, 246. Cited in M. Epstein, op. cit.

[10] Mikhail Lomonosov, 'Predislovie o polze knig tserkovnykh v rossiiskom iazyke', cited from A. M. Dokusov (ed.), *Russkie pisateli o iazyke. Khrestomatiia*, Leningrad: Gos. uch.-ped. izd., 1954, p. 16. Cited in M. Epstein.

[11] M. Epstein, op. cit.

[12] Richard Peace, *Russian Literature and the Fictionalisation of Life*, Hull: The University of Hull, 1976.

[13] Aleksandr Herzen, 'O razvitii revoliutsionnykh idei v Rossii', in A. I. Herzen, *Sobranie sochinenii v 30 tomakh*, vol. VII, Moscow, 1956, p. 198.

[14] M. Epstein, op. cit. (Mandelshtam's quote is also from op. cit.)

Of course, the view of reality as essentially a product of language can be inscribed into the broader theory. Indeed, it forms part of the Structuralist agenda, and represents 'the latest version of the classical idealist doctrine that the world was simply constituted by human consciousness'.[15]

By contrast the materialist view, of which Western rationalist scepticism is a case, shows distrust to the theories that insist on the primacy of language. Thus, Dean S. Worth comments that 'some, perhaps exaggerating, have averred that form of our language determines the form of our thought, while others, more convincingly, maintain that language' (as a general system of selecting and ordering elements) 'is the primary modelling system through which we view all our surroundings and through which all other systems must be filtered'.[16] However, he does concede an important role of language in the underlying culture, and especially in the Russian case: 'At the very least, it is obvious that language plays an essential role in culture, and in defining culture. This is especially true of Russian cultural history'.[17]

Notably, the aforementioned German irrationalist J. G. Hamann in his original theory of language, which found its way to modernity, suggested that 'every language is a way of life, and a way of life is based on a pattern of experience which cannot itself be subjected to criticism, since one cannot find an Archimedean point outside it from which to conduct such a critical examination; at most, all one can do is to examine the symbolism by which the pattern of experience is expressed. [. . .] Above all, content and form cannot be divorced – there is an "organic" connection between all the elements of a medium of communication, and the meaning lies in the individual, ultimately unanalysable whole'.[18] From this Hamann concluded an impossibility of an adequate translation between languages, since form and content are inseparable, and foreign language is a different pattern of experience and way of thinking. As a corollary, Hamann believed, 'one cannot truly understand what men are saying by merely applying grammatical or logical or any other kind of rules, but only by an act of "entering into" – what Hereder called "Einfühlung" – their symbolism, and for that reason only by the preservation of actual usage, past and present'.[19]

In more general terms, the theory that mentality (and hence reality) of a nation is in principle dependent on its language does not appear new in the world practice. Instructively, perceiving language perhaps not as drastically as a magic wand, but at least as a magic mirror that not merely reflects culture, but also speaks back, shaping that culture, is not only far from losing its edge, but instead is becoming ever more topical.

Indeed, while American linguistics developed the subject into the second half of the twentieth century mostly in a rationalist direction – with a vision of language as an object of natural science, European philological tradition 'rejected as crude

---

[15] Terry Eagleton, *Literary Theory. An Introduction*, 2nd ed., Oxford: Blackwell Publishing, 2001, p. 94.

[16] Dean S. Worth, 'Language', in Rzhevsky (ed.), *The Cambridge Companion to Modern Russian Culture*, op. cit., p. 19.

[17] Ibid.

[18] Berlin, op. cit., 130.

[19] See ibid.

any attempts to study language outside the extra-linguistic data of the history and culture of the nation which speaks it'.[20] However, it was also in America that a theory intrinsically uniting language with culture emerged and, although met with scepticism by the main-stream linguistics, gave rise to various related disciplines such as psycho-linguistics, cultural studies, translation theories, culture-through-language studies (culture-oriented linguistics) and others. The theory in question is that of linguistic relativism, authored by Benjamin Lee Whorf (1897–1941), a professional chemist and an amateur linguist, and named after his teacher – a prominent and influential linguist of his time Edward Sapir.

According to the Whorf–Sapir theory, the outlook on life of an individual largely depends on his or her language in that its grammatical as well as semantic categories serve not only as an instrument for transmitting the thoughts of the speakers, but also shape their ideas and govern their mental processes. Thus our picture of the universe, our *Weltanschauung* is linguistically dependant, to the extent that we may find it difficult to have a sufficiently profound and effective communication with a representative of a language which is structurally too distant from ours. Whorf's ideas were developed through his close study of the American Indian tribes, mostly of Hopi, whose native language (Uto-Aztecan branch of Aztec-Tanoan languages) provided a rich ground for investigation.

Notably, despite scepticism from more essentialist quarters with respect to linguistic relativism, up to this day the dialectical relationship between language and culture continues to be a point of serious debate and on-going exploration. Even in the study of the lexical pool alone this topicality 'can be explained by constantly increasing practical demands of the intense intercultural communications of the last decades, as well as by an insufficient amount of general-theoretical research'– we are informed by a contemporary research reported in a doctoral thesis of 2009 at Moscow State University.[21] A paper of 2006 in the Japanese case study demonstrates how Japanese institutional economic structures are based on linguistic structures, and thus how the language reflects the mentality and psychology of the nation.[22]

Instructively, an integrated approach to language study in relation to the underlying culture still represents considerable difficulty, even in restricted areas, such as, for instance, lexical analysis of culturally marked vocabulary. This difficulty apparently arises precisely at the border areas – where an (almost) natural science (linguistics) meets humanities (extra-linguistic disciplines).

Indeed, a cultural side of a language is difficult to objectify, and intuition of those working within language – say, of poets, whose relationship with their tongue (and with language in general) is most intimate – although carries much weight, cannot in itself be an argument in scientific investigation. However, it can serve as a useful

[20] V. Z. Demyankov, 'Dominating Linguistic Theories at the End of the 20th Century', in Iu. S. Stepanov (ed.), *Iazyk i nauka kontsa 20 veka*, Moscow: Institut iazykoznaniia RAN, 1995, p. 242.

[21] M. G. Yashina, 'Analiz i semantizatsiia kulturno-markirovannoi leksiki (na materiale italianskogo iazyka)', PhD Thesis, Department of Italian Studies, School of Foreign Languages and Regional Studies, Moscow State University.

[22] B. A. Erznkian, 'Prostye lingvo-ekonomicheskie osnovaniia slozhnykh institutsialnykh struktur', in O. V. Inshakov (ed.), *Vstrecha s prostotoi*, Volgograd: Volgogradskoe nauchnoe izdanie, 2006.

vantage point, as it were – as empirical data of sorts which can then be tested by more objective – rational (scientific) – means. Furthermore, the weight of these 'empirical' data should not be under-estimated, as often poetic genius is able to grasp – by purely irrational, intuitive, means – the very essence of natural phenomena, even of those which are far from the poet's preoccupations and immediate experience. The professor of physics, Iakov Geguzin, exemplifies this in his lectures on the life of a drop of water, by making constant allusions to literature – predominantly, although not exclusively, Russian literature. In particular, when explaining in the very technical language of crystal physics the mechanism of how a drop can ruin a solid crystal, a rock, he quotes the lines of the French poet Raymond Queneau which describe this phenomenon, and then comments, 'how come that a poet, distant from the physics of liquids and crystals, understands that a dewdrop can break a rock? . . . *maybe this is a sophisticated intuition when the truth, going past logical contemplation, is bursting onto paper?* Indeed, the path of the poetic thought and sources of the poetic images are inscrutable!'[23]

By the same token, a major poet's feeling of a language (especially of his native tongue) certainly merits attention.

Before we turn to it, however, it is worth pointing out that the types of questions which may seem weird today can become completely natural tomorrow. Relative ambiguities of human languages, their gradation according to their 'rationality' may well be written without inverted commas in the future – because the boundary between 'understood' and 'not understood' phenomena shifts as much as that between rational and irrational. For example, some apparently random experiments, such as playing music to house plants, seem crazy at first, but may become an object of scientific research later on, even if surrounded by controversy.[24] Daring thus is a good first step in any enquiry (perhaps even a necessary one, although certainly not sufficient!).

Impressions from within: The language of betrayal?

When asked a question of whether betrayal is a theme for his oeuvre, Joseph Brodsky replied: 'Indeed, it is one of the most essential and eternal themes of Russian literature – which is all about betrayal. In this sense I keep, it seems to me, within the tradition – more that of prose than of poetry. This literature, and frame of mind, are to a large extent balanced out by expectation of betrayal. I believe that, to a certain degree, this makes an impact on the language.'[25]

Having stated this, Brodsky then deems it necessary to make a qualification that he should not really 'venture into these grey areas', but immediately after he does just that: 'In Russian, for example, there is (although this is too strong an accusation) always present an expectation of total rearrangement, probably because

[23] Ia. E. Geguzin, *Kaplia*, Moscow: Nauka, 1977, p. 120. Highlighting with italics is mine.
[24] See for example the ground-breaking study by Dorothy L. Retallack, *The Sound of Music and Plants* (Santa Monika: Devorss & Co, 1973) which evoked substantial resonance, even though it was met predominantly with distrust and scepticism by scholarly world.
[25] Valentina Polukhina (ed.), *Iosif Brodskii. Bolshaia kniga interviiu*, Moscow: Zakharov, 2000, p. 58.

the words are multisyllabic and contain a lot of phonetics. Also an element of self-extermination is present, merely because there are too many syllables to accept this accusation at its face value. The idea of a total rearrangement, of ambivalence and betrayal sneaks into the language. We are now talking about nuances. In fact it is easier, in some sense, to speak Russian in a level tone, regardless of the underlying feeling. The feeling might be a direct one: "I approve of this" or "I do not approve of this". However, simply due to the language, the expression of this feeling acquires a colouring of ambiguity. There appears this light spice, or I would even say, poison. The reader feels it. One can use this endlessly, because almost any statement is coloured with uncertainty'.[26]

These observations over Russian language are then complemented by similar ones concerning English. The interview dates 1980, that is eight years spent in the English-speaking environment – a period during which Brodsky's English developed sufficiently to have started writing essays in it, which only six years later brought him his Nobel prize in literature. This is not to mention that English was the medium into which he strove to submerge, first as a reader and translator (when still in Russia) and then as an active agent (when in emigration in the United States). Brodsky recognizes that English, by contrast to Russian, is an 'analytical language' and characterizes it as the language which 'does not really allow many nuances'. Otherwise, he says, 'one starts being cunning like Henry James, to say the least. There is English and English. On the one hand there are Jane Austin and Orwell, on the other – James, Conrad and Nabokov. I prefer the Austin-Orwell tradition. In James's English the feeling of the texture is similar to Russian. But when you work with texture your statements become . . . well, not exactly compromised, but less significant, as you are striving for a cumulative effect. So, all depends on which English you are talking about. English as such, I think, does not exist'.[27] In the same vein he makes an interesting observation on the impact of English-speaking environment on his Russian: 'When I write, I sense a larger degree of clarity, of rationality in comparison with how I would write while in Russia. The point is that Russian is not an analytical language. [. . .] In English, however, there is something which forces you to clarify your thought, to develop it. And this is now present in my [Russian] poetry'.[28]

Notably, these qualifications of languages are consistent with Brodsky's perception of the underlying cultures, or more precisely of their dominant ways of cognition. Thus he qualifies Russian frame of mind, or a way of perception of the world, as synthetic and English as analytical, and a metaphoric description of this which he gives, although already quoted in the introduction, is too elucidating not to be recalled here again: 'Suppose you cut open an apple and peel off its skin. Now you know what is inside it, but at the same time you lose sight of these two convexities, these two cheeks of the apple. Russian culture, on the contrary, is interested in an apple as a whole, gets delighted in its colour, admires the smoothness of its skin, etc.'[29]

[26] Ibid., pp. 58–9.
[27] Ibid., p. 59.
[28] Ibid., p. 251.
[29] Volkov, *Dialogi s Iosifom Brodskim*, op. cit., p. 198.

The difference between the synthetic and analytical groups of languages is thus usefully summarized by Epstein: 'Normally synthetic languages, such as Russian, are opposed to analytical languages, such as English or French, along the lines of merging or diverging of semantics and syntax. In a synthetic language grammatical and lexical meanings are expressed using one lexical unit, unlike in an analytical language. For example, Russian word "bratu" /"brother", Dative/ contains the lexical meaning "brat" /"brother", Nominative/ together with the grammatical meaning of address, direction, Dative case. In English these two meanings are expressed analytically, using two lexical units: the noun "brother" and preposition "to". One can extend further this distinction between synthetic and analytical designs to the relationship within the language of semantics and pragmatics, i.e. "content"-nominating and expressive-evaluating meanings, of denotation and connotation.[30] Crucially then, 'synthetic design of Russian is manifested, in particular, in the fact that the "content" meaning turns out to be inseparable from the evaluating one, semantics – from pragmatics'.[31]

Vladimir Nabokov's characterization of Russian and English, although strikingly different at first glance from the ideas put forward by Brodsky, when read more attentively still contains the reflections of the same phenomena. Indeed, he sees the two languages metaphorically as follows: 'a venerable genius who combines a motley erudition with an absolute freedom of spirit' (English) and 'a youth of genius, but not yet sufficiently well educated and at times rather tasteless' (Russian). 'Everything tenderly human (strange as it may seem!), but also everything coarse and crude, juicy and bawdy, comes out no worse in Russian than in English, perhaps better; but the subtle reticence so peculiar to English, the poetry of thought, the instantaneous resonance between the most abstract concepts, the swarming of the monosyllabic epithets – all this, and also everything relating to technology, fashion, sports, the natural sciences, and the unnatural passions – in Russian become clumsy, prolix and often repulsive in terms of style and rhythm'.[32] Thus Nabokov is in fact irritated by that very same multi-syllabic structure of Russian which Brodsky sees as the root of ambiguity; and more generally by the inability to carry across the English economy of expression which in Russian disintegrates into a vast and clumsy chaos. In other words, he pays tribute to the laconic and precise features of English as opposed to Russian savage potential.

This admiration with respect to English conceals, it appears, a neophyte type of inadequacy which explains his bias. Indeed, despite his trilingual upbringing, as his afterword to the English edition of *Lolita* (addressed to native English speakers) gives

---

[30] Epstein, 'Slovo i molchanie v russkoi kulture', op. cit.

[31] In this respect, it is interesting to note the difference between the use of swearing language in Russian (*mat*) and in English. While in English it spices up speech in all sorts of registers, but remains largely the way to add extra-colour to one's way of expression, in Russian, even though it is extremely wide-spread, it has not lost its strength and remains *semantically* important. In the Russian context, having emerged as a humane alternative to physical violence, it either still effectively remains such, being intensely charged emotionally, or it becomes another, alternative and all-pervasive discourse, with a life of its own. Either way, in contrast to the Western case, its function is vital.

[32] Vladimir Nabokov, Postscript to the Russian edition of *Lolita*, transl. by Earl D. Sampson, in J. E. Rivers and Charles Nicol (eds), *Nabokov's Fifth Arc: Nabokov and Others on His Life's Work*, Austin: University of Texas Press, 1982, p. 190.

away, Nabokov is much more confident with his Russian than with his English which he regards second-rate: 'My private tragedy, which cannot, and indeed should not, be anybody's concern, is that I had to abandon my natural idiom, my untrammeled, rich, and infinitely docile Russian tongue for a second-rate brand of English, devoid of any of those apparatuses – the baffling mirror, the black velvet backdrop, the implied associations and traditions – which the native illusionist, frac-tails (*sic.*) flying, can magically use to transcend the heritage in his own way'.[33] Curiously, as a result, Nabokov unites in his descriptions what is Lev Shestov's image of the two cultures: Russian – bold and daring in its savage youth, but thus able to seek the truth unreservedly and to have that very freedom of spirit[34] which Nabokov ascribes to English (as a sum-total of its long evolution).

This picture acquires a touch of irony when one recalls that Brodsky ascribed Nabokov's English to the type where it becomes similar to Russian in texture and relies more on the cumulative effect of the text. Even more ironically, we find very different sentiments from the above in Nabokov's 'Drugie berega (Other shores)' which was written almost simultaneously with 'Lolita': 'my memory was tuned to one register – Russian, with its musical understatement, but it was forced to a different register – English, thorough and practical'.[35] Notably, even 20 plus years earlier – in his novel 'Podvig (Glory)' Nabokov expressed similar feelings, being biased in favour of the Russian language and culture: 'Such words, such notions and images, as those that Russia had engendered did not exist in other countries, and it often happened that he would lapse into incoherence, or start to laugh nervously when vainly trying to explain to a foreigner the various meanings of some special term, say, *oskomina* or *poshlost*".[36] In his paper on translation he wrote again of the intrinsic inadequacies of translation into English of certain Russian concepts: "'Yah pom-new" is a deeper and smoother plunge into the past than "I remember," [. . .] "chewed-no-yay" has a lovely Russian "monster" in it, and a whispered "listen", and the dative ending of a "sunbeam", and many other fair relations among Russian words. It belongs phonetically and mentally to a certain series of words, and this Russian series does not correspond to the English series in which "I remember" is found'.[37]

Should we therefore take Nabokov's statements above, of the youth and immaturity of Russian literary language, as conformist, as a mere currying favour with the American public? Or did he, perhaps, change his opinions depending on some external or internal circumstances? One way or another the overall vector of his sentiments still points in the direction of what seems to be a Russian consensus on the comparative characteristics of Russian and English.

[33] Vladimir Nabokov, Postscript to the English edition of *Lolita*, Paris: Olympia Press, 1955, p. 318.
[34] See Lev Shestov, 'All Things Are Possible' ('Apotheosis of Groundlessness'), <http://www.angelfire.com/nb/shestov/all/all_23.html> [accessed 2 August 2013].
[35] Vladimir Nabokov, 'Drugie Berega', <http://www.lib.ru/NABOKOW/drgberega.txt> [accessed 2 August 2013].
[36] Vladimir Nabokov, 'Glory' ('Podvig'), Harmondsworth, Middlesex, England: Penguin Books, 1982, p. 151.
[37] Vladimir Nabokov, 'The Art of Translation', <http://www.newrepublic.com/article/books-and-arts/the-art-translation> [accessed 24 August 2014].

The impression which arises from the above views – particularly for someone looking from the side, especially Western side – is that Russian language (as it is perceived by Russian litterateurs) is fully consistent with the underlying culture in terms of its chaotic element, as it were its almost intrinsic chaos. Indeed, the 'overloaded' Russian speech must seem scary – with its multisyllabic structure, its complex syntax packed in long sentences, endless like Russian trains slowly moving along the vast spaces and at the same time unruly as Russian *troikas* running fast, but largely out of control; its complex grammar and the resulting frighteningly multi-volumed, idiosyncratic literature filled with excessive emotions – all this is reflected in a stereotypical Western perspective on Russia. Curiously, Russian internal view is little different – the distinction is largely in the opposite colouring of the same assessment: one feels at home in the absurdity of existence as wild fish whose gills are used to muddy waters, unlike the refined type, cultivated in a more transparent environment, and frightened off by the dirty lake. By the same token, to Russians their language seems commensurable to infinity, as it were – best suited to handle the irrational of which infinity is an embodiment. Indeed, as Brodsky said about Dostoevsky: 'A born metaphysician, he instinctively realized that for probing infinity, whether an ecclesiastical one or that of the human psyche, there was no tool more far-reaching than his highly inflected mother tongue, with its convoluted syntax'.[38]

Effectively what Epstein speaks about in his contemplation on Russian language equates the standard contemplation on Russian culture: on its notorious obsession with the ultimate questions of existence – the tendency to philosophizing, to a higher, sublime complexity, to the super-meaning at the expense of getting detached from the everyday reality. The following old philosophical fable very much reflects this Russian peculiarity (especially in the light of Czeslaw Milosz's sarcastic comment on Russian national propensity towards passionate, although uneducated and non-academic philosophizing).[39] A witty Thracian handmaid saw Phales, who, while trying to discover mysteries in the sky, had fallen into a well. 'How do you expect to understand what is going on up in the sky if you do not even see what is at your feet?', she asked him laughingly. This striving to the stars at the expense of losing the ground under one's feet metaphorically captures the typical urge of Russian literary tradition towards the edge, to the 'cursed' existential questions, while losing its grip on the everyday reality as a result.[40] It is this Russian tendency, it seems, that Epstein effectively links with the language itself when he writes: '[the writer] Dmitrii Galkovsky observes in the Russian language "predisposition towards the illness of absurdity". However, this

---

[38] Brodsky, 'Catastrophes in the Air' in *Less Than One. Selected Essays*, op. cit., p. 278.

[39] See the introduction where the precise quotation is given: 'no centuries of scholastic theology and philosophy in the past, no university philosophy to speak of – but on the other hand a lot of people philosophizing, and passionately at that, on their own' (Milosz, 'Shestov, or the Purity of Despair', op. cit., p. 101).

[40] This is despite the existence of the Russian proverb 'лучше синица в руке, чем журавль в небе' – literally: 'a tit in the hand is better than a crane in the sky' (the English version – 'bird in the hand is better than two in the bush' – is not really equivalent, as it offers merely a quantitatively better /yet out of reach/ alternative, while in the Russian version it is a qualitatively better, 'higher' alternative) – which reflects the opposite world-view. Isn't this proverb an (unsuccessful) attempt to curtail/oppose the (dangerous) above tendency? Or is it a cunning Russian peasant's logic as opposed to the sublime logic of Russian intelligentsia?

illness of absurdity results from the striving to the supermeaning, when the word does not state a fact (an informative function of speech, according to L. Wittgenstein), but rather exists on its own right, as the "creative let there be" (a formative function of speech according to S. Bulgakov). It is precisely the formative function of speech which creates a domain of silence inside the verbal squall. An informative speech says exactly as much as it says; it does not accumulate silence within itself. The Russian word thus turns out to be formatively excessive and simultaneously informatively insufficient. It swirls around itself and carries an empty funnel of meaning'.[41] Brodsky, effectively, speaks of the same phenomenon when, in his analysis of Platonov's prose, he contemplates the role of utopia in Russian socio-cultural reality: '. . . it should be noted that the first casualty of any discourse about utopia – desired or already attained – is grammar; for language, unable to keep up with this sort of thought, begins to gasp in the subjunctive mood and starts to gravitate toward categories and constructions of a rather timeless denomination. As a consequence of this, the ground starts to slip out from under even the simplest nouns, and they gradually get enveloped in an aura of arbitrariness'.[42]

Brodsky then applies this to Platonov's writings where each phrase 'drives the Russian language into a semantic dead end or, more precisely, *reveals a proclivity for dead ends, a blind-alley mentality in the language itself*.[43] Irrationalism of being is predicated on the irrationalism of the language: thus Platonov's target, as well as the concrete social evil, is the '*sensibility of language that has brought that evil about*'.[44] Through the prism of Platonov's oeuvre Brodsky sees Russian language as the 'very carrier of millenarian sensibility' and speaks of the '*revolutionary eschatology embedded in the language*'.[45]

One way or the other, we have so far, as a dry residue, the (largely intuitive) observations of Russian writers and scholars above of 'rational' and 'precise' English, an 'analytical' language, as opposed to 'ambiguous' and 'treacherous' Russian, a 'synthetic' language, which by nature is predisposed (or even tends) to the irrational (to the apocalyptic and absurd). It would be tempting to explore, from a strictly linguistic perspective, if they conceal objective foundation.

For that one would need a quantifier to measure language's inherent ambiguities – for instance, its distance from (or proximity to) computer languages. But this must be a by-product of the NLP (natural language processing) branch of computational linguistics which is concerned with the interactions between computers and natural languages. Its tasks are to convert information from computer databases into readable human language as well as to convert samples of human language into more formal representations such as parse trees or first-order logic structures that computer can then manipulate. Among multiple problems that arise are those of disambiguation of words' meanings (sometimes multiple) and syntactic (or grammatical) complexities (i.e. choosing between various semantic possibilities).

---

[41] Epstein, op. cit. (Quote from Galkovsky is Dmitrii Galkovsky, *Beskonechnyi tupik*, Moscow: Samizdat, 1997, p. 417.)
[42] Joseph Brodsky, 'Catastrophes in the Air', op. cit., p. 286.
[43] Ibid. Italics is mine.
[44] Ibid., p. 283.
[45] Ibid. Italics is mine.

Intuitively it seems clear to a speaker of both languages – English and Russian – that English is indeed distinguished by a real economy of expression which comes through not only in the (relatively short) length of words, but also in syntactical structures (strict word order, low-inflected grammar and Boolean logic of negation which reflects the rules of formal mathematical logic). Russian is opposite: words are much longer, word order is flexible, word formation is extremely rich (which, in a way, compensates for a significantly smaller vocabulary than in English); it is a highly inflected language and, unlike English, uses double negation: 'I do not want nothing' instead of 'I want nothing'. That is why a bilingual (Russian-English) mathematician invariably knows that mathematical discourse is much easier expressed in English than in Russian – precisely because English leaves much less space for ambiguities. Even articles alone (inherent in a large set of languages, including English, but excluding Russian) can be of considerable help when communicating mathematical statements. Thus to say 'let's take a point' will become in Russian: 'let's take an arbitrary, but fixed point'. Such examples are numerous.

At the same time one suspects in these two languages the buried remnants of the philosophical dilemma of predestination versus free will. Indeed, English appears to be a language of a nominative case, of a subject free to act, while Russian is overwhelmed by Dative, where instead of being an independent agent you are an object to which things happen regardless of your will and are set in motion by some impersonal force. 'I am cold', 'I am in pain', 'I am pleased' and even 'I am forty' is English for what in Russian becomes 'to me it is cold/painful/pleasing' ('мне холодно/больно/приятно') or 'to me it is forty' ('мне сорок лет'). And the fact that English was once different and in Shakespearean times one would say 'to me it is pleasing' only testifies to the particular direction of the evolution English language has undergone in contrast to Russian, where the feeling of a blind force has persisted to this day. This supernatural force pervades Russian grammar in the abundance of impersonal sentences such as 'крышу снесло ветром' (the roof was taken off by the wind), 'город завалило снегом' (the city was snowed down), 'светало' (it was dawning), 'смеркалось' ('it was getting dark'); or, in the same vein, the echo of the pagan sensibility is audible in the descriptions of natural phenomena, where in English 'it' is used: 'it rains/snows', while in Russian the rain and snow themselves are animated: 'шел дождь /или снег'/ (literally: 'the rain/snow was going/walking'). Similarly, one can detect, if one is inclined to reason in such categories, certain a-priori pessimism in the Russian syntactical constructions such as 'Ты не видел моих тапок?' (in English the best approximation would probably be: 'You have not seen my slippers, have you?'); as opposed to the English, full of hope: 'Have you seen my slippers?'. This propensity of the language itself to prompt the (negative in the Russian context) answer, was even used by a brilliant Russian comedian-writer Mikhail Zhvanetsky who wrote about an average Soviet man in the era of Brezhnev stagnation with its ever hopelessly empty shops: 'He himself is to blame for this, as he puts the answer in the mouth of shop assistants – by saying to them: "You do not have any newspapers (or food items) /left/, do you?" And of course they readily say "No, indeed not!"'

By the same token, a literary scholar knows that Russian and English require a different mind-set when writing about the same things. More generally, switching between languages in a conversation often feels like switching your identity – not so much pretending, not wearing a mask, but rather as if opening some locks within your psyche at the expense of closing some other ones – indeed, moving between cultures. However, intuition might easily let us down, and these rather vague empirical observations clearly require a scientific grounding, a qualitative back-up.

So, what is the real state of affairs in the fields of computer science and linguistics with respect to English and Russian? Perhaps not surprisingly, in the area of automated translation there has been relatively little achieved in terms of major qualitative breakthroughs. Thus one is still unable to recognize semantics automatically, despite the diverse attempts to use neural networks and other sophisticated devices. Instead, databases (or 'knowledge bases'), that is organized depositories of data remain the main tool. These databases contain the bilingual equivalents of words, expressions, idioms, grammatical forms, etc., equipped with the weights of these equivalences, as well as with various formal rules and heuristic algorithms for phrase constructions and for selecting 'most probable' translations (i.e. those with maximal weight).

However, the numerical information concerning the current achievements in this area essentially remains a commercial secret, thus leaving us without a genuine authoritative back-up for the conjectures above. If not for that, we could, perhaps, learn – through the comparative lengths and complexity of these databases – as it were, the relative complexities of the languages involved. Some things are known though: for example, the fact that the database for a Russian-English pair considerably exceeds that for the English-German one, while (perhaps instructively in some sense) the results for the former are significantly poorer.

One thing is uncontroversial though – that the (so far) insurmountable difficulties on the route of trying to solve the automated translation problem (which, interestingly, began with a famous attempt to translate between precisely Russian and English back in 1954) hint at the extreme complexity of human languages. It is perhaps not much of a surprise that different languages all have their own complexities and ambivalence in some specific areas, and a certain preservation law takes place: what is absent in one language in comparison to another, is compensated for by different means – like a river meeting an obstacle on its route will make a by-pass to continue its flow. Thus, for instance, grammatical 'poverty' is made up by syntactical 'complexity': in English gerund is effectively borrowed from the continuous tenses verbal form, that is makes for a saving in grammatical forms. This simplifies the grammar, but leads to a more complex syntax, while in Russian *deeprichastie* cannot be used elsewhere, it is a separate, unique verbal form, which makes syntax clearer, but 'burdens' the grammar. And, more generally, language will clearly beat any attempt to 'outwit' it, and will survive no matter what, regardless of the damage which peoples and states may cause to each other, 'because there is a wonderful property of language: it knows better than everything and everybody what is mutation; its ability to mutate is terrifying.'[46] And since language's potential 'is determined not so much by the quantitative body of the nation that speaks it (though it is determined by that, too), as by the quality of

---

[46] Polukhina (ed.), *Iosif Brodskii. Bolshaia kniga interviiu*, op. cit., p. 272.

the poem written in it', both Russian and English will live on and continue to evolve, because 'that which is being created today in Russian or English, for example, secures the existence of these languages over the course of the next millennium'.[47] Thus language needs a human being to actualize its existence as much as a human needs language to actualize his – which by a strange association brings to mind Berdiaev's philosophical ideas that both God and man need each other. It is perhaps not accidental that this comparison springs to mind, as it does in fact have deeper connotations than a mere external resemblance.

Philosophy of language

The connotation implied (where language is paralleled with God) pertains to philosophy of language, which often occupies if not central, then a very significant part in a given philosophical system. Implicitly at least, it gives rise to generalizations of metaphysical character within particular languages and may have far-reaching cultural implications, including a shaping of national identity and self-perception. As with nature, of which philosophies, depending on their position with respect to rationalism, deem humans to be either a product (materialism) or an intrinsic part (idealism), the role attributed to language also varies from being a mere method of communication (as in Marxism, for example) to being a pre-existing objective reality, the substance of being, which precedes every individual existence.

This latter (irrational) stance, which effectively continues the trend of philosophical idealism, essentially amounts to a religious sensibility, where the Divine Logos is placed at the start of things, and language itself thus acquires a Divine status or to a large extent comes to share this status. It takes precedence over existence. Thus, for Epstein (following the whole pleade of Russian philosophers and writers) (Russian) language is Being itself, it is primary and determines the reality around it. For Brodsky, following W. H. Auden, as we shall see, language (per se) is Deity; for Heidegger, whose stance is in many ways similar to Brodsky's, language is a pre-existing reality, a 'House of Being'. By the same token, for the Structuralists reality is a product of language.

Brodsky's train of thought had started, he claims, from reading the lines of Auden: 'Time that is intolerant,// Of the brave and innocent,// And indifferent in a week// to a beautiful physic// Worships language and forgives// Everyone by whom it lives'. He derived from these lines the whole theory of the Divine origin of Language: 'For "worship" is an attitude of the lesser toward the greater. If time worships language, it means that language is greater, or older, than time, which is, in its turn, older and greater than space. That was how I was taught, and I indeed felt that way. So if time – which is synonymous with, nay, even absorbs deity – worships language, where then does language come from? For the gift is always smaller than the giver. And then isn't language a repository of time? And isn't this why time worships it? And isn't a song, or

---

[47]　Joseph Brodsky, 'Uncommon Visage' (the Nobel Lecture) in *On Grief and Reason. Essays*, Harmondsworth: Penguin Books, 1997, p. 57.

a poem, or indeed a speech itself, with its caesuras, pauses, spondees, and so forth, a game language plays to restructure time?'.[48]

In Heidegger's philosophy language 'is not a mere instrument of communication [. . .]: it is the very dimension in which human life moves, that which brings the world to be in the first place'; language 'has an existence of its own in which human beings come to participate', it 'always pre-exists the individual subject, as the very realm in which he or she unfolds'.[49] In his work *Time and Being* Heidegger calls language 'the house of being' and 'clarifying-and-concealing manifestation of being'.[50]

Instructively, in his essay on language[51] Heidegger quotes another intrinsically mystical perception of language, by his fellow German thinker Johann Georg Hamann (1730–88), already mentioned above, from his letter to Johann Gottfried Herder (1744–1803) of 10 August 1784: 'If only I was as eloquent as Demosthenes, I would have to do no more than repeat a single word three times. Reason is language – Logos; I gnaw on this marrowbone and will gnaw myself to death over it. It is still always dark over these depths for me: I am still always awaiting an apocalyptic angel with a key to this abyss.'[52] Heidegger's lecture is in a sense an attempt to respond to this image of language as an abyss.

However, as Brodsky, unlike Heidegger, is indeed a poet, even if a philosophizing one, his relationship with language is more complex, as it acquires not only philosophical, but also, as it were, applied dimensions. Thus Language for him, especially poetic language, is the only means of survival, as well as, likely, the only meaning. Existential fear is overcome by writing: 'scraping of the quill on paper, amidst silence, is fearlessness in miniature'.[53] Moreover, language is substantiated, materialized, it becomes a tangible entity. Thus Yurii and Mikhail Lotman emphasize the role of letters, and more generally – of graphics, in Brodsky's poetics; his tangible, substantiated perception of speech. 'In Brodsky's world, apart from an object and emptiness, there is one more entity – letters; and not as abstract units of the graphic structure of language, but letters-things. [. . .] Graphics constitutes in Brodsky's poetry a substantial element of poetics'.[54]

By the same token Brodsky's conviction throughout his life was that a poet is an instrument of language, and not the other way around. 'A poet always knows that what in vernacular is called the voice of the Muse is, in reality, the dictate of the language; that it's not the language that happens to be his instrument, but that he is language's

---

[48] Brodsky, 'To Please a Shadow', in *Less Than One. Selected Essays*, op. cit., pp. 362–3.

[49] Terry Eagleton, op. cit., p. 55.

[50] Martin Heidegger, *Vremia i bytie* (*Time and Being*), Moscow, 1993. pp. 192, 199.

[51] Martin Heidegger, *Poetry, Language, Thought*, New York: Harper Perennial Modern Classics, 1971, p. 189.

[52] Johann Georg Hamann, *Briefwechsel*, Arthur Henkel (ed.), Wiesbaden/ Frankfurt: Insel Verlag, 1955–75, vol. 5, p. 177. Note that Hamann is strongly linked to irrationalism in its Western form – see, for example, Isaiah Berlin's *The Magus of the North. J.G. Hamann and the Origins of Modern Irrationalism*, op. cit.

[53] Iosif Brodsky, 'Primechaniia paporotnika' (1988), *Forma vremeni. Stikhotvoreniia, esse, piesy v dvukh tomakh*, Minsk: Eridan, 1992, vol. 2, p. 303. In Russian: '. . . скрип пера в тишине по бумаге – бесстрашье в миниатюре'.

[54] Yu. Lotman, M. Lotman, 'Mezhdu veshchiu i pustotoi (Iz nabliudenii nad poetikoi sbornika Iosifa Brodskogo "Uraniia")', in Iu. M. Lotman, *Izbrannye statii*, op. cit., vol. III, pp. 306–7.

means toward the continuation of its existence. [. . .] One who writes a poem writes it because the language prompts, or simply dictates, the next line,[55] he said in his Nobel lecture, and repeated with variations in his poetry, prose and interviews. Thus, by the same token, 'a writer cannot be an avant-gardist, but language is. The only merit of the writer is to understand the internal laws of the language'.[56] This stance, which again indirectly hints at the language's Divine origin and nature, was in fact shared by various artists of various backgrounds, Russian and non-Russian alike. A famous phrase 'I am only God's fife' ('Я божья дудка') by the Russian poet Sergei Esenin (1895–1995) came to symbolize precisely this.[57] Another Russian poet Yuri Levitansky (1922–96) saw it from a different angle: that the poet's duty is to decipher the poetry which once existed, but became obscure, 'covered by ashes and dust': 'our task is precisely in restoring the words, one by one'.[58] More generally, artists who work through different medium than language may still perceive themselves as merely an intermediary between the divine and the earthly, and see their task in discerning the divine message and conveying it intact. Such sentiments are expressed, for instance, by contemporary Russian musicians Alfred Shnitke and Valentin Silvestrov.[59] Similarly, as the philosopher Georgii Gachev wrote, explaining Nikolai Berdiaev's sensibility, 'this intuition, this sensation we find also in St. Augustine, Pascal, Descartes and Frank – that it is not me, but through me some Super-subject is thinking and writing'.[60]

Perhaps ironically (irony is in swapping roles), Heidegger's (i.e. the philosopher's) own writing about language is akin to obscurantist poetry, where one is left with a breadth of interpretations. By contrast, Brodsky (the poet) formulates his convictions with an almost scientific clarity. However, some of Heidegger's statements can be taken as the (strikingly) direct embodiment, or continuation, of Brodsky's ideas: 'Language speaks. Man speaks in as much as he corresponds (matches up) to language. This correspondence means listening. One hears in as much as one listens to the call of silence' (Язык говорит. Человек говорит постольку, поскольку он соответствует языку. Соответствие есть слушание. Слышат постольку, поскольку слушают призывы тиши); and later on: 'All written here is aimed only at teaching to live within the "voice" of language'.[61] (Все написанное направлено лишь на то, чтобы научить жить в говоре языка).

Thus language for Heidegger 'knows' the nature of things much before the human subject and regardless of it. Heidegger's understanding of language is thus as described in Tsvetaeva's poetry: 'This is how one attunes one's ear (the estuary attunes back to the source)';[62] which is reminiscent of Akhmatova's description of

55   Joseph Brodsky, 'Uncommon Visage' (the Nobel Lecture), op. cit., p. 56.
56   Polukhina (ed.), *Iosif Brodskii. Bol'shaia kniga interviiu*, p. 54.
57   Sergei Esenin, *Polnoe sobranie sochinenii*, Moscow: OLMA-Press, 2002, p. 751.
58   Yu. Levitansky, 'ARS POETICA' ('*Vse stikhi odnazhdy uzhe byli . . .*'), <http://levitansky.ouc.ru/ars-poetica.html> [accessed 3 February 2014].
59   See on this Aleksandr Ivashkin's article 'The Paradox of Russian Non-Liberty', op. cit.
60   Georgii Gachev, *Russkaia Duma*, Moscow: Novosti, 1991, p. 195.
61   Martin Heidegger, *Poetry, Language, Thought*, op. cit.
62   Marina Tsveataeva, 'Tak vslushivaiutsa . . .' (1923), <http://tsvetaeva.lit-info.ru/tsvetaeva/stihi/all/stih-806.htm> [accessed 10 February 2014]. In Russian: 'Так вслушиваются (в исток// Вслушивается — устье)'.

poetic creativity: 'A ceaseless striking of a clock is heard; // Far off, a dying peal of thunder. // I somehow sense the groaning and the sorrows // Of unrecognized, imprisoned voices, // A kind of secret circle narrows; // But in the abyss of whispers and ringing // Rises one triumphant sound. // Such an absolute silence surrounds it // That one can hear the grass growing in the woods, // How misfortune with a knapsack plods the earth . . . // But now the words are beginning to be heard'.[63] That is to say – listening to a Divine voice, waiting for poetic inspiration, trying to discern the voice of the Muse . . . – and we have come back to what for Brodsky is the dictate of the language (but what, as he says, is in vernacular called the voice of the Muse).

Considering the language as Deity, the word of God as God himself, was the essence of the dogmatic movement of 'imiaslavie' (name-glorification) within Russian Orthodoxy. It emerged in the early twentieth century, initiated by the schema-monk Illarion, and was supported not only by monks, but also by various Russian philosophers, such as Pavel Florensky, Sergei Bulgakov and Aleksei Losev. Philosophically it is linked to Plato's teaching about ideas and the connection between the names for things and things themselves, as expressed, in particular, in Plato's 'Cratylus'. The magic of the word then implies the vision of language itself as a magic entity, consistent with idealistic philosophical tradition. Thus Pavel Florensky, who created his own philosophy of language, stressing its antinomy and interpreting both language and science as symbolic description (which allowed him to talk – pioneeringly – about science as language), at the same time basically sees in language an elemental force, akin to nature itself. Language as it were may easily lose itself in chaos, merge with it, although this idea is not expressed directly. But if one recalls his views of two conflicting cultures: medieval and renaissance (средневековой and возрожденской), where the latter carries within it the grains of chaos and is subject to the law of entropy – of the spreading of chaos in all areas which are left to their own devices – then language too seems to be inscribable into this model. Indeed, this is what Florensky says: 'everything creative, individual, unique in the language, my personal immediate response to a particular phenomenon of the world – language as created in the very process of speaking, and only as such, leads, via pure emotionality, to excessive cleverness (*zaumnost*) and then to incoherency, and becomes lost in elemental din, banging, whistling, rumble and howling; language's immediacy inevitably turns into meaninglessness and intellectual void. By contrast, the monumental and general in the language, an acceptance of a certain historical tradition, using language as social and general only . . . leads, via reasonableness to convention, and from convention to arbitrariness of the language-giver . . .'.[64] Thus, one way or another we end up in entropy, and if not in absurdity and

---

[63] Anna Akhmatova, 'Creation' ('Tvorchestvo', 1936), in *The Complete Poems of Anna Akhmatova. Expanded Edition*, transl. by Judith Hemschemeyer, Boston, Edinburgh: Zephyr Press, Canongate Press, p. 413. In Russian: 'В ушах не умолкает бой часов;//Вдали раскат стихающего грома.// Неузнанных и пленных голосов//Мне чудятся и жалобы и стоны,//Сужается какой-то тайный круг,//Но в этой бездне шепотов и звонов//Встает один, все победивший звук.//Так вкруг него непоправимо тихо,//Что слышно, как в лесу растет трава,//Как по земле идет с котомкой лихо . . .//Но вот уже послышались слова'.

[64] Pavel Florensky, 'U vodorazdelov mysli', (vol. 1, chapter IV. 'Mysl' I iazyk'), Moscow: 'Pravda', 1990, appendix to *Voprosy filosofii*.

chaos as such (through the general as opposed to the individual in the language), then at least within the possibility of such a chaos, outside any objective constraints – which again points us to the irrational in language, if you like – reveals its irrational side.

Interestingly, one may find parallels between Russian Orthodox 'imiaslavie' and Hamann's irrationalist vision of language with 'the unity of thought and object – [. . .] word and world'.[65] In the Garden of Eden, 'every phenomenon of nature was a name – the sign, the symbol, the promise of a fresh and secret and ineffable but all the more intimate chosen union, communication and communion of divine energies and ideas. All that man in these beginnings heard with his ears, saw with his eyes, contemplated or touched with his hands, all this was the living word. For God was the Word. With the Word in his mouth and in his heart, the origin of language was as natural, as near and as easy as a child's play'.[66]

What are we to make of such mystical understanding of language, ideas of its Divine origin and supernatural functions, which are of a markedly irrational colour? If we put together Brodsky's definition of a poet as someone who falls into dependency on language, on its formative function, with Epstein's theory of the primacy of language in Russian reality, of Russian language replacing and determining this reality, then we are just a step away from making an eccentric and incredible conclusion that Russian consciousness is, as it were, structurally inclined to poetry, to poetic outlook by its very language, as its speakers are simply a function of their native tongue. And the next step would be to see in this the root of the nation's irrationalism, to conclude that it is the language itself which is to be blamed for this irrationalism. Such a conclusion is implausible (because Brodsky's premise (at the foundation of it) should not be taken literally), especially so for a Western reader, for a scholar who belongs to the rationalist tradition and whose reaction is (perhaps rightly so) that this is yet another (Russian) myth to justify the poor social reality by the rich literary tradition. But even more importantly it is implausible because Structuralism (which arose, in its modern form, as, if you like, a joint Russian-Western product conceived by Roman Jakobson together with Claude Lévi-Strauss) became a universal trend which also saw reality as produced by language (not necessarily Russian language!). It simply suggested 'a particular way of carving up the world which was deeply dependent on the sign-systems we had at our command, or more precisely which had us at theirs'.[67]

Yet, as Epstein argues, the radical difference of Russian is that its formative function tragically subsumes the informative one:

There are three levels of the word: sacred, meaningful and vacuous. At the top level word is being or a creation of being, and such a word can be pronounced through silence. At the middle level word informs about being, its pronunciation correlates with reality, states a fact, has meaning. At the bottom level, word does not contain being within it and neither does it inform us of being; it is vacuous, meaningless, and although it sounds in full, it nevertheless conceals muteness inside it. A peculiarity of the word in

[65] See Berlin, op. cit., p. 118.
[66] Georg Hamann, *Sämtliche Werke*, ed. Joseph Nadler, Vienna, 1949–57, vol. 3, p. 32, cited in Berlin, op. cit., p. 118.
[67] Terry Eagleton, op. cit., p. 94.

Russian culture is its hopping between the top and bottom levels, skipping the middle one. Thus spurning the 'human', informative function, and attempting straight away to take on the 'divine' function, word turns into a magic or ideological incantation and, in the end of the day, into a pure figment, into a collection of meaningless sounds'.[68]

Epstein quotes the contemporary Russian writer Viacheslav Pietsukh who too testifies that 'A Russian professes word – and this is at once good and awful'.[69] Epstein then comments:

> It's good if word shapes being, and it's awful if it turns being into a figment. A barrier for such a fall of word from the top, ontological level to the bottom, destructive one, is the middle level – the informative word which does not change or substitute being, but, in so far as possible, gives honest testimonies about it. That is why it is so important for word to secure its meaning at the informative level and then to ascend from it to the formative level – otherwise a fall to the fictious level is inevitable. And then, losing both its formative and informative fullness, word turns into a frenetic sound, surrounded by a loud silence of God, people and nature.[70]

If one were to ground this theory in socio-political reality (or rather, to parallel it by this reality), then this skipping the informative function of language would probably correspond to the virtual absence of a Russian middle class, or even broader: to jumping over the whole stage of development (from serfdom to socialism, skipping capitalism and discovering it so belatedly). A social order and stability of modern Western Europe as opposed to Russian unlawful chaos are asking to enter the equation here. After all, as Fazil Iskander wonderfully put it (and these words serve as an epigraph to our next chapter), 'A Russian person is strong in his ethical striving, but weak in obeying the ethical laws. A mighty ethical striving perhaps results from a horror of encountering the ethical lawlessness. What are the results of all this? These are great literature and feeble statehood'.[71] But aren't we thus back to square one, to asking the question of chicken and egg with respect to Russian language and Russian reality?

Although in a sense even Western scholarly tradition admits that in the Russian case the language effectively defines the national identity, simply because 'to be Russian is primarily to have Russian as one's mother tongue',[72] both sides remain unshakably firm. Of course, as we saw, there exists an irrationalist view of language (and reality) in the West as well; of course in the Russian context one can find a variety of rationalist voices (and one does not have to go far, as the Marxist socialist doctrine is always

---

[68] M. Epstein, op. cit. Note here also a parallel with the speech act theory (developed by Austin, Searle, Mary Louise Pratt and others) who argue for the importance of language as a way of 'doing things with words', not just stating facts. However, their references are not to Russian culture, but primarily to Anglo-American situations, and their focus on the non-referential uses of language differs from the Russian senses in focusing more on the power of language and less on its world-making capabilities.

[69] Viacheslav Pietsukh, Natalia Selivanova. Interviiu s Viacheslavom Pietsukhom, *Izvestiia*, 15 November 1997, p. 2. Cited in Epstein, op. cit.

[70] Epstein, op. cit.

[71] Fazil Iskander, 'Poet', in *Siuzhet sushchestvovaniia*, Moscow: Podkova, 1999, pp. 142–3.

[72] Dean S. Worth, op. cit., p. 19.

conveniently at hand). However (and this is the whole point, perhaps), these are marginalized in the respective national consciousness.

Thus from a Western (rationalist) perspective this fixation on national language and literature, this logo-centrism of Russians is just another excuse for economic and political failures, a compensatory device, into which 'Russian religious and political messianism falls'; and Russian writers, likewise, are forever rendered prophets and interpreted as archetypes to fit the desired ideological ends of Russian spiritual superiority, as Austrian scholar Rudolf Neuhäuser explains giving an example of Dostoevsky.[73] At the same time, the Russian (irrationalist) view suggests that these social failures are to a large degree the consequences of the Russian language itself, which 'exists (бытийствует) at the expense of all the other kinds of being'.[74] 'Everything in Russia is illusion and lies', according to the French historian Michelet.[75] The Russian view in a sense agrees with this extreme premise, tracing the roots of this illusion back to the Russian language. Indeed, as Brodsky expressed in the epigraph above, 'Platonov speaks of the nation which has become in a sense a victim of its language', and hence, as the Russian translation has it, 'blessed is that language into which his work cannot be translated'.[76]

Language and politics

'Blessed is that language into which his work cannot be translated'. Not only is the gruesome Russian past of sophisticated sanctioned tortures concealed in words and phrases (such as 'podnogotnaja', 'verevki vit', 'v podmiotki ne goditsa'),[77] not only do idioms and proverbs breath with national ethos – these are the features of any language – but also the turbulent, dramatic, often tragic and practically always totalitarian political situation in Russia over the last two centuries had forced Russian intellectual and artistic elite into either external or internal exile – and thus indirectly helped to form and cultivate an exclusive attitude towards their native tongue.

Indeed, for those cut off from their country, language often becomes the only island of motherland, the only cultural refuge. Perhaps taken for granted in the land where it is spoken, it starts to be perceived as a real treasure outside it, in conditions of cultural isolation. Hence Nabokov's piercing lines addressed to the lost Russia where, through

---

[73] See Rudolf Neuhäuser, 'Views of Dostoevsky in Today's Russia. Historical Roots and Interpretations', in K. Kroó and Tünde Szabó (eds), *F. M. Dostoevsky in the Context of Cultural Dialogues*, Budapest: ELTE, 2009, p. 369.

[74] M. Epstein, op. cit.

[75] Quoted in Neuhäuser, op. cit., p. 369 (from Michelet, *Le Pologne Martyr*, Paris, 1863).

[76] Iosif Brodsky, 'Katastrofy v vozdukhe' ('Catastrophies in the Air'), transl. by A. Sumerkin, op. cit., p. 204.

[77] *Podnogotnaia* (literally: 'from under the finger-nails') means all the truth, without reservations; *verevki vit'* (out of someone) (literally: 'to weave ropes') means to have his/her will subjugated to your full control, so that it is possible to make them do anything for you; *v podmiotki ne goditsa* means 'not worth to serve as a sole of your shoe'. All these are clearly derived from the time of sanctioned tortures in Russia, when sticking nails under the finger-nails, etc., was normal practice. Of course in modern speech these words and phrases are used without any connotations with this gruesome etymology, the very thought of which makes your hair rise.

the agony of a forced separation and desperate attempts of detachment equating self-abnegation, he acknowledges by the way of negation that all he has is his (Russian) language: 'To make myself bleed, to maim myself, not to touch my favorite books, to exchange all that I have – my language – for any other speak'.[78] Hence also the famous epic lines by Turgenev in his poem in prose 'Russian language': 'In days of doubt, in days of dreary musings on my country's fate, thou alone art my stay and support, mighty, true, free Russian speech!'.[79] This is despite the fact that he was a distinct Westernizer, and valued and enjoyed the civilized European life. His long years of living outside Russia were voluntary. Still, he shared the same longing as the others. After all, as Tsvetaeva aptly noticed, 'Motherland is not a territorial arrangement, it is the inevitability of memory and blood'.[80]

For her the condition of exile was internal, inherent in her personality regardless of her actual place of residence. She professed that poet is always emigrant. Yet, having claimed 'It doesn't matter to me in what tongue I am misunderstood by whoever I meet'[81] and that for her 'German is more native than Russian',[82] she still lets her nostalgia come through in the burning lines of 'Toska po rodine' concluding with 'But if by the side of the path one // Particular bush rises // The rowanberry . . .'.[83] Pain is always greater and more stunning when it is denied, subdued, stranded, but makes its way all the same from under these inner prohibitions and constraints. Thus in a negative sentence referring to Russian – 'And I won't be seduced by the thought of // My native language, its milky call'[84] – it is the last word (the positive qualifier – 'milky') which gives away the longing, subverting the stated meaning – just as in the poem as a whole the concluding lines do.

Brodsky's admiration of his native tongue is much more open and affirmative. He revels in Herodotus's historical account of the tribes inhabiting Skythia – 'these are

[78] Vladimir Nabokov, 'K Rossii' (1939), <http://lib.ru/NABOKOW/stihi.txt> [accessed 11 August 2014]. In Russian: 'обескровить себя, искалечить, не касаться любимейших книг, променять на любое наречье все, что есть у меня, – мой язык'.

[79] Ivan Turgenev, 'The Russian Tongue' ('*Russkii Iazyk*', 1882), *Poems in Prose*, <http://www.readbookonline.net/readOnLine/21262/> [accessed 11 February 2014].

[80] Marina Tsvetaeva (the full quotation in the original reads: 'Родина не есть условность территории, а непреложность памяти и крови. Не быть в России, забыть Россию – может бояться лишь тот, кто Россию мыслит вне себя. В ком она внутри – тот потеряет ее лишь вместе с жизнью . . .' ['Motherland is not a conditionality of the territory, but an inevitability of memory and blood. Not to be in Russia, to forget Russia – this is possible to be afraid of only for those who perceive Russia outside of themselves. Those for whom Russia is within them, will only lose it together with life itself . . .']), in *Sobranie sochinenii v 7 tomakh*, Moscow, 1994, vol. 4, p. 618.

[81] Marina Tsvetaeva, 'Toska po rodine' (1934), <http://tsvetaeva.lit-info.ru/tsvetaeva/stihi/all/stih-909.htm> [accessed 11 February 2014]. In English: 'Homesickness', in *Selected Poems of Marina Tsvetaeva*, transl. and introduced by Elaine Feinstein, Oxford, New York, Melbourne, Toronto: Oxford University Press, 1981, p. 81. (I have rephrased the translation slightly – to be closer to the original; the actual translation reads, 'How can it matter in what tongue I // Am misunderstood by whoever I meet.') In Russian: 'Мне безразлично на каком непонимаемой быть встречным'.

[82] Marina Tsvetaeva, 'Novogodnee' (1927). In Russian: 'русского родней немецкий'. <http://www.tsvetayeva.com/big_poems/po_novogodnee.php> [accessed 11 February 2014].

[83] Marina Tsvetaeva, 'Toska po rodine' ('Homesickness'), op. cit. In Russian: 'Но если на дороге куст встает, особенно рябина . . .'.

[84] Marina Tsvetaeva, 'Toska po rodine' ('Homesickness'), op. cit., p. 82. In Russian: 'Не обольщусь и языком // Родным, его призывом млечным'.

basically our ancestors', Brodsky explains and quotes the source: 'There, up north, there lives a tribe which settles in highly populated areas. They live by hunting and farming, build houses from the material at hand, namely, out of the forest wood; once a year they have white flies flying there (it must be that someone told Herodotus that it snows there). He says further: One of the most interesting details known about them is that they live in a state of constant astonishment at their language'.[85] Again, it is instructive to juxtapose this account with the broader scientific picture. As Russian is an East Slavic language, its 'recorded history begins towards the end of the first millennium AD', 'with the exception of some interesting but unreliable material from the Gothic chronicler Jordan in the sixth century and accounts from Arabic travellers in the eighth'.[86] Herodotus, of course, lived approximately 15 centuries earlier, at the time when on the territory in question there was a single linguistic entity known as Common Slavic. That language was obviously a very distant ancestor of Russian (not to mention its modern form). However, the story is to be taken symbolically rather than literally, and is clearly told by the poet for the last – romantic – statement which he profoundly shares.

Again, physical exile makes the stakes higher, although for Brodsky existence outside language is unthinkable whatever the circumstances. 'The only thing into which I believe and what gives me a foundation in life is language. If I had to create a God for myself, someone who rules undivided, it would be Russian language. At any rate, Russian language would have been its principal part'.[87] At the same time his striving towards English remains extremely powerful, to the extent that, as Brodsky claims, if he were to be confined to just one language (either English or Russian) he would essentially go mad: 'should a situation arisen when I had to live with one language only, be it English or Russian (even if it were Russian), it would upset me, to put it mildly, if not altogether made me go mad'.[88] The double vision which is allowed by bi-culturalism (equivalent – instructively! – in Brodsky's eyes to bilingualism) is extremely precious to him. 'This belonging to two cultures, or – putting it more simply – this bilingualism [. . .] is a wonderful situation in psychological terms. This is as if you are sitting at the top of a mountain and can see both of its slopes [. . .], and this is a very special feeling. If a miracle happened, and I returned to Russia for permanent residency, I would feel extremely nervous without an opportunity to speak another language . . .'.[89] Yet, his poetry is Russian poetry, and he knows that. 'Writing poems in English is for me rather akin to a game, to chess of sorts, to putting little cubes together, if you like . . .'; 'I do write poems in English, but extremely seldom and rather as a form of entertainment'; 'I have written a few poems in English, but have no striving to make a substantial contribution to English literature', he says repeatedly in his interviews.[90]

Apart from physical displacement, there was also an inner emigration, internal exile, strongly present in Russian reality. The language of underground, the ideologically

[85] Polukhina (ed.), *Iosif Brodskii. Bolshaia kniga interviiu*, op. cit., pp. 236–7.
[86] See Dean S. Worth, op. cit., p. 21.
[87] Polukhina (ed.), *Iosif Brodskii. Bolshaia kniga interviiu*, op. cit., p. 204.
[88] Ibid., p. 152.
[89] Solomon Volkov, op. cit., p. 198.
[90] Polukhina (ed.), *Iosif Brodskii. Bolshaia kniga interviiu*, op. cit., pp. 118, 152, 250.

unconstrained, free word became both a weapon of inner resistance or even of political opposition, and a life jacket for spiritual survival, a liberating pass-way. As the Russian context has demonstrated (although not uniquely, but as part of a broader picture of totalitarian regimes) language is a double-edged sword which can both kill and rescue. It can rescue the consciousness and sanity of the nation and of the writing subject, but it can also destroy (or at least undermine) the object and thus bring persecution to the subject, for it is perceived as a real threat by the state, which is thus afraid of any new diction. In a sense ironically, by persecuting its national writers and poets, the state itself thereby mythologizes their word and recognizes its potential deadly power. In Russia 'because the written word was carefully scrutinized and censored by the church and state', David Bethea writes, 'its "sacred" status [was] thereby implicitly recognized and controlled' and 'the list of "martyred" writers is very long'.[91] In the West, on the contrary, while Romanticism extolled creative imagination and offered an escape from the oppressive rationalism of industrial capitalism, it also alienated the writer pushing him ultimately into the margins of society, where he has basically remained, despite different periods of narrowing the gap between literature and politics. In Russia, due to its autocratic tradition, this gap never really existed.

Importantly, as Brodsky remarks, '. . . if a poet is prohibited from publishing, it is because his language is prohibited. The language turns out to be in the state of confrontation and conflict with the (political) system and with the linguistic idiomatics used by that system. In other words, Russian language cannot tolerate the language used by the authorities. This is precisely why genuine poets are not published in our motherland: because the authorities strive to establish a certain linguistic dominance, otherwise they will lose their grip'.[92]

Thus the state on its part creates its own *novojaz* (*newspeak*) to serve its totalitarian ideology – the discourse where, as was the case in the Soviet reality, words are totally divorced from thoughts and equally from deeds. 'Any speech, any conclusion, any decree or law formulated by the state, as a rule use the appropriate vocabulary and stylistics'.[93] Epstein even talks about the kinship of ideology and magic, whereby speech becomes a chant, whose role is to mesmerize, to lull the vigilance, to deceive and to conceal – in other words, to divert speech from reality. He stresses the fictitious nature of the Russian word:

'Word which subjugates semantics to pragmatics is incantation. [. . .] Ideology is a language of spells and curses, verbal magic which quite achieved its aim and transformed the outside world, or more precisely which turned it into a figment. [. . .] Soviet ideology used these features of language to full extent – to surround an object by a spell of words, to stick to it a nickname and to give it an illusion of existence through infinite repetition. [. . .] An even more drastic turn in the relationships between word and being is possible, when these relationships just stop, and words turn into pure figments whose sole function is to mean nothing, but to sound in full, acoustically imitating an act of speech. The sound creates an illusion of safety since in

---

[91] David Bethea, 'Russian Literature', in Rzhevsky (ed.), op. cit., p. 167.
[92] Polukhina (ed.), *Iosif Brodskii. Bolshaia kniga interviiu*, op. cit., p. 236.
[93] Ibid.

it an existence of the other is manifested, while silence is perceived as concealment and hidden threat'.[94]

In a (very restricted) sense parallels can be drawn again with Western Europe where language did serve at times as a weapon in a socio-political struggle, but the beastly face of modern Russian history makes the situation quantitatively (and hence qualitatively) different. Thus in Russia the language came to serve as a battle-field and sacred aid, secret weapon of resistance and means of survival, sentimental treasure and nostalgic home-territory. Furthermore, as the embodiment of Russian culture it became a meeting ground for progressive and reactionary forces, a national symbol to be used by representatives of opposite political and spiritual creeds.

Thus Brodsky believes it to be the principal national value of Russia (and he is the last to be suspected of Russian chauvinism): 'I would say this (even though it is a somewhat risky statement): the best and most precious thing that Russia has, that the Russian nation has is its language. [. . .] The most sacred thing we have is, likely, not our icons and not even our history – it is our language'.[95] Similarly, Dmitrii Likhachev notes that 'the most valuable treasure of a nation is its language – the language in which it writes, speaks and thinks'.[96] At the same time Russian nationalists take up Russian language as a national symbol to epitomize Russia's exclusive role in history, its superior mission and to fight for its cleansing from harmful Western impurities.[97] This too is a facet of Russian irrationalism; which functionally displays some very rational (i.e. well calculated) features. Thus they quote Pushkin say '. . . the language Slavic-Russian has an unquestionable pre-eminence over all European languages . . ', but conveniently forget to cite his famous 'It was the idea of the devil himself that I be born with spirit and talent in Russia!'.[98] They do not, however, forget Western sources such as English queen Elizabeth I or French prose writer Prosper Mérimée:

"'It is the most beautiful of all the European languages, including Greek", the great French prose writer Prosper Mérimée claimed. [. . .] "Russian language is the richest and most elegant language in the world", confessed in the 16 century Jerome Horsey, the envoy of the English queen Elizabeth Tudor. He also testified, together with his contemporary Roman Beckman, about a genuine interest to the Russian language on the part of the Queen herself, who was very much "attracted by the decorated Slavic script, and interested in the pronunciation of written Russian words". Russian language seemed to the English Queen "a famous and richest language in the world"'.

But they do fail to notice a loss of dignity in scratching around for this one-sided and loudly self-promotional material. Perhaps they genuinely do not see how their efforts defeat their purpose – which is in itself a form of irrationalism, at the end of it where it merges with intellectual and cultural blindness. Or, worse yet, this irrationalism could be in fact a cover-up for a cold-bloodedly calculated rationalism on the side of those

---

[94] Epstein, op. cit.
[95] Polukhina (ed.), *Iosif Brodskii. Bolshaia kniga interviiu*, op. cit., p. 237.
[96] Dmitrii Likhachev, *Razdum'ia*, Moscow: Det.Lit., 1991, p. 176.
[97] For the quotes in the sequel, see the following website which exemplifies the point made, <http://urokirus.com/online/articles/2360-vglubrodnogoyazyka.html> [accessed 20 August 2013].
[98] From Pushkin's letter to his wife, of 18 May 1836, <http://rvb.ru/pushkin/01text/10letters/1831_37/01text/1836/1903_715.htm> [15 January 2013].

reactionaries to whose benefit it is to keep up and cultivate the ignorant, superstitious and thus easily manipulated agents of mass irrationalism. In any case, trying to fight Russian language's pollution by Western sources, they pollute it just the same by their undignified touch. However, as in an old poem about the girl who is dancing naked in a night club, surrounded by drunken clients, but whose purity raises above their cruel abuse, the language is equally unharmed.

However, one can see how easily linguistics spills into history, how dangerously culture borders with politics. The examples are endless. Thus Gogol writes in his *Dead Souls*:

> With a deep knowledge of the heart and a wise grasp of life will the word of the Briton resound; like a flippant fop will the ephemeral word of the Frenchman glitter and burst; ingeniously will the German contrive his shrewdly spare word, which is not accessible to all; but there is no word so sweeping, so bold, so torn from under the heart itself, so bubbling and quivering with life, as the aptly uttered Russian word.[99]

The abyss which opens up here pertains to the eternal Russian problem: of its relationship with the West. The obsession with this issue must seem, at least from an outside, completely idiosyncratic (read: irrational), yet for hundreds of years it has troubled the minds of Russian thinkers. It is to this irrational phenomenon, which like a magnifying glass lays bare the facets of Russian irrationalism, that the next chapter is dedicated.

---

[99] Nikolai Gogol, *Dead Souls*, transl. by Robert A. Maguire, London: Penguin Books, 2004, p. 121.

2

Russia and the West. The Power of Illusion

A Russian person is strong in his ethical striving, but weak in obeying the ethical laws. A mighty ethical striving perhaps results from a horror of encountering the ethical lawlessness. What are the results of all this? These are great literature and feeble statehood

Fazil Iskander ('Poet')

Russia
Insane carefreeness
Wherever one looks.
The plain. Infinity.
The cowing of rooks.
Riots. Fires. Secrecy.
Obtuse indifference.
A unique eccentricity.
A terrible grandeur.[1]

Vasilii Grossman ('Life and Fate')

Russia's relationship with Europe, a brief summary

'At the one side of the border one speaks Russian and drinks more, while at the other side one drinks less and speaks in a non-Russian',[2] wrote Venedikt Erofeev in his immortal tale 'Moskva-Petushki'. This sobering-up vision of a drunkard hero is very different from the multifaceted panoramic view arising from the long-established historical debate between the followers of the so-called Slavophiles and Westernizers, and quite intentionally lowers its traditionally lofty patriotic pathos.

---

[1] Vasilii Grossman ('Life and Fate'), transl. by R. Chandler, London: The Harvill Press, 1995, p. 130 (in the original Russian – «Россия»: Безумная беспечность // На все четыре стороны. // Равнина. Бесконечность. // Кричат зловеще вороны. // Разгул. Пожары. Скрытность. // Тупое безразличие. // И всюду самобытность // И жуткое величие. (Василий Гроссман, «Жизнь и судьба»)).

[2] Venedikt Erofeev, *Moskva-Petushki*, <http://lib.rus.ec/b/377009/read> [accessed 13 February 2014].

Due to its crossroads location, Russia experienced a rich variety of external influences largely responsible for its 'structural incompleteness, which caused at times an excessive openness, at times a feverish reserve'. Indeed, Russia 'was influenced in sequence by Byzantium, China (system of taxes – via the Mongols), the cruelty of the Muslim state system and Western cult of freedom. It is an unstable symbiosis of the Byzantium rank, kazak freedom and Tatar's whip. It is eternal incompleteness, inspiring geniuses to seek an unknownly wide finalization and very difficult for the Russians in their search for merely a personal completeness'.[3]

The importance for Russia of assessing its position vis-à-vis Western Europe (and more generally, the outside world) has been always disproportionally large, compared to many other countries. From a Western perspective it looks at best as a compensatory mechanism to make up for Russia's economic and political 'backwardness'; at worst – as an obsession of sorts, where patriotism, exalting a mere coincidence of a birthplace to a sentimental status of the personified Mother-Russia, spills over into Messianism. In any case such a stance in Western European eyes easily borders on irrationalism.

This inflated importance, however, has resulted from a variety of objective historical factors; and yet, it seems, some additional internal, highly subjective characteristics were required to ignite this flammable combination into a real fire. Among the well-known objective causes for Russia's singular situation is its equivocal geographical position as a shield of sorts between East and West. Moreover, with respect to the cultural axis of North-South in the early medieval times, Russia was also geographically in the middle.

In the eleventh century, the church in Rome lost political control over eastern Christendom, and Constantinople emerged as a second focus of power, with Byzantium making a credible claim to be the successor polity of the Roman Empire, though the Holy Roman Empire had similar pretensions. Kievan Rus was an important centre of power. It was simultaneously an Eastern culture, but also culturally European. It suffered repeated attacks from the tribes of the Far East. In a sense, Kievan Rus was a buffer state, effectively protecting Europe from the worst of the depredations of the Mongols. Byzantium was weakened, and Roman Catholic Europe seized the opportunity to conquer it in 1204. Eventually Kievan Rus was taken by the army of Genghis Khan in 1240, extinguishing that branch of Russian culture and putting a tragic end to its Kievan period. Russia regained independence in the fifteenth century, but it has never since fully repaired its cultural and political relations with mainstream European civilization.

Nevertheless, despite the divergence of their paths, the intermediacy of Russia's geographical position can rightly be extended to the cultural context as well, and Russian culture throughout its history never abandoned the view of Western Europe as simultaneously a teacher and potential apprentice. This combined attitude was rooted not only in the external geo-political situation, but also in the country's internal affairs. With conservative Moscow taking over a more cosmopolitan Novgorod in the fifteenth century, Russian cultural distrust against Western Europe intensified, although it was

---

[3]   Grigorii Pomerants, 'O podlosti, o doblesti, o slave', *Vestnik Evropy* 2008, No. 22, <http://magazines. russ.ru/vestnik/2008/22/po3.html> [accessed 14 February 2014].

still combined, for practical rather than cultural reasons, with economic and political rapprochement, allowing for some cultural exchange and employment of Western art and technology. A decisive turn was introduced by Peter the Great's pro-European policies which revolutionized the country in the way that proved eternally controversial. By and large the argument against Peter's reforms is based on the conviction that their nature contradicted Russia's own organic way of development, its national spirit, cultural singularity, customs and ways of life, which were thus forcefully broken and the course of Russian history violated. More crucially, in Dmitrii Likhachev's words, 'Peter made it clear that he himself assumed functions of the patriarch and that he would rule by force. It was Peter the Great who introduced absolutism to Russia; earlier autocracy was limited by councils and an assembly of boyars, the duma, which at times did not submit to the monarch. Strange as it may seem, true despotism came to Russia along with Westernization and Peter was the medium for both one and the other.'[4]

The eighteenth century after Peter's reign saw the continuation of the Europeanization of Russia. In the popular novellas 'Gistoria o rossiiskom matrose Vasilii Koriotskom' written at the time by an unknown author and combining elements of Slavic and Western European cultures, Russia was referred to as 'Russian Europia'. Katherine the Great, who saw herself as an enlightened monarch in tune with the rest of Europe and its Enlightenment, defined Russia unambiguously as a European country. Among her various political measures was a manifesto designed to attract foreigners to move to Russia. European Enlightenment, and Reason in general, were thus cultivated into becoming the dominant way of thinking. However, even the very term 'Enlightenment' in Russian (*Prosveshchenie* Просвещение) was marked with duality, accommodating both the concept of reason and knowledge, of the rational, and, at the same time, the concept of the Divine light, of the spiritual. As A. N. Burmeister writes, the Russian term was 'on the one hand a calque from the German "Aufklärung", and thus connected to the secular humanist values of the Enlightenment, but on the other hand, in the context of the Old Church Slavonic, it was cognate with the Russian Orthodox spirituality – the Light of the Divine Truth which enlightens one spiritually.'[5]

The two meanings eventually diverged, in conjunction with the split and ultimate break-up between the two fundamental schools of thought in the country. Indeed, in basic terms the accomplishments of Peter and his successors for Westernization of Russia were celebrated by the Westernizers and criticized by the Slavophiles, when both movements emerged in Russia in the early nineteenth century, prompted by the philosophical currents flowing from Western Europe, especially from Germany, by the ideas of Shelling, Hegel, Kant and others. Petr Chaadaev's notorious philosophical letters, which declared Russia a grave historical error existing only for the purposes

---

[4] Likhachev, 'Religion: Russian Orthodoxy', in Rzhevsky (ed.), *The Cambridge Companion to Modern Russian Culture*, op. cit., p. 49.

[5] A. N. Burmeister, *Dukhovnost i prosveshchenie: u istokov russkogo samopoznaniia*, Tiumen: Tium. GASU, 2010, p. 96. Cited in A. Medvedev, '"Sviatoi Vladimir" i "Petr Velikii": Russkoe samosoznanie v poiskakh edinstva', in *'Russkaia filosofiia: istoriia, personalii, metodologiia': materialy nauchnykh trudov*, Tiumen: RIO GOU VPO TiumGASU, 2011, p. 3. As Medvedev notes (see ibid.), Nikolai Gogol emphasized and glorified the uniqueness of the Russian term ('Prosveshchenie') in his letter to V. A. Zhukovsky of 1846.

of giving humanity a negative example, served perhaps as a catalyst for the ultimate formation of both schools.

It is then, with the distinctive border forming between the two movements, that the view of Western Europe, promoted by the early Slavophiles, as a highly rationalist structure (as it were, Western mind as opposed to Russian soul) became consolidated. As was explained in the Introduction, Vasilii Zenkovsky traces the derogatory association of Western Europe with pure rationality, to the early Slavophiles' theoretical misconception which ironically originated in Western Europe itself in the 'pre-Romantic' period. 'The fundamental epistemological distinction between reason and mind' – *rassudok/razum*, Verstand/Vernunft, a function of purely logical operations as opposed to a source of ideas – made by German philosophers 'got distorted on Russian soil resulting in identification of rationalism as a phenomenon of general-cultural character with reasoned cognition'.[6]

Having said this, one should not, however, overlook the obvious and directly related question of the ways this misconception further undertook. For if the rationalistic nature of Western European culture was so misconstrued by the Russians as a result of a theoretical error, then surely their stance would be corrected by their own life experience. Indeed, many Russian travellers, most notably writers, visited Western Europe, thus giving themselves a perfect chance to form their impressions directly, either verifying or refuting the above perception as a result. One does not have to go far for examples which illustrate a critical character of Russian travellers' impressions of the 'rationalist' West and prove surprisingly consistent with the above theoretical misconception. Although these impressions vary depending on ideological convictions of their bearers, but, either explicitly or indirectly, they still display ambiguity with respect to Western ways, ranging from an approval muddled by angst and nostalgia to the open suspicion and subversion.

Looking West: Mixed feelings of Russian writers

Dostoevsky was perhaps the champion of the anti-Western critique which found a direct reflection in his 'Winter Notes on Summer Impressions' after he visited Western Europe in 1862. Continuing Fonvizin's critical remarks of almost a century earlier, Dostoevsky spits venom on Western-European idea of progress as purely technological, material achievement epitomized by the famous Crystal Palace of London and impersonated by the self-assured, insensitive preachers of the public good, who themselves live in material comfort and moral complacency, undisturbed by the surrounding misery. Significantly, both Dostoevsky's discourse and the essence of his Slavophile pretensions show strong continuity with subsequent sentiments about Western Europe prevalent in Russia up to the present day, and still strongly opposed by contemporary Westernizers, proponents of 'Western values' and way of life. Equipped by self-denigration as a protective valve of sorts, these sentiments are essentially hostile to Western ways, which is manifested

---

[6] Zenkovsky, *Istoriia russkoi filosofii*, op. cit., vol. 1, 226.

through a display of caustic irony resulting in turn from a profound resentment. The resentment is caused by observing in the West a better living order (at least in terms of technological advances and external social arrangements) without evidence of any real spiritual superiority, which nevertheless does not prevent the Western-European neighbour from a smug feeling. At any rate, such a suspicion of a badly concealed patronizing attitude is strongly present in the heart of a Russian patriot who sees no grounds for it, as the progress of Europe in his eyes is only illusory.

'You see our bridge, you miserable Russian? Well, you are a mere worm in comparison with our bridge and with every German man because you haven't got a bridge like that,'[7] exclaims Dostoevsky imagining a course of thought of a German toll collector at the entrance to the famous bridge in Köln, and acknowledging at that his own insulted patriotic feeling, his 'injured vanity'. 'You are a fool, Erofeev [. . .]. Get! [. . .] Get out of our Sorbonne,'[8] echoes Venedikt Erofeev a century later, with the same mixture of self-irony and sarcasm with respect to Western vanity. Surely enough, Dostoevsky also does not fail to observe the pervasive and idiosyncratic character of such feelings, in his attempts to conceptualize his impressions: 'All such phrases, which put foreigners in their place, contain, even if we come across them now, something irresistibly pleasant for us Russians. We keep this very secret, sometimes, even secret from ourselves. *For there are in this certain overtones of revenge for an evil past.* Maybe this is a bad feeling, but somehow I am convinced it exists in almost everyone of us. Naturally enough, we kick up a fuss if we are suspected of it, and are not one bit insincere, and yet I should imagine Belinsky himself was in this sense a slavophil'.[9]

The last phrase here is significant and by no means accidental. Indeed, as Stanislaw Matskevich aptly observed, Dostoevsky disavowed Russian Westernizers, and Russian revolutionaries more broadly, as those who under the guise of their striving towards Europe in fact ally immediately with Western-European revolutionary movements, whose nature is to deny Europe, to go against it, to fight against its history and traditions. Thus, Dostoevsky concludes, the essence of our Westernizers is more Russian than that of our Slavophiles.[10]

Even Turgenev, one of the most Westernized Russian writers, with his perfect sense of balance and measure, his deep respect for European values and belief in gradual progress, with his aura of true civilization, can be seen as part of this pattern: in 1859 he 'recognized revolution in Italy (and Insarov's planned revolution in Bulgaria) as a holy war',[11] although his rebels and revolutionaries, such as, for instance, Insarov and Bazarov, are certainly tragic figures. With all his Westernized affiliations Turgenev was clearly never free from the power of his Russian origin which made a deep imprint on his personality and hence on his life and writings. Reading this profound influence

---

[7] Fyodor Dostoevsky, *Summer Impressions*, transl. by Kyril Fitzlyon, London: John Calder Publishers, 1955, p. 6.

[8] Venedikt Erofeev, 'Moskva-Petushki', *Moscow to the End of the Line*, transl. by H. William Tjalsma, Evanston, IL: Northwestern University Press, 1980, p. 104.

[9] Dostoevsky, *Summer Impressions*, op. cit., p. 10. Highlighting is mine (O.T.)

[10] See Stanislaw Matskevich, 'Dostoevsky: otryvki iz knigi', *Novaia Polsha*, No. 2, 2011, pp. 19–23.

[11] Frank Friedeberg Seeley, *Turgenev. A Reading of His Fiction*, Cambridge: Cambridge University Press, 1991, p. 333.

between the lines of his troubled personal history, one can argue that despite him feeling ashamed of Russia's serfdom with all its sadomasochistic cruelty,[12] which is not disconnected from him feeling ashamed of his own cruel mother-landowner, Turgenev nevertheless proceeded to fall for a woman equally tough and authoritarian, although Western-European, as if to impose subconsciously the same tormenting pattern on his private life as that already familiar to him from his Russian childhood – drawn from the troubled social reality of his native land. In the same vein, Lev Shestov observed in Turgenev, under a civilized façade of a perfect European, some hidden angst, the Russian 'wild and superstitious soul' with its search for miracles and its torment with the eternal questions of existence.[13]

It is also interesting in this connection that Turgenev 'was clearly looking for a character who could be a genuine Russian European',[14] but, as Natalia Volodina concludes, 'such a character is absent from Turgenev's writings'.[15] She explains that Turgenev's 'heroes who are interested in this or that area of European life did not become Western men' and 'their extended visits to Europe did not necessarily make them Europeans'.[16]

Furthermore, as part of the same pattern, Turgenev also acknowledges – just as Dostoevsky does – Western-European distrust and almost disdain towards Russians: 'there is no point in fooling ourselves – foreigners look at us with a secret distrust, almost with spite', and equally notices the feeling of extreme boredom experienced by majority of Russian travellers in Western Europe – 'bitter, caustic, and yet carefully concealed boredom'.[17] Yet, unlike Dostoevsky, Turgenev sees its roots in the Russian own ignorance, in coming unprepared and unwilling to penetrate deeply into another culture: 'as Pushkin said, we are "laizy and uninquisitive"; but travelling – if one wants to derive some use out of it – requires work as much as anything else in life'.[18] Thus, while Dostoevsky pretending to take the blame for his own gloomy vision of the West, in reality blames Western Europe itself, Turgenev shifts the blame back onto the Russians.

However, as previously mentioned, his attitudes reflect not only the writer's profound concern with Russia's backwardness, but also his inner observations of his own nature which, while longing in many ways for the West, was also too deeply

[12] See Michael Finke, 'Sacher-Masoch, Turgenev, and Other Russians', in Michael Finke and Carl Niekerk (eds), *One Hundred Years of Masochism: Literary Texts, Social and Cultural Contexts*, Amsterdam: Rodopi, 2000, pp. 120–1, where Finke suggests that Turgenev's descriptions of Russian serfdom can be viewed from the point of view of sadomasochistic psychology and physical cruelty inherent in Russian social arrangements. This theme is touched upon again in Chapter 4.

[13] Lev Shestov, *Turgenev*, Ann Arbor: Ardis, 1982, p. 22.

[14] Natalia Volodina, 'Russkii evropeets v tvorchestve I. S. Turgeneva', in *Dinamicheskie modeli prostranstvenno-vremennoi kartiny mira v russkoi literature*, Vologda: Rus', 2006, p. 12.

[15] Ibid.

[16] Natalia Volodina, 'Ivan Turgenev's Characters as Russian Europeans; the Spiritual Experience of the Past', abstract in ICCEES VII World Congress *Europe – Our Common Home?*, Abstracts, Editors: Thomas Bremer, Heike Dörrenbächer, Inken Dose, German Association for East European Studies, 2005, p. 455.

[17] Ivan Turgenev, 'Iz-za granitsy', in *Polnoe sobranie sochinenii i pisem v tridtsati tomakh*, Moscow: Nauka, 1978, vol. 10, p. 307 and p. 303.

[18] Ibid., p. 307.

rooted in Russian soil. 'It is impossible for a Russian not to miss Russia, wherever he goes. There is no other Russia for a Russian. Russia – Russians – is something quite special, quite different. Therefore no-one can understand us adequately',[19] these words (as well as his aforementioned famous short poem of glory to Russian language)[20] by the convinced Westernizer Turgenev could have easily come from the mouth of a dedicated Slavophile.

This irrational stance, grating on Western European taste, a 'Slavophile' utterance of Russia's distinctiveness, rather unusual for Turgenev, is nevertheless a typical Russian sentiment abroad, a specifically Russian angst, experienced by so many and expressed in varied forms throughout Russian literature. When Nikolai Karamzin incorporated (in the form of Notes) into the sixth volume of his 'History of the Russian State' the 'Journey Beyond Three Seas' – a travel account of the Russian fifteenth-century merchant-traveller Afanasii Nikitin, who died on his way back home, longing for Russia – the historian, in particular, documented a common Russian trait of feeling acute nostalgia while abroad. In the twentieth century, with its waves of tragic emigration, it became even more prominent.

Curiously, even when it takes the form of denial, it is hardly believable, subverted by the passion of one's dictum in more indirect discourses. Thus when Joseph Brodsky speaks of no nostalgia experienced in his Western (American) life, of his preference 'to be a total failure in a democracy than a martyr, or *la crème de la crème*, in a tyranny',[21] one feels distrustful, given the underlying, piercing suffering of total solitude in which his émigré poems are steeped – a global, ice-age solitude which is much more than that expressed by Tsvetaeva's formula of a poet's perpetual inner state of a stranger, outsider and exile. And the more monumental Brodsky's poetry abroad becomes, the more stifled scream is heard beneath it. 'One can return to the place of one's crime, but one should not revisit the place of one's love'.[22] 'Here you can live, the calendar forgetting, swallowing your bromine, not venturing outside, and look into the mirror, as a street-lamp in a drying puddle'.[23] And his stubborn and deadly resolve of not stepping his foot in Russia after the fall of communism (i.e. when it became possible) speaks for itself and can hardly be explained by political and social resentment.

Returning to the nineteenth century, equally idiosyncratic are Lev Tolstoy's attitudes to the West which 'take anti-European tendencies of Russian culture to the extreme'.[24]

19 I. S. Turgenev v vospominaniiakh sovremennikov, vols 1–2, Moscow, 1983, <http://philolog.pspu.ru/module/magazine/do/mpub_9_166> [accessed 11 February 2014].

20 'Russian Tongue': 'In days of doubt, in days of dreary musings on my country's fate, thou alone art my stay and support, mighty, true, free Russian speech! But for thee, how not fall into despair, seeing all that is done at home? But who can think that such a tongue is not the gift of a great people!' (*June 1882*) (Ivan Turgenev, 'The Russian Tongue', <http://www.readbookonline.net/readOnLine/21262/> [accessed 11 February 2014]).

21 Joseph Brodsky, 'Ucommon Visage' (the Nobel Lecture) in *On Grief and Reason. Essays*, op. cit., p. 44.

22 From Polukhina (ed.), *Iosif Brodsky. Bolshaia Kniga Interviu*, op. cit.

23 Joseph Brodsky, 'Osennii vecher v skromnom gorodke . . .', 1972. See <http://rupoem.ru/brodskij/all.aspx#osennij-vecher-v> [accessed 11 February 2014]. In Russian: 'Здесь можно жить, забыв про календарь, глотать свой бром, не выходить наружу и в зеркало глядеться, как фонарь глядится в высыхающую лужу'.

24 Vladimir Kantor, 'Lev Tolstoi: Iskushenie neistoriei', op. cit.

Similarly irrational, especially in Western eyes, is the type of unquivering Russian patriotism depicted by Nikolai Leskov. His famous hero, Levsha, a craftsman of magic powers, persistently declines the invitations from the English engineers to remain in England, in prosperous conditions, far superior to those of his native Russia: 'The Englishmen couldn't do anything to make him fancy the English way of life'.[25] To all the temptations offered to him, Levsha replies, '"I thank you humbly for your hospitality. [. . .] I've been very pleased with everything and I've seen all I wanted to see, now I want to get home as quickly as I can". They couldn't persuade him to stay any longer'.[26] His desire to go back home is so strong that he is prepared to travel in a dangerous way, just to speed up his return. 'It's all the same where a man dies', he answered, 'it's the will of God and I want to go home before I go off my head'.[27] In his terms, madness is not in his (irrational) spurning of a (rationally) better existence, but the mental state which for him a separation from his native Russia immediately entails.

Famously, a Westernized Russian of the Chaadaev's type, who was ashamed of Russia's backwardness in comparison to the advanced West, was Aleksandr Herzen – but having found himself in Western Europe, he got profoundly disappointed and expressed ideas which are in essence similar to the Slavophile ideas of Dostoevsky. In the words of Vladimir Kantor, Herzen found in Europe, much to his disillusionment, no creative impulse and no inspiring conception of history,[28] while Dostoevsky saw it as a doomed wasteland which exhausted its moral resources (and thus needs to be revived by the example of Russian Orthodoxy with its ideas of sobornost' and brotherly love).

Thus both camps – of Slavophiles and of Westernizers – were marked by certain resistance to Western Europe, whether conscious or unrecognized. At any rate, Western Europe served for Russian cultural figures as a perpetually irritable spot, and, instructively, this pattern is no less intense in Russia today, with its continuing fierce debates as to the country's future vis-à-vis the West.

However, this resistance was simply another side of the coin of a powerful attraction and appreciation. Turgenev and Tiutchev were among those who spent most of their creative time in Western Europe. The pull of Europe was strong even in the case of writers from the Slavophile camp. Thus Gogol, with all his Slavophile leanings, adored Italy and preferred to write about Russia while living away from it. Dostoevsky's lament also was double-edged – his apocalyptic vision of Western civilization did not prevent him from recognizing a profound kinship between Russia and Europe, referring to the latter as the second motherland and the second mother, and thus implying a feeling of responsibility towards it, which at the same time, arguably, may not be entirely devoid of messianic flavour: 'We Russians have two homelands: our own Russia and Europe, even if we call ourselves Slavophiles.[29] [. . .] Europe is also our mother, just as Russia is;

[25] Nikolai Leskov, 'Lefty' ('Levsha'), in Leskov, *The Enchanted Wanderer and Other Stories*, Moscow: Progress Publishers, transl. by George H. Hanna, ed. by Julius Katzer, 1974, p. 289.

[26] Ibid., pp. 290–1.

[27] Ibid., p. 291.

[28] See Vladimir Kantor, 'Lev Tolstoi: Iskushenie neistoriei', in *Voprosy literatury*, 2000, No. 4, <http://magazines.russ.ru/voplit/2000/4/kantor.html> [accessed 11 February 2014].

[29] Fyodor Dostoevsky, *A Writer's Diary*, transl. and annotated by Kenneth Lantz; Introduction: Gary Saul Morson, Evanston, Illinois: Northwestern University Press, 1993, vol. 1: 1873–6, p. 505.

she is our second mother; we have taken much from her, and we will take still more; we don't wish to be ungrateful to her'.[30] In the same vein, referring to Khomiakov's famous lines about Europe,[31] Dostoevsky expressed pain and concern about its destiny, in the words which give another dimension to his uneasy and castigating lines quoted above: 'Oh, gentlemen, do you know how dear Europe is to us Slavophile-dreamers who, as far as you're concerned, should only hate it, Europe, this "land of holy miracles"! Do you know how dear these "miracles" are to us and how we love and revere, with more than brotherly love and reverence, those great tribes that populate it, together with all the grand and beautiful things they have accomplished? Do you know the many tears we shed and the pangs of heart we suffer at the fate of this dear and *native* country, and how frightened we are by the storm clouds that are ever gathering on her horizon?'.[32]

Nevertheless Russia rather than Europe remained for these and for many other Russian writers their central concern, the source of perpetual love and perpetual torment,[33] to the extent of being personified, of being worshipped as a beloved woman – be it mother or wife. That is why I would suggest that the lines by Evgenii Baratynsky addressed to his beloved can be equally used to describe, with the same force, the underlying affection towards Russia on the part of many of its artists who at the same time admired Western Europe and stayed there for long periods: 'I burnt incense to others, but you I kept most holy in my heart. I worshipped new icons, but unsettled as an Old Believer'.[34]

Against this overly intense background the contemporary Russian writer Andrei Bitov, looking at the nineteenth century, singles out only two Russian writers, Pushkin and Chekhov, who, in his opinion, can be called true Europeans. Indeed, they remained to the end sober and calm with their balanced attitude to Western Europe and their deep, but devoid of idiosyncrasy or hysteria, love towards Russia. As Bitov put it, both were united by being truly civilized: 'Both neither preach, nor are aggressive. Neither of them confuse role with predestination. They are knights of dignity and knights of shame. And dignity and shame are the working instruments of a personality. There is absence of pathos, emotionality and naked idea. Even thought is concealed in such a clear exposition that it may not appear to be a thought at all, until you grow up sufficiently to be able to understand it. [. . .] The miraculous embodiment of the world's

---

[30] Fyodor Dostoevsky, *A Writer's Diary*, op. cit., vol. 2, 1877–81, p. 1373.

[31] Aleksei Khomiakov, 'Mechta': '. . . Ложится тьма густая На дальнем Западе, стране святых чудес' ('. . . A thick darkness is falling on the distant West, the country of holy miracles'), <http://stroki.net/content/view/13209/76/> [accessed 14 February 2014].

[32] Fyodor Dostoevsky, *A Writer's Diary*, op. cit., vol. 2, 1877–81, p. 1066.

[33] In this respect Sergei Esenin's lines, written in 1914, before Bolshevism, are representative both for the nineteenth and twentieth centuries: 'Если крикнет рать святая: «Кинь ты Русь, живи в раю!» Я скажу: «Не надо рая, Дайте родину мою»' ['If the holy men cry out to me: "Leave your Russia and come to live in Paradise!", I'll reply: "I don't need Paradise, just give me my motherland back"'] ('Goi ty, Rus, moia rodnaia'), as well as his 'Stansy' of 1924 which, despite being on the contrary too crudely pro-Soviet, in fact continue the same line, started before the revolution: 'Но более всего Любовь к родному краю Меня томила, Мучила и жгла' ['But more than anything, it is my love toward my native land that tormented, plagued, and burnt me'].

[34] Evgenii Baratynsky, 'Uverenie' ('Net, obmanula Vas molva . . ', 1824), <http://rupoem.ru/baratynskij/all.aspx#net-obmanula-vas> [accessed 14 February 2014]. In Russian: 'Другим курил я фимиам, но Вас носил в святыне сердца. Молился новым образам, но с беспокойством староверца'.

cultural benchmark in a Russian (Pushkin) is equivalent to the miraculous embodiment of civilization in a first-generation member of the Russian intelligentsia (Chekhov). Nobility of spirit and honour; dignity and shame; that is to say, culture. These two cultural heroes were unique in their ability to transcend the typically Russian abyss between artistic culture and civilization'.[35] Thus Bitov, by the way, only reinforces the idea of Russia's idiosyncratic cultural distinctiveness, by making the latter statement of Russian artistic consciousness being divorced from civilization (by which he implicitly means European civilization).

At the same time, Pushkin, with all his perfect sensitivity for Russian and foreign cultures alike, and genius ability to cross-fertilize them, lifting Russian literature to European level and with equal ease inscribing European culture into the Russian context, has always protected his motherland in the best patriotic tradition – by hating its worst features, but not inviting outsiders to share his bitterness, that is to say not allowing his criticism to turn into impure rejoicing in the national weaknesses. 'I of course despise my fatherland from head to foot – but it vexes me if a foreigner shares that feeling with me',[36] he famously exclaimed in a letter to Viazemsky. 'In our dealings with foreigners we have neither dignity nor shame', Pushkin complained in the same letter. And despite his fuming remarks – 'You, who are not on a leash, how can you remain in Russia?'[37] – and threats to leave the country if only he were allowed to by the Tsar, it is clear that these are, as it were, marks of the discourse, appropriate for an intimate chat with a close friend of the same liberal political orientation and critical spirit. Pushkin's response to Chaadaev's philosophical letter is, on the other hand, a much more serious testimony of the poet's stance regarding Russia and its historical place: 'Russia, in its immense expanse, was what absorbed the Mongol conquest. [. . .] and Christian civilization was saved. For this purpose we were obliged to have a life completely apart, one which though leaving us Christians left us such complete strangers to the Christian world that our martyrdom did not provide any distraction to the energetic development of Catholic Europe. [. . .] As for our history being nil, I absolutely cannot be of your opinion. [. . .] not for anything in the world would I be willing to change my fatherland, nor to have any other history than that of our ancestors, such as God gave it to us'.[38]

Able to merge creatively Russian and non-Russian, Pushkin thus advocated a middle, synthesizing way of development, and in many ways served as a reconciling force between the Slavophiles and Westernizers, in a sense deterring them from a radical split. Many Russians believe to this day that if only Pushkin lived longer, into the 1870s and 1880s, the fate of the country may well have been different, and many political upheavals and tragedies might have been avoided.

---

[35] Andrei Bitov, 'Moi dedushka Chekhov i pradedushka Pushkin', in *Chetyrezhdy Chekhov*, Moscow: Emergency Exit, 2004, p. 9.

[36] From Pushkin's letter to P. A. Viazemsky, 27 May 1826, from Pskov to St Petersburg. See *The Letters of Alexander Pushkin. Three Volumes in One*. Transl., with Preface, Introduction and Notes by J. Thomas Shaw, Madison, Milwaukee and London: The University of Wisconsin Press, 1967, p. 311.

[37] Ibid.

[38] From Pushkin's letter to P. Ya. Chaadaev, 19 October 1836. See ibid., pp. 779–80.

Emigration as a magnifying glass of attitude to Russia

Pushkin's remark above, from his rebuff to Chaadaev, that he would never wish to change country, to have another fatherland, is culturally significant. Indeed, the question of emigration, of what from the outside may seem a mere change of geographical location of personal existence, has loomed large among Russian educated classes, even when discussed in speculative terms only. The reason for this was perhaps also rooted in the above tormenting ambiguity with respect to the West, and more generally – in the uneasy opposition of Russia versus Western Europe. It always rose to metaphysical heights, evidently touching on something vitally important for Russian subjects. Feeling culturally European, but clearly distinct, easily misunderstood and often alienated, struggling between the visions of Russia's backwardness from within and from the outside, they experienced inevitable personal pain in their patriotism – to the extent that their love for the country, as previously mentioned above, acquired the form of love for a woman, of the vision of Russia as a mother, wife or sister. Among the famous examples of this phenomenon of country's personification and, furthermore, sanctification are Blok's 'Oh, my Russia! My wife!',[39] socio-political sentiments of *Rodina-mat'* (Motherland-Mother) used most forcefully during the Soviet era, and the formula of 'sacred Russia' (*sviataia Rus'*) attributed to Prince Andrei Kurbsky, a correspondent of Ivan IV.

Chekhov, with his recoil from any philistinism and not inclined to sentimentalism, in his intelligent balanced depictions stayed above any partisan attitudes, and earned admiration in Europe, where his work became highly acclaimed. In this he was similar to Turgenev, but unlike the latter, who was personally accepted and welcomed abroad, Chekhov essentially spent his life in Russia. However, with his appeal to Western readers, Chekhov's oeuvre in essence shows sufficient continuity with the above ambivalent stance. Indeed, he was capable of creating disgracing or ironic portraits of Westerners in his stories, such as an indelicate English woman in 'Doch Albiona' (1883) or a naïve, clueless Frenchman in 'Glupyi frantsuz' (1886), but only alongside no less disgraceful Russians, capable of abasing themselves without even realizing it. In the latter story 'Glupyi frantsuz', the difference is portrayed in comic terms between European sense of caution and measure on the one hand, and Russian wild, and – looking through the Western eyes – barbaric striving to abundance on the other. This story, despite its lightheartedness, raises also the more general question of the implied abyss between two civilizations and their lack of mutual understanding.[40] Russians may be savage in Western eyes, but Western Europeans, in turn, in Russian eyes, are

---

[39] Aleksandr Blok, 'Na pole Kulikovom' (1908), See <http://az.lib.ru/b/blok_a_a/text_0054.shtml#napolekulikovom> [accessed 14 February 2014]. In Russian: 'О, Русь моя! Жена моя!'.

[40] Another way to portray how hopelessly lost Westerners may feel within Russian reality is via their lack of proficiency in the Russian language. Among possible examples – to name but a few – one can list the above Englishwoman from Chekhov's story, or a very memorable character from the film created a century later – 'Osennii marafon' by Georgii Danelia (1979). A Danish Slavist – Dostoevsky scholar Bill Hansen, visiting Leningrad, – is baffled, trying to impose a Western order on the amorphous reality around him, but to a large extent gets absorbed by it instead. His disorientation and naïvete with respect to Russian culture, and above all literature, is portrayed via his poor level of the Russian language.

ridiculous and comic in their naïvete and their sense of measure blown out of measure – an overinflated self-preservation instinct. As Saltykov-Shchedrin remarked, 'there exist many ways to make human existence dismal, but one of the most efficient is to force a person to dedicate himself to the cult of self-preservation, to defeat within himself any wild spirit and to acknowledge his life relegated to the level of a purposeless streaking for all the time during which the temptation of enjoying life lasts'.[41] From this point of view, the 'wild' Russian spirit, a fierce striving to the absolute, gain a deep meaning.

At the same time, Chekhov (and this, perhaps, conceals the roots of his universal appeal), with his shrewd psychological vision, saw people at both sides of the border as lonely individuals, vulnerable in the face of fate and existential tragedy. If in Europe an individual is oppressed by a lack of space, in Russia he is crushed by its vastness: 'The suicide of your Russian youngster is, in my opinion', Chekhov wrote to Grigorovich, 'a specific phenomenon unfamiliar in Europe. It results from a horrific struggle possible in Russia only. All the energy of an artist must be directed towards two forces: man and nature. On the one hand, physical weakness, nervousness, early sexual development, passionate thirst for life and for truth, dreams about activities as broad as a steppe, restless analysis, poverty of knowledge together with the broad span of thought; on the other hand, an endless plain, severe climate, grey and stern people with its heavy, cold history, Tatar invasions, bureaucracy, indigence, ignorance, dampness of the capitals, Slavic apathy and so on and so forth. Russian life smashes a Russian man so much that no trace is left; smashes like a rock of a thousand poods. In Western Europe people perish because it is crowded and suffocating to live; in Russia they die because there is too much space . . . So much space that a little man has no strength to find his way'.[42]

After his European trip Chekhov objected to the rumours that he disliked Western Europe: 'Who announced to the entire world that I did not like it abroad? Goodness gracious me, I haven't uttered a single word about it to anyone [. . .] What was I supposed to do? Roar with delight? Smash windows? Hug the French?'.[43] In his story 'Student', Chekhov summarized with brilliant laconism all Russian history in one sentence: 'shrinking from the cold, he thought that just such a wind had blown in the days of Rurik and in the time of Ivan the Terrible and Peter, and in their time there had been just the same desperate poverty and hunger, the same thatched roofs with holes in them, ignorance, misery, the same desolation around, the same darkness, the same feeling of oppression – all these had existed, did exist, and would exist, and the lapse of a thousand years would make life no better'.[44] These were the student's thoughts at the start of the story, when he remembered his gloomy home. However, at the end, when looking back at his village and filled with higher religious sense that absorbs and subsumes human suffering, he is consumed by a different feeling, which is subtly connected to the topos of his poor motherland. 'When he [. . .] looked at his

[41]   See A. Yu. Kozhevnikov and G. B. Lindberg, *Mudrost vekov. Rossiia*, St Petersburg: Izd. Dom 'Neva', 2006, p. 31.
[42]   Anton Chekhov's letter to D. V. Grigorovich of 05.02.1888, see A. P. Chekhov, *PSSP v 30 tomakh*, vol. 2, Moscow: Nauka, 1975, 190.
[43]   Anton Chekhov, Letter to A. Suvorin of 27 May 1891, Letters, vol. 4, p. 237.
[44]   Anton Chekhov, 'Student', transl. by Constance Garnett. See <http://www.eldritchpress.org/ac/jr/173.htm> [accessed 30 August 2013].

village [. . .], he thought that truth and beauty which had guided human life there in the garden and in the yard of the high priest had continued without interruption to this day, and had evidently always been the chief thing in human life and in all earthly life, indeed; [. . .], and life seemed to him enchanting, marvellous, and full of lofty meaning'.[45]

Moreover, it was also Chekhov, as well as Bunin after him, who expressed a sober and courageous view of the Russian people, of the peasantry, which was idealized and even idolized in the second half of the nineteenth century as 'narod-bogonosets' (God-bearing people), and ultimately corrupted, by the country's intellectual elite, full of guilt and remorse with respect to the working classes – corrupted precisely by this exaltation to an invincible and intrinsically infallible status: 'The notions of the "God-bearing people" and "destiny-bearing people" had been guardedly and for a long time promoted by Russian intelligentsia. [. . .] The good manners of the intelligentsia had it that the people (*narod*) are holy. [. . .] The people themselves did not suspect, even remotely, that they are God-bearing or destiny-bearing. But that group of the people which was in contact with the intelligentsia, turned out to be incredibly depraved. They realised that for some scientific reason all is forgiven, and scorned contemptuously the centuries-long moral principles which they did indeed once have'.[46]

When revolutionary Russian intelligentsia had played its fatal role in nearing the country's ultimate collapse into communist dictatorship facilitated by radicalism of the socialist utopia and the associated utilitarian aesthetics, it caused its own undoing. The old, accumulated over centuries Russian culture was squeezed out of the country and extinguished within it. And the uneasy question of emigration was rendered totally tragic when it turned into exile after the Bolshevik revolution of 1917, because emigration then gained the additional meaning of the catastrophic loss of motherland and a sense of fatality. This new dimension – of viewing your motherland from outside, through the eyes of an exile, destined most probably never to see it again, only reinforced the underlying irrationality of Russian attitude to their country. Zinaida Gippius's piercing words, 'If my Russia dies, I'll die with her',[47] (1918) encapsulate that feeling inherent in the first wave of Russian émigrés. Marina Tsvetaeva expressed the same angst in a subtler, but equally heartbreaking fashion in her 'Toska po Rodine . . .' (1934): 'Houses are alien, churches are empty // Everything is the same: // But if by the side of the path one // Particular bush rises // The rowanberry . . .'.[48]

And much later, in the second half of the century, similar tragic overtones permeated the nostalgia of those who left Russia in the same disaccord with the political regime and with the same unbearable prospect of no-return. 'Then why am I in despair just thinking that never, never again . . . Oh my God, never!', wrote Aleksandr Galich in his cycle of poems created on the brink of his departure – by his own admission, as an

---

[45] Ibid.

[46] Fazil Iskander, 'Poet', op. cit., p. 151.

[47] Zinaida Gippius, 'Esli gasnet svet – ia nichego ne vizhu . . .' (1918), <http://gippius.com/lib/poetry/tak-est.html> [accessed 14 February 2014]. In Russian: 'если кончена моя Россия – я умираю'.

[48] Marina Tsvetaeva, 'Toska po Rodine . . .' ('Homesickness') (1934), op. cit. In Russian: 'Всяк дом мне чужд, всяк храм мне пуст, И все – равно, и все – едино. Но если по дороге – куст Встает, особенно – рябина . . .'.

inoculation of sorts against the imminent nostalgic pangs.[49] The same sentiments are present in the great variety of works by Russian artists leaving the country for good, or those sympathetic with them. To name but a few, Evgenii Kliachkin's poem 'Proshchanie s Rodinoi' (1973) breathes with this tragic spirit, and turned out to be prophetic when he indeed left, but only years later, in 1990, when the borders were opening up thus rendering the previous concept of exile a mere migration: 'I am parting with the country where I've lived a life – I can't tell whose – and for the last time, while I am still here, I am drinking its air as one drinks wine'.[50] Similarly, Fridrikh Gorenshtein, a Russian Jew, contemplated his separation with the country in a seemingly rational tone which nevertheless betrays the same painful sentiments: 'There is always sorrow in the parting glance, always the angst of dying, an attempt to imagine how the world will live without you, and suddenly comes a bitter-sweet pagan feeling of losing yourself in these boggy hollows, in these rust-brown peat hills, as the hollows, wooded- with aspen, alder, birch and fir . . . fir, fir, neverending fir'.[51] The remarkable feature of these farewells is the need to profess love to Russia in view of the imminent separation with it – essentially the same need that one feels towards a woman. In this context the example above of Joseph Brodsky with his rational struggle against this irrational angst, his attempts to overcome nostalgia by denying it (although a wound so clearly heals better when not touched rather than when irritated) only reinforces the above rule.

Putting practice into theory: Conceptions behind experience

The crucial question that Dostoevsky raises at the start of his contemplations on his country's unequal place within European neighbourhood is the question of Russia having preserved its own unique way and character despite the huge influence of Western Europe which served as a paragon and importer of civilization. He stresses the remarkable, almost magical pull and fascination that Europe exercised over Russia, and the fundamental role that it played in Russia's cultural development; yet, Dostoevsky exclaims in astonishment, 'we have not been metamorphosed even after being subjected to such an overwhelming influence'.[52] 'I [. . .] am at a loss to account for it',[53] he repeats. Although one may well question Dostoevsky's convictions of Russia's unique way, of its messianic role to show the disillusioned West the route out of the deadlock of rationalism through the intrinsic humanity and warmth of Russian Orthodoxy – as

---

[49] Aleksandr Galich, 'Opyt nostalgii' (1969–73). <http://radio.vfirsov.pro/component/statistics/index. php?mode=lirictext&text=1373> [accessed 14 February 2014]. In Russian: '. . . Так зачем же я вдруг при одной только мысли шалею, Что уже никогда, никогда . . . Боже мой, никогда! . . .'.

[50] Evgenii Kliachkin, 'Proshchanie s Rodinoi' (1973), <http://www.bards.ru/archives/part. php?id=6325> [accessed 14 February 2014]. In Russian: 'Я прощаюсь со страной, где Прожил жизнь, не разберу чью, И в последний раз – пока здесь – Этот воздух, как вино, пью'.

[51] Fridrikh Gorenshtein, 'Poslednee leto na Volge', in *Iskuplenie. Povesti, rasskazy, piesa*, Moscow: Slovo, 1992, pp. 502, 538.

[52] Dostoevsky, *Summer Impressions*, op. cit., p. 14.

[53] Ibid.

he saw it, – the legitimacy of his question remains and his surprise is indeed valid. Whatever sign one may put to Russia's distinctiveness with respect to Western Europe, one must nevertheless recognize certain truths behind Dostoevsky's sentiments that it takes indeed a lot of spiritual resistance in order to withstand such colossal influence.

What lies at the core of this uniqueness, of this unwillingness (or inability) to conform to Western ways? Is it Russia's dual – Occidental-Oriental – identity? Is it, indeed, a distinctive character of the country's orthodox faith and/or its historical specificity? Many generations of Russian writers and thinkers addressed this question, attempting to capture their land's special nature by concise formulas. In their wrestling with this topic the continuous battle of the same two old, but perpetually evolving, major lines is distinctly audible: new generations of Slavophiles of all sorts are forever debating with the new Westernizers, equally diverse, with various attempts at a synthesis, sought in the middle.

The irrationalism that Tiutchev expressed in the nineteenth century in his immortal and by now hackneyed lines 'Russia cannot be understood with the mind alone [. . .], One can only believe in Russia',[54] was echoed, in particular, a century later by the poet Aleksandr Eremenko in his similarly short verse: 'It is a horizontal country, undescribable by qualifiers. Here a diagonal and a side are forever incommensurable'.[55] Aleksandr Blok, inspired by Vladimir Solov'ev, merged the image of the country with that of the Beautiful Lady (Прекрасная Дама) and at the same time reinforced a distinctive demarcation line between Russia and the West, identifying its underlying spirit as Oriental and wild, which, moreover, deliberately opposes itself to Western Europe: 'Yes, we are Scythians! Yes, we are Asians – With slanted and greedy eyes!'.[56] Earlier, even Pushkin, who generally took the middle ground in these debates, essentially aligning with Griboedov in the attempts to synthesize in Russia Occidental and Oriental mentality, epitomized commonly shared sentiments, in a somewhat similar spirit and genre to that of Blok's Skythians',[57] when he addressed his angry lines to 'Klevetnikam Rossii', as a warning, rather conservative politically, to stay away from Russia's internal problems and its own way of self-determination, even if it spills, for an outsider at least, into dangerous questions of foreign policy.

54 Fedor Tiutchev, 'Umom Rossiiu ne poniat' (1866), <http://rupoem.ru/tyutchev/all.aspx#umom-rossiyu-ne> [accessed 10 February 2014]. In Russian: 'Умом Россию не понять . . . в Россию можно только верить'.

55 Aleksandr Eremenko, 'Gorizontalnaia strana' (1987), <http://modernpoetry.ru/main/aleksandr-eremenko-gorizontalnaya-strana#erema1> [accessed 10 February 2014]. In Russian: 'Горизонтальная страна. Определительные мимо. Здесь вечно несоизмерима диагональ и сторона'.

56 Aleksandr Blok, 'Skify' (1918), <http://az.lib.ru/b/blok_a_a/text_0030.shtml> [accessed 10 February 2014]. In Russian: 'Да, скифы – мы! Да, азиаты – мы, С раскосыми и жадными очами'.

57 Even though Pushkin, in contrast to Blok, in a narrow sense was defending the Empire, not the revolution (in which at the time of writing Blok still believed), some scholars drew a distinct parallel between these poems, rightly placing them in a broader artistic and historical context: 'The monumental revolutionary-patriotic ode by Blok is indeed reminiscent, both in its pathos and its artistic structure, of such powerful works of Russian poetry as Pushkin's 'Klevetnikam Rossii' or Lermontov's 'Poslednee novoselie' (V. N. Orlov, 'Gamaiun. Zhizn Aleksandra Bloka'). See <http://az.lib.ru/b/blok_a_a/text_0430.shtml> [accessed 10 February 2014].

The other – Westernizers' – extreme, of 'Chaadaev's type', denies the existence of any special way, or messianic role, or unique character of Russia and insists on its backwardness which facilitates the above convictions as a defence mechanism. It is noteworthy that Chaadaev's stance itself is partly derivative, as it can be traced to the original Hegelian ideas about the two types of Christian peoples: historical and ahistorical (being outside history), depending on the types of their religious beliefs. Within this theory, Catholicism and Protestantism are opposed to Russian Orthodoxy. Such an opposition enjoys wide popularity among contemporary Russian Westernizers, and blames all Russia's misfortunes on the wrong choice of religious faith with its spirit of humility, subjugation, victim mentality conducive of slavery and preventing a proper national development.[58]

In conjunction with that, Russian Orthodox gravitation from the individual towards the collective is sometimes interpreted in terms of reduced personal responsibility. Thus Viktor Zhivov in his interesting study of Russian cultural history attributes the distinctions between Eastern and Western Christianity to diverging practices of repentance and suggests that in Russia especially, by contrast to Western Europe, the discipline of repentance was substantially less rigorous than in the Catholic West.[59] This, Zhivov argues, could not but give rise to blurred contours of individuality – in other words, to collective spirit and rather porous boundaries between the individual and the collective. The attempts of the seventeenth and eighteenth centuries at religious reforms designed to introduce stricter discipline were appropriated by the state and ultimately proved ineffective. According to Zhivov's argument, 'a concept of individual sin remained vague and of secondary importance. Sin was seen largely as an existential characteristic of human life rather than as a personal guilt'. Therefore any suffering, even that of convicted criminals (in fact, especially that, because of its obvious severity), was viewed in Russia more as manifestation of existential tragedy than a sign of a personal fault. Zhivov spots the same ideas, only taken to the extreme, in Dostoevsky's oeuvre, where everybody is responsible for everybody else thus blurring the idea of individual sin. Both sin and salvation are no longer personal in this interpretation, but common, and this ultimately runs into a contradiction with the spirit of Russian Orthodoxy, Zhivov argues.

Zhivov's conjecture, although perfectly valid, does not seem completely convincing, as it suffers from too formal an interpretation of religious practices and spiritual life

---

[58] Thus, for instance, Vladimir Pozner, a prominent television journalist, has voiced the idea of Russian Orthodoxy lying at the root of Russian misfortunes. Sharing the ideas of Petr Chaadaev, Pozner views it as a religion which slows down national development by its spirit of humility and submissiveness. (See, for instance, Pozner's interview to the journal 'Sher Ami', <http://newsland.com/news/detail/id/536250/> [accessed 7 February 2014], and more elaborate explanations, for example, <http://vladimirpozner.ru/?p=3560> [accessed 7 February 2014]). By the same token, three quarters of a century earlier, Nikolai Berdiaev wrote in the journal 'Put' (No. 59) an article entitled 'Is there in Russian Orthodoxy a freedom of thought and of conscience? (In defence of Georgii Fedotov)' ('Sushchestvuet li v pravoslavii svoboda mysli i sovesti? (v zashchitu Georgiia Fedotova)'), where as an epigraph he tellingly chose a paraphrase of Nietzsche: 'You have become small and will become yet smaller: this is the result of your teachings of humility and submissiveness'. See <http://www.odinblago.ru/path/59/5/> [accessed 7 February 2014].

[59] See Viktor Zhivov's lecture at <http://polit.ru/article/2009/08/13/pokojanije/> [accessed 14 February] for this and other ideas and quotations from Zhivov contained in this entire paragraph.

more generally. Individual's responsibility and guilt for the whole mankind do not as such deny personal responsibility – for what was Christ's example if not taking on the sins of all the others? Suffering for others, accepting responsibility for their sins can be seen indeed as the highest rather than the lowest point of religious faith, and the boundary here is extremely subtle, because it concerns exclusively inner work of the individual soul which may have little connection to external religious practices. By the same token, rigorous practices of repentance in the West, as such, do not prove a superior morality, for practice can always degenerate into a hollow formality, a mere external discharge of responsibility, without any inner work involved. One can think of a physiological analogy here, when a stronger external support may simply weaken our muscles, rendering them obsolete. These thoughts would turn Zhivov's argument on its head, suggesting that the more rigorous the external strictures of religious practices are the lesser moral space they may in fact occupy.

Dostoevsky, on the other hand, was preoccupied, it seems, precisely by the moral space within religion rather than theological or any other facet of it. It is in this sense that he believed Russian Orthodoxy to be superior to Western Christianity and was so focused on Russian Orthodox humility, which he saw not as a sign of weakness and gateway for enslavement, but as a manifestation of extreme inner strength. This found expression in a number of his fictional characters, most notably Aliosha Karamazov, Father Zosima, Prince Myshkin and Krotkaia.

It is interesting that modernism, and especially emerging existentialism, with its propensity to question the old ethical and aesthetic paradigms, questioned precisely these archetypes, showing suspicion and distrust towards them. Thus Lev Shestov consistently dismissed the above Dostoyevskian heroes, especially prince Myshkin, the idiot, as a 'pitiful shadow' and 'cold, anaemic spectre', as 'nothing but idea, i.e., a void'.[60]

At the same time, and equally curiously, Lev Tolstoy combined the principle of non-resistance to evil by force, having understood it as a central premise of human life, with his own immense personal pride (and, possibly, precisely as a way to conquer and control it). It is this devastating individual pride that was associated by Dostoevsky et al. with, simultaneously, the evil inherent in pure reason, and Western civilization and its values. Andre Gide singled out precisely this aspect of Dostoevsky's writing and opposed it, with admiration, to Western culture. Commenting on one of Dostoevsky's private letters, Gide writes: 'Towards the end – drunk with the humility he used to intoxicate the heroes of his novels, that uncanny humility of the Russian, which may be Christ-like, [. . .] and which the Western mind will never fully understand since it reckons self-respect a virtue – towards the end, he asks, "Why should they deny me? I make no demands. I am but a humble petitioner! . . ". [. . .] Western readers will protest in face of such humility and contrition. Our literature, too often tinged with Castilian pride, has so thoroughly taught us to see nobility of character in the non-forgiveness of injury and insult!'.[61]

---

[60] In the Russian original: 'жалкая тень', 'холодное, бескровное привидение', 'одна идея, т.е. пустота' – in Shestov, 'Dostoevsky i Nitzshe: Filosofiia tragedii', in *Sochineniia v dvukh tomakh*, Tomsk: Vodolei, 1996, p. 383.

[61] André Gide, *Dostoevsky*, London: Penguin Books, 1967, p. 37.

In a similar way, the Russian thinker Grigorii Pomerants distinguished humility and selflessness, celebrated by Dostoevsky, as necessary attributes of life, such that without them all the real gifts change into their opposites: 'Without the ability to put yourself in second place, without the ability to be humble, all gifts turn into millstones around the neck'.[62]

At the same time, it is difficult to dismiss the arguments of the opposite side, which blame Russian Orthodoxy, with its tradition of humility being one of the central virtues, for rendering the nation vulnerable and defenceless. Non-resistance to evil by force is, more generally, conducive of facilitating the easy triumph of evil. However, the problem with resisting evil turns into a major (and generally insoluble) philosophical problem, for any such resistance is necessarily conducted – by the good – using the means of evil, and therefore can easily change the very nature of the good.

A more productive approach (already touched upon in the Introduction) to assessing the distinction between Russian Orthodoxy and Western Christianity, and its wide-reaching consequences, has been attempted in a recent book by the Russian scholars Argunova and Tiapkov:

'The birth of Christ is the main event in the religion of Western Christians, which stresses the meaningfulness of earthly life. Arranging earthly life as well as the human relationship with God is based on quite understandable pragmatic foundations. A judicial conception of expiation, according to which Christ's sacrifice was predicated on the need to facilitate Divine punishment for Adam's sin, is dominant. Expiation is interpreted as due justice which is more appropriate for the secular world.

In Russian culture an individual is connected to the perishable world by special transcendental relationships. God is separated from the world by His will. God's ideas of creation are separated from creation itself, just as the will of an artist is separated from the work of art in which it is manifested. For this reason the material world loses its validity. The genuine world is the world of spiritual grace, the kingdom of genuine freedom and equality. In order to become united with God one must dismiss the surrounding world, which exists outside God'.[63]

The authors thus perceive the difference in the above religious sensibilities as responsible for exalting respectively the spiritual and material side of life, heavenly and earthly, ideal and real, disproportionately focusing either on the sublime ideas or on their practical implications, and ultimately resulting in two tangibly different mentalities – in rough terms, 'Russian' and 'Western-European'.

At the same time, as Reiner Grübel argues,[64] Russian irrationalism has manifested itself considerably through sectarianism and heresies being a counter-reaction to the rigidity of Russian Orthodoxy. And it is the Russian Schism in general which may be responsible for many peculiarities of the national historical development. Religious faith, however, is only one, even if extremely significant, facet of the issue with Russia's

---

[62] Grigorii Pomerants, *Otkrytost bezdne. Vstrechi s Dostoevskim*, Moscow: Sovetskii pisatel, 1990, p. 266.

[63] Argunova and Tiapkov, *Innovatsionnoe razvitie regiona: potentsial, instituty, mekhanizmy*, op. cit.

[64] See Reiner Grübel, 'Lev Tolstoi and Vasilii Rozanov: Two Fundamental(ist) Types of Russian Irrationalism', in Olga Tabachnikova (ed.), *Mystery Inside Enigma: Facets of Russian Irrationalism between Art and Life*, op. cit.

distinctiveness vis-à-vis Western Europe, and is absorbed by a more general pattern. In fact, the vigour of the Slavophiles-Westernizers debates, which clearly manifests itself in the wrestling with Russian Orthodoxy, at a deeper level revolves precisely around the place of and relationship with the mind and reason in the national consciousness and culture; in other words – around Russian irrationalism – treating it respectively as a phantom and delusion or as tangible reality.

Rudolf Neuhäuser, the Austrian scholar of Dostoevsky, suggests a model which, in his view, captures best the idiosyncrasy of the Russian mentality and hence Russian cultural consciousness and reality. This model is based on the theory surrounding a psychological disorder of *pseudologia fantastica*, when an illusion (an alternative reality) takes the upper hand over actual reality to the point of severing increasingly more ties with it and then gradually replacing it altogether. Neuhäuser starts with analysing the treatment of Dostoevsky's legacy in Russia, and observes that the novelist's name is used widely to justify and reinforce a predominantly reactionary political agenda.

Interestingly, the Russian Dostoevsky scholar Ludmila Saraskina comments on precisely the same phenomenon – of using Dostoevsky's name as a shield to smuggle one's own reactionary views into the present Russian reality. Saraskina tries to clear Dostoevsky's name and defends the novelist from such abusive attempts, explaining that their authors invariably distort the truth to their own ends.[65]

Neuhäuser draws on the negative impressions of Russia by various famous foreign travellers and historians, such as Jules Michelet or Marquise de Custine, whose views convey a similar idea – of Russia being the country of lies and deception, self-deception in particular. Indeed, Michelet wrote: 'In Russia everybody, from the young to the old, lie: this country is a phantasmagoria, mirage, empire of illusions [. . .]. Russia is an aberration; apotheosis of lies and deceit'.[66] De Custine put it even more eloquently: 'There exist remedies from the primitive savagery; however, there is no treatment against the mania to appear what you are not'.[67]

Dmitrii Likhachev, in a controversial way for some, takes issue with such stereotypical mythology. 'It is not from Marquis de Custine, who spent in Russia just over two months, that we should learn how to perceive Russia!',[68] he exclaims bitterly. With historical facts in hand, Likhachev argues against the image, widely spread in Western Europe, of Russian people's infinite patience and 'slave mentality'. His main claim is that Russian culture 'always, at the depth of its foundation, was committed to the idea of individual freedom'.[69] Likhachev recalls, in particular, *Veche* and *Zemskie sobory* which Russian Princes had to reckon with, and also the process of fleeing to Cossacks from state oppression, as well as the existence of varied literature which 'defended the rights and dignity of an individual', such as 'Legislation'

[65] See <http://www.pravmir.ru/lyudmila-saraskina-o-prityagivanii-citat-i-stalinizacii-golovnogo-mozga/> [accessed 21 April 2013].

[66] See, for instance, <http://www.ukrinform.ua/rus/news/etot_den_v_istorii_21_avgusta_1549058> [accessed 5 May 2013]. Referred to in Rudolf Neuhäuser, op. cit., p. 369.

[67] Marquis de Custine, *Rossiia v 1839 godu: v 2 tomakh*, Moscow: Izd-vo im. Sabashnikovykh, 1996, vol. 1, p. 106.

[68] Dmitrii Likhachev, 'O natsionalnom kharaktere russkikh', *Voprosy filosofii*, 1990, No. 4, pp. 3–6.

[69] Ibid.

('*Zakonodatelstvo*'), 'Russian Truth' ('*Russkaia Pravda*'), 'Code of Law' ('*Sudebniki*') and 'The Code' ('*Ulozhenie*').[70]

He talks also of the 'flourishing of monastery culture [. . .] supported by the large number of saintly ascetics living in the monasteries'. As a result, 'basic Russian ideals of moral conduct were created' and 'most fully embodied in the *Izmaragd*', from which in the sixteenth century *Domostroi* was derived. Although it was not nearly as influential as *Izmaragd*, 'thanks to a lack of discernment on the part of many in the 19th century, it became a source for false evidence regarding the backwardness of Russian mores'.[71]

An example of vital importance which puts into perspective the whole of Russian cultural history is the movement of Old Believers, who, in a totally irrational fashion from an outsider's viewpoint, 'literally went to the stake [. . .] for the sake of the idea which was unprofitable for them in material terms. They preferred to immolate themselves rather than agree to ideological concessions'.[72] Their drive was not in a simple preservation of the old traditions, but in upholding the religious purity. As Florovsky put it, 'not a ritual, but anti-Christ is the theme and mystery of the Russian Schism'.[73] Likhachev, talking of their semiotics of behaviour, stresses in particular honesty and reliability of Old Believers as a consequence of their religiosity: 'As a result of being morally firm in their Faith, the Old Believers in their work were also morally firm. All that Old Believers did [. . .] they did properly. Entering into various business agreements with them was congenial and straightforward, and no written confirmations were necessary. A word given by an Old Believer, a merchant's word, was sufficient, to have everything done without any deceit'.[74] They were industrious not only in physical labour, but also in keeping up cultural continuity: 'Adherents of ancient piety, [. . .] Russian settlers brought with them – along with all the basics, most necessary for their initial settling in, – books, books and books again; and then, in their arduous life on the new lands, they had been engaged in copying books and creating their own new peasant literature'.[75]

One could argue that Likhachev's vision here is one-sided, in that it ignores the problematic aspect – that fanaticism of Old Believers in their defense, as it were, of the 'letter of the law', turned out to be destructive for Russia. In this connection, the views of Maximilian Voloshin, in relation to his poem 'Archpriest Avvakum' (1918) – where Avvakum epitomizes an 'ecstasy of perseverance'[76]– are instructive. In his letter to Aleksandra Petrova of 19 January 1918 Voloshin thus compared Avvakum to Mikhail Bakunin: 'I am perturbed by the personality which I feel behind Avvakum. It

[70]   Ibid.
[71]   Dmitrii S. Likhachev, 'Religion: Russian Orthodoxy', in Rzhevsky (ed.), op. cit., p. 44.
[72]   Dmitrii Likhachev, Interview for *Russkii Kurier*, published on 28.11.2006 – for Likhachev's centenary.
[73]   Georgii Florovsky, 'Puti russkogo bogosloviia', Paris, 1937, p. 58.
[74]   Likhachev, Interview for *Russkii Kurier*, op. cit.
[75]   Dmitrii Likhachev, 'Arkheograficheskoe otkrytie Sibiri', in N. N. Pokrovsky, *Puteshestvie za redkimi knigami*, Novosibirsk: Sova, 2005, p. 3.
[76]   From Voloshin's letter to A. M. Petrova, of 25.12.1917, where he summarizes his vision of Avvakum's personality in this neat formula. See Maximilian Voloshin, *Iz literaturnogo naslediia*, St Petersburg: 'Aleteia', 1999. See <http://az.lib.ru/w/woloshin_m_a/text_1921_pisma_k_petrovoy.shtml> [accessed 24 June 2014].

is Bakunin. I feel their organic connection, but have no idea, how it can be exposed and transmitted – so distant they are now from the public imagination. And yet, they express the main idea of Russian history: Christian anarchism'. [. . .] 'a merger of the church with the Roman empire determined the Latin church. In Slavic cultures, by contrast, Christianity has a tendency to get transferred entirely into an individual feeling and to oppose the state, as the dominion of the beast. That is why in the members of the People's Will and in terrorists there is no less Christianity than in the martyrs of the first centuries, despite their atheism. It is in this dimension that I feel some congenial kinship of Avvakum and Bakunin'.[77] Similar sentiments are expressed in Voloshin's poem 'Rossia' (1924): '. . . Bakunin has fully reflected our true face. All Russia's creative power is in anarchy: Europe was going with the culture of fire, while we are carrying within us the culture of explosion'.[78]

Nevertheless, high ethical principles of the movement of Old Believers are undeniable. A similar phenomenon in ethical terms, and in essence equally irrational and sublime, was holy foolishness which, although not exclusive to Russia, became particularly widespread and popular exactly on the Russian soil. In their disdain towards the earthly comfort, towards all the petty self-indulgences, holy fools rebel against the injustices, lies and temptations of life, and, taking on the intentional madness, they strive to the heavenly, longing for the highest truth and love. While in the West such a revolt led to concrete practical changes – for instance, to social transformations – Russian rebellion was more of a non-applied nature (in this sense akin to art). The main feature of Russian holy foolishness is thus reminiscent of that of Russian philosophy and religiosity as a whole – it is in the hierarchical perception of the universe, where the earthly without the heavenly is worthless (which, again, is akin to the artistic, anti-utilitarian perception). As we shall later see, Russian holy foolishness has crossed the borders between life and art, and profoundly informed many works and authors of Russian literature. In a more narrow sense, with its persistent exposure of dishonesty, 'especially frequently and severely it always attacked state power'.[79]

Speaking more broadly – regardless of the critical Western opinions, in Russia itself, with its increasing political autocracy and deepening existential concerns, the questions of inner freedom, moral code and human dignity gained painful intensity, and many classical Russian writers raised their voices bitterly mocking the 'national vices' in an attempt to redeem the meaning of the above concepts. Thus Anton Chekhov, among others, criticized the Russians precisely for their arrogance and lack of inner freedom: 'With our lack of seriousness, on the part the majority, our inability

---

[77] Maximilian Voloshin, *Iz literaturnogo naslediia*, St Petersburg: 'Aleteia', 1999. See <http://az.lib.ru/w/woloshin_m_a/text_1921_pisma_k_petrovoy.shtml> [accessed 24 June 2014].

[78] Maximilian Voloshin, 'Rossiia', <http://www.all-poems.ru/voloshin1.html> [accessed 24 June 2014]. In Russian: '. . . Бакунин / Наш истый лик отобразил вполне. / В анархии всё творчество России: / Европа шла культурою огня, / А мы в себе несём культуру взрыва'. I am grateful to Dr Aleksandr Medvedev of Tiumen' State University for his valuable comments and for drawing my attention to this material. Notice also in this connection a statement by Yurii Lotman that 'Russian cultural history is seen by Russian cultural imagination as a chain of explosions' (see Yurii Lotman, 'Tezisy k semiotike russkoi kultury', in *Yurii Lotman i tartusko-moskovskaia semioticheskaia shkola*, Moscow: Gnozis, 1994, p. 409).

[79] Zenkovsky, op. cit., p. 47.

and unaccustomedness to peer into and to try to understand the phenomena of life, there is no other place where one would say so often, "What vulgarity!", where one would take other people's achievements or serious questions so lightly, often mockingly. And on the other hand, there is no other place where the pressure of authority would be as burdensome as it is for us, Russians, demeaned by the age-old slavery, afraid of freedom. We are overtired from servility and hypocrisy'.[80] Similar sentiments are expressed earlier in the century, by Pushkin in his response to Chaadaev, alongside the rebuff. 'Many things in your letter are profoundly true. One must admit that our social life is a sad thing. The absence of public opinion, the indifference toward all duty, justice, and truth, the cynical disdain for human thought and dignity are truly distressing'.[81]

Almost a century later, Berdiaev wrote of the same problem of a lack of individual consciousness, of personal dignity and individual rights, linking this to a historically strong collective spirit of Russians. 'The Russian people has a stately gift for submissiveness, of the humbling of the person before the collective. The Russian people does not sense itself a man, it is all ready to be a bride, it senses itself a woman affront the colossus of the state, "strength" makes it submissive. [. . .] The great misfortune of the Russian soul is [. . .] in a womanish passivity, transformed into a "baba-ism", in an insufficiency of manliness [. . .]. The Russian nation lives too much in a popular-element collectivism, and within it there has not yet solidified the consciousness of the person, of its worth and its rights'. [82]

The same idea of the individual subjugating to the collective, as a trademark of the Russian soul, was given an entirely positive sign by Herzen, more than half a century earlier. Herzen felt indignant, provoked precisely by the aforementioned anti-Russian sentiments of Jules Michelet, and came forward with a passionate response. To Michelet's accusations (resonant with Chaadaev's radical criticism), 'Russia does not exist, Russians are not people and they are devoid of moral sensibility', Herzen exclaimed: 'The Russian people, dear sir, are alive, healthy and even not very old, in fact, very young'.[83] He defended the communal spirit of the Russians, their 'extraordinary vitaliy and much promise for the future'; he wrote of their extraordinary honesty and good will in dealings with each other, but not with an oppressive and unjust state.[84] 'The people and the state have nothing in common. [. . .] The peasant finds himself, literally, outside the law. The court will not defend him and his entire participation in the existing order of things consists only in the taxes which weigh heavily upon him and which he pays by sweat and blood. Outcast by all, he understands instinctively that the entire administration is structured to his disadvantage, not to his benefit and that the

[80] A. P. Chekhov, 'Zapisnaia knizhka I', in *Polnoe Sobranie Sochinenii i Pisem v 30 tomakh*, vol. 17, Moscow: Nauka, 1987, p. 102.

[81] *The Letters of Alexander Pushkin. Three Volumes in One*. Transl., with Preface, Introduction and Notes by J. Thomas Shaw, op. cit., p. 780.

[82] Nikolai Berdiaev, 'Concerning the "Eternal Baba" in the Russian Soul', transl. by Fr. S. Janos. <http://www.berdyaev.com/berdiaev/berd_lib/1915_187.html> [accessed 10 December 2013].

[83] Aleksandr Herzen's letter to Jules Michelet of 22 September 1851. See <https://www2.stetson.edu/secure/history/hy308C01/herzen.html> [accessed 17 January 2014].

[84] Ibid.

task of the government and the landowners consists entirely of finding ways to wrest from him more labor, army recruits, and money'.[85] In the end, the Westernizer Herzen strikes a final and distinctly slavophilic chord by opposing Russian 'communism' to the implied Western individualism. 'It is very fortunate for Russia that the peasant commune has not perished, that personal property has not replaced common property. It is very fortunate for the Russian people that it has remained outside all political movements and outside European civilization which, without doubt, would have destroyed the commune'.[86]

Thus Herzen as well as other Russian intellectuals of the time opposed the people (or the country) and the (autocratic and bureaucratic) state (even though he excludes the tsar and the clergy from the state structures). And this opposition has never really lost its relevance. What Belinsky wrote to Gogol in 1847, about the lack of elementary lawful space and basic human rights, still reads as a contemporary analysis: 'You failed to realize that Russia sees her salvation not in mysticism or asceticism or pietism, but in the successes of civilization, enlightenment, and humanity. What she needs is not sermons (she has heard enough of them!) or prayers (she has repeated them too often!), but the awakening in the people of a sense of their human dignity lost for so many centuries amid dirt and refuse; she needs rights and laws conforming not to the preaching of the church but to common sense and justice, and their strictest possible observance. Instead of which she presents the dire spectacle of a country [. . .] where there are not only no guarantees for individuality, honor and property, but even no police order, and where there is nothing but vast corporations of official thieves and robbers of various descriptions. The most vital national problems in Russia today are [. . .] the strictest possible observance of at least those laws that already exist. This is even realized by the government itself [. . .] as is proved by its timid and abortive half-measures for the relief of the white Negroes'.[87]

Thus, a Russian subject has been traditionally far from being protected by the state and remained instead forever vulnerable in the face of history, nature and fate, left to his own devices. Existentially this has had a revealing effect, returning people to their primordial state, where their true nature could be tested to the full. 'A neverending crisis of Russia uprooted people from their everyday'.[88] Such merciless tests exposed most horrific meanness as well as most profound heroism. In Dostoevsky's oeuvre, for example, 'world disorder disturbed even most petty personalities',[89] not just the main heroes, endowed with profound individualities. This state of affairs could have contributed to the grotesquely monstrous pictures of Russia reported by Western travellers.

Curiously, the views above – by Neuhäuser or the earlier Western historians whom he quotes – have one distinctive common feature: with their psychological approach

---

[85] Ibid.
[86] Ibid.
[87] V. G. Belinsky, Letter to Nikolai Gogol of 15/3 July 1847 in N. V. Gogol, *PSS v 14 tomakh* (Moscow-Leningrad: Izd-vo AN SSSR, 1937–52), vol. 8, pp. 501–2; for the English version see <http://www.marxists.org/subject/art/lit_crit/works/belinsky/gogol.htm> [accessed 12 November 2013].
[88] Pomerants, 'O podlosti, o doblesti, o slave', op. cit.
[89] Ibid.

they treat Russia, the country, as a person. This tendency is, in fact, a typical legacy of Romanticism, whose 'teaching of a nation as a person, and realisation of the uniqueness of every individual or national consciousness being the highest value, has prepared ground for a typology of national cultures'.[90] Dostoevsky expressed a related idea in his notebook, 'A nationality is nothing more than a national personality (народная личность)'.[91] The historian Vadim Borisov regards this, essentially Romantic, perception of nation as irrational in character, for he writes, 'Perceiving nation as *person* cannot really be translated into the language of rational categories, and thus remains entirely alien to rationalism and positivism, let alone materialism (we are talking here, I stress, about *world outlooks*, whereas among their concrete bearers exceptions are, of course, possible)'.[92]

Perhaps rather ironically, Neuhäuser's notably rational model follows this very pattern. One could of course continue this line (of applying human psychology to national typology) in a similarly productive way to surmise that in the tormented Russian attitude to the West and obsession with the Russian-Western dichotomy there lies indeed a certain inferiority complex inherent in a relationship of the young to the old, of a child to a parent. This might in particular underlie the sarcastic anti-Western quotations above – by Dostoevsky as well as Venedict Erofeev.

It also squares up with the relative youth of Russian literary culture as a major player on the international stage. What took many centuries for Western Europe, Russian literature accomplished within one. The same motif is observed by Yuri Lotman in Lermontov's oeuvre of the poet's final years: 'From Lermontov's point of view, Russian culture opposes great decrepit civilizations of the West and East as a young culture which is only entering the world scene'.[93] In particular, 'Lermontov connects a young cultural type with its flexibility, its ability to perceive foreign consciousness and to understand foreign customs'.[94] The same idea – of high and sensitive susceptibility – is taken to the extreme by Dmitrii Galkovsky, who believes that 'The Russian soul is [. . .] an absolute void; silence, hiatus. [. . .] But this very emptiness gives rise to immense sensitivity and the ability to illuminate in a remarkable, unequaled way the material that is being absorbed'.[95] Lotman draws a parallel between the ideas of Lermontov and Griboedov with respect to the youth of Russian culture. He refers to Griboedov's lines from the draft of the play 'The Year 1812' where Napoleon was supposed to contemplate

[90]   Yurii Lotman, 'Problema Vostoka i Zapada v tvorchestve pozdnego Lermontova', in *Izbrannye statji*, Tallinn, Alexandra, 1993, p. 9.
[91]   F. M. Dostoevsky, *Polnoe sobranie sochinenii v 30 tomakh*, vol. 21, Leningrad: Nauka, 1980, vol. 21, p. 257.
[92]   Vadim Borisov, 'Lichnost i natsionalnoe samosoznanie', in *Iz-pod glyb. Sbornik statei*, Paris: YMCA-Press, 1974, see <http://www.vehi.net/samizdat/izpodglyb/09.html> [accessed 25 January 2014].
[93]   Y. M. Lotman, 'Problema Vostoka i Zapada v tvorchestve pozdnego Lermontova', *Izbrannye statii*, op. cit., vol. 3, p. 14.
[94]   Ibid.
[95]   Dmitrii Galkovsky, 'Beskonechnyi tupik', List 3 at <http://fictionbook.ru/author/galkovskiyi_dmitriyi_evgenevich/beskonechniyyi_tupik/read_online.html?page=3> [accessed 22 January 2012]. Similar views are expressed by John Shemiakin in his conversation with A. Smirnova and T. Tolstaya in 'Shkola zlosloviia' – see <http://www.youtube.com/watch?v=t7TTIH1lDvE> [accessed 22 January 2012]. In a way, Chekhov's 'Little Darling' portrays the same type of mentality, only at a personal rather than national level.

'on this young, original nation, on the peculiarities of its dress, building, faith and mores. If given to itself, what could it produce?'.[96]

It is also with the (relative) youth of Russian literary culture that Lev Shestov connects its incredible audacity (with all its underlying potential), which is the other side of the coin of absolute ignorance and naïvete of inexperience: 'our simplicity and truthfulness are due to our relatively scanty culture. [. . .] And if we don't know, it seems to us it is only because we haven't tried to find out. Other people's experience is not ours. We are not bound by their conclusions. [. . .] The most skeptical Russian hides a hope at the bottom of his soul. Hence our fearlessness of the truth, realistic truth which so stunned European critics. [. . .] We have wanted to reexamine everything, restate everything. I won't deny that our courage is drawn from our quite uncultured confidence in our own powers'.[97] Behind this inappropriate daring, Shestov argues, there lies 'a lingering belief in the possibility of a final triumph over "evil". [. . .] In the strength of this belief Russian writer goes forth to meet his enemy – he does not hide from him'.[98]

By the same token, Shestov perceives the difference between Russia and Western Europe in the Russian self-assured belief – based on the youth and inexperience of Russian culture – in the miracles of progress, or, in other words, in the Russian infantile propensity to self-delusion. He frames this difference elegantly in the following witty lines:

'Culture is an age-long development, and sudden grafting of it upon a race rarely succeeds. To us in Russia, civilisation came suddenly, whilst we were still savages. [. . .] We quickly submitted. In a short time we were swallowing in enormous doses those poisons which Europe had been gradually accustoming herself to, gradually assimilating through centuries. [. . .] A Russian had only to catch a whiff of European atmosphere, and his head began to swim. He interpreted in his own way, savage-like, whatever he heard of western success. Hearing about railways, agricultural machines, schools, municipalities, his imagination painted miracles: universal happiness, boundless freedom, paradise, wings, etc. And the more impossible his dreams, the more eager he was to believe them real. [. . .] But the Russian bear crept out of his hole and strolled to Europe for the elixir of life, the flying carpet, the seven-leagued shoes, and so on, thinking in all his naïveté that railways and electricity were signs which clearly proved that the old nurse never told a lie in her fairy tales . . . All this happened just at the moment when Europe had finally made away with alchemy and astrology, and started on the positive researches resulting in chemistry and astronomy'.[99] This craving for a fairy-tale or, in other words, this exaltation with illusion – which is another name for day-dreaming – all frame the utopian nature of Russian cultural consciousness and its tragic historical consequences. In a very similar spirit to Shestov, but more than half a century earlier, Khomiakov wrote, 'It is not long ago at all, that we came out

---

[96] A. S. Griboedov, *Polnoe Sobranie Sochinenii*, St Petersburg, 1911, vol. 1, p. 262. Cited in Y. M. Lotman, 'Problema Vostoka i Zapada v tvorchestve pozdnego Lermontova', op. cit.

[97] Lev Shestov, 'All Things Are Possible' ('Apotheosis of Groundlessness'), op. cit. See <http://www. angelfire.com/nb/shestov/all/all_23.html> [accessed 26 October 2013].

[98] Ibid.

[99] Lev Shestov, 'All Things Are Possible' ('Apotheosis of Groundlessness'), op. cit. See <http://www. angelfire.com/nb/shestov/all/all_2.html> [accessed 26 October 2013].

of the epoch of gullible simplicity and intricate folk-tales'.[100] Furthermore, but very much along the same lines, Dmitrii Galkovsky, as we saw earlier, speaks of the intrinsic irrationalism inherent in the very rationalism of Russians:

'In all probability, somewhere in the subconscious of every Russian there is a barbaric aspiration to Western learning, rationality. Moreover, rationality itself is perceived by Russians as something extremely irrational, not grasped by the mind, that provides secret knowledge. Amongst the schismatics there was a superstition that he who reads the whole Bible and understands it completely, would go mad. Stankiewicz read Schelling, Kant and Hegel with the same feeling'.[101] These words continue Shestov's observations of the irrational character of Russian rationality which is linked directly to Russia' ambiguous attitude to Western Europe: 'We wish to draw with a generous hand from fathomless eternity, and all that is limited we leave to European bourgeoisie. With few exceptions Russian writers really despise the pettiness of the West. Even those who have admired Europe most have done so because they failed most completely to understand her. They did not want to understand her. That is why we have always taken over European ideas in such fantastic forms. Take the sixties for example. With its loud ideas of sobriety and modest outlook, it was a most drunken period. Those who awaited the New Messiah and the Second Advent read Darwin and dissected frogs. It is the same to-day'.[102] Thus again Russian dream, illusion and exaggeration, that is all impractical, idealistic qualities, replace Western practical applied approach. This is what Leskov's Levsha also epitomizes – Russian preference for aesthetics and beauty, rather than utilitarian use. 'Nobody doubts the great gifts and talents of the Russians, but all their mastership is somehow out of place and at the wrong time'.[103]

Thus Russian philosophizing happens as if for its own sake, without any practical implications. It is symbolized by a brief dialogue of the two idle passers by at the start of Gogol's 'Dead souls', who discuss if a cart wheel can travel as far as Moscow or Kazan. 'They impersonate the remarkable creative faculty of Russians, so beautifully disclosed by Gogol's own inspiration, of working in a void. Fancy is fertile only when it is futile. The speculation of the two muzhiks is based on nothing tangible and leads to no material results; but philosophy and poetry are born that way',[104] perceptively wrote Nabokov. Philosophy which according to the ancients starts with amazement, in the West leads to practical re-organization of life, while in Russia it simply ends in amazement: 'If a person in holy Russia is struck with amazement, he will freeze stupified, and remain so frozen until his death'.[105]

[100] A. S. Khomiakov, *Sochineniia v 2 tomakh*, Moscow: 'Medium', 1994, vol. 1, p. 131.
[101] Dmitrii Galkovsky, 'Beskonechnyi tupik', List 3, op. cit. (This quotation was first given in the Introduction.)
[102] Lev Shestov, 'All Things Are Possible' ('Apotheosis of Groundlessness'). Op. cit. See <http://www.angelfire.com/nb/shestov/all/all_23.html> [accessed 26 October 2013].
[103] Boris Paramonov, reflecting on Leskov's 'Levsha': see <http://www.svoboda.org/content/transcript/25030578.html> [accessed 26 October 2013].
[104] Vladimir Nabokov, *Lectures on Russian literature*, New York: Harcourt Brace Jovanovich, 1981, p. 20.
[105] A popular phrase, without definite authorship, which is often ascribed to Saltykov-Shchedrin.

The line of the Russian distrust of the mind is still extremely popular with the country's Westernizers. Thus Vladimir Kantor argues that Russian culture altogether dismisses reason as part of its existence.[106] Drawing on German philosophers with their accent on Enlightenment, on the courage, required for making use of human mind (Kant), on the crucial role of reason in the process of mankind reaching adulthood (Hegel), and on the civic infantilism inherent in a totalitarian society (Karl Manheim), Kantor concludes that Russian irrationalism, Russian inability or unwillingness to engage one's mind testifies precisely to such civic infantilism of the country. He notes that if for Chaadaev Russia's alienation from Western syllogism was a tragedy, then for the Slavophile Russian thinkers it became a virtue.

Tiutchev's metaphor of irrelevance of rational cognition in the Russian context, Kantor develops further into a major claim of Russian God being the god of a sacred space, the pagan god of place rather than supra-national, Christian god. Thus the efforts of the late nineteenth-century Russian philosophers, Kantor argues, were largely an attempt of Christianization of Russia which traditionally epitomized a pagan-Christian blend and the kind of knowledge which does not incorporate understanding.

However, such conclusion does not necessarily follow, for the concept of a sacred place does not imply a pagan god, but merely a sanctuary of the past, that is a natural affiliation with the national history and the memory of one's ancestors: 'love for your home and hearth, love for the tombs of your ancestors'.[107] The fact that emotional element seems dominant in Russian culture (if one accepts that premise) – hence the notion of the 'Russian soul' rather than the 'Russian mind' – does not automatically mean that feelings overpower reason and dismiss the mind; it may equally mean that reason is framed and permeated by emotion, is verified by it, and is thus prevented from becoming the mankind's undertaker, its horrible Golem. The interaction between mind and soul is far from being a Boolean relation, and its non-linear character is brilliantly captured by Andrei Platonov in the following description: 'What he felt now in his heart was a dam trembling continuously before the pressure of a rising lake of feelings. Feelings rose high against his heart, then tumbled down to other side, already transformed into a stream of mitigating thought. Still however the duty light of his watchman burnt above the dam, the watchman who takes no part in the life of man, drowsing within him for a pittance of salary. Occasionally this light allowed Dvanov to see both expanses, the warm swelling sea of feelings and the long tumbling thought which ran down the dam, cooling itself with its own speed. It was then that Dvanov could overcome the labor of his heart, which fed his consciousness as it braked it, and could be happy'.[108] Thus a more precise conclusion than Kantor's seems to be supplied by Ivan Ilin, who calls the Russian version of Christianity a 'religion of the heart'.

---

[106] See, for example, Kantor's lecture 'Umom Rossiiu ne poniat' at <http://www.youtube.com/watch?v=Hsup-LyGjds> [accessed 17 July 2013].

[107] Pushkin, 'Chernovye nabroski', in *Sobranie sochinenii v 10 tomakh*, op. cit., vol. 2, 1959. In Russian: 'любовь к родному пепелищу, любовь к отеческим гробам'.

[108] Andrei Platonov, *Chevengur*, transl. by Anthony Olcott, Ann Arbor: Ardis, 1978, p. 120.

Kantor's claims are shared by numerous similar arguments of modern Westernizers who compare unfavourably Russia's intrinsic 'national' shortcomings to the advancements of the West.

The line of modern Slavophiles is, similarly, a natural continuation of their nineteenth-century predecessors (arguing for Russia's special path and messianic role), except for the radical nature of contemporary rhetorics. As Aleksandr Medvedev writes,[109] commenting on the study of A. N. Burmeister,[110] with all the polar opposition of their stance, Russian early Slavophiles and Westernizers had more in common than they had differences. The first and most obvious unifying feature was the very opposition of Russia to Western Europe which both movements considered as their premise. However, in the polemics between Gogol and Belinsky it is the former who is open to a dialogue and is 'capable, in the manner of Pushkin, of uniting the rightness of the "Slavianists" and "Europeists": "they all speak of two sides of the same coin, but it does not occur to them that in fact there is no dispute or contradiction between them'.[111] Moreover, Gogol summons them to put aside their vanity and to recognize the truth of the opponent. Belinsky, on the contrary, is monological and advocating progress through external, revolutionary more than internal, spiritual transformations. 'As a result, his revolutionary theory of socialism and his atheism determined for Russia the route of external, violent transformations: "I am beginning to love mankind in the fashion of Marat: in order to make a tiny part of it happy, I would destroy the other part, it seems to me, by fire and sword . . .'".[112] The rift between the Enlightenment and Spirituality proved fatal to Russia, Burmeister writes. Belinsky's exclamations were taken as 'an extremist political manifesto, which opens up the road for nihilism, i.e. for the radical rejection and total condemnation of the heritage of both Westernisers and Slavophiles'.[113] Subsequently the Slavophiles sunk into Russian orthodox metaphysics, while Westernizers evolved into radical intelligentsia whose line eventually resulted in Bolshevism.[114]

Interestingly, according to the aforementioned pattern, it was Chekhov who continued Pushkin's line of reconciliation, or rather who shared a shrewd Pushkin's vision of spotting undercurrent similarity in things superficially different. Thus it was Chekhov who, in contrast to the commonly accepted opposition of arts and sciences, argued for their intrinsic kinship. Thus he wrote in a letter to Dmitrii Grigorovich, 'an artist's intuition is sometimes worth of a scientist's brain, [. . .] both have the same goals and the same nature'[115] and continued in a letter to Aleksei Suvorin, 'Both anatomy and belles-lettres are of equally noble descent; they have identical goals and an identical

109 Medvedev, '"Sviatoi Vladimir" i "Petr Velikii": Russkoe samosoznanie v poiskakh edinstva', op. cit., pp. 71–2.
110 A. N. Burmeister, *Dukhovnost i prosveshchenie: u istokov russkogo samopoznaniia*, op. cit.
111 N. V. Gogol, 'Spory (iz pisma k L***)', in *Polnoe sobranie sochinenii v 14 tomakh*, Moscow-Leningrad: Izd-vo AN SSSR, 1952, vol. 8, p. 262.
112 V. G. Belinsky, Letter to V. P. Botkin of 28 June 1841 in Polnoe Sobranie Sochinenii v 13 tomakh, Moscow, 1956, vol. 12, p. 179.
113 A. N. Burmeister, *Dukhovnost i prosveshchenie: u istokov russkogo samopoznaniia*, op. cit., p. 388.
114 Ibid.
115 From the draft of Chekhov's letter to Grigorovich of 12.02.1887, see *PSSP v 30 tomakh*, vol. 2, Moscow: Nauka, 1975, pp. 28–31.

enemy – the devil – and there is absolutely no reason for them to fight. [. . .] It is for this reason that geniuses never fought among themselves and Goethe the poet coexisted splendidly with Goethe the naturalist'.[116]

Along the same lines of unification as opposed to polarization of extremes, Lotman views the ideas of Lermontov in the poet's latest years. In the polemics of the 1840s concerning the cultural antithesis of Russia-West, he places Lermontov's stance close to Griboedov and to an extent to Pushkin. 'Russia is thought of as a third, middle, entity, situated between the "old" Europe and the "old" East. It is precisely the in between nature of its cultural (not just geographical) position which allows Russia to be the bearer of cultural synthesis that facilitates the merger of the ("European") Pechorin's and Onegin's craving for happiness, and the Oriental striving for "tranquility"'.[117] In contrast to Tiutchev's dislike of endless steppes which exterminate his personal being, for Lermontov's poetic personality of the latest period, as Lotman observes, the vastness of Russia's spaces only helps to acquire full existence without losing one's individuality.[118]

Contemplating such cultural typology does not, of course, prevent one from formulating a typological existential difference between Russians and Western Europeans. Thus Turgenev, with all his mild, cautious approach and recoil from undue generalizations, was not afraid, when asked directly (by Flaubert and his friends), to express the following instructive formula: 'vous êtes des homes de la loi, de l'honneur; nous . . . nous sommes des homes de l'humanité!'.[119]

The same idea, in a sense, was coded in Pushkin's 'Captain's Daughter', where the writer, poses the question, fundamental for Russian cultural history, of what is superior – mercy or justice – and opts for mercy! 'Opposition between mercy and justice, impossible either for the XVIII century educators, or for the Decembrists, is deeply significant for Pushkin', in whose late works the theme of mercy becomes fundamental.[120] Lotman inscribes Pushkin's preoccupation with this theme, reflected in particular in his famous 'Pamiatnik', where the poet lists his call for mercy among his utmost spiritual achievements, into a broader utopian dream of a better social order.[121] However, this dream is manifested indirectly, by spurning the historical-social reality and celebrating instead those outstanding moments of human existence when the legal norms are violated for the sake of the individual striving for mercy to the fallen. This, as Lotman argues, is the most interesting stage in the history of Russian social utopianism.[122] 'For Pushkin in "The Captain's Daughter" the right way consists not in moving from one camp of modernity to another, but in ascending above the

---

[116] See Simon Karlinsky (ed.), *Anton Chekhov. Life and Thought; Selected Letters and Commentary*, Evanston: Northwestern University Press, 1997, p. 145: Chekhov's letter to A. S. Suvorin of 15.05.1889.

[117] Lotman, 'Problema Vostoka i Zapada v tvorchestve pozdnego Lermontova', op. cit., p. 23.

[118] Ibid.

[119] Edmond and Jules de Goncourt, *Journal*, under 5 March 1876. Cited in Seeley, *Turgenev. A Reading of His Fiction*, op. cit., p. 30.

[120] Yu. Lotman, 'Ideinaia struktura "Kapitanskoi dochki"', in *Izbrannye statii*, op. cit., vol. 2, pp. 425–6.

[121] Ibid., p. 426.

[122] See ibid.

"cruel age", while preserving humaneness, human dignity and respect for the living life of other people'.[123]

Continuity of this line, vital for the Russian always problematic socio-political reality, can be traced far beyond Pushkin's era. Thus, a century and a half later, Sergei Dovlatov wrote in his literary notebooks 'Solo na "Undervude"', 'What can be more important than justice? – More important than justice? At least – mercy to the fallen'.[124]

Olga Sedakova comments on the connection between this phenomenon and Russian traditional attitude to evil, whereby 'evil is seen not as the last reality, but as something that [. . .] can be extinguished by [. . .] pardon – as in Pushkin's "Pir Petra Pervogo", whose protagonist "pardoning the guilty, rejoices, shares a frothy cup with him, kisses him on the forehead, with a lit up face and heart, and celebrates this pardon as a victory over an enemy"'.[125] However, this generous, noble and truly Christian ability 'has its shadow, its dark double [. . .] – a stubborn insistence on not attributing anything ultimately to evil'.[126] Sedakova calls this archetypical Russian feature a 'friendship with evil' or 'unsqueamishness', and distinguishes two kinds of this moral relativism: an apologetics of evil, a pseudophilosophical, demagogical justification of it, and – more seriously and terrifyingly – a deification and admiration of evil, almost worship. At the roots of such devious attitudes Sedakova sees effectively a cowardly attempt to escape from responsibility, delegating it in the latter case to an external force. Especially difficult (and vitally important) is an effort of love, a fulfilment of a simple premise expressed directly in Nikolai Zabolotsky's famous lines: 'dusha obiazana truditsa . . .' (Душа обязана трудиться. . .').[127] Russian 'moral disorientation is linked to the fact that nothing is truly loved, for loving is too hard',[128] Sedakova writes. At the same time, 'while evil always needs good as a false cover, good never needs evil's cooperation'[129] – this formula of Archimandrite Sophrony (Sakharov) is met with suspicion by the mundane thinking which refuses to believe in the independent strength and power of the good.

Taking issue with such attitudes, Sedakova opposes to immoral proverbs of the type 'you cannot sell anything without cheating' (не обманешь – не продашь), the idea of honest trade as being, in particular, more profitable – and this inspiringly resonates with Likhachev's words above on a particular merchant success of the Old Believers with their adherence to strictest morality in their business conduct. A strict delineation of good and evil is what Sedakova calls upon as a way forward for Russia – the country

[123] Ibid., p. 429.
[124] Sergei Dovlatov, 'Zapisnye knizhki', in *Sobranie prozy v 3 tomakh*, St Petersburg: Limbus Press, 1993, vol. 3, p. 303.
[125] Olga Sedakova, 'Net khuda bez dobra', *Znamia* 2009, No. 7, <http://magazines.russ.ru/znamia/2009/7/se17.html> [accessed 17 March 2013]. Pushkin's original: 'Виноватому вину // Отпуская, веселится; // Кружку пенит с ним одну; // И в чело его целует, // Светел сердцем и лицом; // И прощенье торжествует, // Как победу над врагом'.
[126] Ibid.
[127] Nikolai Zabolotsky, 'Ne pozvoliai dushe lenit'sa' (1958), <http://www.ruthenia.ru/60s/zaboloz/dusha.htm> [accessed 15 February 2014].
[128] Sedakova, 'Net khuda bez dobra', op. cit.
[129] Archimandrite Sophrony (Sakharov), *Arkhim. Starets Siluan*, Moscow: Sretenskii Monastyr, 2000, p. 121. Cited in Sedakova, 'Net khuda bez dobra', op. cit.

where, as Konstantin Leont'ev put it over a century ago, 'it is easier to meet a saint than a decent person',[130] and where 'a most sublime ideal' co-exists in one's soul 'with the greatest meanness, and all absolutely sincerely'.[131] Dostoevsky's hero then asks a very reasonable question: 'is this a particular breadth of a Russian person, which will take him far, or simply meanness – this is the question'.[132]

Grigorii Pomerants, while commenting on the treacherous nature of Russian rulers, including those who betrayed Russian interests by playing their dirty games with the Golden Hord (and because of whom Dostoevsky's hero says terrifying words of the 200 years under the Tatars being deserved and basically desired),[133] makes a suggestion concerning the origins of the Russian ambiguous tolerance of evil. 'Hardship, caused by the Tatars' rule, made Russian love and worship their Russian strength. Thus force per se became the greatest good even if it created evil. And gradually this could give rise to the cult of evil'.[134] Dostoevsky, like no other writer, depicted this extraordinary spaciousness of Russian soul that accommodates simultaneously both extremes – an exaltation of mercy which can overpower justice, and 'friendship with evil'.

The opposition of mercy and justice, or judicial system as such, gains particular importance in the Russian context especially because of the weak tradition of legal rights in the Russian state. In the West 'the law is cruel, but it's the law. Similarly the morality of the New Time is "narrow" and merciless towards the fallen. By contrast, in Russia law is overflexible. In its gaps and holes there is always enough room for the royal pardon and people's mercy, but equally – for the Russian revolt, senseless and merciless'.[135] And Russian self-will which 'does not recognise any law' spans 'from the enlightened ascents to barbaric cruelty'.[136]

Much has been said about the concepts of individual and collective unevenly developed in the West and in Russia respectively. Already in the fifteenth century, Nicholas of Cusa in the hospital established under his patronage, gave the philosophical principle of privacy a tangible practical framing by building separate wards for patients. In the old Russian village whole families lived together in one large room of a country house, discharging their natural physical needs, including sex, in the presence of others. The collective spirit of ancient Russia and disrespect for the individual resulting from the long running authoritarian tradition contributed to the imbalance of personal and collective, leaving Russian subjects in the situation of high personal vulnerability.

---

[130] Although these words are ascribed to Leontiev (see, for instance, Nikolai Berdiaev, *Sud'ba Rossii* (part I, Chapter 'O sviatosti i chestnosti', 1918), Moscow-Kharkov, 1998, p. 335; or Grigorii Pomerants, 'O podlosti, o doblesti, o slave', op. cit.), Vladimir Solov'ev attributes this idea to 'some Slavophiles'. See V. S. Solov'ev, *Sochineniia v 2 tomakh*, Moscow: Mysl, 1988, vol. 1, p. 491 and vol. 2, p. 597. I am grateful to Aleksandr Medvedev for bringing this to my attention.

[131] Fedor Dostoevsky, 'Podrostok', <http://az.lib.ru/d/dostoewskij_f_m/text_0090.shtml> [accessed 15 February 2014].

[132] Ibid.

[133] Ibid. The precise quotation reads: 'We have lived through the Tatars' invasion, then two hundred years of slavery, and this is surely because all of this turned out to be to our taste'. Cited in Pomerants, 'O podlosti, o doblesti, o slave', op. cit.

[134] Pomerants, 'O podlosti, o doblesti, o slave', op. cit.

[135] Ibid.

[136] Ibid.

Not surprisingly then, left to his own devices, the individual seeks strategies of survival which circumvent the weak (nominal only) law. Thus, a considerable lack of lawful space, by introducing a random and unpredictable element in life, lays bare its irrationalist aspect, comprised of the irrationalism of all the agents. In other words, in the Russian case it is not the system, but personalities that prevail, exposed to a ready-made existential laboratory which throws into relief the irrationalism of the human nature per se. Hence M. I. Pyliaev's instructive words, already given in the Introduction: 'Being personally weird is a consequence of randomness of life, and the more such randomness reigns in a society which is still non-homogeneous, the more weird personalities it produces'.[137] In the same vein, law is perceived 'as an annoying convention invented by a hostile force', whose name is 'state', 'in its own interests'.[138]

Curiously, a (rather irrational) paradox of the situation is concealed in the subtle and complex balance between one's own conscience being a barometer of morality and the instructions of the law, or, if you like, precisely between mercy and justice. Indeed, as previously mentioned, by contrast to Russia, in the Western law-abiding societies there is an opposite, but equally alarming tendency – of the legal strictures encroaching upon human ability to exercise one's own judgement based on one's own conscience and understanding of good and evil. As Fazil Iskander asks through the mouth of his hero, 'Is it not the case that an infinite development of legislation leads to a gradual atrophy of conscience? [. . .] If law becomes the dominant pathos of life, then conscience fades away. However, no matter how advanced laws can become, there have always been and will be occasions in life when one must behave in accordance with one's conscience. But how can one behave in accordance with one's conscience if it has faded away? And it has faded away precisely because laws have developed well, and people have got used to restricting themselves only by law?'.[139] A similar stance was expressed by Ivan Il'in: 'Law is an *external* order of life. However, if this external order is detached from the *inner* states of human spirit, if it is not created and accepted by them or does not grow from their maturity and their autonomy, then it degenerates, withers, abases a human being, and, when disintegrating, it destroys spiritual life'.[140] These sentiments return us to the polemics with Zhivov's conclusions above, where, similarly, strict Western practices of repentance instead of serving as a guarantee of high morality may, in fact, as we argued, be conducive of reduced moral sense of an individual. In other words, highly developed external framework can make inner development redundant. In the West itself, concerns had been raised regarding its excessively rigid moral system. Thus 'one can recall the great Albert Schweitzer who criticised Western moralism for its

---

[137] M. I. Pyliaev, *Zamechatelnye chudaki i originaly*, Moscow: Interbuk, 1990, p. 3.

[138] The quotation is a contemplation of Boris Akunin's character from 'Ves mir teatr' (Moscow: 'Zakharov', 2009, <http://www.e-reading.co.uk/book.php?book=133385> [accessed 24 August 2013]), and is given in full in the Introduction.

[139] Fazil Iskander, 'Dumaiushchii o Rossii i amerikanets', in *Rasskazy, povest, skazka, dialog, esse, stikhi*, Ekaterinburg: 'U-Faktoriia', 1999, p. 557.

[140] Ivan Il'in, 'O sushchnosti pravosoznaniia', in Ivan Il'in, *Sobranie sochinenii v 10 tomakh*, vol. 4, Moscow: Russkaia kniga, 1993–99, p. 413.

overly judicial character', its oversimplified and unbending dictum which 'hinders the genuine manifestation of humaneness'.[141]

The curious relationship between mercy and justice in the Russian context can be traced back to the archbishop Ilarion of the eleventh century – the first non-Greek Metropolitan of Kiev. In the words of M. S. Airapetian, it is Ilarion's thesis of the correlation between law and morality, which gave rise to a distorted perception of the place of law in human life: 'For the Russian judicial and political tradition the thesis of Metropolitan Ilarion of the middle of the XI century became crucial. This thesis states that law is only a shadow of the truth rather than truth itself, since it was established by state power rather than divine power, and hence it only has judicial, not moral content. Such an approach to the relationship between law and morality became, essentially, the basis for all the subsequent judicial nihilism, radicalism and anarchism in Russia: from the time of Ilarion it has been characteristic for Russian history to acknowledge a limitation of the regulatory possibilities of law in comparison with morality'.[142]

The 'legally unfair' Russian context not only amplifies the problem of mercy versus justice, but also creates a (more obvious) consequence – that of the mimicry and pretence becoming a way of life. It is this protective valve, and simultaneously a dubious feature, of Russian mentality as a facet of the insincere game forever played between the state and its subjects, that must be a significant contributing factor to the aforementioned vision, on the part of Western travellers, of Russia being the empire of lies and evil. And the concepts of delusion and illusion, often being two very different sides of the same coin, are both relevant here.

Indeed, to the above delusion-based model of *pseudologia fantastica* suggested by Neuhäuser in the Russian case, one can juxtapose a different – illusion-based – model, according to which the national mentality is shaped by the national ideal being the unattainable goal imprinted in and sustained by Russian cultural consciousness.

Thus Dmitrii Likhachev comments on a profound connection between the national ideal and the national character: 'The ideal does not always coincide with reality. But the national ideal is nonetheless very important' in that 'the people who are creating this ideal, in the end give birth to their heroes, their geniuses, who are approaching that ideal, and the latter give the tone to national culture as a whole'.[143] Fazil Iskander in his vision of the role of a national genius in a sense complements Likhachev's ideas:

A genius portrays as the fundamental property of his nation such features which are most needed, but least inherent in it. [. . .] It is as if a national genius tells his nation: 'Get up! It is possible. I have shown that it is possible!'.[144]

Therefore instead of an ideal being (mis)taken for reality (Neuhäuser), we have an ideal serving as a driving force for that very reality (Likhachev/Iskander).

[141] Sedakova, 'Net khuda bez dobra', op. cit.

[142] M. S. Airapetian, 'Ekonomicheskaia i politicheskaia modernizatsii i ikh politiço-ideologicheskoe obespechenie (sravnitelno-istoricheskii analiz)', in *Sbornik nauchnykh trudov: Teoriia i praktika institutsionalnykh preobrazovanii v Rossii*, vol. 25, Moscow: TsEMI RAN, 2012.

[143] D. S. Likhachev, *Izbrannoe. Mysli o zhizni, istorii, kulture*, Moscow: PIK, 2006, p. 270.

[144] Fazil Iskander, *Lastochkino gnezdo. Proza. Poeziia. Publitsistika*, Moscow: Fortuna Limited, 1999, p. 347.

Here Pushkin's famous lines, taken as an epigraph to this entire book, are of high relevance, for not only do they help to delineate between delusion and illusion, but, furthermore, they quite possibly capture the very essence of Russian irrationalism, or, at any rate, poeticize its best facet: '*The lofty illusion which elevates us is dearer to me than the darkness of low truths*'.[145]

Aleksei Mashevsky contemplates the multifaceted meaning of this phrase which by now has become an idiom in Russian. He argues that what the poet expresses here is 'not that man will always prefer sweet delusion to bitter truth, but that a spiritual truth does not exist by itself – it is born only through my uplifting effort inside a deception of a certain kind. It is a deception from the point of view of a stranger, of an observer, who, in order to acquire faith in heroism and love, demands first a proof of their existence from others and only then turns towards his own self. No, this is not the way forward, it will lead nowhere. The only reliable method to prove the existence of good in this world is to start immediately creating it yourself'.[146] In other words, the subjective, metaphysical world is part of the objective, physical one in that our spiritual and moral values are sustained only through the actions of our own will – that is, through our personal, real efforts. Unless we inscribe sublime concepts into our personal world, into our own reality, that is unless we ourselves invest them with concrete and tangible meaning through our own spiritual efforts, rendering them an 'elevating illusion', they will remain a destructive delusion which cuts us off from real life.

It is clear, therefore, that this elevating illusion, which grows from the very depth of Russian culture and likely lies at the heart of the phenomenon of Russian irrationalism, dangerously borders on 'Neuhäuser's' self-delusion, with the boundaries remaining forever porous and blurred. In particular it permeates, as was argued, the problem of Russia vis-à-vis Western Europe.

In fact, we have a somewhat ironic situation of certain symmetry of distorted perceptions. On the one hand, Western Europe perceives Russia as dystopia – as a deceptive, illusory country, country-phantom, sunk in its illusion of itself, in utopia, which is obviously never sustainable. And self-mythology is also likely to play a role in this mutual process of constructing a mythology of the Other. Thus Tutchev's sentiments wholeheartedly embraced by the Russians – of the country's irrational nature – as well as his other lines that here 'chelovek lish snitsa sam sebe' (человек лишь снится сам себе) (man sees himself as if in a dream) only reinforce the above vision. On the other hand, Russian view of the West is often a utopia – as (again) an illusory place, a dream-land or promised-land – which is another obviously unsustainable image. More importantly, as we saw, an illusion can be constructive, when it is the type of Pushkin's

---

[145] In Russian: 'Тьмы низких истин мне дороже нас возвышающий обман . . .'.
[146] Aleksei Mashevsky, 'Nas vozvyshaiushchii obman', *Zvezda*, 1999, No. 6, <http://magazines.russ.ru/zvezda/1999/6/mashev.html> [accessed 17 July 2013]. For a more detailed discussion on this issue, see Olga Tabachnikova, 'Patterns of European Irrationalism, from Source to Estuary: Johann Georg Hamann, Lev Shestov and Anton Chekhov – on Both Sides of Reason', in Olga Tabachnikova (ed.), *Mystery Inside Enigma: Facets of Russian Irrationalism between Art and Life*, op. cit.

elevating illusion which is invested with our personal spiritual effort, or it can turn into a destructive delusion, when it is an excuse for spiritual apathy and inactivity, and as such only separates us from actual reality.

These conclusions of the vital role of illusion in Russian culture point us to the need for a closer look at the fermenting force behind this illusion – Russian dreamers of all sorts and creeds that can be traced throughout Russian literary history. While a comprehensive analysis of this topic remains the task for future studies, a brief discussion of Russian literary dreamers is offered in the next chapter.

3

On Russian Dreamers

We are deeply disjoint from existence. We fantasise, we do not want to know reality, we constantly irritate ourselves with dreams . . . Our misfortune is in the divergence between life theoretical and life practical.

Aleksandr Herzen

The conflict between dream and reality has not waned for thousands of years. Instead of the desired harmony, it is chaos and disorder that reign on Earth. Moreover, something similar we have discovered in our own soul . . .

Sergei Dovlatov

*. . . But the hero is not afraid of perishing,
While his dream is raging!*

Aleksandr Blok

It would hardly be an exaggeration to say that the images of dreamers (мечтатели *mechtateli*) are all-pervasive in Russian literary history. A typically Russian propensity for the extremes, striving to the Absolute on the one hand and a tradition of oppressions of all kinds on the other provide a background conducive of dreaming, fantasy, utopian speculations and a desire to escape to alternative reality. At the same time, a traditional preoccupation with the ultimate questions of existence, a habit of philosophizing for its own sake rather than for any pragmatic reason, a tendency of Russian culture for continuous self-reflection (whereby 'looking at its own self' is 'more primary and more essential than contemplating the outside world')[1] also contribute to this cultural phenomenon.

A concept of dream is clearly of multifaceted nature. As well as an elevating illusion which induces a constructive, creative impulse, serves as a guiding star, as an ennobling ideal and sustains human hope, a dream can equally be destructive, carrying a dreamer into the 'bad infinity' of fruitless and exhausting self-reflection, which, if united with

---

[1] Yurii Lotman, 'Tezisy k semiotike russkoi kultury', op. cit., p. 407.

a rationalistic idea, brewed on resentment, can become flammable and devastating. A dream can evolve, can change its nature, can crush or, on the contrary, redeem the dreamer. It can serve as a catalyst for self-fulfilment or as a Pythia, a siren, and destroy the traveller to a dreamland.

To write a comprehensive history of Russian literary dreamers is a task as fascinating as it is enormous, and would require a separate book. Therefore here we shall limit our quest to marking some avenues for such a study and giving a very brief sketch only, with no claims for being exhaustive. Our main interest will remain in exploring the interplay between the rational and irrational, as well as in following the anthropocentric tradition of Russian literature with its focus on the moral problematic.

A collective dream as a complex of national aspirations found expression first of all in folklore. In Chapter 7 dedicated to Russian humour this aspect of a dream will be touched upon, and various interpretations of Russian folk-tales and their heroes, especially such as Emelia, Ivan-The-Fool and the mighty-man Ilya-Muromets, will be discussed. Part of the debate centres around possible interpretations of these tales in terms of national characteristics that they reflect.

Chronologically closer to our scope of study is a dreaming character who is especially traditional for romanticism, and occurs in Russian literature of the 1830s and 1840s, in the works by N. I. Bilevich, S. K. Aksakov, V. F. Odoevsky and N. A. Polevoi. However, more generally, such a hero can be found in sentimental, romantic and realistic traditions alike. Karamzin's 'Bednaia Liza', Pushkin's 'The Queen of Spades' and Gogol's 'Overcoat' can all be considered in this key and supply distinctive examples of dreamers. Another vital source of examples is provided by Lermontov's heroes and, most notably, by Dostoevsky's oeuvre. A dream is also distinctly present in Chekhov's writings as a separate theme, and many of Turgenev's heroes as well as the writer himself were clearly preoccupied by this concept. More generally – and equally applicable to the twentieth-century literature – it is the characteristic Russian themes of the 'superfluous person' and the 'small person' and their later modifications which seem to be intrinsically interwoven with dreaming.

A typology of dreamers is best exemplified by the works of Dostoevsky, who started out as a dreamer himself. Thus in his recollections of the turning point of his life, after Belinsky famously praised his first novel 'Bednye liudi', Dostoevsky mentions his 'passionate dreams' and characterizes himself as being at the time a 'terrible dreamer'.[2] His privileged understanding of the inner world of a dreamer permeates virtually all his writings, giving us a diverse gallery of types from elegiac and humble to feverish and passionate, from hyper-sensitive and selfless to ideologists of crime.

Dostoevsky's reconstruction of his youthful perception of the world and of his own place in it is portrayed in his 'Petersburg Dreams in Verse and Prose' ('Peterburgskie snovideniia v stikhakh i proze') written already after his time in the penal colony. It

---

[2] F. M. Dostoevsky, *Polnoe sobranie sochinenii v 30 tomakh*, Leningrad: Nauka, 1972–90, vol. 25, p. 31.

reflects a markedly artistic view of existence, an inner striving to 'live in poetry' (an expression of Hoffmann borrowed by Yurii Mann to describe Gogol's heroes):[3]

> I was still young then. Approaching the Neva, I stopped for a minute and cast a penetrating glance along the river [. . .]. Night was descending on the city [. . .]. A twenty degree frost was setting in. Frozen steam poured off the tired horses, from the people running to and fro. The compressed air trembled from the slightest sound and from all the roofs of both embankments columns of smoke rose like giants and were carried upwards across the cold sky, interweaving and unweaving as they went, so that it seemed that new buildings were rising above the old ones, that a new city was forming in the air . . . It seemed, finally, that this whole world, with all its inhabitants [. . .] at this twilight hour, resembled a fantastic magical reverie, a dream which in turn would immediately disappear and dissolve in steam up in the dark blue sky. A strange thought suddenly stirred within me. I trembled and my heart was, as it were, suffused at this moment with a hot rush of blood, which suddenly boiled with the surge of a sensation which was powerful but up until then unfamiliar to me. It was as if I realised something in that minute which had up until then only stirred within me but was still not fully comprehended; as if I had had a vision of something new, of a completely new world, which was unfamiliar to me and known only through some dark rumours, some mysterious signs. I suppose it was from that minute that my existence began. . . .[4]

This vision reflects a sensibility already familiar to Dostoevsky's readers from his early works, as if generalizing his 'early dreamers', who later underwent various substantial transformations. In scholarly literature on Dostoevsky, Sergei Kosiakov singles out in particular a cultural-psychological strand, where a dreamer is not only a hero fed on sentimental and romantic traditions, but a figure representing a national archetype, as noted by K. K. Istomin, V. N. Toporov and E. M. Meletinsky.[5] In this perspective the hero of Dostoevsky's 'Khoziaika' rescues not just Katerina, but Russia itself: 'A hero-dreamer is fighting for the "tsar-maiden" (царь-девица *tsar'-devitsa*) who symbolizes national Russian soul – sinful, psychologically unstable, but striving for the good. He is, however, unable to tear her out of the clutches of a perverse fanatic Old Believer, demonic carrier of evil'.[6] Earlier, Viacheslav Ivanov, talking about 'Khoziaika', 'Idiot' and 'Besy', saw this on an even larger – universal – scale: 'A Divine messenger, whatever he might be called, must liberate the Soul of the World'.[7]

Maximalist tendencies, inner intensity and striving to an ideal are all inherent to varying degree in such dreamers. However, more significantly, this points us to an

---

[3] Yu. Mann, 'Gogol', in Yu. B. Vipper et al. (eds), *Istoriia vsemirnoi literatyry v 9 tomakh*, vol. 6, Moscow: Nauka, 1989.

[4] 'Translation of F. M. Dostoevsky's "Petersburg Dreams in Verse and Prose"' by David Foreman, *New Zealand Slavonic Journal*, 2003 (281–99), pp. 282–3.

[5] Sergei Kosiakov, 'Mechtatel i ego transformatsiia v tvorchestve F. M. Dostoevskogo', PhD Thesis, Voronezh: Voronezhskii Gosudarstvennyi Pedagogicheskii Universitet, 2009.

[6] E. M. Meletinsky, *O literaturnykh arkhetipakh*, Moscow: RGGU, 1994, p. 88.

[7] Viacheslav I. Ivanov, 'Dostoevsky. Tragediia – mif – mistika', in *Esse, statii, perevody*, Bruxelles: Foyer Oriental Chrétien, 1985, p. 63.

important, differentiating, aspect concealed in the nature of a dream itself, determined by the character of the dreamer. Crudely speaking, one can talk of two major types of dreamers: those who are at the outset selfless or those who are egotistic. More precisely, the former type encompasses those whose dreams do not envisage an abuse of others as a means for fulfilment, while the latter type consists of those who contemplate striving for their goal at the others' expense.

Also of high significance is a subsequent transformation of a dream and its agent – what started out as a pure and noble ideal often mutates later on, not being able to withstand the harsh reality – a typical literary collision, especially characteristic for romanticism. Thus an artist Piskarev from Gogol's 'Nevsky prospekt' is crushed by the cruelty of life, but even more importantly, 'his lofty dreams turn out to be unsustainable, [. . .] his exalted aspirations to rescue a prostitute from her low life acquire a half-ironic tone – in word, the "life in poetry" fails',[8] although he started out as a selfless type.[9] Equally, Chekhov shows us numerous examples of degeneration of a youthful dream – most notably in 'Ionych', when the hero failed to live up to it and betrayed himself and the high demands of his aspirations.

It would seem that the factor which often facilitates the original striving to 'live in poetry' is a literary influence, literary roots of a dreamer – the role played by reading in the dreamer's life: a young, easily flammable imagination set on fire by romantic books. A distinct example of such influence is Pushkin's Tatiana Larina, to whom we shall yet return here, or famous 'Turgenevan young females' (*turgenevskie devushki* тургеневские девушки). Afterall, the process of creating literature is itself reminiscent of a higher dream of sorts, of an attempt to correct one's personal or world's general reality by creating its imaginary alternative or altogether an attempt to approximate a divine act of creation. Thus Tsvetaeva's words from her letter to Anna Teskova are in a sense a confession of a dream-creation taking precedence over reality: 'I do not love life per se; it begins to be meaningful for me – that is, to gain sense and weight – only when it is transformed into art. If I were taken beyond the ocean – to Paradise – but forbidden to write, I would decline those ocean and paradise. I don't need things as such'.[10]

However, against the above logical expectation of reading (or writing) laying at the basis of a dream, the heroes whose dreams are innocent and elegiac, and imply no harm to others include, in fact, not only educated and sophisticated personalities wishing to bring certain harmony (or happiness) to the world and to themselves but also simple folk, dreaming of fulfilling their small private needs. Thus the famous Bashmachkin from Gogol's 'Overcoat', 'the last one here', also exemplifies the collision

---

[8]   Yu. Mann, 'Gogol', op. cit.

[9]   A different, although related collision is present in the stories of great disillusionment when man's pure and profound feeling for a woman is crushed by her cynical and debasing attitude, her expectation of money in exchange for sex. Such is the story 'Mechtatel' (Aggei) by Aleksei Tolstoy written in a tragic key, and similarly, although more light-heartedly and closer to a farce, is Vladimir Vysotsky's song 'Ia odnazhdy gulial po stolitse . . .'.

[10]   Marina Tsvetaeva, from the letter of 30.12.1925 to Anna Teskova. Cited in Ellendea Proffer, *Tsvetaeva. A Pictorial Biography*, Ann Arbor: Ardis, 1980, p. 31.

of a dream with cruel reality, but his psychological features, despite his low origin, are 'as if borrowed from the emotional palette of the "true musician", "naïve poetic soul", i.e. the man who is not of this world, and who was perceived as a special Hoffmannian type'.[11] Bashmachkin too displays distinct dreamer's qualities, being possessed by his idee-fixe, his single dream of a new overcoat.

'But what an unexpected "idea" it was, daring in the literary sense!', writes Yurii Mann, reflecting on the innovative, even revolutionary devices of Gogol in terms of style and content, his transcending the boundaries of romanticism. 'Similarly to the way in which the lofty theme of madness in "Notes of a madman" was given not to an artist or musician, but to a minor clerk, and was saturated with everyday material and social content, in "Overcoat" too a place of a transcendental striving towards a lofty artistic goal is occupied by the "eternal idea of the future overcoat" with a thick cotton underlining. The transcendental striving is reduced to an elementary need, but the need which is vital, rather than excessive; which is essential and integral in the poor, shelterless life of Akakii Akakievich. Moreover, it ends in the same inevitable failure in which the dreams of an artist or musician ended too'.[12] Notice a drastic difference between this dream of Bashmachkin and the dream of Nikolai Ivanovich, the protagonist of Chekhov's story 'Kryzhovnik', who strove all his life to have an estate of his own with gooseberry bushes on it. While seemingly the desires of both are materialistic, concrete and practical (even though, importantly, for one it is a matter of survival, while for the other it is not), for the 'naïve poetic soul' Bashmachkin his dream acquires the dimensions of the spiritual and lifts him above the everyday, while for Chekhov's character, on the contrary, the wingless and narrow underpinning of his dream lays bare Nikolai's inner poverty, the low origins of his aspirations. Similarly, Gogol's Manilov, a grotesque character, is exposed as dreaming a continuous empty, non-redeeming dream, living in a phantom world of soppy pretence and idleness.

Before returning to the poetic and pure dreamers, it is worth lingering over Chekhov's 'Kryzhovnik' for another reason. An important implication of this story is that it points to a perhaps most cruel scenario of a possible dream destruction – through the dream actually becoming fulfilled. Thus Georgii Gachev, in an interesting, although controversial way, believes that Russian cultural tendency for tormented love is connected to an intuitive, subconscious belief that perfect love is only sustainable while the lovers cannot be together, cannot realize their love. A fulfilment of it, a 'happy' outcome is a guarantee for ruining it. 'What would happen, if Tatiana gave herself to Onegin, in love?', asks Gachev referring to Pushkin's 'Eugene Onegin', and answers unambiguously, 'Well – they would both simply ruin their love by its realization. [. . .] But now this love exists as an eternal wound in Tatiana's heart and in Onegin's soul, and in this mutual pain and divine misfortune they invariably belong to each other and are forever united in Russian cultural imagination. Indeed, all Russian literature is permeated with the lofty poetry of unfulfilled love. However, when love is fulfilled, as in Chernyshevsky's novel "What is to be done?", it is not

[11] Yu. Mann, 'Gogol', op. cit.
[12] Ibid.

beautiful. Similarly, Natasha Rostova – once she is the wife of Pierre and mother of the children – loses poetry too'.[13]

Let us now return to, and look more closely, at the first type of dreamers – those whose dreams are pure and at the core sublime. Whether cultivated on reading or born straight from a simple, but still poetic soul, an idyllic, elegiac dream reflects purity, and often altruism, of the dreamer's inner world. As mentioned previously, a real test begins when the dream collides with life, ideal with reality. Turgenev in his essay 'Hamlet and Don Quixote' opposes thinking and will as two mutually exclusive faculties. Essentially he views Russian 'superfluous people' as dreamers, as Hamlets of sorts – trapped in their thoughts and unable to act. Oscar Wilde perceives Hamlet in a similar light: 'He is a dreamer, and he is called upon to act. He has the nature of the poet, and he is asked to grapple with the common complexity of cause and effect, with life in its practical realisation, of which he knows nothing, not with life in its ideal essence, of which he knows so much'.[14] Interestingly, Iskander notes that while Hamlet preserves his nucleus, for as long as he remains 'Mozart of thought, of analysis',[15] he cannot perpetrate an act of violence – to revenge. As soon as he understands the reality around him, he succumbs to the cruel laws of his time.[16] This leads us to the questions posed above – concerning the evolution of a dream, of the outcome of a clash between the dreamer's imagination and real world.

Most interesting and diverse ways of dreams failing to come true are given by Chekhov's stories and plays which often supply examples of pure irrationality (as explored in Chapter 6). We have already mentioned 'Ionych' where the hero surrenders to the petty life, his personality degenerates, while his dream fades and disappears. The theme of self-betrayal, of an almost invariably losing battle between an individual and his medium (as in the story 'V rodnom uglu' or in Chekhov's first play 'Platonov' ('Bezottsovshchina'), to name just a few), of one's inability to live up to one's ideal is all-pervasive in Chekhov. But even more interestingly, Chekhov's heroes more often than not seem disconnected from their dreams, as if they are afraid of what they think they desire; as if the process of dreaming per se is an end in itself, or a trap, or both. Thus the three sisters with their exclamations 'To Moscow!' do not move a finger to bring the aim closer, do not step an inch towards the fulfilment of their dream. A similar discrepancy, or a lack of proper self-awareness, is brought to its logical end in Andrei Tarkovsky's screening ('Stalker') of the Brothers Strugatsky's novel 'Piknik na obochine', where there is a magic room fulfilling one's wishes. The catch is that it fulfils a real wish, rather than what has been declared as such while in the room. Someone who asked for his daughter's illness to be cured, had become rich instead. The outcome is that since then everyone declined entering the room, in the fear of their true dreams – rather than those pronounced inside the room – being revealed afterwards, above all to them (by coming true). The problem thus goes even deeper than inability to stay faithful to your dream – it lies in not being able (and often being afraid and unwilling) to identify

---

[13] Georgii Gachev, *Russkii Eros ('Roman' mysli s zhizniu)*, Moscow: Interprint, 1994, p. 20.
[14] Oscar Wilde, *De Profundis and Other Writings*, Los Angeles: Indo-European Publishing, 2012.
[15] Fazil Iskander, *Lastochkino gnezdo. Proza. Poeziia. Publitsistika*, op. cit., p. 397.
[16] Ibid.

what your true dream really is. In brief, it lies in life being an irrational hide-and-seek game of the individual with oneself.

Another important and relevant in this context feature of Chekhov is to demonstrate how both night and day dreams, inner thoughts, seemingly ephemeral entities, all constitute an important, integral, inseparable part of us and our existence; in other words, their metaphysical reality is as unquestionable and, if you like, as physical, as the reality of our tangible everyday life. As Anatole France phrased it, a dream is 'a highest reality'.[17] The tangible feature of Chekhov's own dream – and we are not talking here either of the peculiar dreamingness of his heroes, or, on the contrary, of his own authorial sobriety – is his striving for freedom. 'Susan Sontag is surely right when she suggests that Chekhov's writing is a dream of freedom – "an absolute freedom" [. . .] "the freedom from violence and lies".[18] And freedom is not merely political or material in his work. It is a neutral saturate, like air or light. How often he describes a village, and then, at the village's edge – "the open fields!"', James Wood observes.[19] He then also notes Chekhov's awareness of freedom having its painful side; which returns us, implicitly, to the nature of our deepest wishes being often concealed from us.

However, more standard than inscrutability of our most sacred dreams and desires (as in the magic room above) is the theme of their, often somewhat ambiguous, failure. That is, normally, what protagonists believe to be their dreams, chokes up on reality and is extinguished, but leaves behind a taste that is in a sense more sweet than bitter, more precious than that of an easy victory; or, more precisely, whose bitterness the heroes cherish as a sweet memory. This is because the intensity of disappointment gives rise to a strange pleasure of at least being capable of strong passions and intense experiences.[20]

This apparently irrational development is inherent in Turgenev's writings with a gallery of superfluous people whose dreams failed miserably leaving a colourfully burning tail of memories behind. But the writer who takes this much further is Dostoevsky, as he explores the impact of the unfulfilled dream, of rejection and resentment, on an individual psyche. As Iskander notes, 'Dostoevsky was the first to notice that the chemical composition of man had changed. That is why his unnatural heroes are so natural in their unnaturalness. His main discovery is a human being. His novels are an ecological warning to humanity: "Beware of the underground man who is emerging!"'.[21] A similar observation, as we have seen above, was made by Lev Shestov

---

[17] Anatole France, *Thais* (1890), <http://www.gutenberg.org/cache/epub/2078/pg2078.txt> [accessed 10 February 2014].

[18] James Wood, *The Broken Estate. Essays on Literature and Belief*, London: Jonathan Cape, 1999, p. 86. Wood here quotes from Chekhov's letter to A. N. Pleshcheev of 4 October 1888, see *PSSP v 30 tomakh*, op. cit., vol. 3, p. 11.

[19] Ibid.

[20] Of course, in the case of a noble dream, even more important is that it is the kernel of our personality, it is our divine spark, that stays behind as an inexterminable residue, after our hopes were crushed and our sacrifices wasted, or rejected. It is the divine impulse itself that proves immortal and more important that the actual fulfilment of our dream. In other words, the very process of dreaming releases our spiritual energy, elevating us to a different reality, and this experience turns out to be in itself of an ultimate value.

[21] Fazil Iskander, *Lastochkino gnezdo. Proza. Poeziia. Publitsistika*, op. cit., p. 403.

almost a century earlier, when he wrote 'there ends for man the thousand-year reign of "reason and conscience"; a new era begins – that of "psychology", which Dostoevsky was the first in Russia to discover'.[22] Iskander neatly captures the state of mind of this mutated dreamer of Dostoevsky, which evolved from the earlier unpoisoned types, 'In the dampness of the underground, man is warmed up by the fever of a sickly dream. Self-irony disappears, and nothing stops the underground man from regarding himself a Napoleon oppressed by his surroundings. The quantity of humiliation turns into the monstrous quality of vanity. Just give him a chance to get out, and he will take incredible revenge for all the humiliation, as no-one before him'.[23] This is the energy of self-assertion of a disintegrating soul, a chain reaction of scandals, a precursor of nuclear energy. It is by this energy that Dostoevsky's novels are sustained'.[24]

Sergei Kosiakov focusing in his study precisely on those writings of Dostoevsky where the hero can be identified as a dreamer of some sort, distinguishes two separate strands of Dostoevsky's dreamers: the first one 'begins with "Belye nochi" (and then leads to the "Notes from Underground" and "Crime and Punishment"); the second starts with "Netochka Nezvanova" (and leads to "Row Youth")'.[25] In Kosiakov's classification, 'The first strand is focused on studying the dreamer from the point of view of his unique and separate case; the second – on presenting him as generated by an "accidental family"'.[26] Kosiakov singles out the Underground Man as being the first hero among Dostoevsky's dreamers who perverted his dream rendering it ugly, while Raskolnikov underpinned it by a rational foundation (as no other dreamer before him).[27] In the same vein, Kosiakov concludes that a dream which in elegiac culture pertains to memories of the past, in Dostoevsky's novels joins hands with the idea born of the rationalist culture.[28]

However, primary here is not the idea as such, but precisely the so-called Napoleonic complex – a feverish striving for superiority sparked off by humiliated spirit, brewed on inner deficiency and resulting envy. Afterall, Hamlet is also trapped by being 'predominantly perceiving hero; a hero whose entire life was concentrated in the pure function of perceiving himself and the world'[29] – the description which Bakhtin applies to Dostoevsky's Paradoxicalist. For Bakhtin, Dostoevsky seeks to 'unite the artistic dominant of the portrayal with the social-characterological dominant of the

[22] Shestov, 'Dostoevsky i Nitzshe (filosofiia tragedii)', op. cit., p. 352. In translation (by Spencer Roberts), <http://www.angelfire.com/nb/shestov/dtn/dn_7.html> [accessed 12 February 2014].

[23] Recall in this connection Joseph Brodsky's poem 'Odnomu tiranu' (1972), whose protagonist-tyrant 'having later dealt with world culture by arresting the café's regulars, [he] thus in some sense avenged not so much them, as Time itself – for poverty, being demeaned, bad coffee, boredom and lost games of black-jack' (In Russian: 'Арестом завсегдатаев кафе покончив позже с мировой культурой, [он] этим как бы отомстил (не им, но Времени) за бедность, униженья, за скверный кофе, скуку и сраженья в двадцать одно, проигранные им').

[24] Fazil Iskander, *Lastochkino gnezdo. Proza. Poeziia. Publitsistika*, op. cit., p. 403.

[25] Sergei Kosiakov, 'Mechtatel i ego transformatsiia v tvorchestve F.M. Dostoevskogo', op. cit.

[26] Ibid.

[27] Ibid.

[28] Ibid.

[29] Mikhail Bakhtin, *Problems of Dostoevsky's Poetics*, transl. by Caryl Emerson, Minneapolis: University of Minnesota Press, 1999, p. 40.

person portrayed',[30] and finds a perfect occasion for this merging in the categories of 'dreaming' and 'underground', in the consciousness of the underground man and of the unfulfilled dreamer, who is generally incapable of being fulfilled. It is the 'bad infinity' of his consciousness that Bakhtin singles out: 'the "underground man" does not merely dissolve in himself all possible concrete traits of his image by making them the subject of his own reflection – he has no such traits at all, he has no fixed definition, there is nothing to say about him; he figures not as a person taken from life, but rather as a subject of consciousness and dream. And for the author he is not a carrier of qualities and characteristics which are neutral in relation to his self-consciousness and capable of finalizing him; no, the vision of the author is directed precisely at his self-consciousness and at the inescapable unfinalizability and vicious circle (*durnaia beskonechnost'* дурная бесконечность) of that self-consciousness.'[31]

Yet, Hamlet, being caught in the same 'bad infinity', does not resemble the Paradoxicalist. He instinctively recoils from humiliation, because in his innate nobility of spirit he knows that humiliation ultimately comes from within rather than without, and resentment and impotent hatred will humiliate him incomparably more than any external enemies can. Moreover, as previously mentioned, in the end, by choosing revenge he in a sense defeats himself, becoming equal to his foes (as Vysotsky put it in his poem 'My Hamlet', 'But through a murder I debased myself – No better than the man I had to slay').[32] The Underground Man, by contrast, instinctively begins where Hamlet ends: giving up all his inner space to his 'offenders'; and chokes on his helpless resentment and spite. The difference is therefore in the scale of personality, in the noble spirit which refuses for as long as possible to be defeated by sinking into self-indulgence, as opposed to the weak spirit which surrenders to evil with a kind of perverted joy. In the process of scores setting, Hamlet begins with himself, the Paradoxicalist – with the outside world, at the others' expense. Raskolnikov moves even further, but on the same path – by trying to defeat humiliation in principle, once and for all, he gets even more humiliated through the sheer need to prove himself superior.

Thus, the devastating energy of the unfulfilled (and often unfulfillable) dream, the unbearable clash of ideal with reality serve as a test of personality, of its spiritual strength. And, as was stated above, it is in the end the egotistic or otherwise nature of dreaming and of coping with its dramatic consequences that determine the individual. Using, if you like, a descending metaphor, it is useful to recall here a moralizing story from children's literature written in 1969 by Nikolai Nosov. It is called 'Dreamers' (literally 'Фантазеры' rather than 'Мечтатели'), and tells of the difference between fantasies intended as innocent entertainment and self-betterment as opposed to those which are basically lies invented for their teller's egotistic needs. Two boys are telling magic stories to each other when the third comes along and mocks them for

---

[30] Mikhail Bakhtin, *Problemy tvorchestva Dostoevskogo*, Moscow: Alkonost, 1994, p. 42.

[31] Mikhail Bakhtin, *Problems of Dostoevsky's Poetics*, transl. by Caryl Emerson, Minneapolis: University of Minnesota Press, 1999, p. 41.

[32] Vladimir Vysotsky, 'My Hamlet' ('Moi Gamlet') (1972), in *Vladimir Vysotsky: Hamlet with a Guitar*, transl. by Sergei Roy, Moscow: Progress Publishers, 1990, p. 95. In Russian: 'и я себя убийством уравнял с тем, с кем я лег в одну и ту же землю'.

purposeless nature of their preoccupation. He tells them how the other day he shifted the blame for a mischief onto his little sister who was punished as a result, while he was let off. The emotional nerve of the story is the disgust the third boy evokes, and the feeling of purity and happiness exuded by the two 'non-pragmatic' boys, whom the other one obviously deems very stupid. Similarly, the perpetual torment and emotional misery of Raskolnikov or Paradoxicalist, or other heroes with Napoleonic complex, such as, for instance, Lermontov's Pechorin and Pushkin's Herman, the crumpled state of their inner world tell us of their ultimate inner defeat.

The rationalist-irrationalist dichotomy here, important for our purposes, is concealed in particular in the fact that Raskolnikov's calculation was based on the presumption of his total rationalism, whereas his ultimate failure was predicated on the irrational basis of his human nature. In other words, he set out for his crime deeming himself a rationalist, but instead discovered the irrationalism of his nature which ultimately overpowered all his rational calculations. One of the implications concealed here is Dostoevsky's fierce opposition to any grand rationalist projects; that is irrationalism as a rebellion against radical rationalism of the Enlightenment variety. A related situation happens to Pushkin's Hermann. His rational endeavour – a product of his calculating and rational mind – is based on the irrational, mystical scheme, but, even more significantly, does not take into account the intrinsic irrationality of human nature. Consequently, in implementing his rational plan – his purely egotistic striving and merciless exploiting of others as a means for fulfilling his dream of becoming rich – he gets carried away in a completely irrational fashion, and fails miserably. This gives us a different example – that of irrationalism born off excessive rationalism.

While Herman's spontaneous, obsessive actions essentially refute his calculative nature and rational plan, another character of Russian literature, a positive hero Andrei Shtolts from Goncharov's 'Oblomov' demonstrates a true rationalism, implementing in a planned, orderly manner his life strategies and intentions, which can hardly therefore be called dreams.[33] Oblomov himself is, on the contrary, a true dreamer,

---

[33] It is worth noting in this connection that Yurii Lotman finds proximity between the archetypical villain and the archetypical saviour of the classical Russian novel, concealed precisely in their active, non-dreaming component. The villain is 'the hero of calculation, reason and practical activity, combined with demonic egotism' (i.e. possessing the aforementioned Napoleonic complex), which is often associated with the West, while the altruistic saviour is also necessarily practical, active, fully aware of the real life around him and well adjusted: 'Bazarov and Shtolts, as well as Chernyshevsky's heroes, are all practical men. [. . .] Unlike Rudin, Insarov is also a practical man, a man of action rather than of dreams and speculations'. Following Pisarev, Lotman calls these characters 'люди «реалистического труда»' ('men of "realistic labour"'), for whom 'propensity for dreaming is [. . .] disgraceful'. Thus 'Shtolts is not a dreamer, as dreaming is a feature of people who are ill in mind or body, unable to organize their life according to their own will'. (See Yurii Lotman, 'Siuzhetnoe prostranstvo russkogo romana XIX stoletiia', op. cit., pp. 100–1, with Pisarev's quotations taken from D. I. Pisarev, Soch. v 4 tomakh, Moscow, 1956, vol. 1, p. 10.) The above argument, in my view, suffers from a too narrow interpretation of a 'dreamer', as well as too formal understanding of the above heroes. Thus, for example, Bazarov, with all his rational practicality, is in fact a passionate and highly irrational, obsessive character, who is driven precisely by a lofty and utopian dream, and tries, somewhat in Raskolnikov's manner, to overcome his own irrationality. Lev Shestov's ironic remark above, claiming that those who cut open frogs, simultaneously waited for a Messiah, seems more appropriate here.

recognized as typically Russian at that. Gentle and sensitive, attentive to others, full of sublime and profound sentiments, he is at the same time confined to his sofa and his dreams, as if proving the point that Russian history during one thousand years brought about 'very much in order to aid understanding the world, but very little that helps us live in it'.[34] A multi-dimensional character, Oblomov can be viewed within different frameworks, historical, religious, ethical, aesthetic and others, each displaying a different perspective which drastically turns the tables, changing his image from outrageous lazyness to commendable non-pragmatism, from a cowardly rejection of life to a praiseworthy (almost courageous, if only not so caricaturesque) spurning of pointless, unspiritual existence, and so on. It is, of course, the mosaic whole, the sum total of these which give a full-blooded image, as interpreted with profound sympathy, in a somewhat Slavophile spirit, by Nikita Mikhalkov's screen adaptation of Oblomov's novel, where exemplary Shtolts looks in comparison as a bleak and lifeless shadow. A closeness of Oblomov's character – central for Russian culture to the same degree as he is irrational – to Ivan-The-Fool, in many ways his folklore predecessor, is discussed in Chapter 7. In particular, Tsvetaeva's lines, as if demonstrating an inverted logic of a Romantic poet, capture an important philosophical dimension of Oblomov's sensibility: 'Maybe, the best victory over gravity and time is to move through without leaving a trace, without leaving a shadow'.[35] This is resonant with the idea of Andrei Siniavsky who draws a parallel between Ivan-The-Fool's philosophy and 'mystical practices of different religious persuasions. The essence of these beliefs is in rejecting the activity of the controlling mind which hinders the appreciation of the superior truth. This truth (or reality) is revealed to the person by itself, at that happy moment when his consciousness seems to be switched off, and his soul is in a special state – that of the susceptible passivity'.[36] Oblomov's reason is not switched off, but his will is, and as a result he does rest in the state of this 'susceptible passivity'.

As we saw earlier, this quality of 'susceptible passivity' is what best characterizes Russianness in the opinion of some: 'The Russian soul is silent, wordless and shapeless. It is an absolute void; silence, hiatus. Similarly, Russia is fruitless. [. . .] But this very emptiness gives rise to immense sensitivity and the ability to illuminate in a remarkable, unequaled way the material that is being absorbed'.[37] Another, in fact a clearer example of this 'susceptible passivity' is Chekhov's 'Little Darling' – a woman who is forever prepared to lose her identity in the one he loves. Oblomov is not lost in others, but he is open to the world, he accepts it as blissfully given and his pure soul suffers from any violation of the Divine image; yet, he turns himself into a harmlessly loving but paralysed part of it, as a detail of a landscape, as a thankful tree.

[34] The words of a character from Zakhar Prilepin's novel 'San'kia' (2006), Chapter 8 at <http://sankya.ru/chapters/8.html> [accessed 13 December 2013].

[35] Marina Tsvetaeva, the poem 'Prokrastsa' (1923), <http://ouc.ru/cvetaeva/prokrastsia.html> [accessed 20 January 2013]. In Russian: 'А может, лучшая победа Над временем и тяготеньем – Пройти, чтоб не оставить следа, Пройти, чтоб не оставить тени'.

[36] Andrei Siniavsky, *Ivan-Durak: Ocherk russkoi narodnoi very*, Moscow: Agraf, 2001, p. 43.

[37] Dmitrii Galkovsky, 'Beskonechnyi tupik', List 3 at <http://fictionbook.ru/author/galkovskiyI_dmitriyI_evgenevich/beskonechniyyI_tupik/read_online.html?page=3> [accessed 20 January 2013]. We have already encountered this idea and the quotation supporting it in Chapter 2.

Returning to Hermann and other 'Napoleonic' heroes, the case with Lermontov's Pechorin is more interesting than that with Herman or Raskolnikov. Being one of the demonic, romantic characters with a clear Napoleonic complex, he is not a dreamer in a conventional sense, for not only does he act (in fact, he is continuously enwrapped in action), but has a clear vision and sober estimation of his abilities vis-à-vis the goal he is pursuing. He may deem himself omnipotent, in the way a wild dreamer might, but in his case his cynical sense of superiority almost invariably proves to be grounded in reality – indeed, Pechorin carefully prepares, achieves and cherishes his victories. Yet, at the same time, he does have a dream, in a sense, and his entire image is a poetic one rather than pragmatic. His dream is to be free from boredom, from total spiritual isolation, from the feeling of inner emptiness, at times unbearable to death. In other words, instinctively (even though he might never acknowledge that) Pechorin craves a true emotional involvement – to the loss of himself in somebody or something; he simply envies the human race in its ability for a genuine love, for renunciation of self, of the ego – something totally unattainable for him. At the very least he desires a foe who would be his equal.

This burning desire may be concealed even from his own mind (although he knows perfectly well of his ultimate unbreakable inner solitude), and in this sense he is in fact much more of a victim than a victor and tyrant. Indeed, the victims of his cruelty suffer from very human feelings of humiliated love and betrayed trust, while he himself undergoes a much more fundamental suffering – caused by his emotional deficiency, his inability for mercy and true affection, or in other words his inability to be human. Like Maxim Gorky's outcast-hero Larra, a son of an eagle (the neo-romantic character created more than half a century later), who was punished by total exclusion for his icy superiority and murderous neglect of others, Pechorin is truly a 'superfluous person' – not so much in social as in existential terms, superfluous above all to himself. And his concealed dream is doomed, he can never leave the vicious circle of his cold contempt and join the human race, to discover the joy of genuine attachment which rescues one from cosmic indifference and fatal depression. The words from Gorky's narration about Larra precisely capture Pechorin's fate: 'he regards himself as being number one in the world, and sees nothing else, but himself. Everybody almost felt scared, when they realized to what a loneliness he was subjugating himself. He had no tribe, no mother, no cattle, no wife, and he did not want any of these', and his punishment is terrible: 'His punishment is in him! Let him go, let him be free. This is his punishment!'.[38]

A fusion of sorts of the 'small' and 'superfluous' person is to be found in Turgenev's 'Notes of a Superfluous Man', whose protagonist broods over the same resentment against life as his Dostoevsky's counterparts, but without the 'Napoleonic' sting. As many of Turgenev's characters (and in a way as Turgenev himself) he is despondent and non-daring. Such heroes end up by total withdrawal from life, by inner solitude and, more often than not, by misery. At best they confine themselves to a monastery (either a real one or that of their own spirit) and become moving shrines of their deceased

[38] Maxim Gorky, 'Starukha Izergil', <http://az.lib.ru/g/gorxkij_m/text_0012.shtml> [accessed 20 January 2013].

dreams. A different non-daring example is Tolstoy's Karenin, who, like Chekhov's 'man in a case', is afraid of dreaming, of overstepping the line, unable to abandon the narrow 'framework of habits and conventions'[39] which saved him from his emotional haemophilia, as Frank Seeley puts it. However, only at what was perceived as his wife's deathbed, 'did he yield to the temptation to rise above empty gestures – the temptation to experience, however fleetingly, the fullness of his humanity by taking on himself real suffering and real love.'[40] This, as Seeley observes, was a 'surrender from weakness, not from strength.'[41] Had he abandoned the shell of his ego, Karenin 'might have treasured for the rest of his life the memory of that finest hour.'[42]

Apart from the demonic dreams and their fatal evolution, and apart from the innocent dreams – perishing, changing their nature or even unable to be conceived, there exists another, more life-affirming, scenario – shown by Pushkin in the image of Tatiana Larina, the protagonist of 'Eugene Onegin'. This is a distinct example of a dream-crash which does not lead to a disintegration of personality or, in some superior sense, to disintegration of life; an example where the heroine stays faithful to her dream to the end, remaining at the same time faithful to her own self, even though her fate is essentially tragic. As young (and still idealistic) Lev Shestov admiringly and rather grandiloquently put it, commenting on the poet's unique ability to resolve harmoniously the insoluble conflict between art and reality, to unite within him an idealist with realist: 'he was the first not to give way when encountering the terrible sphinx who had already devoured many great fighters for humanity.'[43] The question was formulated sharply, and meant a lot at the end of the nineteenth century when it was repeated by the young thinker: 'how can a poet, without betraying the truth of life, preserve the loftiest, the best aspirations of his soul? Apparently, there isn't (and there cannot be) any choice; apparently, it is impossible to worship two gods simultaneously; one has to either describe the reality as it is, or to escape to the realm of unfulfillable dreams.'[44]

In Shestov's view, in the new Western European literature this question still remained unresolved at the time and produced a clear border-line between the great idealists like Victor Hugo or George Sand, or realists like Flaubert, the Goncourts, Zola and many others. But Russian literature and Pushkin above all, Shestov concludes, managed to answer it positively – one can encounter real life with all its horrors and still believe in truth and good. Ironically, only five years later Shestov was to write his article on Chekhov, having failed to spot the same optimistically heroic ability in the writer. Misled by the 'simplistic' exterior of Chekhov's works and trying to extract a moralistic message from their intangible aesthetic truth, Shestov missed their 'inner diversity and concealed heroism',[45] and remained unaware of the writer's amazing conclusions:

---

[39] Seeley, *Saviour or Superman?*, op. cit., p. 59.
[40] Ibid.
[41] Ibid.
[42] Ibid.
[43] Lev Shestov, 'A. S. Pushkin', in *Umozrenie i otkrovenie*, op. cit., p. 334.
[44] Ibid.
[45] These are quotations from Fazil Iskander's novella 'Poet', op. cit. (where the protagonist defines Chekhov as being 'externally simple, but internally diverse and heroic in a concealed way').

'If you want to become an optimist and to understand life, then stop believing in what others say and write, but instead watch and think for yourself'.[46]

Tatiana Larina was sensitive and pensive – deprived of a kindred spirit, of a deserving interlocutor around her, she grew a dreaming girl, bred on sentimental novels to the extent of 'reading literary stereotypes as the equivalent of reality'.[47] Yet, she managed to escape the danger of relying too heavily on the imaginary world and modelling her life on literary canons – instead she learned to take charge of her own destiny, inspired, but not subdued (or confused) by her reading baggage. Her attempts at understanding of Onegin's inner world are also connected with her discovery of his reading titles. 'Tatiana's road to self-consciousness thus entails becoming a critical reader'.[48] She is a creator herself – writing a letter to Onegin, she merges the sentimental French traditions with her own Russianness and her genuine unpretentious ways, and then, with time, she, as it were, perfects her style and becomes fully an author of her own life.[49] Thus Tatiana is not defeated by her youthful dreams, not taken by them off the path of reality, but strengthened to a perfect maturity. Such a balance is rarely achievable by Russian literary characters, and in classical literature it is more often a woman (like Tatiana or 'Turgenevan young females') who lead the way.

Saltykov-Shchedrin's hero Nagibin (novella 'Protivorechiia', 1848) contemplates the dangers which await a youngster on the road between his dream (often born of lofty literature and sensitive heart) and reality, and which normally prove insurmountable: at first, in idealistic youth, 'Our consuming thirst of attachment does not have as an object something real, on the contrary, we turn away almost with disdain from the environment in which we live, and create for ourselves a special dream world which we inhabit with ghosts of our imagination, in which we find satisfaction for our best, most profound desires, in a word – a world in which we are sorcerers'.[50] It is then very difficult to fall from such heights to the mundane, which seems in comparison dull and undeserving. 'The soul seeks freedom and light, but it is given a room of three yards and windows facing a cesspit. The soul wants to burn of longing and the sorrow of pleasure, yet instead it is offered a very moderate warmth, of twenty degrees Reaumur. Where is there here to burn, to roam? Everywhere is crumped, everywhere is cold'.[51]

The hero then gives an explanation of the source of such propensity for dreaming, tracing its roots not only to the fervency of youth, but also to the wrong upbringing and distorted education which facilitate a certain infantilism of spirit (and evoke the first epigraph to this chapter, taken from Herzen and later shared by Ivan Bunin – about the rift between theory and practice): 'Of course, one should neither burn, nor paint

[46] Anton Chekhov, Dnevnikovye zapisi in A. P. Chekhov, *PSSP v 30 tomakh*, vol. 17, op. cit., p. 102.

[47] Wiiliam Mills Todd III, *Fiction and Society in the Age of Pushkin: Ideology, Institutions, and Narrative*, Cambridge: Harvard University Press, 1986, p. 131.

[48] Marcus Levitt, 'Evgenii Onegin', in Andrew Kahn (ed.), *The Cambridge Companion to Pushkin*, Cambridge: Cambridge University Press, 2006, p. 51.

[49] See more on this topic in Todd, op. cit., and in Olga Peters Hasty's *Pushkin's Tatiana*, Madison: University of Wisconsin Press, 1999, where the ideas of Tatiana's creative potential are developed.

[50] M. E. Saltykov-Shchedrin, 'Protivorechiia', in Sobranie Sochinenii v 20 tomakh, Moscow: Khudozhestvennaia literatura, 1965, vol. 1, p. 73.

[51] Ibid.

the town red; one should instead live and study, but, I repeat, all this is quite forgivable in youth, all is due both to upbringing more inclined to empty dreaming than to a sober outlook at life, as well as to our field of activities which is limited by speculative sciences only, so that man, instead of learning from the beginning, learns from the end, and complains afterwards that he cannot understand anything in this confusion of Babilon'.[52] This upbringing is fatal, for 'depleted by incessant mental depravity, man loses the courage to look reality in the eye, does not have enough energy to expose the secret springs and explain the apparent contradictions of life. Speculative science injects arrogance into the human mind, renders man a sceptic, so that afterwards he even boasts of his scepticism, and says that in it there is all that is chic, the last word of philosophy. Such are the sad results of this sweet youthful naïvete, this ingenuous desire to love no matter what and no matter how, as long as one loves, and beyond that – the whole world can go to hell and be destroyed'.[53]

This decisive crusade against Hamletian type of dreaming inherent in Russian culture in general, and especially prominent in the literature of the mid-nineteenth century, is resonant with Turgenev's views from his aforementioned essay 'Hamlet and Don Quixot' written more than ten years later. Saltykov-Shchedrin through his hero stigmatized fruitless, destructive self-reflection, a sophistication of the mind, not equipped with sufficient spiritual strength, lacking in maturity and resolve, and thus unable to take action and to make responsible choices – unable both to face life in all its ugliness and to appreciate all its real beauty. In the same vein, Turgenev castigated Russian Hamlets – the 'superfluous people' – whose will is paralysed by their sceptical doubts and trapped in the dark labyrinth of their self-analysis. 'For action one needs will as well as idea, but will and idea in our life have become disconnected and continue to drift apart every day . . ;[54] he wrote about the divide between Russian Hamlets and Russian Don Quixotes.[55] Saltykov-Shchedrin's hero Nagibin himself follows the path of inactivity, of excessive thought and passive observation, the path of dreaming, while lamenting it: 'I was not given a practical understanding of reality [. . .] my mind was fed with dreams, without an opportunity to get stronger, to sober up, and then released, unassisted, straight onto the high road of life!'.[56] Just as Dostoevsky's Paradoxicalist, he blames the outside world rather than his own self for his misfortunes. And it is not surprising that so many lines in Saltykov-Shchedrin's novella read as a direct echo and premonition of Dostoevsky's famous 'Notes'

[52] Ibid.
[53] Ibid.
[54] I. S. Turgenev, 'Gamlet i Don Kikhot', in *Polnoe sobranie sochinenii i pisem v 30 tomakh, Sochineniia v 12 tomakh*, Moscow: Nauka, 1980, vol. 5. See <http://az.lib.ru/t/turgenew_I_s/text_0240.shtml> [accessed 17 February 2014].
[55] At the same time, both represent a type of inner heroism, ready to defend the destiny of the world. As Grigorii Pomerants noted, 'Both see a sprawling, crumbling world. Both feel lonely in their struggle against moral chaos. Burden of responsibility rests on the shoulders of both. But Hamlet takes on his impossible task with horror and doubt, while Don Quixote frees the convicts with delight and enthusiasm. No wonder Turgenev wrote his article 'Hamlets and Don Quixotes' when having before him the first members of Russian intelligentsia who threw themselves from the depths of doubt to attacking windmills'. (See Grigorii Pomerants, 'O podlosti, o doblesti, o slave', *Vestnik Evropy* 2008, No. 22.)
[56] M. E. Saltykov-Shchedrin, 'Protivorechiia', op. cit., p. 182.

(written also, just as Turgenev's essay, more than ten years after 'Protivorechiia'), to which Saltykov-Shchedrin in many ways prepared the ground.

Rudolf Neuhäuser studies precisely this phenomenon, placing the discussion into a philosophical framework, and finds numerous parallels between early writings of Saltykov-Shchedrin and Dostoevsky's oeuvre, especially his 'Notes from Underground'.[57] In the protagonists of 'Protivorechiia' Neuhäuser sees an ecounter of Hegelian philosophy and utopian socialism – the leading philosophical currents of the time. Nagibin's convictions are predominantly of Hegelian type, but 'as the social thinkers of the 1840s, he tries, following utopian socialists, to discover a more perfected mode of social organisation'.[58] Saltykov-Shchedrin precipitates a struggle against idols of all kinds, including in equal measure romantic and idealistic world-views on the one hand, and utilitarianism and positivism on the other. Just as Dostoevsky later, he demonstrates a rebellion against the 'stone wall' (in his case – a 'granite mountain') of Necessity, and even appeals to the same formulae of 'two-by-two is four rather than five'. He too deems irrational egotistic strivings, desires and whims of an individual forever more important for humans than the principle of reasonable profit based on the demands of reality. Thus, Neuhäuser concludes, the roots of Dostoevsky's 'Notes' go back to the ideological searches and currents of the previous decades.[59]

Having started with exploration of social and psychological aspects of dreaming, Dostoevsky later expands his analysis to involve a philosophical and historical dimension of this phenomenon. In his own definition, the characters most conducive of dreaming are those who are 'greedy for action, greedy for actual life, greedy for reality, but who are weak, feminine and delicate'.[60] A propensity for dreaming distorts them and turns into weird creatures of 'neuter gender' – into dreamers: 'The dreamer – if you want an exact definition – is not a human being, but a creature of an intermediate sort. For the most part he settles in some inaccessible corner, as though hiding from the light of day; once he slips into his corner, he grows to it like a snail . . .', says the protagonist of 'Belye nochi'.[61] 'We are such dreamers. Without practical activity man will inevitably become a dreamer', wrote Dostoevsky in 1861 jointly with his brother in the article 'Vopros ob universitetakh'.[62] In the years 1876–7 the writer was even contemplating a novel dedicated exclusively to this theme. As G. M. Friedlender comments, 'In his novel "Mechtatel" Dostoevsky intended – judging by his sketches – to show realisation of the tragedy of dreaming by the protagonist himself (in this respect the writer would be returning to the issues raised in his "Belye nochi"). His hero acutely senses evil and injustice of life. By his own admission, these could cause him to "shoot himself", "if he had not been dreaming". But the protagonist's

[57] Rudolf Neuhäuser, 'Ranniaia proza Saltykova-Shchedrina i Dostoevsky (paralleli i otkliki)', in *Dostoevsky. Materialy i issledovaniia*, vol. 2, Leningrad: Nauka, 1976.
[58] Ibid.
[59] Ibid.
[60] Fedor Dostoevsky, 'Peterburgskaia letopis', in Dostoevsky, *Sobranie sochinenii v 15 tomakh*, op. cit., vol. XIII, pp. 30–1.
[61] Fyodor Dostoevsky, 'White Nights', <http://www.online-literature.com/dostoevsky/4394/> [accessed 20 August 2014].
[62] Published in *Vremia*, 1861, No. 12, p. 99.

"dreaming" is not only his strength, but also his curse: helping him to endure the hardship of life and rescuing him "from despair", his dreams take him away from reality into the world of fantasy, thereby mitigating for him the tragedy of existence. Thus they testify to the weakness of the hero, who "does not dare to accept the truth with all its consequences"'.[63] Dostoevsky calls propensity for dreaming a 'desease of the century'. His planned protagonist was supposed to fail in his attempts to 'shake off the paralysis of dreaming and to become a person', and this had to lead to his suicide. It is interesting in this connection, that it was the laconic Pushkin who, long before, commented – by a single epithet: 'ungrateful dream'[64] – on this shadowy side of dreaming, which, through a construction of an imaginary, fantasy world, shutters reality, thus depriving one of its full appreciation.

The hero of the aforementioned novel, planned, but never written by Dostoevsky, is thus tormented by his dreaming as by a weakness and illness of sorts. Dostoevsky's other dreamer – most feverish and sinister – the aforementioned Paradoxicalist, lives in the underground of his dreams, by contrast, aggressively, and instead of suicidal thoughts revels in equal measure in self-disgust and in misanthropy, planning to outlive everybody. Lev Shestov, one of the philosophers with a 'monological' approach to Dostoevsky, using Bakhtin's term, saw the Paradoxicalist as above all Dostoevsky himself, who treads into mud his youthful idealistic convictions, burning all the bridges with his earlier devotion to Belinsky[65] – the interpretation which is, as it were, much more intense and tendentious than a popular perception of the novel as, in particular, a polemical parody of Chernyshevsky's rationalism and positivism. In other words, the story of this dreamer for Shestov exemplifies, among other things, the premise that there is no greater cynic than a disillusioned idealist. A paraphrase of Brodsky's formula – that cynicism is just a form of despair[66] – fits in this context as a framework of a sad existential story of a large variety of dreamers.

The new dreams of social nature, which Dostoevsky mocks in his 'Notes' and warns about in his 'Demons', are rooted deeply in the utilitarianism and positivism of the radical intelligentsia. Their helpless aesthetics, as in Chernyshevsky's 'Chto delat'?' and their calls, as in Pisarev's famous article, to renounce aesthetics altogether, result, not surprisingly, in unconvincing and utopian ethics. Yet, in Russia, as we saw, even the time of the 1860s 'with its loud ideas of sobriety and modest outlook, [. . .] was a most drunken period. Those who awaited the New Messiah and the Second Advent read Darwin and dissected frogs'.[67] Equally, Russian Slavophiles suffered from utopian dreaming, as reflected in Dostoevsky's aforementioned words coloured

---

[63] Commentary by G. M. Fridlender in F. M. Dostoevsky, *Sobranie Sochinenii v 15 tomakh*, vol. 10, Leningrad: Nauka, 1991, pp. 432–3.

[64] See A. S. Pushkin, 'Mechtateliu', in *Sobranie sochinenii v 10 tomakh*, op. cit., vol. 1, 1959, p. 59.

[65] See Lev Shestov, 'Dostoevsky i Nitzshe. Filosofiia tragedii', op. cit.

[66] The authentic quotation says, 'Snobbery? But it's only a form of despair' (Joseph Brodsky, *Less Than One*, op. cit., p. 403).

[67] Lev Shestov, 'All Things Are Possible' ('Apotheosis of Groundlessness'). Op. cit. See <http://www.angelfire.com/nb/shestov/all/all_23.html> [accessed 26 October 2013].

with self-irony: 'Oh, gentlemen, do you know how dear Europe is to us Slavophile-dreamers who, as far as you're concerned, should only hate it, Europe, this "land of holy miracles"!'.[68]

It is tempting to see the ancient Russian folktales which traditionally embodied a desire for truth and justice, for a kind Tsar and merciful God, for material wealth and personal happiness, as remaining alive in the Russian blood towards the end of the nineteenth century, just as paganism never died underneath Russian Orthodoxy. Flooded with the Enlightenment ideas from Western Europe and the air of great disillusionment which marked the crisis of speculative philosophy, Russian thought still (and regardless of its Slavophile or Westernizers variety) preserved that aura of a fairy-tale, a desire for a miracle which Dostoevsky refers to and which Shestov captured so aptly in his words, already quoted previously – about a peculiar Russian perception of Western European scientific progress and a Russian persistent refusal to part with illusions.

A related idea, also mentioned earlier, is that of the relative youth of Russian literary culture resulting in its daring, boldness and in 'a lingering belief in the possibility of a final triumph over evil'.[69] By the same token, 'the most skeptical Russian hides a hope at the bottom of his soul'.[70] Thus German remarkable conceptual achievements, crowned by Hegel whose philosophical character 'at first glance, could not be more suited to the tastes of even his Russian disciples',[71] were misinterpreted in the usual Russian way, and taken to their logical extreme. Hegel's 'Absolute was a spitting image of a Russian sorcerer who can do anything, but does not want to yet; and seemed to open up that infinite expanse, which crowned the dreams of overstays of Ilya-Muromets type. Needless to say that this time too Russians misunderstood Germans, or rather understood them too well'.[72]

In theological terms, as Erich Auerbach believes, Russian literary realism with its belated character 'is fundamentally related rather to old-Christian than to modern occidental realism'.[73] And Joseph Frank observes a specifically Russian rift between the Christian ethos and the demands of secular life, which in Western Europe, on the contrary, had been reconciled over a long period of time following the Renaissance.[74] Thus A. V. Kartashov writes that 'the Russian people saw in Christianity a revelation about the Saviour's coming to Earth and about creating, through the power of ecclesiastical piety, instead of this sinful, impure world another world – thoroughly holy'.[75] This dream is the 'Russian civitas Dei, paradisical existence with all the

---

[68]   Fyodor Dostoevsky, *A Writer's Diary*, op. cit., vol. 2, 1877–81, p. 1066.

[69]   Lev Shestov, 'All Things Are Possible' ('Apotheosis of Groundlessness'), <http://www.angelfire.com/nb/shestov/all/all_23.html> [accessed 2 August 2013].

[70]   Ibid.

[71]   Lev Shestov, *Turgenev*, Ann Arbor: Ardis, 1982, pp. 19–20.

[72]   Ibid., p. 20.

[73]   Erich Auerbach, *Mimesis: The Representation of Reality in Western Literature*, Princeton: Princeton University Press, 2003, 521.

[74]   See Joseph Frank, *Between Religion and Rationality. Essays in Russian Literature and Culture*, Princeton and Oxford: Princeton University Press, 2010.

[75]   A. V. Kartashov, 'Smysl staroobriadchestva' in the Collective Volume of articles in honour of P.B. Struve, Prague, 1925, p. 378. Cited in Zenkovsky, op. cit., p. 59.

fullness of life's diversity – except for sin'.[76] As Zenkovsky comments, writing about the Schism, 'In all this one should see a dead-end of the utopia, of the dream about the "holy kingdom", but the utopia itself flourished from the theocratic idea precious to all Christianity. In the Old Belief, with its sad history [. . .], Russian ecclesiastic imagination paid dearly for its dream, for the utopian understanding of the Christian theocratic idea. In essence, together with the Old Belief, the idea of the holy Russia, understood as reality already fulfilled in history, was also sidelined'.[77]

Consequently, 'while the nineteenth-century English novel may portray the difficulties of its characters to live up to the prescriptions of Christian morality, one does not find in it the same depiction of the struggle with the source of that morality itself, the Christian faith'.[78] In Frank's view, it is first of all the echoes of this struggle and its social and existential implications that Dostoevsky managed to bring up to genuinely tragic heights. In this light Frank comments on the connection between the ideological flavour of Russian literature and the country's socio-political reality. Apart from the politically motivated lack of an open platform for any non-literary discourse, Frank finds a deeper reason, essentially reiterating the thoughts of Shestov, quoted above, as he talks of 'the novelty of such ideas suddenly intruding on a world totally unprepared to receive them by any period of transition and compromise, such as had been worked out in European literature for several centuries'.[79] Thus 'the "radical" ideas of the West, when they came to Russia, were immediately driven to their most extreme consequences; they were not merely theories to be discussed [. . .], but plans to be put into action'.[80] What could be added to these words though, is the thought that the roots of such extremism may have well been concealed in the hypertrophied national dreaming (cultivated by the conditions of hardship and injustice) with its intrinsic larger than life properties. For such a fertilized ground it only takes a tiny spark blown up by 'demons' of any kind to flare up an extreme fire. 'Hamlet' turns into 'Don Quixote', a subdued dreamer – into a rebellious fighter; the mighty man Ilia Muromets gets up from the stove where he was laying for the best part of his life and springs into action.

Thus towards the end of the nineteenth century the ideological ground was ripe in Russia for any rational global solutions. When new 'local' gods of mankind, such as Marx, Freud and Nietzsche, replaced the old Biblical God, they channelled traditional human aspirations onto more concrete paths, having on the one hand earthed them, bringing from the metaphysical to a physical realm, and yet rendering them even more feverish and urgent, on the other. Rationalistic at the core, they at the same time were wildly irrational in their naïve hope to reduce human nature to a system much more trivial than the reality – as it were, to squeeze the infinite into the finite. Saltykov-Shchedrin's words from the same novella 'Protivorechiia' on the all-absorbing fatality of irresponsible dreaming, pronounced in the middle of the nineteenth century, remained no less relevant towards its end: '. . . what is understandable and forgivable in youth, is not always decent

---

[76] Ibid.
[77] See Zenkovsky, op. cit., p. 59.
[78] Frank, *Between Religion and Rationality: Essays in Russian Literature and Culture*, op. cit., pp. 2–3.
[79] Ibid., p. 4.
[80] Ibid.

for a man who grew out, at least to an extent, of the nappies of habit. [. . .] to remain the same student, the same fiery admirer of an abstract entity, to speak only of mankind and forget about a particular man is stupid, and not only stupid, but also vile.[81] A century later, after the radical dreams of a final solution to mankind's predicament had been put into practice, into morbid reality, Vasilii Grossman's character repeated essentially the same thought: 'I do not believe in good, I believe in kindness'.[82] And Herzen, earlier, wrote about Russia, 'Here the people respect the idea, but not the person'.[83] As soon as 'a compassion for a human being was replaced by a compassion to a fairy-tale understood as a new truth',[84] then private man was replaced by a general mankind, private kindness – by the general good, and a private dream turned into a communal, state dream. Ultimately dehumanizing humanity, Marxism and 'Nietzscheism' led to the respective totalitarian societies stamping down a private individual for the sake of which these systems were supposedly constructed (while Freudism, arguably, eventually paved the way to post-modernism with its disintegration of meaning and deconstructive conception of man).

It is instructive that, contemplating the nature of Russian revolution and its ultimate victory, Fazil Iskander appeals to the concept of a dream: 'One can say that the revolutionaries had infected with the sin of theorizing a sufficiently large proportion of the population, which followed them. Maybe our Asiatic dreamingness, not too burdensome relationship with a production of practical values of life made this process easier? [. . .] in principle, in certain historical circumstances, this could happen to any nation, because wanting to shake off the load of tragic consciousness, at least to shout: let everything go to hell! – is peculiar to people in general. [. . .] After the revolution in Russia everything got reversed. Poets, being horrified by the surrounding chaos, began to call for the sobriety of the state'.[85] A famous phrase of H. G. Wells, calling Lenin a 'Kremlin dreamer' (after their personal meeting in Russia in 1920), links with Iskander's elaborations on the subject which sum up the course of Russian history in the twentieth century: 'But what a poetic (as well as graphomaniac) sweep in the dreams of the state: world revolution, total collectivisation, electrification, "chekization". [. . .] It is a frenzy of dreaming'.[86] And finally, a theoretical premise underlying the mechanism behind excessive dreaming and explaining the writers' mission in the totalitarian conditions is as follows: 'This naturally leads one to suspect that such an inflammation of dreams is caused by a subconscious fear of reality. A builder who is unable to build a henhouse, declares that he is going to build a magic palace, with a place for a henhouse as well. Thus the responsibility for the final result is moved to infinity. In these circumstances our best writers took upon themselves an impossible burden of sobering up the authorities – by ranging from irony over the unmeasurable futuristic pathos to compassion toward a person crushed by the state dream'.[87]

[81] Saltykov-Shchedrin, 'Protivorechiia', op. cit., pp. 73–4.
[82] Vasilii Grossman, *Zhizn i sud'ba*, <http://lib.ru/PROZA/GROSSMAN/lifefate.txt> [accessed 10 February 2014].
[83] Herzen's letter to Jules Michelet, op. cit.
[84] Iskander, *Rasskazy, povest, skazka, dialog, esse, stikhi*, op. cit., p. 592.
[85] Ibid.
[86] Ibid., p. 382.
[87] Ibid.

These agonies of a person crushed by the state dream, trying to adjust to it at one's own expense, are visible in many high calibre post-revolutionary Russian literary works. Nikolai Kavalerov from Yurii Olesha's novel 'Zavist' embodies a sensibility of an artistic individual lost and disoriented in the new system of values, and reduced to tormenting envy leading him to the anabiosis state of indifference. A subtlety of his perception of the world, his – at once fearful and colourful – dreaming, his angst and trepidation in the face of existence are totally out of place in the new shiningly polished mechanism of a state preoccupied by the material and materialistic, which are exalted to the new spiritual.

In the humorous genre, Ostap Bender, the famous Ilf's and Petrov's hero, a dreamer and poet at heart, a gambler and a wanderer, ends up defeated by the iron laws of the world around him, his colourful game in sharp contrast to the aesthetics of the new regime, which in fact he mocks vivaciously by using its attributes to his advantage. And although his role is to reveal, as litmus paper, all the malfunctioning elements stuck to the healthy body of a new state, his own individualist game looks far more attractive than the collective Socialist reality of the time of the New Economic Policy which is redeemed largely because it is portrayed through the prism of Bender's cheerful outlook.

But the time of an individual dreamer is over. A dreaming hero is replaced by a dreaming author, who is doing his best to believe in the new world order, but falls a victim of it, either directly or figuratively. For no matter how loyal and well meaning his authorial intentions, they come into conflict with his literary talent depicting things with merciless authenticity. Thus Andrei Platonov mirrors the tragedy of the new life with its perdition of a dream. And neo-romantic Aleksandr Grin (Grinevsky) simply escapes from the havoc and bloodshed of the military communism, from the hardship of unsettled, hungry and unjust Soviet years into the dreamland, an imaginary country, a parallel universe. In his novels, especially in 'Begushchaia po volnam' (1928), he is defending precisely a profound human need for an elevating dream, which he is clearly unable to connect to the Soviet reality.

Yet, this elevating dream is what the new ideology offered in epic, mythological proportions. The aforementioned 'unmeasurable futuristic pathos' seductively attracted all those who were romantic dreamers at heart with a profound need to believe in a higher realm, refusing to part with their dream and to face the ever gloomier reality.

A fierce resistance to disillusionment, to disintegration of a dream were put up by most stubborn, I would say – convinced – dreamers, for whom dreaming was an ideology, a way of life. This is perhaps best seen from the lifepath of Maxim Gorky, who was prepared to hate the truth if it contradicted his dream. From early on, as Vladislav Khodasevich observes, 'Philosophizing and speaking through his characters, Gorky endowed them in the highest degree with a dream of a better life – the dream, that is, of finding a moral and social truth that might cast its radiance over everything and arrange everything for the good of humanity'.[88] This truth, which Gorky searched for,

---

[88] Vladislav Khodasevich, 'Gorky', in Donald Fanger, *Gorky's Tolstoy and Other Reminiscences; Key Writings By and About Maxim Gorky*, New Haven: Yale University Press, 2008, p. 239.

shifted from ideology to ideology, starting from religion, and moving on to Marxism. A dream, an illusion were of personal, private, acute importance to him. In a penetrating description of this phenomenon, Khodasevich lifts a curtain over a psychological mechanism underpinning social processes of Bolshevism in Russia.

Gorky 'did not bear despondency, and demanded from people a hope – against all odds, and in this his peculiar, stubborn egoism manifested itself: in exchange for his involvement, he demanded for himself the right to dream about the better future of the person to whom he was trying to help. [. . .] A destroyed dream, like a corps, evoked in him squeamishness and fear, as if he felt in it something impure. This fear, accompanied by anger was evoked in him by all those who were guilty of destroying illusions, those who disturbed emotional comfort, based on a dream, those who spoilt a festive elevated mood. [. . .] He felt it his duty to respect creative impulse, or a dream, or an illusion even in those cases when all this manifested itself in the most pitiful or repulsive fashion. The exposure of a petty lie evoked in him the same annoyed boredom as the destruction of a lofty dream. Re-establishing the truth appeared to him the banal and vulgar triumph of prose over poetry'.[89]

The conclusion reached by Khodasevich is also of a general application: 'Gorky was fated to live in an age when the "golden dream" came down to a dream of social revolution as panacea for all human suffering. He subscribed to this myth and became its spokesman not because he believed so firmly in revolution but because he believed in the saving power of the dream as such. In another time he would have defended other beliefs and other hopes just as passionately. He passed through the Russian liberation movement, and then through the revolution, as a fomentor and upholder of the dream – as Luka, the wily wanderer. [. . .] his life and work alike testify to a sentimental love for all kinds of lies and a stubborn, persistent dislike for truth'.[90]

Various other cultural heroes of the early Soviet years showed a more courageous attitude by facing the inevitable disillusionment, a collapse of a dream, and going down with it themselves. Ultimately a history of Soviet literature, especially of its early period, is in essence a history of disillusionment. Thus Sergei Esenin, 'the prophet of the unfulfilled miracles, turns into a holy fool, but this is not his last fall. The last one came when Esenin went out, painted the town red. He imagined that the whole of Russia drowned its sorrow, and for the same reason as he did: because her hopes for something that is "greater than revolution", "more left than the Bolsheviks", did not come true: because she destroyed her past, but did not get any closer to her dreams'.[91]

The ways out were sharply different – either to carry on believing despite any evidence to the contrary, to continue uniting the European knightly romanticism with the aesthetics of revolutionary communism, as did, for example, Arkadii Gaidar (Golikov) – that is to maintain the grandeur of futuristic pathos; or to return to the pre-revolutionary themes, to extinguish the epic pretence of the militant state by

---

[89] V. F. Khodasevich, *Nekropol*. See <http://az.lib.ru/h/hodasewich_w_f/text_0020.shtml> [accessed 30 June 2013].

[90] Vladislav Khodasevich, 'Gorky', in Donald Fanger, *Gorky's Tolstoy and Other Reminiscences*, op. cit., p. 241.

[91] V. F. Khodasevich, *Nekropol*, op. cit.

the unquivering ironic resolve, as did in particular Fedor Sologub, or many émigré writers.

Dmitrii Bykov views Gaidar as a direct heir of Aleksandr Grin – 'with the same mania of distant travels, with the same affection for the prose of Gustave Aimard and Louis Boussenard, with the same amazing psychological precision and authenticity, and with the same, a bit childish, cruelty, which is present in Grin and from which you cannot hide'.[92] Yet, what Bykov does not say is that Grin believed that violence cannot be overcome by violent means and recoiled from Bolshevism, while Gaidar continued on the path of romantic revolutionary strength, armed with weapons and christened in bloodshed – the way of thinking which 'Boris Natanovich Strugatsky so accurately labelled a cheerful and infantile Soviet militarism'.[93] For Bykov, Gaidar's is a classical example of an 'epic stylistics of rearranging the world which begins anew',[94] and the writer for him is one of its many faithful knights. Moreover, Bykov believes provocatively that in not so many years from now 'a grateful posterity – all those aware of what the Soviet power was like, what it had done, what all of us, its miserable recklings, had been like – will be obliterated and evaporated. But many more generations of children', when reading Gaidar's lines, will encounter the purity of his dream and, 'experience strong feelings, for the sake of which, in fact, a human being is born'.[95]

The path, chosen by Sologub among others, was drastically different, failing the ideologically driven attempts of state mythology to appropriate a personal, individual romantic dream: 'Gritting his teeth, stubborn dreamer, confident, solid, steady master, he uttered, in the days of the "proletarian art", with a grin over enemies, and himself, and the "bitter life":

"Tirsis under the shadow of willow
Is dreaming of Nanette,
And bowing his head,
He is playing on his musette:
I am tormented by love,
And driven to the grave".[96]

Decades later, Yurii Dombrovsky's hero, also a romantic dreamer at heart, opposed his sharp wit and caustic irony to the murderous machine of the state, for which the fundamental concepts of humanness became useless knowledge.[97] Dreamers of the Thaw resumed and continued the anthropocentric moral tradition of Russian

---

92   Dmitrii Bykov, 'Strana, kotoruiu pridumal Gaidar', <http://gaidarfund.ru/articles/1154> [accessed 25 February 2013].
93   Ibid.
94   Ibid.
95   Ibid.
96   Khodasevich, *Nekropol*, op. cit. The quotation is from Fedor Sologub's poem of 1921; in Russian: 'Тирсис под сенью ив // Мечтает о Нанетте,// И голову склонив,// Выводит на мюзетте:// Любовью я, – тра, та, там, та, – томлюсь, // К могиле я, – тра, та, там, та, – клонюсь'.
97   The reference is to Dombrovsky's novel 'Fakultet nenuzhnykh veshchei' (completed in 1975).

literature, but they no longer shared a futuristic pathos. Shameful and discredited, it was extinguished by irony which became their inseparable attribute. Most striking is Venedikt Erofeev's lyrical hero,[98] who, under the holy-foolish disguise of an alcoholic haze, lives in the divine presence, tormented by the tragic farce of existence and dreaming of the unattainable. As a miniature and a metaphor of human life, he is never reaching his desired destination, being both reduced and elevated to a dream: searching for Kremlin, but ending up invariably at the Kursky railway station; striving for Petushki, but never arriving there, and perishing instead. And just as the words of Adam Gussow about Dovlatov – 'his heroes are burning as brightly as the heroes of Dostoevsky only in a much more frivolous hell'[99] – are equally applicable to Erofeev, Ludmila Petrushevskaya's heroes too are close to Dostoevsky, but gravitating towards his infernal dreamers, and with no light-hearted concessions in this case.

A different continuation of the old national tradition, rooted in folklore, portrays selfless dreamers – humble (like early Dostoevsky's heroes), but at the same time with a fiery, explosive potential – as can be found in Vasilii Shukshin's 'chudiki', confused, misunderstood and tormented home-made philosophers. Ridiculous from the philistine, mundane point of view, they are in fact salt of the earth, authentic, ingenious and deeply humane. In their warm and spiteless attitude to mankind they stand next to the aforementioned lyrical heroes of Sergei Dovlatov and Venedikt Erofeev, as their spiritual brothers from a different social stratum, without a privilege and burden of education, but with the same highly sensitive, disquieting and non-conformist soul. Some of them, by their rebellious nature and elemental force, evoke the memory of Russian turbulent history. They refuse to live mechanically, they constantly search for meaning, otherwise their soul aches: 'Where can man go if his soul is disturbed? The soul, it aches, you know. If you get toothache in the night, you will run headlong to those, well, emergency-dentists, who will extract the achy tooth. But what about your soul, where do you go? Where will they listen to you, and display compassion?' ('At night, in a boiler house').[100] '"But a person's also got something else – a soul! Right here!" – Maksim pointed at his chest – "and it aches! I'm not makin' it up! I can actually feel it – it aches!" [. . .] Maksim [. . .] suddenly realized that he could never explain what was happening to him, and his wife Lyuda would never understand him. Never! If he ripped into his chest with a knife, extracted his soul and held it out to her on the palms of his hands, she'd just say, "What a lot of tripe!"' ('I believe!').[101] 'And the ache in his soul would rise up. But it was a strange kind of ache – one he longed for. Something was missing without it' ('Meditations').[102]

[98]   The reference is to Erofeev's poem in prose 'Moskva-Petushki' (completed in 1970).

[99]   From Gussow on the American edition of Dovlatov's 'Kompromis'. Cited in Andrei Arev, 'Nasha malenkaia zhizn' – Foreword to Sergei Dovlatov, *Sobranie Sochinenii v 3 tomakh*, op. cit., vol. 1, pp. 15–16.

[100] Vasilii Shukshin, 'Noch'iu v boilernoi' ('At Night, in a Boiler House'), <http://lib.rus.ec/b/97967/read> [accessed 15 February 2014].

[101] Vasilii Shukshin, 'I Believe!' ('Veruiu'), in *Stories from a Siberian Village*, transl. by Laura Michael and John Givens, DeKalb, IL: Northern Illinois University Press, 1996, p. 12.

[102] Vasilii Shukshin, 'Meditations' ('Dumy'), in *Stories from a Siberian Village*, op. cit., p. 102.

They are often lost, but driven by innate inner integrity, by love – deeply Christian in spirit – for their fellow being, and by striving to the divine heights from the suffocating routine of false values. They are, if you like, a new type of 'small' and at once 'superfluous' people – not so much superfluous to themselves as the old nineteenth-century types, but rather estranged from the society that lost genuine faith. And faith here should be understood not in a direct religious sense, but as an authenticity of feelings, a sensibility of uncorrupt spiritual values, of a typically Russian desperate striving to find meaning to existence, to pose the 'cursed questions' and face their torment. 'OK, let's presume that it is necessary that we live, but then why were we not denied this cursed gift – forever, tormentingly and fruitlessly, trying to understand: "What is all this for?"' ('Once there lived a man').[103] These 'strange' and confused Shukshin's heroes, who in a sense represent a long-desired fusion of Hamlet and Don Quixote – an active nucleus, but with a self-reflective propensity – have about them something inspirationally Mozartian. 'For me Mozart is not so much an ideal of a sunny talent, as an ideal of a sunny unselfishness',[104] says Iskander. Fulfilling his highly demanding role of total creative selflessness, Mozart acts at the fatal, crucial moment, about to be poisoned, essentially against himself, unable to distort the integrity of his genius: he is trying to rescue Salieri from his treacherous, murderous plan. All his life Mozart has been teaching good with his great art, 'but when it turned out that art was not enough, he added his own life to his system of proof, because life for Mozart was a continuation of art. Such are colossal integrity and purposefulness of a great artist'.[105]

Similarly, Shukshin's *chudiki* exemplify, as it were, a Mozartian embryo. On a different scale, they intuitively serve an ideal of selflessness, and are ready to sacrifice if not their life, then certainly their interests for the sake of that ideal – of human dignity and integrity. When Vasilii Kniazev (Chudik) drops a banknote, likely worth half his monthly salary, and mistakes it for someone else's, he then voices his witty surprise: '"You live well, citizens!" he said loudly and cheerfully. [. . .] "Where I am from, for instance, we don't just toss around bills like that"'.[106] But having realized that it was actually his own, he is unable to bring himself to asking for it to be returned to him. This is, thus, in miniature, a story of human integrity as epic as Pushkinian 'Little Tragedies', engraved in a seemingly ordinary 'simple' life of a seemingly ordinary 'simple' person. In fact it is a hymn, gentle and humble, to human nobility of spirit. 'There is no contradiction between the unquestioning credulity of Mozart and his unexpected permeation in heinous plans of Salieri. As soon as he realized that Salieri has lost his humanity and needs to be revived, he involves Salieri's life into the sphere of his creative task'.[107] By the same token, Kniazev, by trying to warm up his stern and down-to-earth sister-in-law, is, in fact, intuitively trying to redeem her humane nature, to bring her soul back to kindness and generosity of spirit. In a Mozartian organic way

[103] Vasilii Shukshin, 'Zhil chelovek' ('Once There Lived a Man'), <http://lib.ru/SHUKSHIN/rasskazy2.txt_with-big-pictures.html#51> [accessed 15 February 2014].
[104] Iskander, *Lastochkino gnezdo. Proza. Poeziia. Publitsistika*, op. cit., p. 390.
[105] Ibid., p. 394.
[106] Vasilii Shukshin, 'Oddball' ('Chudik'), in *Stories from a Siberian Village*, op. cit., p. 82.
[107] Iskander, *Lastochkino gnezdo. Proza. Poeziia. Publitsistika*, op. cit., p. 393.

Shukshin's 'chudiki' love and enjoy life and people, even though their soul constantly aches in a very physical, tangible way. They are unsettled dreamers, whose dreams simultaneously stir, disquieten, inspire and move the reader.

A similar catharsis is present in Alla Sokolova's famous play 'Fariatiev's fantasies' (1978), which was screened and staged widely, and became an international hit. Its protagonist, the provincial dreamer Fariatiev, is a dentist, but with a profoundly poetic soul, capable of true self-sacrificial love. His outlook at life, his stunning ability to love another person not in a petty and egotistically demanding way, but in a truly religious one, as if opens the eyes of everybody around him to the real purpose and substance of existence.

These dreamers, the heroes of Erofeev and Dovlatov, Shukshin and Vysotsky (who cried, screamed and roaringly laughed in poetry, as Shukshin did in prose) – are all examples of a different type of irrationalism – what I would call a specifically Russian type. In contrast to an irrationalist reaction against the rationalist spirit of the Enlightenment variety, or to the irrationalism born of excessive rationalism, this third type is irrationalism pure and with no apparent underlying reason. It is born just out of the burning sense of being alive – of having soul and conscience, compassion and anguish, of searching for the Truth, eternally and without compromise, and of being tragically and forever separated from the final answers.

> I now know: man is . . . an accidental, beautiful, agonizing attempt on Nature's part to know itself. But a fruitless one, I assure you [. . .] Nature will never understand itself . . . [. . .] it's gone on a rampage and is avenging itself in the form of man.[108] (Shukshin)

> And I look, and I see, and for that reason, I'm sorrowful. And I don't believe that any one of you has dragged around within himself this bitter, bitter mishmash. I'm in a quandary over saying what this mishmash is composed of, and, all the same, you would never understand, but mostly there's "sorrow" and "fear" in it. "Sorrow" and "fear" most of all and, then, muteness.[109] (Ven. Erofeev)

> Horses dancing all along, Smoothly dance the horses. On the road it seems all wrong, At the end much worser. Nothing's holy anymore, Neither drink nor prayer. It's all wrong, boys, by the Lord, No, boys, it's not fair . . ..[110] (Vysotsky)

> Suddenly my throat contracted painfully. For the first time I was part of my unique, unprecedented country. I was entirely made of cruelty, hunger, memory, malice . . . Because of my tears I couldn't see for a moment.[111] (Dovlatov)

[108] Vasilii Shukshin, 'Passing Through' ('Zaletnyi'), in *Stories from a Siberian Village*, op. cit., p. 161.
[109] Venedikt Erofeev, *Moscow to the End of the Line*, transl. by H. William Tjalsma, Evanston, IL: Northwestern University Press, 1992, p. 46.
[110] Vladimir Vysotsky, 'My Gypsy Song' ('V son mne zheltye ogni . . .') (1967–8), in *Vladimir Vysotsky: Hamlet with a Guitar*, transl. by Sergei Roy, op. cit., p. 145. In Russian: 'Где-то кони пляшут в такт, нехотя и плавно. Вдоль дороги всё не так, а в конце подавно! И ни церковь, ни кабак – ничего не свято! Эх, ребята, всё не так! Всё не так, ребята!'.
[111] Sergei Dovlatov, *The Zone*, transl. by Anne Frydman, Berkeley: Counterpoint Press, 2012, p. 162.

They are all ill at heart, but this is a lofty illness, a disease of being a human being. Instead of running away from the tragic existential abyss, they run towards it, they balance at its edge, peering down with a merciless intent and boldness, with a roar of laughter and sob.

Has it all died out with globalization, consumerism, post-modernist loss of meaning and its aftermath? Did dreaming degenerate, did it shift into fantasy genre and science-fiction only? What is clear is that the futuristic emotion is no more. It was rather replaced by an apocalyptic eschatological sentiment, akin to that at the start of the last century, only with an excruciatingly higher rate of mass devastation potential, and of technological scientific progress. Yet, the tradition of lofty Russian dreamers has it roots in the sacred, and 'righteousness does not exist without dedication to faith, and ultimately, without martyrdom', says Averintsev contemplating a 'specific constant of the moral landscape of Russian culture'.[112] In a deep sense, many of the selfless dreamers in Russian culture continue its ascetic tradition, the flame of which is clearly cast on Shukshin's and Vysotsky's characters. 'This is the way it was. Now we are told that this will be no more; that the feature of almost sainthood in Russian culture, suspicious for severe adherents of the faith and funny for people without any faith, has forever become the thing of the past. Forever. Well, we shall see about that, if we are still around', wrote Averintsev, 'but we shall not forget to bow down in front of each and every one of the elders, who yesterday alone, secluded, singlehanded, just by the strength of their personality, defended, in the face of fear and indifference, the tradition of Russian ascetics, the tradition of St. Stephen'.[113] And Joseph Frank, talking about the strength of Russian religious faith and its oppositional, dissenting aspects, recalled 'the unforgettable scene in Andrey Sinyavsky's [. . .] encounter with the *Raskol* (Old Believers) in his prison camp, who meet secretly at night in the boiler room to recite *Apocalypse*, each of them having memorized a chapter'.[114]

This is again an example of the purely Russian irrationalism, pointless, almost nonsensical on the outside and deeply meaningful on the inside. 'A little unquenchable icing lamp, once lit by someone somewhere, is still burning. It burns and never goes out, and voluntary wanderers, unnoticed by others, pour oil into it',[115] wrote Lev Shestov almost a hundred years ago – and the flame of a sacred dream is still burning today.

[112] Averintsev, *Sviaz vremen*, op. cit.
[113] Ibid.
[114] Frank, *Between Religion and Rationality: Essays in Russian Literature and Culture*, op. cit., p. 5.
[115] See Olga Tabachnikova (ed.), *Perepiska Lva Shestova s Borisom Schloezerom*, YMCA-Press, Paris, 2011, pp. 50–1.

4

Russian Eros: Love in the Context of Moral Philosophy

The mystery of love is greater than the mystery of death

Salomea

Body and soul: Theoretical prelude

What does mankind know about love, which formulas has it developed during its thousands-years-long history for this most palpitating and most irrational element apart from the sacramental 'this is a great mystery'? The idea of love – which in essence is a religious idea – to a greater or lesser extent permeates any national culture and largely determines it, giving an orientation to the spiritual life of the people. Rooted in both pagan and Christian mythologies, Russian idea of love is an integral part of the whole of Russian cultural history and contributes to the famous 'cursed questions', inseparable from the meaning of life itself. Within Russian literary–philosophical tradition, personal love is intrinsically connected to a broader concept of devotion to 'Mother Russia', the Russian-Orthodox ideas of compassion, mercy, justice, self-sacrifice and self-denial, to the dreams about justice, truth and beauty, about Christ's exploit and personality translated onto a lyrical hero. But equally it is brewed on the demonic agonies of pride, vanity, 'spiritual lust' and master–slave relationships. Clearly, without comprehending the idea of love, all the other spheres of human existence will remain closed and impenetrable, for it involves all human faculties, including mind, will power, conscience and sensual sphere, and thus organically belongs by its very nature to the most irrational phenomena of human life. Indeed, appearing from nowhere and departing nowhere, it is not subject to anything – and least of all to human reason and will.

It has been noted that in contrast to Western literature which endowed the world with such stunning examples of eternal and absolute love as Romeo and Juliette or Tristan and Isolde, there has been virtually nothing comparable in Russian letters.[1]

---

[1] See, for instance, Nikolai Berdiaev, 'Mirosozertsanie Dostoevskogo' (Chapter V: 'Liubov': <http://www.magister.msk.ru/library/philos/berdyaev/berdn008.htm> [accessed 1 February 2014]), repeated by Viacheslav Shestakov (ed.), Introduction to *Russkii eros, ili Filosofiia lubvi v Rossii*, Moscow: 'Progress', 1991, p. 5.

Yet, examples of individuals who exude most passionate and devoted love for their chosen ones, and are ready to sacrifice their life for them, are abound in Russian culture too, and scattered across national literature. But, unlike Romeo and Juliette, whose love is tragic by the virtue of the external plot rather than by its inner intrinsic qualities, Russian characters are usually involved in the cases of love which is tragic from inside much more than from outside. That is to say, it is either unrequited or poisoned by the heroes' own suffocating imagination, consumed by doubt and disturbed at the roots by some moral considerations or existential torment, as if their beings are intrinsically incapable of happiness and completeness. Moreover, even in the cases of intense and mutual love, the romance per se is not normally central to the literary work in terms of that work's main idea or the scope of issues it discusses. At best the love story constitutes a back-bone of the plot-line, as in Lev Tolstoy's 'Anna Karenina' or Mikhail Bulgakov's 'Master and Margarita', while opening up to deeper concerns, or serves as a background for a much broader narrative, preoccupied with general existential investigations and probing into the tragic human predicament and complexity of human nature.[2] But the most remarkable feature here is that, despite the existence of fully capable protagonists and their individual situations, in Russian cultural consciousness it is not the cases of perfect mutual love, boundless, total, unique (if only cut short by external circumstances, as in Romeo and Juliette's story), which form its spinal cord, but on the contrary – intrinsically tragic and unhappy love stories, broken destines, wrecked personalities. It is the latter which sustain Russian literary canon as far as the phenomenon of love is concerned. In other words, this is as if love for Russian writers is not a theme worthy of discussion in its own right, but only an excuse to contemplate the nature of life and man more generally, a springboard to propel the thought into the same undying 'cursed' questions, which, in turn, inevitably highlight the intrinsic tragedy of existence. Of course, literary traditions as such have a substantial part to play in this distinction, but only in so much as they reflect the nation's cultural imagination. Thus Western European novel was, as Saltykov-Shchedrin noted, predominantly centred around the family: 'In a positive sense (English novel), or in a negative sense (French novel), but the family has always played a leading role in a novel.'[3] Russian novel, by contrast, was by and large socially oriented: 'drama [. . .] started with kissing of two loving hearts, but ended with Siberian exile.'[4] And, as Lotman writes, 'with all the relative value of such generalized characteristics, it still, undoubtedly, contains some profound truth.'[5] By the same token, Russian literature was profoundly steeped in ethical problematics, growing from religious roots, and stayed unwaveringly obsessed and tormented by the validity of those roots in terms of their implications for human morality.

---

[2] For Lev Shestov, as we saw from the quotations earlier, it is the neophyte state of Russian literature, its belated character, that were to a large extent responsible for this wild, fearless and excessively ambitious striving.

[3] Mikhail Saltykov-Shchedrin, 'Gospoda Tashkenttsy'. <http://lib.rus.ec/b/205534/read#t2> [accessed 10 January 2014].

[4] Ibid.

[5] Lotman, 'Siuzhetnoe prostranstvo russkogo romana XIX stoletiia', op. cit., p. 97.

Thus, in Russian classical literature at least, love has turned, as it were, into a separate moral philosophy (and quite original at that), much more so than being just a feeling, emotion or passion per se. In other words, in Russian cultural tradition, love is above all a cultural construct. Even the epoch of Modernism with its 'Walpurgis', Dionysian spirit and open sexual revolution did not change this perception. The old – classical – view is distinctly audible later on as well – for instance, in Joseph Brodsky's definition of love as 'the most elitist of passions. It acquires its stereoscopic substance and perspective only in the context of culture, for it takes up more space in the mind than it does in the bed'.[6] Andrei Platonov's vision of love clearly springs from the same root: 'Love is a measure of how much one is endowed with a gift of life. It is, despite conventional assumptions, least of all about sexuality'.[7] By the same token, Vladimir Solov'ev in his teaching on love, without dismissing its physical aspect, claims that it is, nevertheless, neither necessary nor sufficient for the authenticity of love. At the same time, the existing Anglophone scholarship of love in the case study of Russia has predominantly considered it from the gender perspective or sexuality angle rather than treating the concept of love as an indicator of cultural values in literary–philosophical terms.[8] This chapter intends to redress the balance, while making connection between a specifically Russian idea of love and the theme of Russian irrationalism.

The quintessence of Russian stereotypical model of love as stemming from love's tragic side and concealed in the inscrutable injustice of non-coincidence, non-meetings, unhappiness and impossibility – in all those negating prefixes resonant as they are with the suffering intrinsically present in human predicament, with the ideas of human finiteness against divine infinity and the abyss between reality and ideal – this quintessence is suitably captured in Olesia Nikolaeva's poetic formula of Russia's 'selfless Eros':

Russia is all the way through – parting and separation,
For its passion is unrequited and fatal,
And any arrow shot from a bow,
file-hard and curved, misses the target . . .[9]

---

[6] Brodsky, 'Nadezhda Mandelshtam (1899–1980): An Obituary', in *Less Than One. Selected Essays*, op. cit., p. 154.

[7] Andrei Platonov, 'Odnazhdy lubivshie', in *Kotlovan. Izbrannaia proza*, Moscow: Knizhnaia palata, 1988, p. 4.

[8] Such are, for instance, the studies by Laura Engelstein, Eric Naiman and Aleksandr Etkind, whose works, full of useful insights and valuable theories, still focus on love as stemming predominantly from sexual drive, rather than as a branch of original moral philosophy. At the same time, Anna Lisa Crone masterfully details the efforts of the Silver Age philosophers (Vladimir Solov'ev, Vasily Rozanov, Nikolai Berdyaev and Boris Vysheslavtsev) to establish the importance of the sex drive in human life and to reinterpret Christianity as a religion of the flesh as well as the spirit, while Valeria Sobol studies the cultural connection between love and illness, physical and emotional, literature and medicine – or more broadly, between scientific and cultural developments.

[9] Olesia Nikolaeva, 'Beskorystnyi eros', <http://magazines.russ.ru/novyI_mi/2006/1/nik3.html> [accessed 20 July 2013]. In Russian: 'Вся она, выходит, как бы сплошь – разлука, // ибо страсть ее – без отклика, роковая, // и стрела любая, пущенная из лука, // попадает мимо, каленая и кривая . . .'

Nikolai Berdiaev's verdict, of almost a century earlier, is even harsher: 'In Russian love there is something dark and torturous, unenlightened and often ugly.'[10] In the same category is also Viacheslav Ivanov's term of the 'Eros of the impossible', taken up by Aleksandr Etkind in his book of the same name. This is, notably, an extension of the basically Freudian idea of sublimation, that is to say, of the erotic which finds its applications in diverse areas of existence, not directly related to sexual activity or the concept of love as such. This squares well with the Russian phenomenon of mythological approach to love, most evident in the nineteenth-century Russian literary culture, when the erotic is simultaneously feared and castigated, on the one hand, and sanctified and spiritualized on the other. Hence Ivanov's term, coined for describing the spirit of the Russian Modernism of the pre-revolutionary years, which evidently encapsulated this very tendency – the agonizing contemplation inherited from Russian classical literature where Eros was a deeply problematic concept full of insoluble contradictions. Such highly strung, tormented attitudes, rooted in Russian religious beliefs, not just Christian Orthodox, but also pagan, were summarized by David Bethea in the following paradigmatic model of Eros-cum-national-myth. Extending the inversion of the pagan mythology as a way of its accommodation into the Russian version of Christianity, observed by Boris Uspensky, Bethea notices how the pagan concept of Mother Earth and the Christian concept of Holy Russia were 'made extensions of each other', and how this resulted in the development of a major literary plot involving the 'rescuing/redeeming of a heroine, who represents the country's vast potential, by a Christ-like paladin'.[11] In this Bethea traces the unified logic of the fairy-tale and Christian hierogamy, and concludes that 'the national Russian myth has, at its core, become profoundly eroticized and at the same time strangely sublimated/abstracted: personal love cannot have meaning outside this higher calling.'[12]

While the suggested unified plot is, in my view, in need of further qualifications, the conclusion is not. The higher calling of personal love in Russian letters is indeed its trademark. And the argument undermining Bethea's model is only partly due to the fact that in a great majority of Russian literary works, especially of the nineteenth century, the plot is actually reversed, so that it is not the hero, but the heroine herself who rescues or redeems her beloved, as did, most notably, Sonia Marmeladova to Raskolnikov in Dostoevsky's 'Crime and Punishment' (and the point that such a heroine indeed represents the country's vast potential only reinforces her strong position). Or perhaps, even more precisely and more subtly, a process of rescue or redemption, especially within the framework of love, just like a relation of possession, is mutual, it always cuts both ways. Hence, Tsvetaeva's 'Pod laskoi plushevogo pleda'[13] ('who was defeated?/in this battle of love/, who was the hunter and who was the prey?'), or Brodsky's 'Podsvechnik'[14]

[10]   Berdiaev, 'Mirosozertsanie Dostoevskogo' (chapter V: 'Liubov'), op. cit.
[11]   David Bethea, 'Literature', in Nicholas Rzhevsky (ed.), *The Cambridge Companion to Modern Russian Culture*, Cambridge: Cambridge University Press, 1998, pp. 172–3.
[12]   Ibid.
[13]   Marina Tsvetaeva, 'Pod laskoi pliushevogo pleda . . .' (1914), <http://slova.org.ru/cvetaeva/pod_laskoi_plushevogo_pleda/> [accessed 12 February 2014].
[14]   Joseph Brodsky, 'Podsvechnik' (1968), <http://music.lib.ru/k/kapustin_m_a/alb4.shtml> [accessed 12 February 2014].

(where the Satire clasps the candle-holder as the thing he possesses, and simultaneously to which he belongs, as part belongs to the whole). Also, as Chernyshevsky noticed in his famous 'Russkii chelovek na randevu', a Russian man in his relationship with a woman often behaves in a pathetic way (as is reflected by his literary projection – the 'superfluous man'), revealing what Berdiaev later referred to as 'eternal *baba*' in the Russian soul.[15] At the same time, a Russian woman, glorified among others by Nekrasov and through many of Turgenev's heroines, exemplifies strong 'manly' characteristics such as courage and heroic, self-sacrificial abilities. That is why it is almost stereotypical nowadays to speak of a 'superfluous man' and 'strong woman' in Russian literature (and this implicit gendered imbalance may also go some way to account psychologically for the enthusiasm with which the idea of androgyny – rooted in ancient Greek mythology as depicted in Plato's Symposium, and absorbed by various philosophies – was met by some Russian thinkers, including Vladimir Solov'ev, Viacheslav Ivanov, Zinaida Gippius and Nikolai Berdiaev, who drew it from Jakob Böhme).[16] Moreover, as indicated in Chapter 2, the image of Russia itself is often personified and feminised, and endowed – especially in the male-authored literature – with the features of a beloved female, be it mother or wife. Thus a lyrical heroine and Russia itself merge together and reinforce one another's rescuing and caring abilities, as if incorporating not only the pagan Earth, but also various variations of Solov'ev's Beautiful Lady.

However, more crucial, perhaps, than the role reversal as a modification to the model suggested by Bethea, is a consideration that it is love itself which is, metaphorically speaking, the main hero of Russian literature. Love, just like war, serves as a severe existential test, as litmus paper, which, by providing extreme conditions, lays bare the true personalities of all the agents and allows the writer to penetrate deep into their psyche, to explore in general, as it were anthropologically, the enigma of human soul. Love thus acquires a philosophical dimension and almost entirely loses meaning outside it.

That is why love is the main aspect of plot formation in many of Dostoevsky's works – because it provides a perfect existential laboratory for conducting his speculative experiments and often cruel probing into the nature of man. Love thus tests the characters to the utmost and more often than not it breaks them, it appears to be an insurmountable hurdle for their inner selves. Similarly for Tolstoy with all his merciless strivings for intellectual honesty in contemplations of morality, philosophy or religion,

---

[15] See Berdiaev, 'Concerning the "Eternal *Baba*" in the Russian Soul' (1915), <http://www.berdyaev. com/berdiaev/berd_lib/1915_187.html> [accessed 12 February 2014]; Writing about Vasilii Rozanov and his (then recent) book *The War of 1914 and the Russian Renaissance*, Berdiaev characterizes Rozanov as endowed with this frustrating feature of being 'eternal *baba*' which, in Berdiaev's view, is so typically and unfortunately Russian. It is 'the *baba* and the slave, the national-pagan, the pre-Christian'; 'primordial biology experienced as mysticism'; an absence of 'resistance of the spirit in regards to the soul and the processes of life'; 'the raw cheese of his soul' without any logos; and so on., <http://www.vehi.net/berdyaev/rozanov.html> [accessed 12 February 2014].

[16] See, for instance, N. Berdiaev, 'Razmyshlenie ob Erose', in V. Shestakov (ed.), op. cit., p. 271, or 'Tainye sily liubvi' (*Filosofiia liubvi. Sbornik, part 2*, Moscow, 1990), <http://www.aquarun.ru/psih/ psex/ps5.html> [accessed 12 February 2014]; V. Solov'ev, 'Smysl liubvi' and Z. Gippius, 'O liubvi', in V. Shestakov (ed.), op. cit., pp. 40–1 and pp. 192–3, respectively. See also Viacheslav Ivanov, 'Ty iesi', in *Sobranie sochinenii v 4 tomakh*, Bruxels, 1979, vol. 3, pp. 262–8.

and with all his exposure of the modern society's horror and hypocrisy, love ultimately reveals its existential rather than social roots, and the characters, trapped as they are within social strictures, are at the end of the day much more seriously trapped within themselves, failing to deal above all with their own nature than with the externally imposed boundaries. 'Anna Karenina' perhaps illustrates this best.

Thus love itself has a transforming effect on the protagonists – either redeeming (even if fleetingly, like with Karenin at Anna's bedside) or demonic. This has a parallel in Fazil Iskander's metaphor of the first love which occurs to people before they are psychologically mature and ready for it, and has the effect akin to that of a person taken to the shore of a stormy sea – either one will drown, or one will learn to swim.[17] This image need not in fact be restricted to the first love only, it clearly is applicable to love more generally. Such a role of love in Russian letters as, above all, a dramatic, often fatal, existential test which opens up to truly philosophical and anthropological discoveries squares well with Yurii Lotman's contemplation on the nineteenth-century Russian novel. An archetype of a Western-European novel at the time was modelled on a fairy-tale of the 'Cinderella' kind, Lotman observes.[18] More precisely, 'it involved a change in hero's position in life rather than a change of that life itself or of the hero himself'.[19] By contrast, a Russian novel, Lotman argues, 'was oriented at a myth rather than a fairy-tale'.[20] Thus its time is cyclic and therefore the concept of the end of text loses significance. But more importantly, 'Russian novel poses a problem not of a change of the hero's position, but of a transformation of his inner essence, or of a remaking of the surrounding life, or both'.[21]

In this context, love is a force which almost invariably facilitates an inner transformation of the hero and can even lead to a transformation in the surrounding life (certainly in terms of the changes in the outlook, perceptions and behaviour of those involved, as, for example, in Tolstoy's 'Resurrection' and Dostoevsky's 'Crime and Punishment', Kuprin's 'Granatovyi braslet' and Chekhov's 'Dama s sobachkoi', Gorenshtein's 'Iskuplenie' and Iskander's 'Stoianka cheloveka', to name but a few) – as part of that higher calling of personal love in Russian literary culture, as mentioned earlier. In these terms the eros-cum-national myth at the same time reiterates, from a literary perspective, the anthropocentric ideas of Russian philosophical thought (where 'Human being is more important than any "business". Human being is himself the only "business"').[22] Indeed, recall again Vasilii Zenkovsky's words of the mystical realism inherent in Russian religiosity: both spheres of existence – empirical and mystical – are

---

[17] Fazil Iskander, 'Chelovek i ego okrestnosti', <http://lib.rus.ec/b/132545/read#t5> [accessed 24 April 2013].

[18] Lotman, 'Siuzhetnoe prostranstvo russkogo romana XIX stoletiia', op. cit., p. 97.

[19] Ibid.

[20] Ibid.

[21] Ibid., p. 98.

[22] This is a quotation from Berdiaev reflecting on Dostoevsky's oeuvre, where, as Berdiaev explains, protagonists' only preoccupation is concerned with their inner lives, with human relationships, with getting to the bottom of an individual soul; and no other preoccupation can equal this one in importance. See Nikolai Berdiaev, 'Mirosozertsanie Dostoevskogo', op. cit. This interpretation, of course, squares up with Dostoevsky's own (famous) words that 'man is a mystery: if you spend your

real, but hierarchically non-equivalent; empirical existence is sustained only because of its involvement into the mystical reality, and everything in the empirical world must be enlightened through its connectedness to the mystical sphere, through a transforming act of the Divine force.[23]

The same phenomenon is described by Tatiana Chumakova in her study of ancient Russian culture: 'since for the whole of the Byzantine macro-region it was typical, "in contrast to the West, [. . .] not a separation of two levels of consciousness that characterised the medieval dichotomy of the 'earthly world' and 'heavenly world', but on the contrary – their rapprochement",[24] a sacralisation of the everyday phenomena, including, of course, physical love, was quite natural. Physical love had to be sanctified by the church marriage, and was unthinkable outside the family. [. . .] For the ancient Russian culture it was characteristic not to deny the world of physicality, but to consecrate it. Therefore, despite a critical attitude to the phenomena of the sensual sphere, it was not regarded as a creation of evil, and earthly love was not an antagonist of heavenly love; flashes of divine fire shimmered through it.'[25]

However, by the time of blossoming of Russian literary culture in the nineteenth century, a tormenting attitude to sexual aspect of love prevailed, and, in essence, drastically opposed body and soul (what Berdiaev was to call a 'vulgar duality' and 'not only moral, but also metaphysical mistake').[26] Despite Pushkin's masterful ease in handling these intimate issues, despite his seemingly effortless adjustment to the Russian soil of Western patterns (which, in fact, in contrast to the Russian one, allowed the treatment of Eros as a mere source of pleasure and procreation), this line, combining irony, wisdom and ease with respect to such a delicate and palpitating theme, was essentially discontinued. The subsequent development of the theme of love, of relationship between sexes, was marked in Russian literature by what might appear in Western eyes as mere repression. As Bethea justly observes, 'the fear was not so much sin, as in the Catholic and Protestant West, but cosmic indifference, meaninglessness.'[27]

Moreover, a suggestion, offered by Freud's teaching, of an all-pervasive sexual underpinning of the human world, was met by severe resistance in Russian letters, with the classical tradition still alive in the veins of the new – Modernist – blood, no longer restrained by repression. While in the West a psycho-analytical Freudian approach rapidly gained popularity and made its way into literary studies, 'in Russia – although it has always been very susceptible to all the branches of Western philosophy – Freudian teaching [. . .] which placed human biological needs above social ones [. . .],

entire life trying to puzzle it out, then do not say that you have wasted your time' (from the letter to his brother Mikhail of 16.08.1839).

[23] Zenkovsky, op. cit., vol. 1, p. 45.

[24] Kseniia Khvostova, 'Sakralnyi smysl naimenovaniia nekotorykh vizantiiiskikh sotsialno-ekonomicheskikh institutov. K voprosu o roli bogosloviia v formirovanii sotsialno-ekonomicheskikh institutov Vizantii', in *Vizantiiskii vremennik*, vol. 59 (84). Moscow, 2000, p. 25.

[25] Tatiana Chumakova, 'Lubov kak etiko-antropologicheskaia kategoriia', in *Religiia i nravstvennost v sekuliarnom mire. Volume of Conference Proceedings.* St Petersburg: St Petersburg Philosophical Society, 2001, pp. 236, 239.

[26] Nikolai Berdiaev, 'Metafizika pola i lubvi', in V. Shestakov (ed.), op. cit., p. 236.

[27] Bethea, op. cit., p. 174.

did not gain popularity.'[28] For instance, for Lev Shestov, who was arguably a forerunner of a psycho-analytical approach to literature, any literary creation was, as it were, a self-narrative and self-myth which required a hermeneutic decoding. In doing this deciphering, Shestov was interested predominantly in the authorial 'philosophical psycho-biography' of sorts, in the writer's way of inner development, read off his fiction. This is what mattered in Shestov's literary–philosophical analysis, whereas a sexual dimension was not an issue.[29]

Boris Vysheslavtsev, another Russian thinker of the Silver Age, objected to Freudian teaching in theoretical terms. In his book 'Etika preobrazhennogo Erosa', Vysheslavtsev argues that Freud's gravest error is in trying to explain the highest human faculties and abilities (the spiritual sphere) via the lowest ones (instincts), and furthermore, that the profound irrationalism of human nature is not amenable to the rationalist and naturalist means suggested by Freudian theory.[30] Calling this 'descending' theory a 'profanation', Vysheslavtsev writes with disdain that for Freud 'in essence, as for any naturalism and materialism, everything "lofty" and sublime is an *illusion* (a superstructure over the sexual foundation); religion, and love for the Almighty, are also just an *illusion* and a sophisticated form of sexuality ("Diezukunfteiner Illusion"). Then what is not an *illusion*? It is sexual drive and its normal fulfilment. This is, basically, in a nutshell, all the therapeutics and all the "morality" of Freud.'[31] Thus, he concludes, for Freud, with his essential denial of the sublime sphere, sublimation is simply not possible. He argues that a proper sublimation is in fact in raising (ἀναγωγή) of the low to the high, thus creating a qualitatively new level of being. However, to understand this, one has to have a hierarchical system of values and of existential categories, so familiar to Christian ascetics or to ancient Greek philosophers, but of which 'Freud and his school have no idea.'[32] Of similarly negative opinion is Vysheslavtsev's fellow-philosopher Semen Frank, who talks of the 'sexual materialism' and 'cynical outlook' of Freudean conceptions.[33] In his words, 'psychoanalysis in philosophical terms proved unable to cope with the trove of the concealed spiritual life which it itself discovered. The platitude of its rationalistic and naturalistic concerns is inadequate to the depth and irrationality of the spiritual material that it exposed.'[34] Interestingly, Berdiaev too in essence repeats Vysheslavtsev's premise above when he writes that although erotic love is rooted in sex and gender, it nevertheless 'transcends the sexual, it brings in a new element and redemption of the sexual.'[35]

[28] Shestakov, op. cit., p. 7.
[29] Of course, Shestov's silence over it can be itself semantically loaded (see, for instance, Olga Tabachnikova, 'Between Tragedy and Aesthetics: Shestov's Reading of Chekhov – A Look Directed Within', in Olga Tabachnikova (ed.), *Anton Chekhov through the eyes of Russian thinkers: Vasilii Rozanov, Dmitrii Merezhkovskii and Lev Shestov*, op. cit., pp. 175–97); still, the principle of not exalting the sexual remains.
[30] See Boris Vysheslavtsev, *Etika preobrazhennogo Erosa*, chapter 7 'Soprotivlenie proizvola i sublimatsiia svobody' ('Resistance of self-will and sublimation of freedom'), YMCA-Press: Paris, 1931, pp. 186–90.
[31] Ibid., p. 189.
[32] Ibid., pp. 189–90.
[33] Semen Frank, 'Psikhoanaliz kak mirosozertsanie', *Put*, No. 25, December 1930.
[34] Ibid.
[35] Berdiaev, 'Razmyshlenie ob Erose', in V. Shestakov (ed.), op. cit., p. 267.

More generally, it was also in the Silver Age when a process of theoretical conceptualization of love, of elaborating philosophically on relationships between sexes first emerged in Russian culture, following, in turn, the break-through made by Vladimir Solov'ev, whose philosophy – in particular his work 'Smysl liubvi' – crowned the development of this theme by classical Russian literature and thought of the nineteenth century. As Viacheslav Shestakov rightly notes, it is surprising that it is only in the early twentieth century that the theme of love transgressed the borders of artistic genres and spilled over into the journalistic and philosophical discourse.[36] Equally surprising is the fact that, despite a clear tendency towards synthesis generally inherent in the Silver Age, there were two distinguished trends in the Russian development of philosophy of love, which did not merge.[37] These trends can be described as branching, respectively, from Vladimir Solov'ev and from Pavel Florensky. The former camp included such Russian thinkers as Lev Karsavin, Boris Vysheslavtsev and Nikolai Berdiaev, whose theories were based on the humanist ideas derived from antiquity, and developed a neo-Platonic concept of love-Eros. The other camp, to which, among others, Sergei Bulgakov and Ivan Il'in belonged, built on the Christian concept of caritas (love as pity, mercy and compassion). Solov'ev's followers attempted 'to enlighten and elevate human sensuality, to protect individual, personal love, denying ascetics and establishing a connection between Eros and creativity',[38] while Florensky's adherents, who represented an orthodox–theological line, were drawing 'on the ideas of Christian ethics pertaining to family and marriage'.[39]

Interestingly, both camps, while being in acute polemics with one another, were closely connected in their ponderings to Russian literary culture and commented at length on the treatment of love by Russian classics, most notably Dostoevsky and Tolstoy. By the same token, they all displayed a certain continuity of the classical line, above all in their acknowledgement of not only love's joys and delights, but also, and predominantly, of its intrinsically tragic nature. Thus Sergei Bulgakov saw the dark side of love in its sexual dimension which results in the overall disharmony of love relationship. He claimed that our love life has on it 'a stamp of a tragic hopelessness and antinomical pain'.[40] More profoundly, Bulgakov, in his polemics with the Solov'ev's 'school', insisted on the ineradicable nature of evil and therefore on the ideas of suffering, compassion and patience as the only possible form of Christian love.[41] Equally, Berdiaev, although representing an opposite camp, saw Eros not only as potentially creative and pertaining to beauty,[42] but also as intrinsically cruel, which thus has to be

---

[36] Shestakov (ed.), Introduction to *Russkii eros, ili Filosofiia lubvi v Rossii*, op. cit., pp. 5–7.
[37] Ibid., p. 17.
[38] Shestakov, op. cit., p. 14.
[39] Ibid.
[40] Sergei Bulgakov, *Svet nevechernii*, Section III.2: 'Pol v cheloveke', <http://www.vehi.net/bulgakov/svet/003.html> [accessed 18 December 2013].
[41] See Shestakov, op. cit., p. 16.
[42] See for these ideas Berdiaev's 'Smysl tvorchestva', <http://www.vehi.net/berdyaev/tvorch/> [accessed 18 December 2013].

tamed by compassion, to avoid otherwise 'tormenting and destructive' results.[43] Even Solov'ev, whose teaching is optimistic and enlightened at the core, for he sees love in the Platonic light as an action of two Aphrodites, earthly and heavenly, where the Divine image eventually triumphs and elucidates human life with outbursts of incomparable happiness; even he saw love in an essentially utopian, and thus ultimately tragic light – as a total eradication of selfishness, a justification and resurrection of individuality through a sacrifice of egoism.

Examples of such sacrifice are indeed present in the world literature in general, and Russian literature in particular, but rather as unequalled and rare exceptions. This rarity is not surprising, as 'true love is a rare flower',[44] in Berdiaev's words. These rare examples, as was mentioned earlier, seem to be unrestrained from within in the stories of Romeo and Juliette, and others of the kind. However, in Russian letters they are almost invariably undermined – either by the unrequited nature of such profound and sacrificial love (as, for instance, in Kuprin's novella 'Granatovyi braslet' or in the late twentieth-century screen-play 'Fantazii Fariatieva'[45]), or, more generally, by the sobering up truth expressed in Akhmatova's verses of the limits to human kinship, and thus of the ultimate solitude of the individual: 'There is a sacred boundary between those who are close, // And it cannot be crossed by passion or love . . .'.[46] The restricted nature of human companionship implies that a total transcendence of the 'I' on its way to the beloved Other is never possible completely. Lev Shestov speaks of the same existential solitude, 'that horrible loneliness from which not even the most devoted and loving heart is able to deliver you'.[47] For him, it is depicted by Tolstoy in the 'Death of Ivan Iliich' and 'Master and Man': 'that kind of solitude which is more total than that at the bottom of the sea or under the ground'.[48]

In love such a lament over the ineradicable separating line between people is only possible precisely as a result of the extreme striving to the outmost, to a total union of the two Platonic halves. A notion of privacy, so deeply respected in Western European culture, gravitating towards individualism, is absent from the Russian language, surely because it has been absent from Russian mentality. In contrast to the treasured and in a sense sacred personal bubble there is present a dream of an absolute fusion of the two beloved. The impossibility of such a totality – in love and in life more generally – and the perpetual craving of it might be responsible for the typical Russian *nadryv* (that appears particularly irrational to the Western eyes) – a painful and passionate agitation of an almost unnatural strength – present in a vast majority of Russian literary works, especially those concerned with love.

---

[43]   Berdiaev, *Samopoznanie*, Paris, 1949, p. 87.

[44]   Berdiaev, 'Razmyshleniia ob Erose', in V. Shestakov (ed.), op. cit., p. 267.

[45]   This work was mentioned in the previous chapter. Fariatiev is an idealist dreamer, who gives himself completely to his love, and although it is unrequited, the higher, almost religious, truth behind his feelings casts its light on the world around him.

[46]   Anna Akhmatova, 'There is a sacred boundary between those who are close . . .', in *The Complete Poems of Anna Akhmatova*, Expanded Edition, transl. by Judith Hemschemeyer, op. cit., p. 181. In Russian: 'Есть в близости людей заветная черта, Её не перейти влюбленности и страсти . . .'.

[47]   Shestov, 'Dostoevsky i Nitzshe', op. cit., p. 369.

[48]   Ibid.

It is, undoubtedly, Dostoevsky who tops the list. Love in his novels is tragic and obsessive, it is, as Berdiaev observed, of a Dionysian, volcanic nature. 'All Dostoevsky's oeuvre is saturated with burning and passionate love', he writes, and adds that the novelist 'opens in the Russian elements a passionate and lustful aspect, [. . .] not to be found in the works of any other Russian writer'.[49] Georgii Gachev, however, extends this quality to Russian Eros in general, even though he exemplifies his point still using Dostoevsky's works. But lust here, as Gachev explains, is – crucially – of a very different nature than in Western literature; sex as such means little – this is instead, an art, developed like in no other culture, 'of loving and copulating verbally' ('via a Word').[50] A spiritual investigation constitutes a real love game in Russian letters, Gachev asserts. He views love depicted by Dostoevsky as a battle of egos, of vanities, as a game of power, spiritual enslavement and psychological manipulation. 'Love here is a mutual torment, a suffering which causes enjoyment.'[51] Gachev sums it up in a laconic formula: 'there is no bodily lust, but there is instead a lust of spirit.'[52] Thus he implicitly describes a peculiar (in a certain sense even sadomasochistic – but in spiritual rather than sensual terms!) attitude where 'above lust there lies a tormented happiness'.[53] At the same time, Gachev emphasizes that in the Russian love context 'tenderness is more precious than passion'[54] and recalls the concepts of pity and compassion (already discussed earlier within the philosophical frame), which were synonymous of love in Russian language, and to say 'I love you' used to be identical to saying 'I pity you.' However, as Berdiaev observes, in Dostoevsky's novels there is a dichotomy of compassion and desire, and the writer does not know the 'mystery of two souls merging into one and two bodies becoming one', and therefore love of his heroes is destined to destruction.[55] 'Men and women remain tragically separated and torment each other.'[56] Moreover, 'Man experiences female nature only as a theme of his own duality'[57] and is unable to break away from it; 'male nature remains separated from female nature.'[58]

Interestingly, an echo of the same somewhat sadomasochistic relationships based on the spiritual rather than sensuality-centred battles can be found in the works of another Russian classic, aesthetically and temperamentally very different to Dostoevsky – namely, in Turgenev. A perception of love as an irrational fatality, as tragedy, obsession, illness (and profusely autobiographical at that) is acutely present in Turgenev's writings, and the hero of the 'Correspondence' states unambiguously, 'Love, indeed, is not a feeling at all, it's a malady, a certain condition of soul and body. It does not develop gradually. One cannot doubt about it, one cannot outwit it, though it does not always come in the same way. Usually it takes possession of a person without

---

[49]   N. Berdiaev, 'Lubov'u Dostoevskogo', in V. Shestakov (ed.), *Russkii Eros*, op. cit., pp. 273–4.
[50]   Georgii Gachev, 'Russkii Eros. "Roman" mysli s zhizn'iu', 1994, pp. 21–3.
[51]   Ibid.
[52]   Ibid.
[53]   Ibid.
[54]   Ibid.
[55]   Berdiaev, 'Lubov u Dostoevskogo', op. cit., p. 277.
[56]   Ibid.
[57]   Ibid., p. 275.
[58]   Ibid., p. 278.

question, suddenly, against his will – for all the world like cholera or fever . . . It clutches him, poor dear, as the hawk pounces on the chicken, and bears him off at its will, however he struggles or resists . . . In love, there's no equality, none of the so-called free union of souls, and such idealisms, concocted at their leisure by German professors . . . No, in love, one person is slave, and the other master; and well may the poets talk of the fetters put on by love. Yes, love is a fetter, and the heaviest to bear. At least I have come to this conviction, and have come to it by the path of experience; I have bought this conviction at the cost of my life, since I am dying in my slavery.'[59]

Margarita Odesskaia, notably, stresses the parallel drawn at the time between Turgenev and Zacher-Masoch in their depiction of master–slave relationship, in the perverted pleasure of cruelty, and traces the roots of it to Turgenev's upbringing that unfolded in the atmosphere of Russian serfdom, with his mother being a cruel and psychopathic landowner.[60] The American scholar Michael Finke, in conjunction with physical cruelty of Russian social arrangements on the part of the landowners as well as within the peasant community, talks also of a mental slavery and abuse as a Western way of perceiving Russian life[61] (as was briefly mentioned in Chapter 2). It is also noteworthy in the same context that Turgenev depicts two types of women in his works – good and bad: noble-spirited and compassionate on the one hand, and rotten at the core by egotistic passions on the other – and his male heroes often find themselves mentally split, torn between the two, or perhaps more precisely lured by the evil one away from the virtuous. Odesskaia refers to these two female types as 'light-aesthetic' and 'darkly instinctive', and notes that 'women [. . .] destroyers [. . .] possess a hidden, irrational power which knocks the weak male characters from their path. A woman who carries the light, Apollonian principle is the ideal, she embodies the trinity of *truth, good and beauty*, and resembles a classical statue. At the end of the novel, Turgenev tries to return to the Apollonian spirit some of his heroes who have been driven from the path and ended up in a whirlpool of passions. His characters seek forgiveness and make peace with their women-ideals. Before his death, Aleksei Petrovich explains his behaviour to Maria Aleksandrovna; Litvinov returns to Tat′iana; and Sanin tries to find Gemma and writes her a repentant letter.'[62] (Notably, these idyllic attempts of Turgenev were met with scepticism by some critics.[63]) Such inner split, a confused and painful dialectics of male consciousness, resonates with (although is not identical to) the duality of Dostoevsky's heroes, mentioned earlier. In Berdiaev's words, this 'splitting in halves, dual love', love-passion and love-pity 'is not a transcendence

[59] Ivan Turgenev, 'A Correspondence', <http://www.online-literature.com/turgenev/2702/> [accessed 21 August 2014].

[60] See Margarita Odesskaia, 'The Concept of Love and Beauty in the Works of Turgenev', in Olga Tabachnikova (ed.), *Mystery inside Enigma: Facets of Russian Irrationalism between Art and Life*, op. cit.

[61] See, Michael S. Finke, 'Sacher-Masoch, Turgenev, and Other Russians', in Michael Finke and Carl Niekerk (eds), *One Hundred Years of Masochism: Literary Texts, Social and Cultural Contexts*, Amsterdam: Rodopi, 2000, pp. 120–1. Discussed in Odesskaia, op. cit.

[62] Odesskaia, op. cit.

[63] For example, Lev Shestov found them artificial and not trustworthy, and ascribed such tendency of Turgenev to his European convictions. See Lev Shestov, *Turgenev*, op. cit., p. 199.

of one's own "I", is not turning towards the Other and uniting with the Other'; it is instead a process of 'setting scores with one's own self, one's own, closed, destiny'.[64] Thus, as a counterweight to Solov'ev's theory, rather utopian in its moral beauty, the Russian classics, who came before him, offered – like a fascinating textbook of human anthropology – multiple depictions of a ruthless battle and the ultimate defeat of one's own ego to transgress its borders, to overcome itself on its way to the Other.

Resonant with the earlier sentiments of spiritual battle and tormenting passion, but devoid of Dostoevskyan claustrophobic soreness – a dry flame as opposed to the volcanic lava is a shrewd analysis of love in the Russian context provided by Tiutchev's poetry, especially by his immortal poetic formulas: 'Oh, how murderously do we love, How in a tempestuous blindness of passions, We destroy most surely that which is dearest to our heart . . .' and 'Love, love – as legend has it – a union of a soul with another, kindred, soul – their merging together, their combining, and their fatal unification, and . . . their fatal battle'.[65] Once again, rather than focusing on the delights of love or re-creating a romantic cult of female beauty, it emphasizes love's tragic dialectics – as a fatal wrestling of two beings, of two wills, in their striving to a total fusion and the impossibility of it, as a burning and unruly passion driven by irrational forces.

Notably, Tiutchev is talking exclusively of a union of two souls, and neither the body, nor even the mind is mentioned, even if it might be implied. This is not surprising, given the genre and the times, and does not as such indicate a tendency to exalt the spiritual and to disregard the physical, sexual aspect of love. However, he is the poet of brutal honesty, and lust is present in his poetry – he recognizes its power and, notably, its charm! – yet, the description of a sexual desire itself, perhaps even against the poet's intentions and contradictory to the semantics and aesthetics of charm, has a clear negative (almost repulsive in its animal one dimensionality) ring to it: 'gloomy and dim flame of desire'.[66]

Furthermore, Gachev, in his analysis of Dostoevsky's *femme fatale* heroine Nastasya Filippovna, insists on her hatred towards sensuality and on her lustfulness being concentrated in refusal and rejection: 'sex in her is mutilated and trampled from the outset, and sensuality is hateful. And it just seems that she is the victim. For her, given her type of personality, this is precisely what she wants. That is to say, that her ultimate sensuality is not copulation, but breaking apart: walking at the edge of the abyss of sex, inflaming everybody, but not letting herself be sucked into it. In other words, this is an outrage of Russian wind, of Russian spiritual Eros upon the fiery-wet ground of sex. That is why instead of bodily embraces, hurlings, turnings over, passionate poses there is a pandemonium of spiritual passions.'[67]

The other side of the same coin is to be found in the passionate exclamation (which caused a roar of laughter and immediately became immortal) of a fiercely patriotic

---

64. Berdiaev, 'Lubov u Dostoevskogo', op. cit., p. 277.
65. Fedor Tiutchev, 'O kak ubiistvenno my liubim . . .' (1851) and 'Predopredelen'e' (1854). See <http://rupoem.ru/tyutchev/all.aspx#o-kak-ubijstvenno> and <http://rupoem.ru/tyutchev/all.aspx#lyubov-lyubov-glasit> [accessed 14 February 2014].
66. F. I. Tiutchev, 'Liubliu glaza tvoi, moi drug . . .' (1836) <http://rupoem.ru/tyutchev/all.aspx#lyublyu-glaza-tvoi> [accessed 10 January 2014].
67. Gachev, op. cit., p. 22.

Russian woman during one of the first TV bridges between Russia and the West, soon after the fall of the iron curtain: 'In the USSR there is no sex!'[68] Despite the obvious explanation, this, in my view, reflects not so much a Bolshevik-style sanctimony and hypocrisy, as a fiery continuation of and insistence on the classical Russian tradition with its exaltation of the spiritual at the expense of the physical. It is, if you like, worship to the same gods. Sex is trampled and on its bones a spirit, separated from the body, is dancing a rather demonic dance. As Tolstoy, a champion of this hatred towards the physical aspect of love, a continuous wrestler with it, said to Gorky, 'the most tormenting tragedy of man is forever a tragedy of the bedroom',[69] and 'be afraid not of the woman who holds you by your penis, but be afraid of the one who holds you by your soul'.[70]

The problem with a sexual aspect of love, that Tolstoy – himself acutely tormented by it – depicted with such brilliancy and passion, was not born in Victorian times and did not stop with them. For example, Marchionites and Manicheans despised an act of copulation and saw it as a creation by a malicious demiurge. For the nineteenth-century Russian writers an abyss opening up in the physical act, its emptiness and darkness, the burned lands beyond it were simply unbearable. Its otherworldly nature, brutal, degrading, animal-like, was hardly compatible with the Divine image and likeness, just as later on, as we saw, Freudean theories in the eyes of Russian thinkers seemed insulting to the loftiness and grandeur of human spirit. Various forms of denial of sex evolved, including the ascetic monks and such sects as castratees (*skoptsy*) and *khlysty*, taking shape in the seventeenth and eighteenth centuries and incorporating uniquely Russian motives into the universal ones. As Panchenko writes, 'obviously, castration motifs were, in one way or another, incorporated into the system of ascetic practices of the Christian Middle Ages', and yet, 'the teaching of mass castration for religious reasons is, for the European tradition, a very rare, if not unique, event. [. . .] analysis of castration metaphors and symbols of the literature of *skoptsy* demonstrates that myphologisation of emasculation combines and associates, in a complex way, the images traditional for peasant culture with eschatological and apocalyptic themes.'[71]

The Silver Age, in conjunction to its wild, newly found sexual freedom, saw a rise in the opposite tendency as well – several famous marital unions, including Berdiaev's, were formed without consummation, for ideological reasons. In the typical Russian manner, as described by Gachev, 'ethical passions exceeded erotic passions'[72] in Berdiaev, and his own vision of the physical act of love is most instructive: 'A fleeting phantom of being united by a sexual act is always accompanied by a reaction, a backward motion,

---

[68]   It happened in 1986 during a TV bridge USSR–USA, organized by the journalists Vladimir Pozner and Phil Donahue. The phrase is attributed to Ludmila Ivanova, a representative of the 'Committee of Soviet Women'. Allegedly Ivanova was answering a question from the American audiences about sex in the commercials (non-existent in Russia at the time) and added that instead of sex there is love. However, the phrase became wide-spread in the above form, epitomizing the sanctimony and pharisaism of the Soviet ideology, as mentioned earlier.

[69]   Maksim Gorky, *Sobranie sochinenii*, Moscow, Leningrad, 1933, vol. XXII, p. 55.

[70]   Ibid.

[71]   Aleksandr Panchenko, 'Antiseksualnost v russkoi narodnoi culture: ideologiia i mifologiia skopchestva', <http://ec-dejavu.ru/s/Skopcy.html> [accessed 30 January 2014].

[72]   Berdiaev, 'Razmyshlenie ob Erose', in V. Shestakov (ed.), op. cit., p. 266.

breaking apart. After a sexual act, a feeling of disunity is stronger than before it. A painful alienation so often afflicts those who awaited the ecstasy of copulation, of being united';[73] and generally, 'there is something degrading for a human being in sexual life' and 'something ugly' in the sexual act.[74] In the same vein, Akhmatova's poetic lines quoted earlier are often interpreted as a warning against the emptiness which ensues after the sacred line between two people has been crossed, meaning that love was thus desecrated, violated by a sexual intervention. This feeling of a loss of something elusive, but crucial, of some primordial purity and holiness of love, the loss that comes after a sexual intercourse, is captured best, in a poignant, piercing way, in the poem by Yurii Dombrovsky, half a century on after the Silver Age. This poem is so important for understanding this anti-sexual stance, which persists through Russian letters, that we shall quote here its substantial part:

> . . . What fool, what drunken smith,
> What ugly clown from some dark alley,
> Invented this pump and plug,
> Like the piston action of hearts?!
> My flower! My swan-like beauty!
> The light of unfurled wings,
> Me and you once flew there,
> Where even the stars do not shine!
> But the double-bed appeared
> And we suffocated together in one tomb . . .
> [. . .]
> Stupid triumph has ended!
> A pig looks at the sky, frowning.
> Well, having lost your likeness to God,
> Get up, go to some racy anecdote,
> Some cheery French picture.
> My God is severe, and the torture is never-ending,
> The falling of the angels, thrown down from their heights.
> But now fear nothing:
> Live, grow plumper and prettier from happiness.
> Such is the end – all people on the day of communion
> Always devour their God.[75]

---

[73] Berdiaev, *Filosofiia lubvi. Sbornik*, vol. 2, Moscow, 1990. See <http://www.aquarun.ru/psih/psex/ps5.html> [accessed 28 January 2014].

[74] Berdiaev, 'Razmyshlenie ob Erose', in V. Shestakov (ed.), op. cit., p. 266.

[75] Yurii Dombrovsky, 'Rekviem', <http://gondolier.ru/073/73dombr_1.html> [accessed 30 January 2014]. In Russian: '. . . Какой дурак, какой хмельной кузнец, // Урод и шут с кривого переулка // Изобрели насос и эту втулку – // Как поршневое действие сердец?! // Моя краса! Моя лебяжья стать! // Свечение распахнутых надкрылий, // Ведь мы с тобой могли туда взлетать, // Куда и звезды даже не светили! // Но подошла двуспальная кровать – // И задохнулись мы в одной

Venedict Erofeev, Dombrovsky's contemporary, translates the sorrowful truth into his own self-ironic discourse, repeating in Russian, 'Omnia animalia post coitum opressus est' ('every creature after a copulation becomes sad').[76] Equally striking is the 'erotic-philosophical' novel-contemplation 'Chok–Chok' by Fridrikh Gorenshtein, which, through tracing a life story of its protagonist, reveals among other discoveries, the incredibly small (in terms of the number of its addressees) capacity for love of a human soul – as opposed to a human body; virtually a uniqueness of love in human life (and, instructively, here, in this particular novel, once again a flow of a perfect love is ruined by the intrusion of sexual attempts). This uniqueness is epitomized in the classical Russian romance 'Tol'ko raz byvaet v zhizni vstrecha . . .'[77] which has had a sequence of 'ideological follow-ups' in diverse genres (from the implicit 'Kto sgorel, togo ne podozzesh . . .'[78] to the unambiguous 'Vesnu lubvi odin raz zhdut . . .',[79] and 'I tu, kotoraja odna, nedolubil . . .'[80] or 'Ty u menia odna . . .'[81] and so on).

Thus the love agonies of the classical Russian literature – most notably of its pillars: Tolstoy and Dostoevsky – permeated by the irrational torment of a self-reflective consciousness, by the 'verbal' rather than physical lust, a battle of wills and egos, were marked by the persistent and uneasy wrestling of human spirit and human body, of physical and spiritual, by the resistance that mind, in its search for the sublime beauty and divine image, tried to put up against enslaving and abasing sensuality. However, the situation has changed in more than one way with the coming of Modernism. Not only because of Vladimir Solov'ev's highly influential Neo-platonic theories leading to the enlightening of the dark Russian Eros (recall Berdiaev's labelling Russian love dark and 'non-enlightened'), but also because of the times per se, of the loosening of cultural taboos and weakening of Victorian Puritanism.

This made possible emergence of such unique (in the Russian context) thinkers as Vasilii Rozanov with his exaltation of the sexual. Recognizing Rozanov's daring spirit in his exposure of the contradictions within Christian doctrine that encouraged procreation and family, but at the same time condemned sex, his Russian fellow-thinkers disagreed with Rozanov's implicit neglect of the personal, individual kernel of love at the expense of the gender, of the generally sexual. Indeed, he placed the question of sex and gender at the centre of existence, as the main human question underpinning

---

могиле . . . // [. . .] Окончено тупое торжество! // Свинья на небо смотрит исподлобья. // Что ж, с Богом утерявшее подобье, // Бескрылое, слепое существо, // Вставай, иди в скабрезный анекдот, // Веселая французская открытка. // Мой Бог суров, и бесконечна пытка – // Лет ангелов, низверженных с высот! // Зато теперь не бойся ничего: // Живи, полней и хорошей от счастья. // Таков конец – все люди в день причастья // Всегда сжирают Бога своего'.

[76] See Venedikt Erofeev, 'Vasilii Rozanov glazami ekstsentrika', in *Ostavte moiu dushu v pokoe*, Moscow: Kh.G.S., 1995, pp. 150–1.

[77] 'Tol'ko raz byvaet v zhizni vstrecha . . .', lyrics by P. German, music by B. Fomin.

[78] Sergei Esenin, 'Ty menia ne liubish, ne zhaleesh' (1925), <http://feb-web.ru/feb/esenin/texts/e74/e74-238-.htm> [accessed 30 January 2014].

[79] A popular song of 1976, performed by Anna German, 'Kogda tsveli sady', lyrics by M. Riabinin, music by V. Shainsky.

[80] Vladimir Vysotsky, 'Kto-to vysmotrel plod . . .' (1973), <http://otblesk.com/vysotsky/-kto-to.htm> [accessed 30 January 2014].

[81] Yurii Vizbor, 'Ty u menia odna . . .' (1964), <http://music.lib.ru/k/kulikow_s_k/alb26.shtml> [accessed 30 January 2014].

all religions and situated far above any other human concerns, such as social, political, economic, judicial and so on. In Rozanov's view, human being, as a union of physical and spiritual, is linked to Logos not via the universal reason but via the sphere of sexual love. Rozanov thus incurred accusations of erotic madness, although it is also possible to view his theories as passionate attempts to raise the carnal, the physical to the level of the spiritual – as if to sanctify the life of the body.

While Rozanov, with his – as seen by many – sexual folly, remained to a large extent a white craw in Russian thought, Chekhov and Bunin were much more exponents of the Modernist spirit with regards to moral norms and major changes in the cultural paradigm. They, as it were, attempted to redress the balance by re-uniting body and spirit into one integral whole, and their vision of man was marked first of all by striving to infinite freedom, including sexual freedom in particular, which became a singular trait of the time. One can venture to say that this leap for freedom, in its unrestrained rebellion, went too far and signified a new era – of moral relativism, when the old Biblical truths were shaken and undermined – and had a significant impact, in both theory and practice, on the Russian idea of love, as will be discussed shortly. While Chekhov, brought up on the old (classical) canon, was not seduced by the Dionysian spirit of the emerging Silver Age, Bunin – the talent of the next generation – went a step further and his deeply involved investigations of human sexuality are, arguably, as suspiciously pregnant with their own undoing as Dostoevsky's probing into the nature of evil border on moral ambivalence. Indeed, as Brodsky perceptively remarked on the latter, 'Of course, he was a great defender of the "good cause", the cause of Christianity. But come to think of it, there hardly ever was a better devil's advocate. From classicism, he took the principle that before you come forth with your argument, however right or righteous you may feel, you have to list all the arguments of the opposite side. It is not that in the process of listing them one is being swayed by the opposite side; it is simply that the listing itself is a mightily absorbing process. One may not in the end drift away from one's original stance, but after having exhausted all the arguments on behalf of evil, one utters the creed's dictums with nostalgia rather than with fervor. This, in its own way, also fosters the case of verisimilitude.'[82]

Similarly, Bunin seems internally so carried away with the theme (and mystery) of the physical aspect of love, that his persistent attempts to sanctify it are somewhat lost in the profound swirls of his investigations into the nature of sexual desire. In contrast to the more romantic writers, such as, for example, Aleksandr Grin, Mikhail Prishvin, Yurii Dombrovsky or Fazil Iskander as well as the whole pleiad of song-writing poets starting with Aleksandr Vertinsky and culminating in Bulat Okudzhava, Vladimir Vysotsky and Yurii Vizbor – that is, those who in a sense recreated the romantic cult of a Beautiful Lady – Bunin, invariably focusing on physicality in his portrayal of love, lingering over it a touch longer than psychologically justified, may evoke a subconscious intuitive distrust in the attentive reader, a wondering of what will come of the lyrical hero's feeling with fading of the natural beauty of the heroine, through whatever cause – illness, accident or simply an old age. It is not surprising that Zinaida Gippius

---

[82] Joseph Brodsky, 'The Power of the Elements', in *Less Than One. Selected Essays*, op. cit., p. 162.

found Bunin's brilliantly written novella 'Mitina lubov' psychologically unconvincing, because the young hero's obsession with his beloved, his total worship of her, his feverish madness and constant dreams can hardly be compatible with his deliberate copulating with another girl simply out of lust, despair and curiosity. Explaining her doubts, Gippius writes, 'The thing is that a young man in love – precisely a young man, who sensed for the first time the "wafting of unearthly joy" – necessarily becomes chaste to the utmost, passionately chaste.'[83] However, Mitia's behaviour testifies to the contrary, and hence 'either his love for Katia – for her alone – is a lie, and all that, from the outset to the end, had been nothing but a sensual excitement, blood on fire, for which no Eros is necessary, or it is a lie that at the last moment his *physiological* will did not abandon him, that love did not defend itself here and a nakedly fleshy act with another's "baba" for a fiver (which he handed to her right there) *could* take place.'[84] Therefore Gippius expresses essentially the same suspicion with respect to Bunin, as that we voiced earlier: 'The world in his depiction becomes truly horrible by the eternal victory of lust over love, death over life; horrible – and *un*real, *un*authentic.'[85]

However, in some sense Bunin's excessive leaning towards the physical only reinforces the point of the changing paradigms, of body stepping to the forefront in reassertion of its rights from the previous, for some – hypocritical – neglect (or, more precisely, denigration) by classical Russian literature.

Yet, the true holistic vision of man, the vision not tortured, or even concerned, by the body–soul problem, which neither exalted the physical, nor the spiritual, and thus did not have to reconcile the two, came from unexpected quarters – not from the Modernist or neo-romantic writers as such, but from a single, unequalled and singular genius of Andrei Platonov. Indeed, in Platonov's universe no distinction exists between physical and spiritual, and man is simply an organic whole, a part of nature which itself has feeling, consciousness and mind. Stones and animals, people and their creations, such as intricate machinery – all are equal, alive and at once simple and enigmatic. 'During lunch breaks Zakhar Pavlovich would not take his eyes of the engine, silently suffering within himself his love for it. [. . .] Zakhar Pavlovich was not solitary – machines were his people, constantly arousing within him feelings, thoughts, and desires. The forward slope of the engine, which they called the spool, forced Zakhar Pavlovich to worry about the infinity of space. He went out specially at night to look at the stars, to see if the world is spacious, to see if there is enough space for the wheels to live and turn eternally. The stars shone passionately, but each in solitude. Zakhar Pavlovich thought, "What does the sky resemble?" Then he remembered the switching yard where he had been sent for some banding. One could see from the station platform a sea of solitary signals; there were the switches, signals, crossings, warning lights, the watch houses, the shining searchlights, the moving trains. The sky was the same, only farther away, and somehow the hitches barring smooth work had been better worked out. Then Zakhar Pavlovich began to do an eye-count of the number of miles to a blue flickering

[83]   Zinaida Gippius, 'O liubvi', in V. Shestakov (ed.), op. cit., p. 204.
[84]   Ibid., p. 205.
[85]   Ibid., p. 206.

star. He divided his hands into a scale, and wisely applied this scale to the space. The star turned at the height of two hundred miles. This disturbed him, though he had read that the world is endless. He wanted the world really to be endless, so that wheels would always be necessary, ever preparing the way for general happiness, but Zakhar Pavlovich simply could not feel infinity.'[86]

This, primordial, almost pagan perception of life, which while based on human values is at the same time free of civilizational blinkers, as if illuminates the universe anew, providing a singular, independent vision, a fresh portrait of existence, thus depicting, if you like, an anthropologically novel, unfamiliar face of the Earth and of mankind. Contrary to a widely shared view that it is Platonov's unique usage of language, virtually his own self-invented version of Russian, which is responsible for the uniqueness of his poetics and wisdom,[87] I would argue that it is his vision which is primary here, while his language is secondary – a mere way of verbalising his sensibility, a corollary of it. In my view, Platonov simply disavows the conventional at the most profound levels, laying bare the imposture of civilization, a fundamental distortion of its approach. In other words, he sheds a clear light of some divine wisdom on the darkness of our perceptions, for his supreme sight just x-rays things down to their true essence. Platonov's vision could be called cosmic if it were not rooted in human moral sense, and furthermore in his culturally Russian origin.

Thus his understanding of love shows certain continuity with the classical tradition, asserting, as in the citation earlier in this chapter, love's minimal dependency on the sexual, and in echoing Solov'ev's fusion of the neo-platonic and Christian elements, as will be seen in the sequel.[88] In Platonov's eyes, love is dissolved in the very texture of the universe, and is synonymous with life, for love is, as we saw, 'a measure of how much one is endowed with a gift of life'.[89] Just as for Vladimir Vysotsky later on, love is primary, it permeates the air we breathe and thus 'I am breathing, that means I'm in love! I'm in love, and that means I'm alive!'[90] By contrast to René Descartes's rationalist formula 'Cogito, ergo sum' ('I think, hence I exist'), we encounter here a different approach to existence: 'I love, hence I live.' However, in this model of the universe love requires an intense inner work of one's whole being, a strain of all human faculties, in order for the human heart to break free both from the earthly limitations imposed by self-interest and from the unearthly delusion (self-deception), reaching for the ultimate sobriety and sensitivity, that is for the highest degree of perceptive intelligence, or, if you like, for the next level of being in evolutionary terms. 'Love is terribly shrewd, and those in

---

[86] Andrei Platonov, 'Chevengur', op. cit., p. 27.
[87] As Brodsky put it, Platonov can be regarded as 'an embodiment of language temporarily occupying a piece of time and reporting from within. [. . .] Like no other Russian writer before or after him, Platonov was able to reveal a self-destructive, eschatological element within the language itself, and that, in turn, was of extremely revealing consequence to the revolutionary eschatology with which history supplied him as his subject matter'. See Joseph Brodsky, 'Catastrophes in the Air', in *Less Than One. Selected Essays*, op. cit., pp. 287–8.
[88] See the next chapter.
[89] Andrei Platonov, 'Odnazhdy liubivshie', <http://www.hrono.ru/proza/platonov_a/rozhenzeva1. html> [accessed 16 January 2014].
[90] Vladimir Vysotsky, 'Ballada o liubvi' ('A Ballad about Love'), in *Vladimir Vysotsky: Hamlet with a Guitar*, op. cit., p. 183. In Russian: 'Я дышу и значит я люблю; я люблю – и значит я живу!'

love see one another completely – with all their vices, and do not bestow each other with adoration.'[91] Its hallmark is sincerity, which 'makes love similar to work (from creating a symphony to doing a brickwork) – both require sincerity, that is, a total accord between actions and internal, as well as external, natural design; otherwise love will turn into a business-like ignobility, and a brick will fall out of the wall, causing the house to collapse.'[92] Love is 'an ulcer of the heart, which renders us clever, strong, strange and wonderful people.'[93] It involves a miracle of transcending the poor limits of the 'I', as happens to one of Platonov's protagonists: 'Previously, he had sensed the life of others through a barrier of pride and self-interest, but now, all of a sudden, he had touched another life with his naked heart.'[94]

Thus Platonov's oeuvre, with all the uniqueness of the writer's vision, in many ways stays within Russian classical tradition which regards love above all in the key of moral philosophy. One of the important distinctions within the tradition, however – which, in particular, sets Platonov apart from, say, Mikhail Bulgakov – lays in the distinction labelled below as that between 'nature' and 'culture', and which will be discussed, as promised, in the next chapter. But before we move on to it, we shall first demonstrate through most representative examples how the tradition itself, as a resilient organic whole, survives some paradigmatic shifts and continues well into the future.

Russian idea of love as ethical category

As the discussion earlier implies, the root of genuine love is always religious, hence, in particular, its inner intensity. The idealistic and maximalist tradition inherent in Russian letters fosters and magnifies this intensity. What Nadezhda Mandelshtam wrote about Tsvetaeva to a large extent summarizes this tradition: 'in everything and everywhere she sought emotional fullness and enravishment. She craved enravishment not only in love, but also in abandonment, desertion and failure.'[95] Pasternak's famous sentiments grow from the same root: 'In everything I want to reach // The very essence: // In work, in seeking a way, // In passion's turbulence.'[96] These uncompromising strivings permeate popular culture just as well, as in Aleksandr Rozenbaum's lines: 'if you cure someone – then do that to its full extent! If you love – then really love! If you

[91] Andrei Platonov, 'Odnazhdy liubivshie', op. cit.

[92] Ibid.

[93] Ibid.

[94] This is a quotation from Platonov's story 'Vozvrashchenie' (The Return) (see *The Return and Other Stories*, transl. by Robert and Elizabeth Chandler, and Angela Livingstone, London: The Harvill Press, 1999, p. 203), which will be discussed in more detail in the next chapter.

[95] Nadezhda Mandelshtam, *Vtoraia kniga: Vospominaniia*, Moscow: 'Moskovskii rabochii', 1990, p. 376.

[96] Boris Pasternak, 'In everything I want to reach . . .' ('Vo vsiom mne khochetsa doiti do samoi suti . . .'), in *Selected Poems*, transl. by Jon Stallworthy and Peter France, London: Allen Lane, 1983, p. 143. In Russian: 'Во всем мне хочется дойти // До самой сути. // В работе, в поисках пути, // В сердечной смуте'.

celebrate wildly – then truly celebrate! If you shoot – then shoot properly!'[97] Such a religious temperament of love can often be encountered in the Russian context.

As Berdiaev put it, 'Any kind of love, and sexual love in particular, predominantly belongs to the sphere of religious mysticism. In this sphere we encounter the mysterious and sacramental,[98] and 'in a strong emotion of love there is a depth of infinity.'[99] This also leads to love being organically close to such mysteries of existence as death and creativity. 'A profound inner tragic element is inherent in love, and it is not accidental that love is related to death.'[100] Indeed, love is always dangerously close to death if only because it is woven out of life, and the border between love and death is often crossed at the peaks of human experience, at the limits of human strength. A mark of this proximity is also reflected in the language – in the rhymed pun of *lubov'-krov'* (любовь-кровь), which conceals, in particular, numerous examples of a truly religious readiness for self-sacrifice for the sake of love (as in Vladimir Vysotsky's 'Ballada o liubvi': 'You cannot drive the madmen – they say, Just name the price, and we will promptly pay. They'll pay the highest price – they'll risk their lives To keep the thread from breaking, to prevent The magic golden thread from being rent – The flimsiest and strongest of all ties').[101] At the same time, in Berdiaev's words, 'There exists a tragic conflict between love and creativity. This theme has been expressed by Ibsen in a genius way.'[102]

The evident and deeply meaningful links between love, death, religious impulse and creativity are multiple and profound, but the task of their detailed investigation lies outside the scope of our present enquiry. We shall, however, make just a brief observation in this respect. 'Christianity is a religion of love. And Dostoevsky accepted Christianity as first and foremost religion of love', Berdiaev remarked. At the same time, he noted that Dostoevsky lays bare inner contradictions of love between man and woman, as well as between people more generally. In Versilov's dream of the Golden Age, Dostoevsky draws a picture of love without God. 'This love is opposite to Christian; it comes from the meaninglessness of existence, not from the meaning of it.'[103] For Berdiaev, this is a 'fantastical utopia'[104] which is never to be in godless mankind. However, this atheistic society indeed came into being in the twentieth century and, interestingly, while religion was largely removed from the individual consciousness, religious impulse did not vanish, but became transformed, and revealed itself above all in creativity (and, in particular, through the religious temperament of genuine love which in itself is also a creative process). In this respect one could talk about artistic

[97] Aleksandr Rozenbaum, 'Utinaia okhota', <http://www.karaoke.ru/song/1011.htm> [accessed 26 January 2014]. In Russian: 'Лечить – так лечить! Любить – так любить! Гулять – так гулять! Стрелять – так стрелять!'

[98] Berdiaev, 'Metafizika pola i lubvi', in V. Shestakov (ed.), op. cit., p. 259.

[99] Berdiaev, 'Razmyshlenie ob Erose', in V. Shestakov (ed.), op. cit., pp. 271–2.

[100] Ibid., p. 273.

[101] Vladimir Vysotsky, 'Ballada o liubvi' ('A Ballad about Love'), op. cit., p. 183. In Russian: 'Но вспять безумцев не поворотить, Они уже согласны заплатить. Любой ценой и жизнью бы рискнули, Чтобы не дать порвать, чтоб сохранить Волшебную невидимую нить, Которую меж ними протянули'.

[102] Berdiaev, 'Razmyshlenie ob Erose', in V. Shestakov (ed.), op. cit., p. 273.

[103] Berdaiev, 'Lubov u Dostoevskogo', in V. Shestakov (ed.), op. cit., p. 282.

[104] Ibid.

creativity as a form of the religious, or, in the same vein, of art understood as religious service. This, in fact, is a continuation of the long-standing Russian tradition which David Bethea labels as 'writer as secular saint'.[105] Joseph Brodsky when talking about his generation's relationship with culture expresses this as a particular sensibility – a product of the Christian civilization – which is becoming extinct: 'This is the last generation for whom culture has been, and continues to be, the ultimate value of all the values available to mankind in general. These are the people for whom Christian civilisation is more important than anything else in the world. They have put a lot of efforts into preserving these values, while spurning the values of the world that arises in front of their eyes'.[106] Czeslaw Milosz characterized Brodsky's oeuvre as 'the poetry of two polarities of human existence: love [. . .] and death'.[107] The poet's attitude to both of these categories is 'with trepidation, expressed through inspired incantations, far from secular' – despite the fact that 'Brodsky did not have a talisman of faith'.[108]

A paradigmatic shift of values, to which Brodsky refers, in fact relates to the process which began much earlier – at the brink of the twentieth century, at the time of Chekhov, and it is these tectonic cultural shifts and their impact on the idea of love, that this section discusses.

Undoubtedly, it would be both an important and fascinating endeavour to trace fully an evolution of the idea of love in Russia precisely in the context of the moral and spiritual values. However, the scope of such a task would require a separate book, or possibly a collection of books. Therefore, here we shall give only a very sketchy and partial version of such an analysis. Our aim is to uncover a tendency in the way the idea of love has correlated with the moral canon of the epoch and with the changes in the cultural paradigm. To this end, we shall consider the image of Pushkin's Tatiana Larina – the protagonist of 'Evgenii Onegin' (which has long since become canonical) – in Dostoevsky's interpretation, and then compare his conclusions with the views on love of Chekhov's heroes, and finish off with some contemporary parallels.

*   *   *

It is precisely Dostoevsky's reading, explained in his famous Pushkin speech of 1880, which became rooted in Russian cultural consciousness as canonical. Yet, the writer gives us here the image of Tatiana, perceived through the prism of his own moral values and hard won convictions, raising it to a cultural metaphor and ethical paragon, stripped of Pushkinian lightness and irony. In Dostoevsky's interpretation, Tatiana's character is epic; and this epos is fully tragic, even if enlightened. This is solely because Dostoevsky is interested above all in the ethical, moral side of the question, or, putting it differently, love as a moral category. In this sense, the famous phrase, sacramental

---

[105] Bethea, op. cit., p. 167.
[106] A quotation from the French film on Joseph Brodsky 'Poete russe – citoyen americain' (1989), by Victor Loupan and Christophe de Ponfilly.
[107] Czeslaw Milosz, 'Bor'ba s udushiem', in Petr Vail' and Lev Losev (eds), *Iosif Brodsky. Trudy i dni*, Moscow: Nezavisimaia Gazeta, 1998, p. 244.
[108] Ibid.

for the whole Russian culture: 'Now am I to another given: To him I will be faithful unto death' is a foundation for an entire philosophy. This philosophy comprises the most sacred and innermost idea of Dostoevsky – on the paradoxical relationship of the private and the general, on the tear of a child, which cannot be sacrificed even for the sake of universal happiness of mankind.

'To whom, to what will she be true?'[109] – Dostoevsky exclaims, – 'To what obligations be faithful? Is it to that old general whom she cannot possibly love, because she loves Onegin.'[110] Himself answers the question: 'Yes, she is true to that general. [. . .] She married him out of despair. But now he is her husband, and her perfidy will cover him with disgrace and shame and will kill him.' Next, the most fundamental Dostoevsky's question is voiced: 'Can anyone build his happiness on the unhappiness of another?' As an answer another question is asked, equally rhetorical: 'What kind of happiness would that be, based on the unhappiness of another?' A moral conclusion follows: 'Happiness is not in the delights of love alone, but also in the spirit's highest harmony. How could the spirit be appeased if behind it stood a dishonourable, merciless, inhuman action?'[111]

Then Dostoevsky brings us explicitly to the vital connection between the deed (and outlook) of Tatiana and the principal philosophical questions of his own works: 'Imagine that you yourself are building a palace of human destiny for the final end of making all men happy, and of giving them peace and rest at last. And imagine also that for that purpose it is necessary and inevitable to torture to death one single human being, and him not a great soul, but even in someone's eyes a ridiculous being [. . .]. Would you consent to be the architect on this condition? That is the question. [. . .] Could Tatiana's great soul, which had so deeply suffered, have chosen otherwise? No, a pure, Russian soul decides thus: "Let me, let me alone be deprived of happiness, let my happiness be infinitely greater than the unhappiness of this old man, and finally let no one, not this old man, know and appreciate my sacrifice: but I will not be happy through having ruined another". Here is a tragedy in act, the line cannot be passed, and Tatiana sends Onegin away.'[112]

Hitherto Pushkin would probably agree with Dostoevsky in principle, if he heard the latter's words. However, Dostoevsky goes further, and makes the next step, quite speculative and far from uncontroversial – he says: 'I think that even if Tatiana had been free and her old husband had died and she become a widow, even then she would not have gone away with Onegin. One must understand the essential substance of this

---

[109] Fedor Dostoevsky, 'Pushkin', speech of 8 June 1880, <http://az.lib.ru/d/dostoewskij_f_m/text_0340. shtml> [accessed 3 December 2014]. For the English translation, see <http://www.linda-goodman. com/ubb/Forum7/HTML/010678.html> [accessed 12 June 2014].

[110] Here, in the swift and simple logic of this phrase, it is interesting to note also that Dostoevsky, who created a number of depictions of a bifurcated tormenting love even in the cases of his most positive heroes, when talking of Tatiana's love, assumes an immutable thesis of love's uniqueness! This, obviously, does not contain a contradiction, for duality (bifurcation) of love always testifies to its fatality, to its dubious and self-destructive nature, and invariably ends in disintegration – if not of the feeling, then certainly of the person. At the same time, Tatiana is regarded by Dostoevsky as an ideal, wholesome soul, free of the fatal canker of duality.

[111] Fedor Dostoevsky, 'Pushkin', speech, op. cit.

[112] Dostoevsky, 'Pushkin', speech, op. cit.

character! [. . .] She knows that [. . .] if she were to follow him, then tomorrow he would be disillusioned and look with mockery upon his infatuation. He has no root at all, he is a blade of grass, borne on the wind. She is otherwise: even in her despair, in the painful consciousness that her life has been ruined, she still has something solid and unshakable upon which her soul may bear. These are the memories of her childhood, the reminiscences of her country, her remote village, in which her pure and humble life had begun: "it is the woven shade Of branches that overhang her nurse's grave". [. . .] There is here a whole foundation, unshakable and indestructible. Here is contact with her own land, with her own people, and with their sanctities. And he-what has he and what is he? Could she possibly follow him merely out of compassion, [. . .] knowing well beforehand that tomorrow he would look on his happiness with mockery? No, these are deep, firm souls, which cannot deliberately give their sanctities to dishonour, even from infinite compassion. No, Tatiana could not follow Onegin.'[113]

In other words, for Dostoevsky the image of Tatiana is first of all a confirmation of the fact that in human morality (applied to individual life) there exists something sacred which stands above our personal happiness. It is our debt to a higher principle, be it our duty to another or to a community of others, or even to an ideal as such, a betrayal of which equates self-betrayal. Let us stop at this fundamental conclusion for now, and move on to a representative of the next generation – to Chekhov, and to his understanding of love in the context of morality. To this end, we shall look at the two characteristic Chekhovian stories on this theme: 'O Liubvi' and 'Dama s sobachkoi'.

Both stories were written almost two decades after Dostoevsky's Pushkin speech. By that time the epoch has changed in Russia, and, for that matter, in the world. God was dead, the idea of scientific–technical progress very much alive, but speculative philosophy had run into the dead-end, exhausted itself, having cleared the space for the counter wave – the wave of the irrational and psychological, for mystical moods, for Symbolism in art and for new religious search. Chekhov remains sober, and yet he breathes new life into realism, as if turning it inside out, and the exposed underside turns out to be quite irrational. He is regarded as a bridge between the old and the new, as a transitional stage on the way to Modernism, the writer who brought about a new sensibility, both ethically and aesthetically – a sensibility of a modern man. In many ways continuing Russian classical tradition, Chekhov at the same time moved away from it at considerable distance – by making a literary narrative didactics-free, by removing from it any moralizing judgements, up to withdrawing the authorial voice itself. Moreover, he recoiled also from pondering intently over the 'cursed' questions, traditional for (and inseparable from) Russian literature before him.

Thus in his story 'O liubvi' the hero (Alekhin) not only openly raises such a stance into a point of principle, but also ridicules the very tradition itself, applied precisely to the question of love: 'We Russians of the educated class have a partiality for these questions that remain unanswered. Love is usually poeticized, decorated with roses,

---

[113] Ibid.

nightingales; we Russians decorate our loves with these fateful questions, and select the most uninteresting of them, too. In Moscow, when I was a student, I had a companion, a charming lady, and every time I took her in my arms she was thinking what I would allow her a month for housekeeping and what was the price of beef a pound. In the same way, when we are in love we are never tired of asking ourselves questions: whether it is honourable or dishonourable, sensible or stupid, what this love is leading up to, and so on. Whether it is a good thing or not I don't know, but that it is in the way, unsatisfactory, and irritating, I do know.'[114]

But does such an open mockery of the philosophizing tradition mean that the questions of morality have fallen out of use and that the hero is now free from moral torment? Not at all! For Chekhov's world is essentially rebelling not against the cursed questions as such, but against speculations with them, against using them as shields and excuses (although the tendency of recoiling from the accursed questions is in itself symptomatic and fraught with disastrous consequences). This story illustrates precisely how love is crushed under the burden of moral insolubility. This is how Alekhin describes his feeling:

'My love was deep and tender, but I reflected and kept asking myself what our love could lead to if we had not the strength to fight against it. It seemed to be incredible that my gentle, sad love could all at once coarsely break up the even tenor of the life of her husband, her children, and all the household in which I was so loved and trusted. Would it be honourable? [. . .] And how long would our happiness last? What would happen to her in case I was ill, in case I died, or if we simply stopped loving one another? And she apparently reasoned in the same way. She thought of her husband, her children, and of her mother, who loved the husband like a son. If she abandoned herself to her feelings she would have to lie, or else to tell the truth, and in her position either would have been equally terrible and inconvenient. And she was tormented by the question whether her love would bring me happiness – would she not complicate my life, which, as it was, was hard enough and full of all sorts of trouble?'[115]

But how does this love story end? What is the outcome of this moral drama? 'When our eyes met in the compartment our spiritual fortitude deserted us both [. . .] – I confessed my love for her, and *with a burning pain in my heart I realized how unnecessary, how petty, and how deceptive all that had hindered us from loving was. I understood that when you love you must either, in your reasonings about that love, start from what is highest, from what is more important than happiness or unhappiness, sin or virtue in their accepted meaning, or you must not reason at all.'*[116]

Thus Chekhov's hero asserts here the idea of the ultimate value of love. This idea at first glance contradicts Dostoevsky's convictions, and solves Tatiana Larina's dilemma, even if purely theoretically, in an opposite way. But is it really so?

---

[114] Anton Chekhov, 'About love' ('O liubvi'), <http://www.classicreader.com/book/1597/1/> [accessed 17 November 2014].
[115] Ibid.
[116] Ibid. Highlighting here and for the rest of this chapter, unless otherwise stated, is mine. O.T.

Let us turn once again to Dostoevsky's conclusions. Essentially there are two of them:

1.   'What kind of happiness would that be, based on the unhappiness of another?'
2.   There are 'deep, firm souls, which cannot deliberately give their sanctities to dishonour' (that is to say, one cannot betray oneself, one's ideal and convictions, i.e. the basis of one's personality).

At the same time, Chekhov's Alekhin proclaims, 'I understood that when you love you must either, in your reasonings about that love, start from what is highest, from what is more important than happiness or unhappiness, sin or virtue in their accepted meaning, or you must not reason at all.'

However, based on Alekhin's logic, if love is the ultimate value, if it is situated above everything else in the hierarchy of human values, then it is in it that the meaning of human existence is concealed, and hence, by betraying our love we are betraying our own essence! Thus a betrayal of love is equivalent to self-betrayal, and hence the pathos of Chekhov's story coincides with the pathos of Dostoevsky – in what concerns his second conclusion. However, what is the situation with regard to his first statement – on our moral duty to others, on the impossibility to erect the building of our own happiness on the foundation of the unhappiness of another? On this issue there is a clear divergence, and it is, apparently, not accidental.

Indeed, Chekhov's time is the time of the dusk, of a profound disillusionment within Russian as well as generally European culture. With the death of the tsar-reformer, a painful period of reforms in Russia is replaced by a lifeless period of repression; great hopes and illusions of the previous generations are shattered. But even more broadly, with the death of God, there ensues the time to Nietzsche and Freud, of Marx and Einstein, of the profound shift of the cultural paradigm. It is the time of a new outlook, of a new state of mind – of man trapped in the agonies of modernization, when Biblical truths collapse, and with them the ethical foundations of life are destroyed as well.[117] Black and white, good and evil are no longer absolute categories; a blurring of shades and relativism of concepts come to occupy the centre-stage. European civilization shifts from the sacred paradigms to the areligious, abstract humanism. Henceforth, man does not have another guide except his own conscience. But where does one stop in the individual attempts to discern good from evil, where is now the border to be situated, when it is no longer prescribed from the superior (divine) heights? One could even venture to say, without a fear of too excessive an exaggeration, that all the tragic history of the twentieth century, full of humanitarian catastrophes, is an illustration of the consequences of this shift to relativism.

Despite the fact that Chekhov's hero proclaims love as the highest value, no category in the world of the writer – a representative of this new time – is any longer absolute.

---

[117] In her article on Chekhov Svetlana Evdokimova thus characterizes his outlook: 'Chekhov's oeuvre as a whole reflects the agony of modernization as culture changes from sacred paradigms to a new secular humanism' (see Svetlana Evdokimova, 'Philosophy's enemies: Chekhov and Shestov', in Olga Tabachnikova (ed.), *Anton Chekhov Through The Eyes Of Russian Thinkers: Vasilii Rozanov, Dmitrii Merezhkovskii and Lev Shestov*, op. cit., p. 220).

In Simon Karlinsky's words, for Chekhov 'sex, like religion, is also a morally neutral quantity, whose moral and ethical implications depend on the circumstances and the attitudes of the people involved.'[118] Thus everything becomes subjective, exclusively individual, as Chekhov's Alekhin indeed asserts:

> So far only one incontestable truth has been uttered about love: 'This is a great mystery.' Everything else that has been written or said about love is not a conclusion, but only a statement of questions which have remained unanswered. The explanation which would seem to fit one case does not apply in a dozen others, and the very best thing, to my mind, would be to explain every case individually without attempting to generalize. *We ought*, as the doctors say, *to individualize each case.*[119]

Chekhov himself, as a man who was brought up in one epoch and writing in another, when the eternal values got shaken and fell, undoubtedly felt the cultural shift taking place. Thus, for example, in his famous letter to Suvorin, he says, 'The writers we call eternal or simply good, the writers who intoxicate us, have one highly important trait in common: they are moving forward something definite and beckon you to follow, and you feel with your entire being, not only with your mind, that they have a certain goal. [. . .] The best of them are realistic and describe life as it is, but because each line is saturated with the consciousness of its goal, you feel life as it should be in addition to life as it is, and you are captivated by it. But what about us? Us! We describe life as it is and stop dead right there. We wouldn't lift a hoof if you lit into us with a whip. We have neither immediate, nor remote goals, and there is emptiness in our souls. We have no politics, we don't believe in revolution, there is no God, we're not afraid of ghosts, and I personally am not even afraid of death or blindness.'[120]

But if sin and virtue ('in their accepted meaning'), of which Chekhov's Alekhin is talking and which he places beneath love, are blurred at the edges and can easily swap places, then what about happiness, which he also deems a category to which love is unaccountable? This question for the writer himself was probably devoid of meaning: 'Seeing how Chekhov crossed out everything he deemed superfluous in his works, striving for the utmost brevity, his friends exclaimed: "his manuscripts should be rescued from him – otherwise he will leave in his story only the following: they were young and fell for each other, but then got married and lived unhappily". To this sarcasm Chekhov replied: "But listen – this is precisely how it is in reality!"'[121]

---

[118] Karlinsky (ed.), Introduction to *Anton Chekhov. Life and Thought; Selected Letters and Commentary*, op. cit., p. 15.

[119] Chekhov, 'About love', op. cit.

[120] See Karlinsky (ed.), *Anton Chekhov. Life and Thought; Selected Letters and Commentary*, op. cit., p. 243 (Chekhov's letter to A. S. Suvorin of 25.11.1892).

[121] See Boris Eikhenbaum, 'O Chekhove' (1944), <http://feb-web.ru/feb/chekhov/critics/eih-357/eih-357-.htm> [accessed 24 May 2013]. Similar sentiments of Nikolai Berdiaev are relevant here: 'It always seemed strange to me when people talked of the joys of love. It would be more natural, if one looks at life more profoundly, to talk about the tragedy and sadness of love. When I see a happy loving couple I feel a mortal sorrow. Love, in essense, does not know fulfilled hopes.' Berdiaev, 'Razmyshlenie ob Erose', in V. Shestakov (ed.), op. cit., p. 273.

Thus, while diverging, but not breaking up completely with the preceding classical tradition, Chekhov brings about to Russian culture a qualitatively new vision of love – and essentially performs a quiet, bloodless revolution! In lieu of a happy dream and clear moral regulations there comes an individual freedom – in particular, a freedom of interpretation of the previously immutable categories – but also an individual responsibility that accompanies it. Without God, man is alone in this world, and cannot rely on anyone, but himself. In essence, Chekhov offers us a new type of individualism – not a tormented, self-obsessed individualism of a Romantic hero, but calm and sober individualism of a 'civilized European', who votes for personal freedom and independence of thought. To the uneasy attitude to sex, to extra-marital affairs, to Victorian puritanism, Chekhov opposes an individual's right (not very familiar to Russian culture) for privacy, for a personal mystery. This stance of his is expressed most explicitly in his 'The Lady with a Lapdog' ('Dama s sobachkoi'): 'He had two lives: one, open [. . .], full of relative truth and of relative falsehood, exactly like the lives of his friends and acquaintances; and another life running its course in secret. [. . .] And he judged of others by himself, not believing in what he saw, and always believing that every man had his real, most interesting life under the cover of secrecy like under the cover of night. All personal existence rests on secrecy, and possibly it is partly on that account that civilised man is so nervously anxious that personal privacy should be respected.'[122]

Moreover, Chekhov brings to Russian literature an unusual for it extreme sobriety. Thus, against the tradition (mostly idealistic, maximalist, or, simply speaking, utopian) he talks about finiteness – and hence about a potential non-uniqueness! – of love.

Even the story 'The Lady with a Lapdog' – which has become a symbol of sorts of an ideal, true, all-conquering and authentic love not only in Russian, but also in world culture – contains that 'subversive' sentiment: 'It was evident to him that this love of theirs would not be over soon [. . .]. Anna Sergeevna grew more and more attached to him. She adored him, and it was unthinkable to say to her that *it was bound to have an end some day . . .*'[123]

The same idea, even if differently framed, we find in the story 'About Love': 'Luckily or unluckily, *there is nothing in our lives that does not end sooner or later*.' What is most striking is that even at the peak of love, in its full bloom, Alekhin concedes that this love can die a natural death, may fade away at its own accord: 'And how long would our happiness last? What would happen to her in case I was ill, in case I died, *or if we simply stopped loving one another*?'[124]

Thus Chekhov evidently changes the canonical views on love inherent in the Russian classical tradition, as if removing from it some vital links. Characterized at the same time by a new attitude to physical love – free from the torment typical for Tolstoy and Dostoevsky with their perpetual, unending fatal struggle between body and soul – Chekhov views sex as natural and devoid of the agonizing subtext. This, however, is

[122] Anton Chekhov, 'The Lady with a Lapdog' ('Dama s sobachkoi'), <http://www.ilibrary.ru/text/976/p.1/index.html> [accessed 4 March 2013].
[123] Chekhov, 'The Lady with a Lapdog', op. cit.
[124] Chekhov, 'About Love', op. cit.

perhaps less interesting, considering that Russia was anyway on the brink of sexual revolution, even though Chekhov remained distant from its wild and largely barbaric Dionysian element. Much more important are those metaphysical links which Chekhov removed from the tradition, thus having considerably 'earthed' it and sobered it up, but not having degraded it! Indeed, he has transformed not the scale of moral values itself, but only our attitude to it, and hence to life as a whole – shifting the accent from the scrolls to our personal conscience, professing everyone's right to their own hard won path. However, in the new time, when in the absence of God man finds himself in total solitude, this shift is turning fatal, because what for Chekhov and his contemporaries was still rested on the immutable principles of the Bible, becomes hanging in the air in subsequent generations. Our conscience alone, devoid of divine support, collapses in search of reliable guiding stars. Although Chekhov himself is by no means poisoned by relativism, and, as Vladimir Kataev formulated, '"the real truth" for Chekhov is a synonym of God',[125] but he could not help but feel that the coming time itself – the time of muddled morality and dried up sources – is infected with relativism. In particular, the role of our duty to others turns out to be a shaky rather than absolute category; no more than an object of our own assessment. This is so in particular because 'a religious person, no matter how gifted, tends to assert himself at the expense of others to a much lesser extent than non-religious. His ambition is directed vertically and always restricted by the loving admission of the impossibility to catch up with the Teacher. He is forever pulling himself up, knowing at the same time that the peak is unattainable. By the very spirit of his nature, he cannot [. . .] and does not want to replace the Teacher.'[126] Chekhov, as it were, calls for vigilance in the new situation of faithlessness; he offers a courageous approach to this existential solitude, the approach that essentially requires from each person – in an atmosphere of freedom and emptiness – an even greater effort of mental strengths than in the previous situation of freedom as simultaneously a divine mercy and divine test.[127]

---

[125] Vladimir Kataev, 'Istinnyi mudrets', in Anatolii Sobennikov (ed.), *Filosofiia A.P. Chekhova*, Irkutsk: ISU Publishers, 2008, p. 74.

[126] Iskander, *Lastochkino gnezdo. Proza. Poeziia. Publitsistika*, op. cit., p. 366.

[127] One can, of course, easily enter here into a discussion of some objective differences between Chekhov and Dostoevsky, of the two types of religious (or quasi-religious) sensibility (or, at any rate, of an intrinsic sensitivity to the religious ethos) that they represent (along the lines described earlier) and of their different solutions to the problem of the private versus the general; by the same token, one can discuss the patriarchal model of marriage as opposed to an emancipated idea of personality as an aim in itself rather than a means. However, while perfectly valid, this would be, at the same time, entirely missing the point. After all, from a 'modern' perspective (see, for instance, the book *Pushkin tselilsia v tsaria. Tsar, poet i Natali* by Nikolai Petrakov/Moscow: Algoritm, 2013). Tatiana's problem may seem ridiculously contrived – if she really loves Onegin, then she should just follow her heart, be with her beloved, leaving behind her odious husband and her loveless (and hence, arguably, altogether immoral) marriage. But the point is not whether it is moral or immoral to live with a husband whom you do not love – that is *fait accompli*; the point is the scale where two things are juxtaposed: on the one hand, there is a betrayal of others (even if you joined your life with theirs by mistake) for the sake of your personal happiness, and, on the other, there is self-sacrifice as a means to avoid such a betrayal. The choice is thus precisely between self-sacrifice and sacrificing others. Dostoevsky, following the Bible, maintains that there is something sacred which is higher than our personal happiness. Receding from this premise may prove ultimately fatal for humanity.

However, what I deem remarkable, and with what I would like to finish this discussion of the evolution of Russian treatment of love as moral category, is the later restoration of these removed (or 'earthed') links by Russian followers of Chekhov. I shall restrict myself to just one example: In Chekhov's 'Dama s sobachkoi' we read, 'All the time the audience were coming in and taking their seats Gurov looked at them eagerly. Anna Sergeyevna, too, came in. She sat down in the third row, and when Gurov looked at her his heart contracted, and he understood clearly that there was in the whole world no creature so near, so precious, and so important to him; she, *this little woman*, in no way remarkable, lost in a provincial crowd, with a vulgar lorgnette in her hand, *filled his whole life now, was his sorrow and his joy, the one happiness that he now desired for himself.*[128]

Now let us look at Vasilii Grossman's celebrated novel 'Zhizn' i sud'ba' (1959), written more than half a century later: 'She got up from the bench and walked away without looking back. He sat there, thinking that for the first time in his life he had seen happiness, light [. . .]. *This woman* whose fingers he had just kissed *could have replaced everything he had ever wanted, everything he had ever dreamed of – science, fame, the joy of recognition . . .*'.[129] A similarity of feelings expressed in the two works is almost literal, but what lies behind these feelings in the moral sphere?

In Chekhov's story, we read:

'Anna Sergeevna and he loved each other like people very close and akin, like husband and wife, like tender friends; *it seemed to them that fate itself had meant them for one another*, and they could not understand why he had a wife and she a husband; and it was as though they were a pair of birds of passage, caught and forced to live in different cages. They forgave each other for what they were ashamed of in their past, they forgave everything in the present, and felt that this love of theirs had changed them both. [. . .]

Then they spent a long while taking counsel together, talked of how to avoid the necessity for secrecy, for deception, for living in different towns and not seeing each other for long at a time. How could they be free from this intolerable bondage? "How? How?" he asked, clutching his head. "How?"

And it seemed as though in a little while the solution would be found, and then a new and splendid life would begin; and it was clear to both of them that they had still a long, long road before them, and that the most complicated and difficult part of it was only just beginning.'[130]

Let us recall also the following lines from the same page of 'The Lady with a Lapdog': 'It was evident to him that this love of theirs would not be over soon [. . .]. Anna Sergeyevna grew more and more attached to him. She adored him, and it was unthinkable to say to her that *it was bound to have an end some day*; besides, she would not have believed it!'[131]

At the same time, Grossman writes: 'What was happening depended only on them, but *it seemed like a fate they were powerless to oppose*. What lay between them was true

---

[128] Checkhov, 'The Lady with a Lapdog', op. cit.
[129] Vasilii Grossman, *Life and Fate*, op. cit., p. 708.
[130] Checkhov, 'The Lady with a Lapdog', op. cit.
[131] Ibid.

and natural, they were no more responsible for it than a man is responsible for the light of day – and yet this truth inevitably engendered insincerity, deceit and cruelty towards those dearest to them. It was in their power to avoid deceit and cruelty; all they had to do was renounce this clear and natural light. One thing was plain: he had lost his piece of mind *forever*. Whatever happened, he would *never* know peace. Whether he hid his love for the woman beside him or whether it became his destiny, he would not know peace. Whether he was with her, feeling guilty, or whether he was apart from her, aching for her, he would have no peace.'[132]

The two texts indeed display a strong kinship and continuity, in particular in the recognition of love's fatality, its, if you like, divine nature, as if it is sent from above regardless of the will and wishes of its agents. At the same time, there are clear differences. First of all, let us note again that in Chekhov's text there is a feeling of finiteness of all creation, in particular, of love. This means that in principle non-uniqueness of love is admitted too, whereas in Grossman's work love becomes again, in line with the Russian classical tradition, infinite, unique and inviolable: 'he had lost his piece of mind *forever* . . ', 'he would *never* know peace . . .' and so on. The most important thing, however, is not even this, but the fact that the heroes of Chekhov's story do not reason in moral categories, but merely suffer in their dream to be together, while in Grossman's text the protagonists' moral torment unstoppably and powerfully comes to the forefront and is inseparable from the suffering of great love, striving for fulfilment. As in Bulat Okudzhava's song later on, and continuing Dostoevsky's line: 'no, your happiness cannot be built and settled on someone else's unhappiness.'[133]

Thus classical tradition which can be symbolized by Tatiana Larina seen through Dostoevsky's eyes, the tradition of sacred paradigms, of maximalist strivings to the absolute and sublime, to the ideal of morality and spiritual beauty, of the uniqueness and eternity of love, and of self-renunciation for the sake of the highest principle, lives on. It survives and returns despite most brutal historical conditions. The ideal proves resilient and imperishable, and bursts through as grass through pavement!

However, the ideal is unattainable, and uncompromising striving to it is always tragic. Chekhov's heroes, who recoil from the cursed questions, are not in any way free from them, and are as unhappy as their classical predecessors, as well as, for that matter, their followers, openly facing those questions. But in this unhappiness – and in many ways thanks to it – they remain nevertheless invisibly connected to the higher principle. And perhaps, the root of both Russian misfortunes and Russian happiness (or, more precisely, a happy flight of a Russian dream) is concealed in this – in the intuitive understanding of the inseparability of one from the other, in the instinctive desire 'so that the secret flow of suffering warms up the coldness of existence.'[134] And maybe this determines a special character of Russian love and the peculiar position which it occupies on the scale between the rational and the irrational.

---

[132] Grossman, op. cit., p. 707.
[133] Bulat Okudzhava, 'Stat` bogateem inoi norovit . . ', <http://matyuhin2.narod.ru/okujava.html> [accessed July 2013].
[134] Boris Pasternak, 'Zemlia', <http://pasternak.niv.ru/pasternak/stihi/207.htm> [accessed 13 March 2014]. In Russian: 'чтоб тайная струя страданья согрела холод бытия'.

5

Towards the Question of the 'Man of Nature' and 'Man of Culture' in Russian Literature

Because, for wind, the eagle, or the female heart,
There is no law

Aleksandr Pushkin, 'Egyptian nights'[1]

Herds of horses neigh happily in the meadows
And the valley has rusted as Rome did.
The transparent river bears away
Dry gold: the spring days of the classics

Osip Mandelshtam, 'Herds of horses neigh happily
in the meadows . . .'[2]

An opposition 'nature-culture' is multifaceted, although contrasting these two concepts is neither necessary, nor obvious. Nevertheless our aim here is to focus precisely on such a contrast, having first restricted it in some specific way.

Namely, we shall consider two polar outlooks at life which can be encountered particularly in Russian literature of the last two centuries. Let us call them for convenience a 'man of nature' and a 'man of culture'. As Yurii Lotman notes, 'antithesis "a savage – a civilized person" with which a modern researcher operates in order to clarify the range of ideas of the end of the 18th – the beginning of the 19th century, is too simplified and does not reflect the wealth of ideas of that epoch.'[3] Tracing the complex history of the issue, Lotman moves from the idea of a 'natural' man of Rousseau to the works of the young Gorky with his 'distinct utopian-socialist sympathies', where 'the humanist ideal of harmonious personality' turns out to be closely connected 'not with

---

[1] In Russian: '. . . Затем, что ветру и орлу // И сердцу девы нет закона . . .'
[2] Osip Mandelstam, 'S veselym rzhaniem pasutsa tabuny . . .' (Herds of horses neigh happily in the meadows . . .'), in *Selected Poems*, transl. by Clarence Brown and W. S. Merwin, Harmondsworth, Middlesex, England: Penguin Books, 1977, p. 31. In Russian: 'С веселым ржанием пасутся табуны,// И римской ржавчиной окрасилась долина;// Сухое золото классической весны // Уносит времени прозрачная стремнина.'
[3] Yurii Lotman (jointly with Z. G. Mints), '"Chelovek prirody" v russkoi literature XIX veka i "tsyganskaia tema" u Bloka', in Lotman, *Izbrannye statii*, op. cit., vol. 3, p. 248.

the Romantic traditions', but with Russian realism of the nineteenth century with its 'search for an ideal of the "natural", "normal" life'.[4]

An ethical aspect of the problem is essential here. It is linked, among other things, with the range of concepts such as freedom, integrity, strength, which, akin to a litmus paper, reveal in particular inadequacy of civilization. However, we are interested in posing the problem somewhat differently, whereby we look at the watershed between a reflective person and a person who is, in essence, free from reflection. This means that we are preoccupied above all by the question of the role and functions of reason in human consciousness.

Two main tendencies exist here, which can tentatively be labelled as rational and irrational (if you like, pro-Enlightenment and anti-Enlightenment). The former was concisely expressed by Fazil Iskander through the mouth of his hero, as we saw in the Introduction: 'a Russian person is stupid not because he is stupid, but because he does not respect reason!'.[5] At the same time, the hierarchy suggested by the same writer – 'mind without morality is not intelligent, whereas morality is intelligent even without the mind'[6] – can easily be inscribed into the opposite – irrational – tradition by its apologets.

The irrational tendency assigns reason, in a rather radical fashion, quite an unenviable place, and tracks its pernicious role in human life. Among the convinced defenders of this stance was Dostoevsky, who persistently demonstrated how excessive reflection invariably departs from its sensible beginnings and corrodes the person from within, destroying his will and, even more importantly, distorting his moral compass. Lev Shestov, a devout follower of Dostoevsky on this path, often illustrated his idea of the impotence of reason in solving the most pressing questions of human existence by using precisely quotations from Dostoevsky. 'Reason has never been powerful enough to define good and evil or to demarcate good from evil, even approximately; on the contrary, it's always confused them shamefully and pitifully; science has always provided solutions by brute force',[7] Shatov says to Stavrogin in 'The Possessed', and Shestov comments, 'This means that a force, which in the last analysis is soulless, or more precisely, indifferent to everything, had acquired – through science – the power over destinies of the universe and of man. [. . .] This idea [. . .] has permeated all our culture'.[8] Regarding Original Sin as a victory of deadening reason over living life, Shestov believes that in 'Son smeshnogo cheloveka' ('The Dream of a Ridiculous Man') Dostoevsky showed an alternative – non-rational – and (therefore) harmonious development of our civilization – what Cheslaw Milosz calls 'a metaphysical state of man before the Fall'.[9]

[4]   Lotman and Mints, '"Chelovek prirody" v russkoi literature XIX veka i "tsyganskaia tema" u Bloka', op. cit. pp. 266–7.
[5]   Iskander, 'Poet', op. cit. p. 142.
[6]   Fazil Iskander, 'Ponemnogu o mnogom. Sluchainye zapiski', op. cit., p. 122.
[7]   Fedor Dostoevsky, 'Devils', transl. by M. Katz, Oxford: Oxford University Press, 1992, 171–96 (264). Cited in Lev Shestov, 'O "pererozhdenii ubezhdenii" u Dostoevskogo' in *Umozrenie i otkrovenie*, Paris: YMCA-Press, 1964, 193.
[8]   Shestov, 'O "pererozhdenii ubezhdenii" u Dostoevskogo', op. cit., p. 193.
[9]   Milosz, 'Shestov, or the Purity of Despair', op. cit., p. 106.

One of the principal ideas of Shestov is that reason deprives man of freedom. This is, undoubtedly, a radical point of view, as the type of reason which is implied is not a reflecting reason, that is to say it is not the type which is constantly peeping and critically monitoring its own self, but reason more generally – as it were, reason per se. With regards to the reflecting reason, it was Shakespeare who expressed his stance through the lips of Hamlet, emphasizing, in contrast to Dostoevsky, above all the paralysis of one's will rather than weakening of one's moral principles (although one is undoubtedly linked to the other): 'Thus conscience does make cowards of us all, And thus the native hue of resolution Is sicklied o'er with the pale cast of thought'.[10] These Hamletian inner split and restless nature are the most characteristic features of reflective consciousness which is indeed capable of enslaving man by poisoning his mental activity. But even more generally – culture itself already deprives a person of freedom, for it can serve, as Vyacheslav Ivanov aptly remarked in his correspondence with Mikhail Gershenzon, as 'a system of most subtle enforcements'.[11] However, clearly, one can go too far on this path, since ethics and morality also 'imprison' man, and here subtle philosophical questions of free will, self-will (i.e. unrestrained will) and all-permissiveness duly arise.

We are, on the contrary, interested in the opposite – in a certain sense liberating – role of culture in human consciousness, which, as it were, opens up additional degrees of freedom. More precisely, in our view the main difference between the 'man of culture' and the 'man of nature' is that the former, thanks to his constant reflection, as it were creates an alternative narrative (or alternative interpretations) of his life, which are as real for him as the life itself. They also serve as a protective buffer between him and reality, because they leave him the option to re-think all the happenings from a different perspective, if you like – to convince himself differently, to 're-write' his own personal history. Basically, through rationalization of his personal experience the 'man of culture' gains creative power over this experience. As a result, for the 'man of culture' his feelings and experience – as objects of interpretation and reflection – are almost always relative. It is precisely for that reason that Goncharov's Shtolts (from 'Oblomov') 'was never swept off his feet and always felt strong enough to wrench himself free if need be'[12] Similarly, Olga – believed in her chosen man 'and *therefore* loved him; but once she stopped believing in him, she would stop loving him'![13] But in the same sense the 'man of culture' is not only a creator, but also a prisoner of his own interpretations. And here a notorious danger is concealed – of getting trapped in a vicious circle, in the 'bad infinity' of reflection. The suffering 'superfluous' people, doomed Russian Hamlets, supply an endless series of such tragic examples.

Thus culture simultaneously liberates and enslaves its bearer. 'Oh, how late did I realise', utters in the twentieth century the lyrical hero of David Samoilov, '. . . that sometimes I should not have pacified my passions, and that it's wrong to protect

---

[10] William Shakespeare, 'Hamlet', Act 3, Scene 1.
[11] Mikhail Gershenzon and Viacheslav Ivanov, *Perepiska iz dvukh uglov*, St Petersburg, 1921, p. 386.
[12] Ivan Goncharov, *Oblomov*, transl. by Natalie Duddington, London: Everyman's Publishers, 1932 (reprinted 1992), p. 183.
[13] Ivan Goncharov, *Oblomov*, Moscow, 1967, p. 470. Highlighting is mine. O.T.

yourself emotionally . . .'[14] – thus revealing again an existence of a conscious choice of life strategies for a bearer of culture. This pressing choice is emphasized once again in a different poem of the same period – by Yurii Vizbor: 'Get up – the world is awaiting your decision: to be or not to be, to love or not to love'.[15] And here one could recall Chekhov with his irony regarding a fragile inner organization of the 'man of culture', with his scepticism with respect to the thin 'cultural coating' that so easily rubs off in the face of a real danger.

However, if the 'man of culture' has at least a theoretical possibility to escape from the 'inevitable', the 'man of nature' does not have such a choice, because (in our terminology) the 'man of nature' is the one for whom life categories are absolute. Hence a sarcastic question 'to love or not to love' is in principle inapplicable to him! Quite on the contrary, his characteristic formula is opposite: 'If you love – then really love! If you celebrate wildly – then truly celebrate!'.[16] For him love, as well as wild revellings, and all his feelings and passions, as for that matter life itself, are akin to natural phenomena – like rain showers, drought or blizzard. If the 'man of nature' is a prisoner, then he is a prisoner of his own inner elements only. He is denied a choice of interpretations. Reflection is alien to him, and the saying 'you can't control your heart' is immutable, as, similarly, the famous phrase of Antoine de Saint-Exupéry 'only the heart can truly see'[17] is for him beyond doubt. Absence of choice is, in a sense, imprinted in the language itself – through existence of cases and impersonal constructions, which, if you like, mirror the fate of man, first conceived precisely as part of nature, as an object of action of the higher powers rather than as a demiurge-subject. Object rather than subject is man's 'grammatical' role: «его накрыло волной нежности» ['a wave of tenderness swept him'], «его захлестнула ярость» ['wrath came over him'], «ему стало весело» ['joy overwhelmed him'] (with the same higher inevitability with which «снесло крышу» ['the roof was blown off'] or «затопило дорогу» ['the road got flooded']).[18]

Of course, the most distinctive and distilled examples of 'men of nature' are strong and passionate men of integrity – from Pushkin's gypsies to the heroes of the young Gorky. Many of them feature in the writings by Vladimir Vysotsky and Vasilii Shukshin. However, in the latter case we are dealing with a different (but no less important) type of the 'man of nature' whose rich history can also be traced in Russian literature starting from the nineteenth century. This is a quiet, unremarkable type, but who lives a 'natural' life, that is to say not based on reason, but based instead on the 'intelligence of the soul'

[14] David Samoilov, 'Davai poedem v gorod', in Samoilov, *Izbrannoe: stikhotvoreniia i poemy*, Rostov-on-Don, 1999, p. 73. In Russian: 'О, как я поздно понял'; '. . . что, порой, напрасно Давал страстям улечься, И что нельзя беречься . . .'

[15] Yurii Vizbor, 'Vstavaite, graf, rassvet uzhe poloshchetsa . . .', in Yurii Vizbor (edited by A. Azarov), *Veriu v semistrunnuiu gitaru*, Moscow, 1994, p. 129. In Russian:'Вставайте, мир ждёт вашего решения: Быть иль не быть, любить иль не любить'.

[16] This is a quotation, already mentioned in the previous chapter, from Aleksandr Rozenbaum's popular song 'Utinaia okhota', op. cit. In Russian: 'Любить – так любить; гулять, так гулять'.

[17] Antoine de Saint-Exupéry , 'Malenkii Prints' ('Little Prince'), see <http://lib.ru/EKZUPERY/mprinc.txt.>

[18] Of course such a phenomenon is not exclusive to Russian – as reflected in the specially selected translations – but the difference remains in the frequency of such expressions and in the impersonal Russian constructions with no subject.

(which Aglaia Epanchina in Dostoevsky's 'The Idiot' calls 'the main intelligence') and capable of instinctively and unmistakably distinguishing good from evil.

The 'man of nature' of the 'gypsy type' is in the thick of what Dostoevsky called a 'living life', and yet he does not embody the human dream of a metaphysical paradise depicted in 'Son smeshnogo cheloveka', for the recklessness of passion (in particular, a passion for freedom!) restricts and ruins him in the same way as reflection 'destroys' the 'man of culture'. However, basically devoid of the rational buffer, the 'man of nature' turns out to be more vulnerable than the 'man of culture', and can perish at once. At the same time, the 'quiet' 'man of nature', who embodies the Russian Orthodox ideal and symbolizes inner strength, is nevertheless often killed, falling prey to the cruel world and, in a sense, repeating the redemptive feat of Christ.

In some sense the antithesis 'man of nature – man of culture' is reflected in Turgenev's opposition between Hamlet and Don Quixote – the man of thought versus the man of action. Interestingly, a collision of these two types in Russian literature is often associated with conflict: the 'man of culture' feels guilty with respect to the 'simple folk' – the children of nature. In Lev Tolstoy's 'Kazaki', it is precisely the cultured hero who feels lost and defeated in the face of the 'natural' people – those who sense the juicy fullness of existence, are not poisoned by reflection and stand firmly on their feet. It is thus not surprising that Acmeists in their manifesto were striving to return to the 'man of nature', having spurned the neurotic essence of the 'man of culture': 'as adamists we are forest beasts a little, and in any case we shall not give away our animal features in exchange for neurosthenia',[19] Gumilev wrote.

Equally, the 'man of nature', if he has already swallowed the hook of civilization, feels uncomfortable with the 'men of culture', who 'oppress' him with their intellect and weigh him down with their implied superiority. The 'man of nature' then perceives the 'man of culture' as a crafty trickster with his tongue-in-cheek (for excessive reflection is always crafty), even if the latter is selfless and not cunning. A struggle of the 'man of nature' against the 'man of culture' in its futility and doom is by and large reminiscent of the desperate struggle of Don Quixote against the wind-mills, and is depicted with genius in Vasilii Shukshin's story 'Srezal'. Its protagonist, an intellectual popinjay of the village, sadly unaware of his limitations, self-assuredly enters into debates with an occasional educated visitor, without realizing that their dialogue is in principle impossible and that his efforts are pathetic. A true 'man of nature', however, remains grandly and proudly rising above the 'man of culture' as a cliff over a hut.

Already from the above it should be clear that the antithesis the 'man of nature – man of culture' is interesting in its own right, and represents just a tip of an iceberg. However, we would like to make another significant step and move from this opposition to the qualitatively different one: to a comparison along the same lines not only of the protagonists, but of the texts per se. Especially productive here is a juxtaposition of Andrei Platonov and Mikhail Bulgakov – as representatives respectively of these two currents: 'natural' and 'cultural'.

---

[19] Nikolai Gumilev, 'Nasledie simvolizma i akmeizm', in N. S. Gumilev, *Pisma o russkoi poezii*, Moscow, 1990, p. 57.

What do we mean by that? Platonov's works sometimes create an illusion of the flow of raw life, portrayed as it is, so that the very text, paradoxically though it may sound, appears to be a natural rather than cultural phenomenon. It gives an impression of a Biblical text – if the latter is to be understood as a fable, as an unprocessed life material with a moral law encoded within it. At the same time, Bulgakov's text is undoubtedly inscribed into the space of culture – as if filtered through the ethical and aesthetic filters of the author openly (rather than covertly, as in Platonov's case), and is replete with culturological references.

It is believed that the cause of this is above all in the language. For, just as Russia is often named as the main hero of Gogol's 'Dead Souls', the main hero of Platonov's oeuvre, one can venture to say, is the language itself. Indeed, Platonov, if you like, genetically modifies it (thus for some this writer altogether 'left the boundaries of verbal thinking [. . .] and demonstrated a total absurdity not only of reality, but also of the words, using which people describe this reality').[20] For Joseph Brodsky, Platonov obviously illustrated an enormous 'ability of language to mutate',[21] – because only language managed to reflect adequately a 'mutating reality' of those years. Maybe this is another reason why Platonov's texts give the impression of the elements, of the unprocessed raw material of life in its primordial form – for the very elements of language are audible in his writings.

A parallel with the types of humour inherent in the oeuvre of Vladimir Vysotsky and Mikhail Zhvanetsky is relevant here: Zhvanetsky's humour is semantic in nature, while Vysotsky's – often – linguistic. More precisely, Vysotsky, if you like, opens and releases humour concealed in the language itself, while Zhvanetsky constructs humorous content using language as essential, yet traditional instrument. (This is akin to the distinction between physics and chemistry in that the former is concerned with the external transformations of matter, whereas the latter – with the internal ones.) Similarly, Platonov releases the energy of the language itself; he extracts the precious semantic mollusc from inside the linguistic shell. Bulgakov, on the other hand, subjugates language in the same way as one cultivates a plant, without penetrating into the linguistic kernel.

But Platonov has another 'mystery' as well, which reveals itself not in his main works, such as the novels 'Chevengur' or 'Kotlovan', but, for instance, in the story 'Vozvrashchenie'. Its protagonist, who has an intentionally typical, 'ordinary' and 'natural' – close to the roots – surname Ivanov, is returning from the war front to his wife and children. In comparison to the sophisticatedly ornamented, 'temple'-like works of Bulgakov, this story by Platonov is more akin to a petroglyph mural. Indeed, in Bulgakov's text an ethical message is mediated, that is to say, it is enclosed into an aesthetic cocoon; it is a whole cultural universe. By contrast, in Platonov's 'Vozvrashchenie' we are struck by an apparent minimalism of resources. However, a

---

[20] Mikhail Volokhov, Interview. Cited in Andrei Shcherbakov, 'Udarim Platonovym po pokhabshchine!', <http://www.pravda.ru/culture/literature/rusliterature/26–09–2006/198230-platonov-1/> [accessed 18 March 2013].

[21] Joseph Brodsky, 'Poet bogotvorit tolko iazyk', Interview to David Montenegro, in Polukhina (ed.), *Iosif Brodskii. Bolshaia kniga interviiu*, op. cit., p. 272.

psychological (one is tempted to say 'metaphysical') accuracy is so high that it does not leave any room for aesthetic embellishments, as if they can destroy or hinder it.[22]

As a result, the ethical breakthrough happens as if without mediators and with the minimum of resources – namely, thanks to the author's ability to penetrate directly into the very kernel of life – into that Biblical, exposed essence of phenomena. Here is one of the last paragraphs of 'Vozvrashchenie': 'Ivanov closed his eyes, not wanting to see and feel the pain of the exhausted children now lying on the ground, and then felt a kind of heat in his chest, as if the heart imprisoned and pining within him had been beating long and in vain all his life and had only now beaten its way to freedom, filling his entire being with warmth and awe. He suddenly recognized everything he had ever known before, but much more precisely and more truthfully. Previously, he had sensed the life of others through a barrier of pride and self-interest, but now, all of a sudden, he had touched another life with his naked heart'.[23]

It appears that what Platonov does is similar: with his naked, bare heart he touches life itself, and therefore sees straight to the roots of things, to the essence of phenomena, in order to pull out to the light of day the naked grain of the Biblical truth. And this truth – which may seem to be uncunningly simple – turns out to be the shortest distance to the reader's heart, which, as it were, opens up and becomes bare in response. It is the concentrated wisdom about man, delivered in its purest form, that creates a resonance with the New Testament here. Of course such a resonance is also evoked when reading Bulgakov's works, especially 'Master i Margarita'. However, in the latter case we encounter a perception of the Bible, or even its re-production, above all as an object of culture and in the framework of high culture. If you like, this is precisely a reflection of the 'man of culture' on the Biblical theme, where the author's approach is culturological in character. It is a New Testament of sorts, framed by the author's ethics and aesthetics. Any plot-line here is saturated with historical and religious-philosophical references. Thus, for example, the unforgettable story of the highest compassion displayed by Margarita – the story of Frida – is based, as is known, on the real historical material. Two women served as Frida's prototypes – Frida Keller from Switzerland and Konietsko from Silesia. And although Maragarita's act of compassion is spontaneous, just as the catharsis experienced by Ivanov in 'Vozvrashchenie' ('Margarita caught her breath. She was about to utter her secret wish when she suddenly turned pale, opened her mouth and stared. "Frieda! Frieda, Frieda!" a sobbing, imploring voice cried in her ear. "My name is Frieda!"'),[24] it is nevertheless accompanied by comprehension, inherent in a cultured person who knows that her scores with her own self, the pangs of her conscience are more unbearable than a loss

---

[22]   In the same line of 'hidden' devices there is concealed also a precise value hierarchy: Ivanov has not yet become fully a human being – therefore he is only designated by a (common) surname. Masha is given a (girl's) name and a fleeting role. At the same time, Lubov' (which is Russian for Love) Vasilievna – Ivanov's wife – who embodies motherhood, humanity and Love in its highest sense (hence the capital letter) is endowed with full individuality – with both name and patronymic.

[23]   Andrey Platonov, *The Return and Other Stories*, transl. by Robert and Elizabeth Chandler, and Angela Livingstone, London: The Harvill Press, 1999, p. 203.

[24]   Mikhail Bulgakov, 'The Master and Margarita', transl. by Michael Glenny, London: Collins and Harvill Press, 1967, p. 147.

of personal happiness: 'I am a careless person. I only asked you about Frieda because I was rash enough to give her a firm hope. She's waiting, messire, she believes in my power. And if she's cheated I shall be in a terrible position. I shall have no peace for the rest of my life. I can't help it – it just happened'.[25]

In Platonov's story, wisdom, by contrast, is not a corollary of culture. It emerges in front of the reader in a simple and inevitable way, as a phenomenon of nature, whose integral part man is as well. This wisdom is inescapable, and cannot be misinterpreted. It is naked, undressed, and devoid of Bulgakov's cultural references: 'There was nothing to divert or comfort a human heart except another human heart'; Masha 'trusted herself to Ivanov in the goodness of her heart, with no thought beyond the moment'; Ivanov's thoughts prior to the catharsis: 'All love comes from need and yearning; if human beings never felt need or yearning, they would never love', and suddenly, the catharsis itself, whereby 'previously, he had sensed the life of others through a barrier of pride and self-interest, but now, all of a sudden, he had touched another life with his naked heart'.[26]

Thus the whole plot of 'Vozvrashchenie' is also in a full sense a New Testament story – on mercy and compassion, on overcoming your own ego on the way to the Other, that is to say – on love in its highest sense. This story, as it were, is permeated with the very nature of man, just as Bulgakov's text is permeated with culture.

These preliminary remarks by no means exhaust the theme, but merely mark the path for a comparative characteristic of the 'culturological' and 'natural' texts (authorial approaches), as well as their protagonists, which appears productive. Akin to the binary classification, possibly controversial, but certainly captivating, which Fazil Iskander applies to the world (and in particular, to Russian) literature, dividing it into the 'literature of homeliness' (Pushkin, Tolstoy, Akhmatova) and 'literature of homelessness' (Lermontov, Dostoevsky, Tsvetaeva),[27] one could also undertake a large-scale classification based on the 'nature-culture' dichotomy, indicated above. However, this task clearly requires a separate major study.

[25] Bulgakov, op. cit.
[26] Andrey Platonov, *The Return and Other Stories*, transl. by Robert and Elizabeth Chandler, and Angela Livingstone, London: The Harvill Press, 1999, pp. 174, 176, 201–2, 203.
[27] Fazil Iskander, *Lastochkino gnezdo. Proza. Poeziia. Publitsistika*, op. cit., p. 342.

6

Cases of Subversion: Chekhov and Brodsky (Under the Veneer of Rationalism, or On the Concepts of Hot and Cold Blood as Philosophical Categories)

[I feel that I will never read Chekhov again]. It is a dry mind . . .

Innokentii Annensky

Mr Chekhov dabbles in writing with cold blood . . .

Nikolai Mikhailovsky

Despite reproaches in indifference and arrogance [. . .] he (Brodsky) was extremely responsive and generous.

Valentina Polukhina

Many times I have heard the opinion that Brodsky is a cold poet – too rational, too reserved . . .

Svetlana Klimova

In this technique of his Brodsky is very rational . . .

Evgenii Rein

In which way are these two Russian classics – Anton Chekhov and Joseph Brodsky – relevant to our investigation of irrationalism; and what unites them other than the title above? Brodsky's (documented) dislike of Chekhov is discussed, at least to some extent, in scholarly literature, as well as, interestingly, the points of kinship in their artistic worlds. It is not my goal here to analyse the roots and nature of Brodsky's negative attitude to Chekhov. The poet's interest in the writer was profound enough to express it (even if negatively) not only in his non-fiction, but also in his poetry. He dedicated to Chekhov a poem called explicitly 'Posviashaetsa Chekhovu' ('Dedicated to Chekhov'), in which he deliberately reduces and simplifies Chekhov's world to the point of ridicule, but at the same time appropriates it and filters it out through his own poetic and philosophical sensibility, ending up with what looks as their (Brodsky's and Chekhov's) common ground. Both artists signify the same era – of which Chekhov was a precursor and foresaw it intuitively, while Brodsky became its singer, even if his songs are not those of praise. Furthermore, unlike some explicitly mystical, religious or anti-rationalist writers, both Chekhov and Brodsky appear to be rationalists, at least on the outside – with their respect for scientific knowledge, connected to positivism and atheism, and in the very nature of their enquiry – sober and disillusioned. Yet, I want to prove that this impression is deceptive and to reveal their hidden irrationalism – or, more precisely, their complex relationships with the irrational.

The irrational age

Brodsky characterized the divide between the new – modern and Modernist – and the old age by a rapidly widening gulf between a human being and his thoughts about himself (directly proportional to the increase of the technological speeds):

> What we call the nineteenth century marks what appears to be the last period in the history of our species when its scale of reality was quantitatively human. Numerically at least, an individual's interplay with his likes was not any different from that in, say, antiquity. [. . .] The acceleration of pace (subject more of enjoyment than of manly regret) has set us clearly apart, if only due to its curtailing effects on any form of commitment or concentration. For a man travelling at bullet or supersonic speed to his destination, it is difficult to comprehend wounded honour, the grid of class barriers, someone's brooding over a ruined estate, the contemplation of a single tree, or ambivalence at prayer.[1]

The loss of humanness in humanity, the loss of old traditional morality and culture, the encroaching disintegration and chaos were all marks of the new – twentieth – century, of the crisis of Christianity and 'old' civilization. Aleksandr Etkind and the school of thought to which he belongs, traces the roots of this rift to the perversions in sexual and psychological spheres, to the sadomasochistic scale of values with its irrational subversion of Puritan morality of the Enlightenment, when suffering and joy, as it were, swapped places.[2] For Dostoevsky, who was among the first to sense and transmit the tectonic shifts of cultural paradigm, these ideas are absorbed into a wider cultural–philosophical perception with an understanding of intrinsic contradictions of human nature (subversive of positivism) whereby man loves destruction no less than creation, and treasures his right to be capricious, to be irrational, to opt for suffering as a source of consciousness and thus of life. It is such paradoxes of

---

[1] Joseph Brodsky, 'Foreword' to *An Age Ago, A Selection of Nineteenth-Century Russian Poetry*, selected and translated by Alan Myers, New York: Farrar-Straus-Giroux, 1988, pp. xii–xiv.
[2] See Aleksandr Etkind, *Sodom i Psikheia. Ocherki intellektualnoi istorii Serebrianogo veka*, Moscow: Garant, 1995.

human psyche (and/or the acute realization of them) that determine this new 'era of psychology' marked by the reversal of the predictable 'linearity of emotions'.[3]

Chekhov is ascribed precisely to this transitional period of the turn of the centuries, when 'the old value system was crumbling down and the realisation dawned that Truth, Good and Beauty do not constitute a trinity'.[4] Consequently, Chekhov, as yet intuitively, while Brodsky – due to chronology – post-factum, documented the New Age, the end of Culture through its turning into subculture, into the product for mass consumption. In brief, they documented the 'end of a beautiful epoch' (*Konets prekrasnoi epokhi*), using Brodsky's words; not so much the age of reason, as the age of faithlessness. For the poet it was a reality, a fact of life; for the writer – just a premonition. As Andrei Bitov wrote, Chekhov 'felt with his skin, like that Japanese fish which predicts earthquakes, what the twentieth century would bring to Russia'.[5]

As already mentioned in Chapter 4, in this new era, later labelled Modernism and Post-modernism, absolute values no longer exist – relativist principle and random accidentality reign in the universe. Thus the meaninglessness and emptiness of existence become a pressing issue giving rise to existentialist trend in European culture, with the Irrational and the Absurd coming to the forefront.

Irina Plekhanova in this connection identifies a shift of cultural self-identification of an individual from space to time. According to her, the 'man of time' (and moreover, of the New Time, volatile and unstable) is 'oriented toward the relative, and is opposite to the "man of space", who is oriented toward the obvious. [. . .] To the man of time it is more important to feel and to encompass continuing time spans with his thoughts, rather than to see. This means an existence not so much in the external, as in the internal [. . .] while being in search of the hidden content simultaneously of the movement within him and without. This means living with a certain degree of alienation from here and now, as if in parallel fields; not belonging fully to this reality'.[6]

Those characteristics of the 'man of time' which Plekhanova lists in relation to Chekhov are applicable precisely to Brodsky as well: 'space is exhausted, it no longer contains a mystery; pressure is applied by civilization, with its striving to other dimensions; a shift of cultural paradigm, Nietzschean idea of a break-through to the future, combined with the idea of eternal return; the epoch of individualism; relativism of the value system; a search, despite everything, for an absolute freedom here and now, i.e. there, where it is physically impossible, but can be attained by emotion; mystical, metaphysical and existential moods of the authors'.[7]

---

[3] See the Introduction for a more detailed quotation expressing this idea of Lidia Ginzburg. See also Chapter 3 (as well as the Introduction), where the term 'era of psychology' used by Lev Shestov in relation to Dostoevsky is cited in context.

[4] Margarita Odesskaia, 'Byli li idealy u gospodina Chekhova?' in *Vestnik RGGU*, Series: 'Zhurnalistika. Literaturnaia kritika', 2008, No. 11, pp. 219–27.

[5] Andrei Bitov, 'Moi dedushka Chekhov i pradedushka Pushkin', in *Chetyrezhdy Chekhov (Four Times Chekhov)*, Moscow: Emergency Exit, 2004, p. 11.

[6] Irina Plekhanova, 'Chelovek vremeni v proze Chekhova', in Sobennikov (ed.), *Filosofiia Chekhova*, op. cit., pp. 133–4.

[7] Ibid.

By the same token, the Lotmans notice that for Brodsky 'time can be interpreted as a continuation of space. [. . .] Time is more material than space. At any rate it always has some material equivalent.'[8] Moreover, 'despite the fact that natural-philosophy of Brodsky's poetry reveals Platonic foundation', in his poetry 'the essence of existence is not in orderliness, but in disorder, not in regularity, but in accidentality.'[9] These are precisely the features that Chekhov's writings were accused of by the literary criticism of his contemporaries, and which ascribe both writers to the new – existentialist – era.

Existentialist features have indeed been identified in the artistic worlds of both Chekhov and Brodsky, and are undoubtedly relevant to a discussion of the irrationalist elements in their outlook. However, before examining the belonging of both authors to Existentialism, or, for that matter, any other philosophical school, let us look at an interesting paradigm which reveals a rational–irrational duality in their artistic worlds.

Duality of the rational and irrational

If we deem irrationalism to defy or ignore logic (the voice of reason), or, more precisely, to encompass actions and phenomena whose logic we cannot grasp, then we are immediately faced with its underlying relativity. As was mentioned previously,[10] Chekhov certainly has 'an understanding of the reciprocal relationship between the rational and irrational', thus his characters 'when they act rationally from their own point of view, continually perform deeds which are completely irrational from other people's viewpoints.'[11] The same is inherent in Brodsky for whom God's logic is unintelligible for man, for as long as mankind exists. Indeed, it looks to a human as a game without rules; in other words, as absurdity: 'Here lies a merchant from Asia. He knew his craft – a merchant was he practical, but inconspicuous. He died quickly: fever. On merchant business had he sailed here, and not for this. Laid by him, a legionary, beneath rough quartz. In war he had brought glory to the Empire. How many times they could have killed him! Yet, he died an old man. Even here, Postum, there are no rules.'[12]

Curiously, there appears to be a certain duality linking the concepts of the rational and irrational together in an interesting dialectical relationship. Indeed, in many of

---

[8]   Yurii Lotman and Mikhail Lotman, 'Mezhdu veshchiiu i pustotoi', op. cit., vol. 3, p. 297.

[9]   Ibid., p. 296.

[10] See the discussion in the introduction on methodological difficulties of defining the irrationalism concept.

[11] Stepanov, 'Lev Shestov on Chekhov', in Olga Tabachnikova (ed.), *Anton Chekhov Through The Eyes Of Russian Thinkers: Vasilii Rozanov, Dmitrii Merezhkovskii and Lev Shestov*, op. cit., p. 171.

[12] Iosif Brodsky, 'Pisma rimskomu drugu', in Brodsky, *Forma vremeni. Stikhotvoreniia, esse, piesy v 2-kh tomakh*, Minsk: Eridan, 1992, vol. 1, p. 269. In Russian: 'Здесь лежит купец из Азии. Толковым// был купцом он – деловит, но незаметен.// Умер быстро: лихорадка.// По торговым// он делам сюда приплыл, а не за этим.// Рядом с ним – легионер, под грубым кварцем.// Он в сражениях Империю прославил.// Столько раз могли убить! а умер старцем.// Даже здесь не существует, Постум, правил'.

Chekhov's stories excessive rationalism, which knows no restraints and is brought to its logical conclusion, turns into irrationalism. Thus a humble clerk in Chekhov's '*Smert' chinovnika*' ('A Death of a Clerk') who accidentally sneezes, while in the theatre, at a bold patch of an authority figure (someone else's boss), at first behaves rationally, feels suitably (for his mentality) anxious and frightened and apologizes profusely. But having received forgiving assurances from the boss, he persists with his apologies, gradually driving his superior to the state of an utter rage, which leads our humble hero to his death. This is an example of how rationalism, like a car without brakes, speeds up out of control and becomes irrationalism. Similarly, 'The Man in a Case' strikes us as a totally irrational individual, but predominantly because his utterly rational – sensible and cautious – actions are taken to their logical extreme. In other words, it is precisely his rationality, which knows no measure, that appears comically and tragically irrational.

On the other hand, irrationalism which is 'restrained' by the 'brakes' of morality and culture reveals certain rationale to it. In this vein noble deeds which appear irrationally suicidal – like saving someone else's life at the risk of losing one's own – in fact have their own logic in the fact that if one refrains from that noble act and let the other die, he then will be unable to live with himself, with the knowledge of his own self-betrayal, with the loss of dignity/integrity. Thus Dymov from '*Poprygun'ia*' ('Grasshopper') loses his life due to his basically irrational behaviour – non-cautiously treating diphtheria of a child – but this is simply the result of his day-to-day quiet exploit, of his nobility of spirit, where the well-being of others matters much more to him than his own. He simply cannot live otherwise. To use Max Weber's notation (within his division of rationalism into value-oriented and purpose-oriented types), Dymov's irrationalism can perhaps be classified as purpose-oriented (to save a child, possibly at the expense of your own life), which, on the other hand, can be deemed a value-oriented rationalism (the logic of which lies in following some high moral values that are crucial for maintaining self-respect).

However, the earlier examples concern only the outer (if you like – thematic) layer of irrationalism in Chekhov's world. A much more subtle irrationalism is inherent in his very sensibility and manifested in his poetics. As Aleksandr Chudakov put it, 'Chekhov is a bigger irrationalist and mystagogue' than many of the Symbolists.[13]

Indeed Chekhov's authorial withdrawal is accompanied by constant subversions of one layer of meaning by another – deeper – layer, thus denying any statement its absolute value. What seems at first rationally based turns out to conceal an irrational foundation. Thus, the notorious answer of the old professor Nikolai Stepanovich to the desperate outcry ('what should I do?!') of his 'almost-daughter' Katia: 'I don't know, Katia, I don't know' (which drove a lot of 'monological' critics to unambiguous condemning conclusions) is subverted by the professor's inner thought which immediately follows: 'Farewell, my treasure!'[14] By the same token, the story 'Kryzhovnik'

---

[13] Aleksandr Chudakov, 'Chekhov and Merezhkovskii: Two Types of Artistic-Philosophical Consciousness', in Olga Tabachnikova (ed.), *Anton Chekhov Through The Eyes Of Russian Thinkers: Vasilii Rozanov, Dmitrii Merezhkovskii and Lev Shestov*, op. cit., p. 101.

[14] See Anatoly Sobennikov, 'Chekhov i stoiki', in Sobennikov (ed.), *Filosofiia Chekhova*, op. cit., p. 178. The reference is to Chekhov's story 'Skuchnaia istoriia'.

ends with ambivalence when a clear-cut humanist message of Ivan Ivanovich is undermined by the very environment, the interior of the room, the circumstances of the other protagonists and the authorial words:

> Ivan Ivanich's story had satisfied neither Bourkin nor Aliokhin. With the generals and ladies looking down from their gilt frames, seeming alive in the firelight, it was tedious to hear the story of a miserable official who ate gooseberries. Somehow they had a longing to hear and to speak of charming people, and of women. And the mere fact of sitting in the drawing-room where everything – the lamp with its coloured shade, the chairs, and the carpet under their feet – told how the very people who now looked down at them from their frames once walked, and sat and had tea there, and the fact that pretty Pelagueya was near – was much better than any story.[15]

Moreover, a further subversion is introduced by the heavy smell from Ivan Ivanovich's pipe which creates an uneasy contrast with his 'clean' and lofty consciousness, as well as with the smell of fresh linen for the other guests, who are not taken so much by his highly moral sermon: 'A smell of burning tobacco came from his pipe which lay on the table, and Bourkin could not sleep for a long time and was worried because he could not make out where the unpleasant smell came from.'[16]

Similarly, in the story 'Nevesta' just two authorial words subvert the previous utterly positive message: 'The next morning [...] she [Nadia] left the town, *as she supposed* (как полагала), forever.'[17] Equally, the story 'In Exile' ('V ssylke') ends with the phrase 'The door remained unclosed,'[18] which again subverts the individual truths (just delivered by the two heroes) and reinforces their relativity.

The latter story is interesting also as an illustration of another profoundly Chekhovian feature, directly linked to the irrationalism problem: that which can be labelled a conflict of Hot and Cold Blood.

Philosophical opposition of 'Hot and Cold Blood' in relation to the opposition of rational–irrational

Indeed, in a great variety of works Chekhov seems to be deliberately portraying a clashing encounter of two philosophies: Stoicism and 'Lyricism'; acceptance and resignation on the one hand, which seem to be equated to being emotionally static, and rebellion

---

[15] Anton Chekhov (ed.), 'Gooseberries' ('Kryzhovnik', 1898), from *The House with the Mezzanine and other Stories*, transl. by Samuel Koteliansky and Gilbert Cannan, Charles Scribner's Sons, 1917, <http://www.eldritchpress.org/ac/gooseb.html> [accessed 15 August 2014].

[16] Ibid.

[17] Anton Chekhov, 'The Bethrothed' ('Nevesta', 1903), <http://ilibrary.ru/text/1184/p.1/index.html> [accessed 12 August 2014].

[18] Anton Chekhov, 'In Exile' ('V ssylke', 1892), transl. by Constance Garnett, from *The Cook's Wedding and Other Stories*, 1922, Macmillan Company, <http://www.eldritchpress.org/ac/iex.htm> [accessed 15 August 2014].

and suffering on the other hand, which apparently represent emotional dynamics. The importance of this theme for Chekhov is reflected by the fact that sometimes its recurrences have an almost word-by-word similarity. Thus in the aforementioned story 'V ssylke' (1892) we have a debate between a 'stoic' Semen and a 'lyric' – young Tatar convict. Semen claims that he has understood himself fully (that is to say, he fulfilled the commandment of the Oracle of Delphi: познай самого себя ('get to know yourself') (*poznai samogo sebia*: 'Gnothi seauton')), and that he is totally adjusted and self-sufficient – he does not need anything or anybody, and there is no-one richer and more liberated than him. His words, however, are undermined by his actions (another very frequent Chekhov's device) – of actively seeking human contact; by his over-verbosity and his very narrative: repetitive, excessive and authoritarian. As Durkin aptly notices, it is Semen of all the characters who is least dynamic – both physically and psychologically.[19] He is opposed to the young Tatar, unjustly convicted, who, on the contrary, laments and cries, who speaks of his distant home and his beautiful and clever wife, whom he misses terribly. His passions, akin to that of Job, clash with Semen's apparent stoicism. Moreover, he denounces Semen's stance as lifeless and unnatural, referring to the suffering of the impractical барин (*barin*) from Semen's story, of whom the latter spoke with a condescending sarcasm:

> He is good . . . good; but you are bad! You are bad! The gentleman is a good soul, excellent, and you are a beast, bad! The gentleman is alive, but you are a dead carcass. . . God created man to be alive, and to have joy and grief and sorrow; but you want nothing, so you are not alive, you are stone, clay! A stone wants nothing and you want nothing. You are a stone, and God does not love you, but He loves the gentleman![20]

This monologue, the passion of which is further stressed by its broken Russian, is, in terms of its semantics, strikingly similar to that of Gromov in 'Palata No 6' (notably, written in the same year, 1892), despite the fact that the latter is delivered in a different register and through the use of a different (much more sophisticated) vocabulary. Gromov's indignation here is his response to Dr Ragin's philosophy of indifference (or, in other words, to his proclamation of a stoic stance – of acceptance and resignation):

> 'Comprehension . . ', repeated Ivan Dmitritch frowning. 'External, internal . . . Excuse me, but I don t understand it. I only know', he said, getting up and looking angrily at the doctor – 'I only know that God has created me of warm blood and nerves, yes, indeed! If organic tissue is capable of life it must react to every stimulus. And I do! To pain I respond with tears and outcries, to baseness with indignation, to filth with loathing. To my mind, that is just what is called life. The lower the organism, the less sensitive it is, and the more feebly it reacts to stimulus; and the higher it is, the more responsively and vigorously it reacts to reality. How is it you don't know that? A doctor, and not know such trifles! To despise suffering, to be

---

[19] See Andrew Durkin, 'Modeli khudozhestvennogo slova v chekhovskikh rasskazakh "V ssylke" i "Student"', in Sobennikov (ed.), *Filosofiia Chekhova*, op. cit., p. 50.

[20] Anton Chekhov, 'In Exile', op. cit.

always contented, and to be surprised at nothing, one must reach this condition' – and Ivan Dmitritch pointed to the peasant who was a mass of fat – 'or to harden oneself by suffering to such a point that one loses all sensibility to it – that is, in other words, to cease to live.'[21]

Thus what we have here is an opposition of an open, deliberately unsuppressed (and moreover, promoted into a life credo) passion and suffering on the one hand, and what appears to be a wise resignation come indifference, on the other; in brief: an opposition of Hot and Cold Blood. However, this Cold Blood trend is more contradictory than it lets on, for it can, perhaps more suitably, be renamed as Cooled Down Blood, reflecting a (more subconsciously than consciously) suppressed, contradictory stance. Importantly, I am not talking here of the unambiguous instances of utterly inhuman behaviour – of representatives, as it were, of the animal kingdom (those Chekhov's protagonists which Veniamin Albov described as 'completely solid, animal figures, sometimes more nimble, clever and cruel than those animals, which they resemble'[22] or of the heroes whose indifference appears genuinely unnatural and disturbing, like in the story deliberately entitled 'Cold Blood'. Rather, I am talking about those Chekhov's characters who are fully capable of sensations, but lack inner harmony and hide behind various philosophical facades. They cannot bring themselves to face their true feelings – instead they flee from their inner selves, they try to escape, often without even being able to identify their genuine desires. Their lifelessness, their state of being emotionally static come in two different disguises: either of aggression and excessive self-assurance or passivity and apathy. The former can be observed in endless sequence of Chekhov's heroes who 'know how', 'know the way' (знают, как надо, '*znaiut, kak nado*') and therefore loudly preach, like Lida Volchaninova from 'Dom s mezoninom'. The latter, like Dr Ragin, quote Mark Aurelius and turn away from transient existence, deeming struggle pointless.

Nikolai Stepanovich from the aforementioned 'Skuchnaiia istoriia' seems to undergo the same conflict of Hot and Cold Blood, of passion and indifference, only diachronically: when young, he professes Mark Aurelius's principles: 'I have never judged, I have been indulgent, I have readily forgiven every one, right and left',[23] and lists Aurelius explicitly among the classics, whereas at the threshold of death he laments stoic philosophy, seeing it as lifeless.

One could be tempted to associate irrationalism with the concept of Hot Blood and rationalism, accordingly, with Cold Blood. Indeed, the former is permeated with pure passion, while the latter is steeped in rational thought and filtering one's emotions

---

[21] Anton Chekhov, 'Ward No. 6' ('Palata No. 6', 1892), transl. by Constance Garnett, *The Horse Stealers and Other Stories*, 1921, Macmillan Company, renewed 1949, David Garnett, as reprinted in The Modern Library Edition, *Longer Stories from the Last Decade*, 1993, by Random House, Inc., pp. 146–98, <http://www.eldritchpress.org/ac/w6–10.html> [accessed 12 August 2014].

[22] Veniamin Albov, 'Dva momenta v razvitii tvorchestva Antona Pavlovicha Chekhova', in Igor' Sukhikh and Andrei Stepanov (eds), *A.P. Chekhov: Pro et Contra. Tvorchestvo A.P. Chekhova v russkoi mysli kontsa XIX – nachala XX v. (1887–1914)*, Anthology, St Petersburg: Izdatel'stvo Russkogo Khristianskogo gumanitarnogo Instituta, 2002, p. 376.

[23] Anton Chekhov, 'A Boring Story', <http://www.eastoftheweb.com/short-stories/UBooks/BoriStor.shtml> [accessed 10 August 2014].

through a particular philosophical teaching. However, interestingly, the watershed between rational and irrational, it seems to me, does not lay at the boundary between Hot and Cold Blood. This is because, looking deeper, one can conclude that passion has its own logic, it is connected with the aforementioned linearity (or predictability) of emotions to which Lidia Ginzburg referred.[24] By contrast, the concept of Cold Blood turns out invariably to conceal within it not only an underlying conflict (after all passion tears one apart too), but a sense of being disconnected from one's true self – precisely 'not knowing oneself'. It thus points to human attempts to escape the discrepancy between inner desires (ideals) and the outside reality. As such it is much more irrational, for it is brewed on contradiction, on the state of affairs when things 'are happening in reverse', using again Ginzburg's words. Moreover, it looks as if Chekhov, with his acute artistic intuition, inadvertently depicted in his Cold Blood characters a variety of cases of (low-burning) clinical depression (ranging from aggression to apathy), just as in his story 'Chernyi monakh' he turned out to have described, up to tiny clinical detail, a case of megalomania, as Kluge noticed.[25] If so, it points again at the profound irrationalism of human psyche, captured in fictional writing through the reflected instances of concealed psychiatric diseases (note, by the way, frequent use in the popular book *Accentuated Personalities*, by Karl Leonhard,[26] of Dostoevsky's characters as examples of various types of psychic abnormality).

Interestingly, in Brodsky's writings this clashing encounter of Hot and Cold, of Stoicism and 'Lyricism', can be found, as in the last example earlier (of the old professor), within one lyrical hero, but in contrast to the above character of Chekhov, here it happens synchronically. Indeed, for Brodsky, with his almost scientific vocabulary and high philosophical saturate of his poetry, with his propensity, especially in his later writings, to fall into monumentality, almost coldness, one can suspect the apparently rational Cold Blood pattern. And his credo, inspired by Akhmatova, of following the grandeur of idea (величие замысла) only reinforces that. However, at the same time his poetry can be highly intense, virtually boiling with passion: 'I'm howling "youuu" through my pillow dike // many seas away that are milling nearer // with my limbs in the dark playing your double like // an insanity-stricken mirror.'[27] Even sarcasm under his pen can acquire an intensely passionate slant: 'the bloodstream fire, the bone-crushing creeps, // which melt the lead in fillings with desire // to touch – "your hips", I must delete – you lips.'[28] And his lines 'I loved not

---

[24] See the Introduction for the precise quotation.

[25] See R.-D. Kluge, 'Zagadka "Chernogo monakha"', in Anatoly Sobennikov (ed.), *Filosofiia Chekhova*, op. cit., p. 101 and ref. 3 there (p. 106).

[26] Karl Leonhard, *Akzentuierte Personlichkeiten*, Frankfurt-On-Mein: Fischer, 1976.

[27] Joseph Brodsky, 'From nowhere with love . . .', transl. by the author, <http://www-users.cs.umn.edu/~safonov/brodsky/part_of_speech/from_nowhere_auto.html> [accessed 1 August 2014]. In Russian: 'я взбиваю подушку мычащим "ты",// за горами, которым конца и края,// в темноте всем телом твои черты,// как безумное зеркало, повторяя'.

[28] Joseph Brodsky, 'Twenty Sonnets to Mary Queen of Scots' ('Dvadtsat sonetov k Marii Stuart'), in *To Urania*, transl. by Joseph Brodsky and Peter France, Harmondsworth, Middlesex, England: Penguin Books, 1988, p. 20. In Russian: '. . . сей жар в груди, ширококостный хруст, чтоб пломбы в пасти плавились от жажды коснуться – "бюст" зачеркиваю – уст!'

many, but strongly'[29] are pronounced almost through gritted teeth, as if to withhold pain. In general, it appears that his at times almost mathematical discourse is only a device for containing despair, it is a straight-jacket of sorts, a banister which allows the author to hold on, to stay on top of his own insanity. This is akin to hiding one's tears behind a smile; an attempt of courage. 'I am merely nervous [. . .], but observant person'[30] is Brodsky's self-portrait in one of his essays. His phrase 'What is snobbery? Only a form of despair'[31] is a testimony to the above and a significant clue to his own confessions – whether in his creativity or in real life, where on the one hand he can be denying any feelings of nostalgia (as in his interviews and lectures) and on the other he can love the same woman for more than a quarter of a century, and continue to dedicate poetry to her, repeating that one can return to the place of one's crime, but never to the place of one's love. Thus his whole life seems more as an attempt of exercising (or rather imitating) control, of restraining his own despair and taming his own pain, reconciling with loss and with death – in brief, spurning the irrational – the more so, the more he is captured by it. In other words, Brodsky not so much strives to escape from the irrational to the rational as to frame the former with the latter, to overcome irrationalism and the Absurd, the tragic human predicament, by rational means – as if walking through the irrational wasteland of existence dressed in the protective space-suit of rationalism.

As Sergei Gandlevsky put it, 'a set of words, in order to become alive and turn into a poem, needs to release energy, to acquire temperature – oppositely charged poles, a conflict are necessary. [. . .] For Brodsky [. . .] such a life-giving difficulty was a Classicistic contradiction between duty and feeling. When his Olympic reserve abandons Brodsky, and the poet gives in to the most common human weakness – love – he knows no equals. Most of Brodsky's creative successes [. . .] are due to betrayal of oath, to defection from the ranks of heaven-dwellers. If not for the severe, to the point of zealotry, self-discipline of Brodsky, there would be no "break-downs" either – masterpieces of love lyrics and "The hawk's cry in autumn" ("Osennii krik iastreba").'[32]

Thus, although rationalism and irrationalism are naturally interwoven in the artistic worlds of both writers, it appears that the vectors of transmutation of one into the other are somewhat differently directed. More precisely, Chekhov discovers the irrational layer under all sorts of rational disguises, he leads us from rational to irrational; Brodsky, on the contrary, as if is trying to protect himself from the irrational through the refuge in the rational. Furthermore, Chekhov, encouraged among other things by the scientifically oriented aspirations of his epoch, sets out, as it were, with a hope of

[29] Iosif Brodsky, 'Ia vsegda tverdil, chto sudba – igra . . ', in Brodsky, *Forma vremeni. Stikhotvoreniia, esse, piesy v 2-kh tomakh*, op. cit., vol. 1, p. 254. In Russian: 'Я любил немногих, однако сильно'.

[30] Joseph Brodsky, *Fondamenta degli incurabili*, <http://lib.ru/BRODSKIJ/brodsky_prose.txt> [accessed 18 March 2014].

[31] Iosif Brodsky, 'Puteshestvie v Stambul', in *Sochineniia Iosifa Brodskogo*, St Petersburg: Pushkinskii Fond, 1999, vol. 5, p. 288.

[32] Sergei Gandlevsky, in *Iosif Brodskii: Tvorchestvo, lichnost', sud'ba*, Zvezda: St-Petersburg, 1998, p. 118.

understanding the world by rational means, but constantly runs (in frustration) into the deadlocks of the irrational and unknowable. Brodsky (advantaged by chronology itself) knows only too well about the irrational nature of the universe, but tries to order it rationally, to organize the chaos – by language at least. Thus both are intrinsically preoccupied by the epistemological question.

The role of epistemology for Chekhov and Brodsky

The Enlightenment hopes, laid on science and technological progress; the thriving of positivism, of Darwinism and Marxism; rapid industrialization of Western Europe inspired some and terrified others. While Dostoevsky and Tolstoy were appalled by the prospects of human degradation in the face of sweeping forces of 'civilization', Chekhov belonged to a new generation and welcomed scientific advances, at least as a doctor.

However, quite soon after Chekhov's death it started to become increasingly clear that the universe is irrational, in that it is not amenable to complete cognition by rational means. However, Chekhov's vantage point still was, apparently, that rational enquiry is the answer to human search for truth; but his hopes were crashed, his worship of scientific knowledge proved misplaced. What Dostoevsky knew by heart, it seems, Chekhov kept discovering for himself with a tinge of annoyance, if not disappointment. His artistic intuition turned out truer than his science-based hopes. Just as a vast number of literary heroes (most notably Dostoevsky's) Chekhov seems to have started with rationalism, but was proved wrong by the irrational nature of existence, and above all – of man. He then acknowledged with a sober courage the impenetrability of the universe.

As Svetlana Evdokimova convincingly shows, 'Chekhov laments the disproportion between the human need for understanding and the world's unintelligibility, what Camus calls "the unreasonable silence of the world".'[33] Moreover, he combines 'a sober acknowledgment of our inability to know the truth' with 'the realization that "there is nothing beyond reason", to use Camus' words.'[34] Fascinatingly, Evdokimova uses Masha's stance from Chekhov's *Three Sisters*: 'Either you know why you live, or else nothing matters, all the same' to compare Chekhov's rebellion against human inability to know (which deprives life of meaning) with Dostoevsky's famous premise expressed through Ivan Karamazov and usually summarized as 'if there is no God, then everything is permitted.' In Evdokimova's words, 'While Dostoevsky places the questions of ethics in the ontological context, Chekov is more interested in considering the ethical questions in the context of epistemology.'[35] Her conclusion is that 'Chekhov recognizes that Truth and God are inaccessible to thought. Yet the tragedy of man is

---

[33] Svetlana Evdokimova, 'Philosophy's Enemies: Chekhov and Shestov', in Olga Tabachnikova (ed.), *Anton Chekhov Through the Eyes of Russian Thinkers: Rozanov, Merezhkovskii and Shestov*, op. cit., p. 229.
[34] Ibid., p. 230.
[35] Ibid., p. 231.

precisely in his striving to transcend the limits of our knowledge and penetrate the inaccessible realm of Truth. If Ivan Karamazov rebels because there is suffering in the world, Chekhov's heroes rebel because they do not know the meaning of the world.'[36] Thus, 'it is not suffering per se that Chekhov considers a challenge to religion, but rather the lack of knowledge.'[37]

Thus Chekhov in his consistent and honest, 'rational' search for truth, invariably running into the limitations of reason, ends up by penetrating more deeply into the irrational than those who are tuned from the start to a mystical and religious mode and have irrationalism as their point of origin – indeed, an outsider can see better, observing things which are indistinguishable from within. As a result of a similar 'dynamics of resistance' Brodsky, as we saw earlier, speaking from within the self-imposed emotional restraints and bursting out of them, turns out to be more irrational in his acute and painful passion than many 'professional, outright lyricists': 'such pathos, tormentingly bursting through from the pressure of dispassion, affects one stronger than a quick-to-start emotional outpouring of some outright lyricist.'[38]

Brodsky, a product of безвременье (*bezvremen'e*), of the era when mass murder became technologically possible, and genocide – almost a norm, has no illusions as to the narrow capabilities of scientific enquiry and is fully aware of a flimsy nature of human fate. That is why he values Shestov as a philosopher (named by Camus among the thinkers most important for the new Man of the Absurd), and just like him is prepared to fight and mock his own and everybody else's idealism to the utmost. Like Chekhov, Brodsky accepts the tragedy, evil and suffering in the world, but for him human lack of knowledge, the impossibility of full cognition is merely a fact of life, a starting point. How can one cope with that? By becoming indistinguishable, by melting within the landscape, by subtracting oneself from nature – constantly exercising one's own absence – these are Brodsky's methods, at least on paper: 'Draw on a sheet a plain circle. That will be me: nothing inside. Look at it – and then erase it';[39] 'Which is the essence of self-portraiture. // A step aside from one's own flesh and frame, // the profile of a footstool kicked toward // you, a long view on life when dues are paid';[40] 'A complete nobody, a man in a raincoat, who had lost his memory, motherland, son . . .".[41] There is no question of knowing, only of coping. Tragedy reigns in the universe in the form

[36]   Ibid., p. 232.

[37]   Ibid.

[38]   Sergei Gandlevsky, 'Olimpiiskaia igra Iosifa Brodskogo', in *Iosif Brodsky: tvorchestvo, lichnost, sudba. Itogi triokh konferentsii*, St Petersburg: Zvezda, 1998, p. 118.

[39]   Iosif Brodsky, 'To ne Muza vody nabiraet v rot . . .', in *Forma vremeni. Stikhotvoreniia, esse, piesy v dvukh tomakh*, op. cit., vol. 1, p. 464. In Russian: 'Нарисуй на бумаге простой кружок. Это буду я: ничего внутри. Посмотри на него – и потом сотри'.

[40]   Joseph Brodsky, 'At Karel Weilink's Exhibition', in *To Urania. Selected Poems 1965–1985*, transl. by Jamey Gambrell, Harmondsworth, Middlesex, England: Penguin Books, 1988, pp. 119–121, p. 121. In Russian: 'Что, в сущности, и есть автопортрет. Шаг в сторону от собственного тела, повернутый к вам в профиль табурет, вид издали на жизнь, что пролетела'.

[41]   Iosif Brodsky, 'Laguna', in *Forma vremeni. Stikhotvoreniia, esse, piesy v dvukh tomakh*, op. cit., vol. 1, p. 290. In Russian: 'совершенный никто, человек в плаще, потерявший память, отчизну, сына . . .'.

of our senseless temporality. 'Our imagination is rooted in our eschatological dread: the dread of thinking that we are without precedence or consequence.'[42] The absurd is evident, the meaninglessness is the prerequisite of existence, local hope might be possible in the form of poetry and intensity of emotions, but global hope is certainly absent. The country where Brodsky was born he describes as a huge existential laboratory, but even more importantly and more generally: 'human being is a tester of pain' (и человек есть испытатель боли) (*i chelovek est' ispytatel' boli*).[43] Where does this lead us? Pointing suggestively to a mixture of an existentialist and stoic outlook, it very much takes us back to Chekhov. But there is more to Brodsky's (and for that matter, Chekhov's) philosophical outlook than this, which ultimately lands us in the irrationalist realm of the religious – be it within or outside its actual territory.

'All faith is no more than one-way post' (*Vsia vera est' ne bolee, chem pochta v odin konets*)[44] – Silence of the Gods. Chekhov's and Brodsky's philosophies: kinship and divergence.

A good deal of what can be easily observed in Brodsky as a fully fledged result of his *Weltanschauung* is also clearly present in Chekhov, but rather in an embryonic form. It is first of all the existentialist texture of their artistic worlds. R. S. Spivak, in the essay 'Chekhov and existentialism', lists the following characteristics of Chekhov's 'general perception of life', some of which have already been mentioned earlier: 'absurdity of the world, its impenetrability by reason and indifference towards a human being; exclusive value of every individual, profound alienation of a human being from society and equally from the other, acute attention to the problem of choice in critical conditions, tragically sensitive feeling of temporality and unrepeatability of every single existence.'[45] All of these are also and quite clearly the trademarks of Brodsky's sensibility, as we have seen. His profound sense of individualism has become a commonplace in scholarly discussions. Perhaps, a most expressive elaboration of it can be found in the following words written by Brodsky about his whole generation:

> The idea of individualism, of man per se, separately and in pure form, was our own idea. The possibility of its physical realisation was negligible, if it existed at all. [. . .] When it did become possible, for many of us it was too late: we no longer needed physical realisation of this idea. For the idea of individualism by that time had become for us indeed an idea – if you like, an abstract, metaphysical category. In this respect we have achieved both in consciousness and on paper much greater authonomy than it is possible to achieve in physical reality anywhere.[46]

---

42   Joseph Brodsky, 'Homage to Marcus Aurelius', in *On Grief and Reason. Essays*, op. cit., p. 269.
43   Iosif Brodsky, 'Razgovor s nebozhitelem', in *Forma vremeni. Stikhotvoreniia, esse, piesy v dvukh tomakh*, op. cit., vol. 1, p. 220.
44   Вся вера есть не более, чем почта в один конец.
45   Rita Spivak, 'Chekhov i ekzistentsializm', in Anatolii Sobennikov (ed.), *Filosofia Chekhova*, op. cit., pp. 193–4.
46   Iosif Brodsky, 'O Serezhe Dovlatove': 'Mir urodliv I liudi grustny', in Sergei Dovlatov, *Sobranie Prozy v triokh tomakh*, op. cit., vol. 3, p. 361.

The traits of individualism are projected, not surprisingly, into the very texture of Brodsky's poetics. Thus, as the Lotmans point out, his usual trademark is in that 'a transformation [of a thing] into an abstract category is connected not to ascending to the general, but to strengthening the singular, private and individual.'[47]

The existentialist outlook, that Brodsky shares with Chekhov, entails common motifs, such as boredom of existence mixed with existential fear, restrictions imposed by civilization and equally by nature, alienation from one another, solitude and non-communicability.[48] As Spivak points out, 'boredom, sooner or later, gets the majority of Chekhov's characters, it constitutes an inescapable attribute of their life regardless of the social, material or intellectual barriers.'[49] Moreover, it features in the very titles of Chekhov's stories: 'Tedium of Life' ('*Skuka zhizni*'), 'A Boring Story' ('*Skuchnaia istoria*'). Similarly, Brodsky has entitled one of his essays, given as an address to the youth, 'In praise of boredom', opening it by the lines: 'A substantial part of what lies ahead of you is going to be claimed by boredom' and explaining further that life's 'main medium – nay, idiom – is tedium.'[50] However, the most valuable lesson, Brodsky says, which boredom teaches us, being itself a 'window on time', is the 'lesson of your utter insignificance.'[51] Thus, he suggests further, it can be viewed effectively as a source of inspiration, as it is boredom, born of infinity, which creates the contrasting background to human finiteness: 'You are insignificant because you are finite. Yet the more finite a thing is, the more it is charged with life, emotions, joy, fears, compassion. For infinity is not terribly lively, not terribly emotional. Your boredom, at least, tells you that much. Because your boredom is the boredom of infinity.'[52] Brodsky then concludes that 'passion is the privilege of the insignificant'; hence his advice to his young listeners: 'So try to stay passionate, leave your cool to constellations.'[53]

Brodsky thus turns his praise of boredom into praise of passion and in doing so comes very close to Chekhov's Hot-Blooded heroes. Yet, as previously mentioned, often in his poetry he tries, on the contrary, to extinguish this passion, when he professes Cold-Blooded stoicism by his perpetual attempts to develop indifference to the state of non-being, to get used in advance to his pending absence in the universe. Chekhov, by contrast, promotes Cold-Blooded stoicism in his private addresses (his personal correspondence), but signals a somewhat different – Hot-Blooded – message when it comes to his fiction. At any rate, this is the conclusion one reaches when comparing his lines from the letter to his brother Aleksandr: 'Those who are indifferent are either philosophers, or petty, egotistical individuals. The attitude toward the latter would be negative, toward the former positive'[54] with the old professor's words from 'A Boring

47 Yu. Lotman, M. Lotman, 'Mezhdu veshchiu i pustotoi . . ', op. cit., p. 296.
48 See Spivak, 'Chekhov i ekzistentsializm', in Anatolii Sobennikov (ed.), *Filosofia Chekhova*, op. cit., pp. 193–208.
49 Ibid., p. 194.
50 Joseph Brodsky, 'In praise of boredom', in *On Grief and Reason. Essays*, op. cit., pp. 104–5.
51 Ibid., p. 109.
52 Ibid., p. 110.
53 Ibid., pp. 110–11.
54 Anton Chekhov, from the letter to his brother Aleksandr, of 8 May 1889, *Letters of Anton Chekhov*, Avraham Yarmolinsky (ed.), New York: The Viking Press, p. 116.

Story': 'They say philosophers and the truly wise are indifferent. It is false: indifference is the paralysis of the soul; it is premature death.'[55] This is connected to another layer of subversion in Chekhov, whereby the kind of 'stoicism', which we labelled here as 'Cold Blood', and which is so often proclaimed by his characters, in fact serves, more often than not, as a shield for a 'cemetery-like' philosophy that justifies inactivity and indifference. In fact, as Skaftymov aptly observes, it corrupts Marcus Aurelius's teaching which is much more selfless, directed outwards and thus hostile to apathy.[56] But tracing this kind of corruption is, of course, a usual Chekhovian theme, and the writer's sympathies, one can thus argue, are more on the side of the 'hot-blooded'.

In the same way Chekhov seems to take the side of Hot Blood again when he, as many claimed, aligns himself with the Tatar in the aforementioned story 'In exile'. Yet, as Spivak believes (perhaps, not noticing the subversion revealed by Skaftymov), this identification only takes place in the plane of the mundane, of the everyday reality, while existentially, abstractly and theoretically Chekhov is sympathetic to Semen with his professed stoicism.[57] This ambivalence, this multitude of interpretations, is bound to prevail in the perception of the writer, with his avoidance of direct statements, and given the (not always consistent) diversity of his views, as expressed in his letters and in stories. Hence both writers, arguably, exemplify a contradictory (and thus not fully rational) stance which may reflect their inner struggle regarding the problem of 'stoic' and 'lyric' opposition, of Cold and Hot Blood.

Interestingly, according to Durkin, both Semen and the Tatar illustrate a faulty mode of discourse resulting in a failed communication.[58] For Semen it is the falsity of his position, his alienation from his true self which prevents a genuine exchange. For the Tatar it is, more subtly, a monological, self-absorbed lyricism, which ultimately departs from reality just as well, making a proper dialogue impossible. This irrationalist theme of non-communicability is one of the central for Chekhov. In his universe, famously (which is particularly evident in his plays), all are speaking, but no-one hears the other. In Brodsky's world, this theme is further advanced: the fact that communication is futile becomes an axiom; man is alone in the universe, he is just a statistical entity, a speck of dust to be wiped from the surface of eternity, and to return to dust again; as quoted earlier: 'without precedence or consequence'; 'We will continue as a crumpled cigarette butt, a spit, in the shade under a bench, where the angle will let through no ray of light. And integrate with the dirt, counting the days, into humus, residue, a cultural layer. "Carrion", he [*an archaeologist of the future*] will exhale, clutching his stomach, but he will be further away from us than the earth is from birds, because carrion is the freedom from cells, from completeness – an apotheosis of particles.'[59] Even scholarly

---

55 Anton Chekhov, 'A Boring Story', op. cit. See Sobennikov, in *Filosofia Chekhova*, p. 173 for his interpretation of this comparison.

56 Aleksandr Skaftymov, *Nravstvennye iskaniia russkikh pisatelei. Statii i issledovaniia o russkikh klassikakh*, Moscow: Khudozhestvennaia literatura, 1972, pp. 381–403.

57 See Spivak, 'Chekhov i ekzistentsializm', op. cit., pp. 200–1.

58 See Andrew Durkin, 'Modeli khudozhestvennogo slova v chekhovskikh rasskazakh "V ssylke" i "Student"', op. cit., pp. 51–4.

59 Iosif Brodsky, 'Tolko pepel znaet, chto znachit sgoret dotla . . .', in Brodsky, *Forma vremeni. Stikhotvoreniia, esse, piesy v dvukh tomakh*, op. cit., vol. 2, p. 192. In Russian: 'Мы останемся

essays on Brodsky speak for themselves: '*Spustit'sa nizhe mira zhivykh*' ('To descend beneath the world of the living') (Keis Verheil),[60] '*Mezhdu veshiu i pustotoï*' ('Between an object and emptiness') (Yu. and M. Lotman)[61] and so on.

Thus Brodsky is oscillating between, on the one hand, stoic resignation, exercises in indifference, understanding of total pointlessness of existence and, on the other, passionate discharge, resistance to Time by Language, by outbursts of poetry and love. Love is secondary though, just as life itself. As for Tsvetaeva, for Brodsky too, it seems that a reflection of reality in art exceeds that actual reality not only in intensity,[62] but also in importance. 'I do not love life per se; it begins to be meaningful for me – that is, to gain sense and weight – only when it is transformed into art', Tsvetaeva wrote, as we saw earlier.[63] Brodsky treasured Auden's words on the superiority of Language over Time: '*Time* that is intolerant, // Of the brave and innocent, // And indifferent in a week // to a beautiful physic // *Worships language* and forgives // Everyone by whom it lives.'[64] He derived from these lines, as was discussed in Chapter 1, the whole theory of the Divine origin of Language, which for him became the only means of survival (and came close to being the only meaning of existence).[65]

Chekhov is different, although he too seems to oscillate between stoicism and 'lyricism', Cold and Hot Blood, gently opting for the latter (or rather non-obtrusively suggesting this option to the reader, leaving enough clues for the preference of this stance). However, for him life is of ultimate meaning, art is only a documentation of it and as such is secondary, even though a writer is compelled to write (like Trigorin in *Chaika*). With all his stoic resignation and his self-restrictive behaviour (he tied himself to the chair as an act of a writer's self-discipline), Chekhov understands hedonism well, as is clear from his numerous remarks, either in his note-books, letters or stories 'you should write about women in such a way, that the reader feels that your waistcoat is unbuttoned and you are not wearing a tie',[66] 'their wide, cool beds, made by pretty Pelagueya, smelled sweetly of clean linen.'[67] For Brodsky hedonism

---

смятым окурком, плевком, в тени // под скамьей, куда угол проникнуть лучу не даст. // И слежимся в обнимку с грязью, считая дни, // в перегной, в осадок, в культурный пласт. [. . .] "Падаль!" выдохнет он, обхватив живот, // но окажется дальше от нас, чем земля от птиц,// потому что падаль – свобода от клеток, свобода от// целого: апофеоз частиц.'

[60] For this essay see *Iosif Brodsky: tvorchestvo, lichnost, sudba. Itogi triokh konferentsii*, op. cit., pp. 30–6.

[61] References to this essay have been given earlier.

[62] As Brodsky wrote: 'it is a question of the differences between art and reality. One of them is that in art, owing to the properties of the material itself, it is possible to attain a degree of lyricism that has no physical equivalent in the real world. Nor, in the same way, does there exist in the real world an equivalent of the tragic in art' (Joseph Brodsky, 'A Poet and Prose', in *Less Than One. Selected Essays*, op. cit., p. 183).

[63] Marina Tsvetaeva, from the letter of 30.12.1925 to Anna Teskova, op. cit.

[64] Wystan Hugh Auden, 'In Memory of W. B. Yeats (January 1939)', in Edward Mendelson (ed.), *The English Auden. Poems, Essays and Dramatic Writings 1927–1939*, London: Faber & Faber, 1977, p. 242.

[65] See Chapter 1 for more detailed analysis.

[66] From Chekhov's letter of 20 October 1888 to A. S. Lazarev-Gruzinsky, *PSSP v 30 tomakh*, op. cit., 1976, vol. 3, p. 40.

[67] Chekhov, 'Gooseberries', op. cit.

is certainly accessible, but steeped in disillusionment, and thus devoid of its ultimate value. It is a self-mocking hedonism, almost with disgust, almost out of spite or despair: 'Having hoicked up the dress of a beauty, you see what you were after, and not new wonderful wonders . . ',[68] which, paradoxically, only reinforces once again his hidden idealistic, lyrical, passionate aspirations, suppressed by apparent cynicism, by deliberate coldness.

Curiously, in Dostoevsky's artistic world the dichotomy between Hot and Cold Blood does not really exist, since all his characters are so passionately hot-blooded, regardless of their philosophies and moralities. Thus the oscillation for him happens not between stoicism and 'lyricism', but between faith and faithlessness. The question if there is God or not is central for Dostoevsky. The situation with Chekhov and Brodsky is very different.

Impossibility of genuine human contact, the doom of ultimate solitude (most strikingly in Chekhov's story '*Toska*' of a horse-driver who speaks to his horse about his son's death) point to the perception of God as absent, to understanding of the universe as God-forsaken; or at least to His extreme remoteness from man, remoteness of such an extent that it can be equated to absence. This stance is evident at least in some of Chekhov's writings, although perhaps not in many. Rather it is alleviated, at least at some narrative level, by the Russian Orthodox motifs of hope and love. For Brodsky this absence is also ambivalent, as he put it himself, 'all faith is no more than a one-way post.' Theologically speaking, what we have here is a complex mixture of influences: from Russian Orthodoxy to obscure form of Protestantism, such as Calvinism; notwithstanding also the God of the Old Testament and even Hinduism.

Keis Verheil speaks of Brodsky's 'ethics of the Absurd',[69] and derives it from the poet's Calvinism – a reformist religion initiated by Calvin, which is characterized most of all by two central premises: God's impenetrability for a human, the unquestionable, but unintelligible logic of His will, which makes Him infinitely remote from human life; and an acute feeling of individual, personal responsibility for your everyday actions in the eyes of this unattainable God. Brodsky was indeed much preoccupied by the concept of Calvinism and assigned Tsvetaeva to this particular trend, speaking of her subjugating herself to an every day analogue of the Ultimate Judgement. However, Verheil is right – the same is applicable to Brodsky with equal force (and the poet actually acknowledged himself as a Calvinist in various interviews, although sometimes aligned himself with Hinduism in its detachment).[70] The only difference is that while Tsvetaeva is completely open in her tragic outcry (for some – shamelessly and 'exhibitionistly' so), Brodsky hides more often than not, as was mentioned, under artificial restraints, such as mockery, irony, almost cynicism. However, the universe remains threatening, lifeless and indifferent; death annihilates every human effort, the crushing force of

[68] Iosif Brodsky, 'Konets prekrasnoi epokhi', in Brodsky, *Forma vremeni. Stikhotvoreniia, esse, piesy v dvukh tomakh*, op. cit., vol. 1, p. 218. In Russian: 'Красавице платье задрав, видишь то, что искал, а не новые дивные дивы . . .'

[69] Keis Verheil, 'Kal'vinizm, poeziia i zhivopis'', in *Iosif Brodskii: Tvorchestvo, lichnost', sud'ba*, op. cit., p. 36.

[70] See, for instance, Polukhina (ed.), *Iosif Brodskii. Bolshaia kniga interviiu*, op. cit.

necessity which does not take man into account reigns everywhere. True human contact is impossible, tragic solitude, from birth to death, is our predicament. These existentialist premises lead to the religious sentiments of Calvin. But isn't it the same in Chekhov's world, at least in the 'shadowy', hopeless and sober side of it?

As Andrei Stepanov writes about Chekhov's proximity to Lev Shestov's philosophy of tragedy where universal Necessity plays a central role, 'an obvious metaphor of Necessity' is 'the "peaceful green vastness", which tries to swallow the life of Vera Kardina ("At Home")'; the 'unseen oppressive force' which binds nature in 'The Steppe'; the 'unknown and mysterious force' which created a similar world in the story 'A Doctor's Visit'.[71] Perhaps, Shestov here is the bridge which unites Brodsky with Chekhov. The invincible force of both social and natural laws, and most of all the annihilating force of time which destroys every living being, is acutely felt in Brodsky's universe. His preoccupation with the theme of death Iskander labelled as the unprecedented in Russian literature: 'in Brodsky's world everything is inside death, even life itself'.[72] Brodsky seems dual in his treatment of the Divine. On the one hand, his is certainly not the case of Lev Tolstoy with the latter's theomachy, stemming from the immense pride: 'God by god goes out discrowned and disanointed', as Tolstoy 'is driven to cast down and destroy existing authorities – or to put himself in their place'.[73] Brodsky is not engaged in a struggle against God, rather he has an intimate relationship with Him, he enters into an open, heart-breaking in its sincerity dialogue with this Heaven-Dweller (Razgovor s nebozhitelem). There is immense tenderness in his Christmas poems. On the other hand, when Brodsky looks (philosophically) at human futility and transience, he ascends, as it were, to those outer spheres which seem beyond space and time; in other words, he joins (or even replaces) Him in such down-casted visions, viewing the human world from the superior position of eternity. This is not disconnected from Brodsky's sentiments, inherited from Akhmatova, of a privileged position of a Poet, of a certain Guild of the dedicated, of Artists, who are on a mission by the virtue of their vocation, and thus have special privileges over simple mortals. And Brodsky's premise that a poet is merely an instrument of Language seems more like yet another device to restrain his own pride (without renouncing the exclusiveness of the poet's role!) than a case of true humility.

Perhaps for a related (but reversed) reason – of not overestimating his own significance as well as the value of art and artists – Chekhov does not wrestle with death so much, he is reconciled with finiteness and insignificance of his own and everybody else's existence. Yet, he shares with Brodsky the stance of Marcus Aurelius of man's duty to be prepared for death: 'One should live in accordance with Marcus Aurelius teaching, so that one is ready at any minute to meet death calmly'.[74] However,

---

[71] Andrei Stepanov, 'Lev Shestov on Chekhov', in Olga Tabachnikova (ed.), *Anton Chekhov Through The Eyes Of Russian Thinkers: Vasilii Rozanov, Dmitrii Merezhkovskii and Lev Shestov*, op. cit., p. 172.

[72] Iskander, 'Poet', op. cit., p. 143.

[73] Frank Seeley, 'Tolstoy's Philosophy of History', in *Saviour or Superman. Old and New Essays on Tolstoy and Dostoevsky*, Nottingham: Astra Press, 1999, p. 10.

[74] Aleksandr Izmailov, 'Vera ili neverie (Religiia Chekhova)', in Igor' Sukhikh and Andrei Stepanov (eds), *A.P. Chekhov: Pro et Contra*, op. cit.

the terror of Chekhov's characters is perhaps more subtle and even more frightening than a natural human fear of death – it is a fear of life:

> 'Why, when we want to tell some terrifying, mysterious, fantastic story, we don't draw on life for our subject-matter, but invariably on the world of ghosts, on beyond the grave?' – 'What we *don't* understand – that's what scares us' – 'But we don't really understand life, do we? Tell me if we understand this life any better than the world beyond?'[75]

(Curiously, mysticism as such, which is traditionally connected with the after-life and with the theme of death, especially fear of death, in Chekhov's writings can play almost an opposite role. Thus in 'Black Monk' it is the elevations of the soul that are connected to mystical visions, whereas psychic normality is linked to the dull and mundane existence.[76])

However, despite a lack of fixation on death in Chekhov, of the type that we see in Brodsky, oblivion plays a major role in Chekhov's writings: 'The years will pass, and we shall all be gone for good and quite forgotten . . . Our faces and our voices will be forgotten and people won't even know that there were once three of us here',[77] says Olga in 'Tri sestry' ('Three Sisters'). In the story 'Arkhierei' ('The Bishop') after the new bishop is appointed, 'no one remembered Bishop Peter any more.'[78] As Sobennikov points out, even in Chekhov's early story 'Na kladbishche' ('At the cemetery') visitors read on a cross over a grave '"to the forgettable friend Mushkin". Time had erased the prefix "un" and corrected the human lie',[79] says the narrator. This is undoubtedly a very Brodskyan motif. Furthermore, Chekhov's story 'Strakh' ('Terror') illustrates precisely the incomprehensible Divine logic, the threat and dread exuded by existence, by that omnipotent God whose presence is questionable to the point of irrelevancy. 'There's an illness, fear of open spaces: mine is fear of life. When I lie on grass and look for a long time at a small insect that was born only yesterday and understands nothing, I think its life must be just one never-ending horror, and in this insect I can see myself'; 'I watched the crows, and their flight struck me as strange and terrifying.'[80] Man is left in this meaningless, absurd universe, all by himself, and yet – accountable for his actions; faced with his own conscience, with his inner moral sense. This is perhaps the most Calvinistic of all Chekhov's stories. This fear of life rather than death, quite new in Russian literature, is as much irrationalist, as it is terrifying.

Yet, Chekhov ascends above oppositions, above problems posed in his writings; he withdraws. This authorial withdrawal can be equated in a sense to Brodsky's

---

[75] Anton Chekhov, 'Terror' ('Strakh'), in *The Duel and Other Stories*, transl. by Ronald Wilks, Harmondsworth, Middlesex, England: Penguin Books, 1984, p. 226.

[76] Further on this see Kluge, 'Zagadka "Chernogo monakha"', in *Filosofia Chekhova*, op. cit., p. 105.

[77] Anton Chekhov, 'Three Sisters' ('Tri sestry'), in *Chekhov. Plays*, transl. by Elisaveta Fen, Harmondsworth, Middlesex, England: Penguin Books, 1951, 1954, p. 329.

[78] Anton Chekhov, 'The Bishop' ('Arkhierei'), in *The Kiss and Other Stories*, transl. by Ronald Wilks, Harmondsworth, Middlesex, England: Penguin Books, p. 97.

[79] See Anatoly Sobennikov, 'Chekhov i stoiki', in Sobennikov (ed.), *Filosofiia Chekhova*, op. cit., p. 171. The quotation is from Anton Chekhov, 'At the cemetery' ('Na kladbishche').

[80] Anton Chekhov, 'Terror', op. cit., pp. 227, 234.

games with emptiness, exercises in his own physical withdrawal from the world. Only Chekhov is projected onto others, away from himself – towards the world; Brodsky, in the narcissistic, even egocentric stance of a poet is directed on the contrary from the world to his own self. In this sense he is a truly Romantic hero; profoundly lyrical, yet epic, while Chekhov, by contrast, is profoundly epic (at least in the democratic multitude of his characters and their life occurrences), yet lyrical.

However, Chekhov's understanding of God is as pluralistic as his outlook in general. For him, a master of semi-shades, of tinges of meaning, of the continuous, his famous statement 'between "there is God" and "there is no God" there lies an enormously vast field which the truly wise man traverses with great difficulty'[81] is only natural. The idea of one's personal individual God is also rather to be expected: 'Until he finds his own God, man will be disoriented, will search for an aim, and will remain dissatisfied. [. . .] Man must either have faith or search for faith, otherwise he is a shallow person.'[82] This is connected in Chekhov's universe to the question of personal responsibility, for if man is alienated from God, forsaken by Him, it is largely man's own fault – of forgetting of whose image and likeness he was created. Also, and this distinguishes Chekhov from Brodsky most profoundly, the former is not so much a captive of *Logos*, for him actions indeed speak louder than words, his universe is quiet, things happen covertly ('people are having their lunch, just having their lunch, but at the same time their happiness is taking shape or their lives are getting shattered,'[83] or, as Venedikt Erofeev later said: 'Everything should take place slowly and incorrectly so that man doesn't get a chance to start feeling proud, so that man is sad and perplexed.'[84] That is precisely how things happen in Chekhov's artistic world. Brodsky, on the contrary, is immersed in *Logos*, in poetry, in words, even in letters, as we have discussed. His God is, interestingly, more intimate, although absolutely mute. In Brodsky's favourite genre of epistolary, the imprint of which is felt in most of his poems, God is perhaps the ultimate addressee. Even though a response is out of the question, Brodsky's 'Razgovor s nebozhitelem' is very instructive in this respect: 'all things hang on the hooks of their questions', 'from tenderness to frenzy all forms of life are adaptation', 'a yearning to merge with God as with a landscape, in which we are being sought by, say, a marksman'.[85] Yet, highly instructive and equally valid are his lines from another poem: 'Only with sorrow I feel solidarity. But until my mouth is stuffed with clay, it will utter only words of gratitude.'[86]

Here we come to the influence of Christianity and particularly Russian Orthodoxy, with its warmth and compassion, with feeling the caring palms of God – something

---

[81] Chekhov, Diary (1897), in *PSSP v 30 tomakh*, op. cit., vol. 17, pp. 33–4.

[82] Ibid., Chekhov, *PSSP v 30 tomakh*, op. cit., vol. 17, pp. 215–16.

[83] See Vospominaniia Ars. G. (I. Ya. Gurliand), in *Teatr i Iskusstvo*, 1904, No. 28.

[84] Venedikt Erofeev, *Moscow to the End of the Line*, op. cit., p. 14.

[85] Brodsky, 'Razgovor s nebozhitelem', op. cit., p. 221. In Russian: 'все виснет на крюках своих вопросов'; 'от нежности до умоисступленья все формы жизни есть приспособленье'; 'жажда слиться с Богом, как с пейзажем, в котором нас разыскивает, скажем, один стрелок'.

[86] Iosif Brodsky, 'Ia vkhodil vmesto dikogo zveria v kletku . . ', in *Forma vremeni. Stikhotvoreniia, esse, piesy v dvukh tomakh*, op. cit., p. 147. In Russian: 'Только с горем я чувствую солидарность. Но пока мне рот не забили глиной, из него раздаваться будет лишь благодарность'.

that is very anti-Calvinist. Although Brodsky noted often that he prefers the capricious and unpredictable God of the Old Testament as being truer to life of man, he still wrote his Christmas poetry with an outstanding annual devotion. His personal statements remain, as in the case of Chekhov, very diverse and contradictory – from total atheism (there is no afterlife at all) to a virtually opposite stance, even if it seems at a first glance as a figure of speech: 'If the next life exists – and I can no more deny them [*his great poetic predecessors*] the possibility of eternal life than I can forget their existence in this one . . .';[87] and even somewhat pagan sentiments – perceiving two ravens, who frequented his house after the death of both his mother and father, as his parents reincarnated. Yet, Brodsky is clearly beyond any denominations; his religious sentiments are as cosmopolitan, or better yet: as cosmic, as his general concerns. After all, he seems to be more rooted (or more comfortable) in antiquity than in modernity. 'Iudei i Ellin? Ni Iudei, ni Ellin?'[88] as Shimon Markish entitled his essay on Brodsky.

By contrast, Chekhov's rootedness in Russian Orthodoxy is substantial and profound, as was discussed numerous times. Most explicitly it is evident in those of his characters which are permeated with harmony and light: father Christopher in 'Steppe', Lipa, Praskovia and the old peasant from the story 'In the ravine', priest in 'Duel', Petr in 'The Bishop' and various others.[89] As Aleksandr Medvedev writes, quoting Pavel P. Bitsilli: 'Chekhov, just as Pushkin, managed to express a "humble and quiet poetry" of Russian orthodoxy, to give us the gifts of the spirit of "meekness, mercy and compassion" which Chekhov is steeped in'; '*The Captain's Daughter* is lit up with the same dim, warm and steady light of the "everyday" Russian orthodoxy which the best works of Chekhov exude. In a certain sense these two are the most "Russian" of all Russian writers'.[90] These motifs of organic unity of all things alive and of God within and above them, of nature and man, of heaven and earth being at piece with each other can be found in Brodsky too, even if rarely. Thus the poem of John Donne on the unity of all things alive, his famous words: 'I am involved in mankind. Therefore, send not to know For whom the bell tolls, It tolls for thee'[91] were clearly appreciated by Brodsky, as he confessed in his interviews, but even more instructively – as is expressed in his 'The Great Elegy for John Donne' ('*Bolshaia Elegiia Dzhony Donnu*'). This poem grows magically like a snowball, widening the circles, covering the whole world with snow, sewing heaven and earth, as if putting the universe back together from debris, from the state of disintegration – like a broken and split human soul must gather itself together

[87] Joseph Brodsky, 'Uncommon Visage (The Nobel Lecture)', in *On Grief and Reason*, op. cit., p. 45.

[88] See Shimon Markish, '"Iudei i Ellin"? "Ni Iudei, ni Ellin"? ("Hebrew and Hellene? Neither Hebrew, nor Hellene?")', in Petr Vail and Lev Losev (eds), *Iosif Brodsky. Trudy i dni*, op. cit., pp. 207–14.

[89] See more on this in Spivak, 'Chekhov i ekzistentsializm', in Sobennikov (ed.), *Filosofiia Chekhova*, op. cit., pp. 201–6.

[90] See Aleksandr Medvedev, 'Kind and Quiet: Vasilii Rozanov's Reading of Chekhov', in Olga Tabachnikova (ed.), *Anton Chekhov Through the Eyes of Russian Thinkers: Rozanov, Merezhkovskii and Shestov*, op. cit., p. 27. The quotation is from Petr Bitsilli, 'Chekhov', in *Chisla* (Paris, 1930), No. 1, p. 168.

[91] John Donne, 'Meditation VII', in Henry Alford (ed.), *The Works of John Donne*, London: John W. Parker, 1839, vol. III, pp. 574–5.

in one Divine whole. Thus the sermon of John Donne, of the universal unity, gets, as it were, materialized and developed in Brodsky's verses.

These themes, in a sense, are linked with the theme of Hot Blood, when lyricism, intensity, emotionalism are attenuated by Christian humility which reconciles man with the world. The irrationalism here is again, as it were, thematic, as it is encapsulated in the nature of religious feeling, in suffering and humility. This irrationalism is connected to straightening the soul, unburdening the psyche – like Lipa from 'V ovrage' ('In the Hollow') who is carrying her dead child on the way back from hospital, but whose intense grief is absorbed by her religious sensibility. The latter finds its expression in being intrinsically open to human tenderness and love, despite all the incredible cruelty that she endured: "'Are you holy men?" Lipa asked the old fellow – "No. We are from Firsanovo" – "When you looked at me just now my heart melted. And the lad's so quiet – so I thought these must be holy men'".[92] At the same time the irrationalism of Cold Blood, as was discussed earlier, is, as it were, essential rather than thematic; it is about entangling rather than unburdening; if you like, it is Dostoevsky's type of irrationalism: of struggle and pride, of caprice and *svoevolie* (unrestrained will), of pusillanimity and escape from oneself.

It is also the peculiarities of Russian Orthodoxy that render Chekhov's existentialism typically Russian rather than generally European – by investing it with influences of Solov'ev's philosophy, by sustaining a glimmering religious hope, as Spivak aptly notices.[93] Again, along the lines of Russian spirituality where empirical sphere cannot exist without a higher – religious, divine – reality and is justified by it alone, both authors are marked by a characteristic striving to the ideal; if you like – from rational to the irrational, even if in Brodsky this happens at a very deep, concealed level – as if through a semantic spiral: a conscious move from the irrational substance to the rational frame, but than a leap into the deeper and ultimate irrationalism. By the same token, for Eikhenbaum the main driving force of Chekhov's creativity is in trying to penetrate the spheres of the trivial, abased and horrible, only in order to be pushed up ever more powerfully into the domain of dreams. In this for Eikhenbaum lies the main alcohol of Chekhov's artistic creativity.[94] Andrei Belyi meant a similar thing when he described Chekhov's art as thinning the reality and opening a flight to eternity.[95] In the same vein, Andrei Stepanov, when comparing Chekhov and Shestov, describes their convergence by their ultimate striving for a miracle: 'There are harmonious fragments in Chekhov when his desperate heroes hope despite everything. Such are the finales of "The Lady with the Lapdog", "Uncle Vania", "Three Sisters" and a whole number of

[92] See Spivak, 'Chekhov i ekzistentsializm', in Sobennikov (ed.), *Filosofiia Chekhova*, op. cit., p. 207, for a narratological analysis of this scene (the quotation is from Chekhov's story 'In the Hollow' (sometimes translated as 'In the Ravine'), in *A Woman's Kingdom and Other Stories*, transl. by Ronald Hingley, Oxford, New York: Oxford University Press, 1989, p. 270).

[93] Ibid., p. 208.

[94] Boris Eikhenbaum, 'O Chekhove', in Igor' Sukhikh and Andrei Stepanov (eds), *Chekhov: Pro et Contra*, op. cit., p. 965.

[95] Andrei Belyi, 'A.P. Chekhov', in Igor' Sukhikh and Andrei Stepanov (eds), *Chekhov: Pro et Contra*, op. cit.

other episodes. In this desperate hope for the realization of the impossible lies a deep kinship between the writer and the philosopher.'[96]

Brodsky too, as we saw, is bursting out of the self-imposed emotional boundaries into a different realm: 'The essence of life is not in what there is, but in faith in what there should be.'[97] Under the mask of indifference and reserve, almost misanthropy ('There is something in their faces, which is repellent to the mind; which expresses flattery to God knows whom . . .'),[98] he holds back a scream of angst, tenderness and love ('I loved you better than angels and Him Himself // and am farther off due to that from you than I am from both').[99] This is a deliberate bursting out, into the outer spheres, beyond earthly human limits – in brief, a bid for an absolute (irrational?) freedom – just like Chekhov's perpetual striving – into the 'freedom from violence and lies',[100] to shake off the shackles of 'civilisation'. As Susanne Sontag put it (as we saw earlier), Chekhov's oeuvre is a dream of freedom. And the hawk over the valley of Connecticut is striving in the same direction – up and away – even if towards his own death.

Linked to this is also an idea, common for both writers, that our dreams and fantasies constitute reality as objective as that of the actual events. As Lotman pointed out, in Brodsky's world (quite irrationally, one should note) 'the most real is that which never happened; the immortal is that which has been lost.' For Chekhov, furthermore, like in the 'Black Monk' a fantasy may take precedence over reality, with the latter being often, if not always deceptive. Hence the idea of deceptive appearances, of a secret – and truest – existence, of a private mystery – like in the 'Lady with a lapdog'; the idea which is inseparable from that of hope and redemption, of the divine image in which a human was cast – in brief, the idea of beauty. But is it ethical or aesthetic, and as such is it rational or irrational?

Mapping ethics and aesthetics in relation to irrationalism

'One of the most characteristic human features is a fear of truth', wrote the irrationalist philosopher Lev Shestov. He saw civilization, especially Western, as hiding behind the

[96] A. Stepanov, 'Lev Shestov on Chekhov', in Olga Tabachnikova (ed.), *Anton Chekhov Through the Eyes of Russian Thinkers: Rozanov, Merezhkovskii and Shestov*, op. cit., p. 173.

[97] Iosif Brodsky, 'Penie bez muzyki', in *Forma vremeni. Stikhotvoreniia, esse, piesy v dvukh tomakh*, op. cit., vol. I, p. 235. In Russian: 'Не в том суть жизни, что в ней есть, но в вере в то, что в ней должно быть'.

[98] Iosif Brodsky, 'Natiurmort', in *Forma vremeni. Stikhotvoreniia, esse, piesy v dvukh tomakh*, op. cit., p. 257. In Russian:'Что-то в их лицах есть, что противно уму. Что выражает лесть неизвестно кому . . .'

[99] Joseph Brodsky, 'From nowhere with love . . .', transl. by the author, <http://www-users.cs.umn. edu/~safonov/brodsky/part_of_speech/from_nowhere_auto.html> [accessed 1 August 2014]. In Russian: 'я любил тебя больше, чем ангелов и Самого,// И я дальше теперь от тебя, чем от них обоих'.

[100] From Chekhov's letter to A. N. Pleshcheev of 4 October 1888, see *PSSP v 30 tomakh*, op. cit., vol. 3, p. 11.

shield of rationalism, of using reason in order to lull down existential fear, to escape from the tragedy of life. He blamed Lev Tolstoy for the same vice – of trying to equal the mediocre, to renounce his own genius – just in order to flee from the horrors of existence. Nikolai Berdiaev sympathized with this general vision, calling Tolstoyan Christianity 'the ideal of settled mankind' and 'a denial of the tragic experience of Tolstoy's own life, a rescuing escape to the commonness from the abyss, from the horrors of all things problematic'. Like a man with a little hummer from Chekhov's story 'Gooseberry', Shestov knocked at every door, screaming that there are miserable and forsaken people in these world, that there is tragedy. Chekhov, and Brodsky alike, attempted to see the truth, as it is, with all the horrors, evil, tragedy and pain, as Czeslaw Milosz put it about Brodsky – 'without consolations of calm clarity'.[101]

Chekhov especially, in his disdain for ready-made ideologies, was not afraid to recognize the relativity of ideas and values, the entropy of life, to acknowledge that everything is inseparably mixed in the universe, including good and evil. Such stance effectively is a challenge to the openly moral imperative of Russian literature with its prophetic and preaching character as well as to Russian philosophy in which, using Vasilii Zenkovsky's words, 'moral doctrine prevails';[102] (and, one should note in brackets, prevails overtly, while in Chekhov it prevails covertly, it is subtle and carefully concealed). This is linked to the main challenge of Chekhov – his elusiveness. As in Tsvetaeva's poem, already quoted in Chapter 3, 'Maybe the best victory over gravity and time is to move through without leaving a trace, without leaving a shadow . . .'.[103] Chekhov left almost no mark of his own self, no footprint of his soul. Like a smile of the Cheshire Cat from *Alice in Wonderland*, he reigns up there, looking from above with his usual irony at how bewildered critics, scholars and readers are arguing to this day, where is the true Chekhov. Andrei Stepanov called him 'the mirror of Russian criticism',[104] implying that everyone speaking about the writer ends up ascribing to Chekhov his own convictions and views. And a mirror he was; the kind of mirror that reveals, like an x-ray, our hidden weaknesses and shortcomings, of which we ourselves are often only half-aware. If Elena Tolstoy is right in her judgement that Chekhov's poetics is that of annoyance (поэтика раздражения) (*poetika razdrazheniia*),[105] then it is well transmitted to many of Chekhov's readers, leaving them in a state of deafened, unclear annoyance with themselves and the world; the annoyance the source of which is almost indistinguishable. Yet, it might lie precisely in our state of self-denial, when we try to turn away from Chekhov's truthful mirror, from his ethics of a doctor, who needs 'to be merciless in order to be kind'. As Andrei Arev noticed about Sergei Dovlatov (arguably, a true heir of Chekhov), he wanted merely to show how people live, instead,

---

[101] Milosz, 'Borba s udushiem', in Petr Vail and Lev Losev (eds), *Iosif Brodsky. Trudy i dni*, op. cit., p. 245.

[102] Zenkovsky, *Istoriia russkoi filosofii*, op. cit., vol. I, pp. 18–19.

[103] Tsvetaeva, the poem 'Prokrastsa', op. cit. In Russian: 'А может, лучшая победа Над временем и тяготеньем – Пройти, чтоб не оставить следа, Пройти, чтоб не оставить тени . . .'

[104] See Andrei Stepanov, 'Anton Chekhov kak zerkalo russkoi kritiki', in Igor' Sukhikh and Andrei Stepanov (eds), *A.P. Chekhov: Pro et Contra*, op. cit., pp. 976–1007.

[105] Elena Tolstaia, 'Poetika razdrazheniia. Chekhov v kontse 1880-kh – v nachale 1890-kh godov', Moscow: Radix, 1994.

however, he showed how they are unable to live.[106] By the same token, Chekhov left a canvas of human disharmony, but at the background of infinite possibilities: universal harmony, absolute freedom and natural beauty. Thus his Gurov from the 'Lady with a Lapdog' thinks of how 'everything in the world is beautiful really, everything but our own thoughts and actions, when we lose sight of the higher aims of life, and of our dignity as human beings'.[107]

Brodsky's mirror is different, more akin to the one described in his poem: '. . . and look into the mirror, as a street-lamp in a drying puddle'.[108] It reflects the devastating impact of time on human life and human soul (also a very Chekhovian motif); in short, it reflects Brodsky's 'ethics of the absurd', using Verheil's words again. Yet, ethics for Brodsky is derivative, it stems from aesthetics, and, given his craft, where form largely determines content, this stance is hardly surprising. In his Nobel lecture, Brodsky famously claimed that '. . . aesthetics is the mother of ethics. [. . .] The categories of "good" and "bad" are, first and foremost, aesthetic ones, at least etymologically preceding the categories of "good" and "evil". If in ethics not "all is permitted", it is precisely because not "all is permitted" in aesthetics, because the number of colours in the spectrum is limited. The tender babe who cries and rejects the stranger who, on the contrary, reaches out to him, does so instinctively, makes an aesthetic choice, not a moral one. [. . .] The more substantial an individual's aesthetic experience is, the sounder his taste, the sharper his moral focus, the freer – though not necessarily the happier – he is. It is precisely in this applied, rather than Platonic, sense that we should understand Dostoevsky's remark that beauty will save the world, or Matthew Arnold's belief that we shall be saved by poetry'.[109]

This interesting stance met with a strong opposition in the contemporary Russian writer Fazil Iskander who argued, through the mouth of his hero, that Brodsky's claim that 'a baby starts perceiving the world first of all aesthetically' is 'the opposite of the truth. A baby starts smiling first of all to his mother and stretches his hands to her as being a source of good. It is entirely obvious. And it is only later that the source of good starts to be perceived by the baby as a source of beauty. [. . .] A later split in human consciousness of ethics and aesthetics is a sign of man's tragic fall. But even now a person who is morally healthy when looking at a sophisticatedly coloured snake does not feel its beauty – instead he feels disgusted by its colourful pattern. He perceives it as a repulsive camouflage of evil. Good is primary and therefore a rose is beautiful. If good was not primary we would not have realized that a rose is beautiful. Aesthetics is a child of ethics – a child sometimes rebelling against his parents'.[110]

Thus Iskander stresses the tragic split of ethics from aesthetics. As indicated at the start of this discussion, the era when beauty and good (and truth), that is, ethics

[106] Andrei Arev, 'Nasha malenkaia zhizn', op. cit., p. 7.
[107] Anton Chekhov, 'The Lady with the Dog' (1899), transl by Ivy Litvinov, see <http://www.ibiblio.org/eldritch/ac/lapdog.html> [accessed 5 May 2012].
[108] Brodsky, 'Osennii vecher v skromnom gorodke . . .', op. cit. In Russian: 'И в зеркало глядеться, как фонарь глядится в высыхающую лужу'.
[109] Brodsky, 'Uncommon visage. Nobel Lecture', op. cit., pp. 49–50.
[110] Iskander, 'Poet', op. cit., pp. 143–4.

and aesthetics, constituted a trinity ended with the end of the nineteenth century. Interestingly, Chekhov, despite his elusiveness, is mapped on the above scale (as far as his poetics is concerned) next to Brodsky. Thus Andrew Durkin writes about Chekhov that in his artistic world 'aesthetics lays at the basis of ethics; the way in which a hero speaks or tells something turns into a metaphor of his life'.[111] Does this give us the right to claim the dominance of the irrational in the artistic worlds of both writers? Not quite.

On the one hand, aesthetics is clearly much more irrational than ethics. The following Russian anecdote illustrates this rather beautifully: a religious believer practices his religion dutifully throughout his life, without fail. Yet his path is full of disasters. In the end he cannot take any more and cries out to God, 'Why are you being so cruel to me? What have I done to deserve it? All I did was to serve you with my utmost!' In response, God leans down from the cloud and says, 'Ну, не люблю я тебя!' ('I simply dislike you – I can't help it!').

On the other hand, ethics is not fully rational, even though many, including Nietzsche and Shestov, denounced autonomous ethics, derived from the Western speculative philosophy and saw it as a utilitarian tool to serve the conveniently settled bourgeois ideology. Still, to speak of the antinomy of ethics and aesthetics in terms of the dichotomy of rational–irrational, although tempting, is hardly legitimate. Culture and the associated ethical norms can be viewed indeed as purely rational utilitarian constructions, in place to restrain barbarity and to make social co-existence possible. Freud regarded this cultural layer as superficial, thin and flimsy, not able to withstand any significant existential tests. Chekhov's writings exemplify this point to a large extent. Aesthetics, on the contrary, appears irrational. Yet, within ethics, perhaps at the root of it, there lays a concept of совесть (*sovest'*) (good conscience, moral sense) which appears basically as irrational as aesthetics. As in the mocking song by Yulii Kim, this moral sense is supposed to be highly subjective and individual, built-in deep into the human psyche: 'I recently made a discovery: I have opened a dictionary. And it turns out that conscience (совесть) is a moral category that allows one unmistakably to distinguish between good and evil.'[112]

The following anecdotal story from Fazil Iskander testifies to the same irrational root of *sovest'* (conscience): 'The most cannibalistic states, which suppressed conscience, never denied it theoretically, but merely distorted it to their own advantage. Even they were afraid to deny it directly and loudly. In this respect, an interesting dialogue took place between our famous priest and surgeon Voino-Iasenevsky and Stalin. Here it is in a nutshell. "Why are you saying all the time – soul, soul. It does not exist. Nobody has ever seen it", Stalin said to the priest. "But nobody has seen conscience either", the famous surgeon-priest has replied. – "However, you won't deny that it does exist". And

[111] Durkin, 'Modeli khudozhestvennogo slova v chekhovskikh rasskazakh "V ssylke" i "Student"', in Sobennikov (ed.), *Filosofiia Chekhova*, op. cit., p. 46.
[112] Yulii Kim, 'Dialog o sovesti', <http://www.bards.ru/archives/part.php?id=6082> [accessed 15 February 2014]. In Russian: 'Я недавно сделал открытие: Открыл я недавно словарь – Оказывается, "совесть" – Это нравственная категория, Позволяющая безошибочно Отличать дурное от доброго'.

Stalin remained silent in response. He did not dare to say that conscience did not exist. This is a great, invincible mystery of conscience.'[113]

Thus the dichotomy here is hardly appropriate, and, just like with the concepts of Hot and Cold Blood ('lyric' and stoic trends), the boundary between the rational and the irrational does not coincide with the boundary between ethics and aesthetics, the watershed lies elsewhere. Or, better yet, that watershed does not really exist, as in T. S. Elliot's 'The Waste Land', 'mixing memory and desire'[114] – a projection of what has been with what one would like to have been. And shouldn't we thus pose the question differently – as that of a fusion of rational and irrational, of mind and soul, reason and faith, rather than attempting to divide them?

Recall that for irrationalist Shestov an understanding of the Fall as 'a choice of an inferior faculty with its passion for [. . .] general ideas [. . .] and [. . .] synthetic judgments *a priori*' was the source of universal tragedy leading to the irreconcilable opposition between faith and reason, Athens and Jerusalem. At the same time, as we also saw earlier, Russian religious doctrine is, instead, consistent with the synthetic and thus reconciliatory tendency of Russian culture, and faith occupies in Russian Orthodoxy unique position being 'the highest kind of cognition – it exceeds the mind, but does not contradict it'.

This differs from Western analytical tradition which, perhaps inevitably, ends up with a division (just as Shestov does, paradoxically, while attempting to fight it). Maybe because Reason is so distilled, so isolated in Western philosophy, it gets perfected as a pacifying utilitarian tool in human adjustment to existential horrors. In Russia perhaps, due to its 'synthetic' culture (of which the cult of 'collectiveness' might be a consequence), it is not available in such a pure form, and thus existential dissatisfaction prevails, because ethical feeling, untamed by reason, rebels against the horrors imposed by the chaos of both social and natural origin. The resulting 'great literature and feeble statehood' are complemented in a strong and burning spa of Russian irrationalism, inseparable from the everyday existence, from any rational endeavours. Thus the suspicion creeps in that irrationalism, at least in the Russian context, permeates any rational discourse, just as aesthetics, very likely, permeates our ethical judgements (and vice versa!).

Therefore the premise that in Chekhov, just as in Brodsky, aesthetics is primary, doesn't really give us any conclusions as to the degree of their irrationalism. Moreover, it does not really help us much in understanding their ethics either. Indeed, Chekhov left us to guess whether he is behind the Cold or Hot Blood; whether his ethics is Christian or no ethics at all. Simon Karlinsky argued passionately against the 'standardized' image of 'gloomy and morose Chekhov' which numerous 'Russian Anti-Chekhovians', as he calls them, created.[115] Similarly, Bitov urged not to forget that Chekhov should not be an invention of the Soviet literary canon, that he was 'sharp dresser and womaniser'

---

[113] Iskander, *Lastochkino gnezdo. Proza. Poeziia. Publitsistika*, op. cit., p. 431.

[114] Thomas Stearns Eliot, 'The Waste Land' (1922), <http://www.poetryfoundation.org/poem/176735> [accessed 18 February 2014].

[115] Simon Karlinsky, 'Russian Anti-Chekhovians', in *Russian Literature* (15) 1984, pp. 183–202.

nearly 2 meters in height.[116] Kornei Chukovsky joins in with his depictions of Chekhov's gaiety, his love for practical jokes, performances, parties and so on, as well as his highly noble and courageous actions of a doctor and social devotee.[117] But this does not extinguish opposite voices proclaiming Chekhov's misanthropy and indifference. His plays, which are full of apparent irrationalism, of people day-dreaming, speaking at once and not hearing each other, of absurd coincidences and disjoint events, are discussed as parodies of decadence, mistaken by the decadents themselves for the real thing, so much so that they became a paragon of life-creation.

Similarly, Brodsky left entangled clues of himself, with the uncertain gap between the author and his lyrical hero. Combative and dynamic, he was at the same time constant in his true affections. Both writers escape from the finalizing pen, both dissolve within their own contradictions, revealing irrational substance under the rational veneer; or rather (much more precisely) – the inseparable mix of rational and irrational in human life.

As the most perceptive critics started to notice early on, and in spite of the accusations of dryness and coldness which Chekhov was snowed down with: 'Chekhov is the first of our artists who consciously opposed the rational activity of man to that organic thinking which takes its origins in the irrational depths of our spirit, and rejects the validity of any purely rational thought.'[118] This is perhaps the key to the frequent ambivalence of his characters, to what seems their contradictory nature, when their words and their actions are at odds with each other. Keis Verheil, in connection to Brodsky, wrote about poetry creation that it is akin to having (night-time) dreams – irrational par excellence.[119] As a poet, Brodsky had to work within the irrational. Notably, Chekhov's prose is also first of all poetic, and the vices he was blamed for included precisely those features which characterize poetry writing: accidentality, lack of thematic hierarchy and of causal connections. Evgenii Rein, himself a poet and Brodsky's friend, commented on the latter's personality that it combined immense intellect with immense intuition – again, a symbiosis of rational and irrational, like life itself.

This echoes the lines from Brodsky's essay, entitled as if to suit our purposes: 'On grief and reason' (which is also – instructively – the title for the entire book of his prose): 'the story, as it were marries grief to reason [. . .] the poem ["Home Burial" by Robert Frost] in other words plays fate'; 'while the characters may stand respectively for reason and for grief, the narrator stands for their fusion.'[120] And this is perhaps an ideal closing line to the present discussion.

However, I am going to spoil the idyll by one final point, even though I declared it at the start as being outside the scope of the chapter's concerns. Why did Brodsky so loudly dislike Chekhov – his kin in many more ways than one? Was it simply a vogue,

[116] Andrei Bitov, 'Moi dedushka Chekhov i pradedushka Pushkin', op. cit.
[117] See Kornei Chukovsky, *O Chekhove*, Moscow: Khudozhestvennaia literatura, 1967.
[118] Lubov Gurevich, *Literatura i estetika*, Moscow, 1912, p. 47.
[119] Keis Verheil, 'Spustit'sa nizhe mira zhivykh', in *Iosif Brodsky: tvorchestvo, lichnost, sudba. Itogi triokh konferentsii*, op. cit., p. 33.
[120] Joseph Brodsky, 'On Grief and Reason', in Brodsky, *On Grief and Reason. Essays*, op. cit., p. 260.

inherited from Akhmatova? Even if so, there must have been more to it – because too persistent were his expressions of this dislike to be merely an echo. As Bitov said about Chekhov – его ревновали ('many were jealous of him').[121] For all the improbability of this statement with respect to Brodsky, I think it may carry some weight. Indeed, like Tolstoy for Isaia Berlin is a fox which strives to be a hedgehog,[122] Brodsky may have been striving to be free – above all from his own inner restraints, almost from his own nature. Because for all his outer nihilism, for all the apparent cynicism of his dictum, his carefully protected inner self appears to be most sensitive and vulnerable – the more so, the more protection in sarcasm it needs. Like Lev Shestov, whom he lovingly respected, and in the same paradoxical way, Brodsky is 'ideologically' committed, he is a prisoner of his passions (in a very subtle sense one could even venture to say – of his underlying idealism, even if the surface of it is disenchanted). Tsvetaeva's piercing lines could easily have been said about him: 'Whistle out your boyish // pain, your heart squeezed in your hand. // My cool one, my vehement one . . .'.[123]

At the same time Chekhov, in his quiet pluralism, *really*, intrinsically does not need a pillar of ideology to hold together his inner world, he *indeed* allows for fluidity of life and human psyche, almost for fluidity of good and evil. He is thus much more post-modern than post-modernists; certainly more than Brodsky whose attachment to the things and people he loved was unquestionable ('I loved not many, but strongly'),[124] whose true loyalty was absolute. He was after all a man of single love (однолюб), while Chekhov was more genuinely akin to a cat – a creature so worshipped by Brodsky, a creature he wanted to resemble. His ideal of a woman was also, it seems, feline: women and cats untied by being beautiful, capricious and unattached. He favoured this type of God – capricious and unpredictable God of the Old Testament; he wanted himself to be of this image and likeness. But he was not; for all his inner freedom and dynamism, he was not. Chekhov apparently was. It is perhaps this (almost unethical; almost 'beyond good and evil') freedom, intrinsically unattainable by Brodsky, which he found hard to forgive in Chekhov. Highly irrational, one might say; and probably rightly so.

---

[121] Bitov, 'Moi dedushka Chekhov i pradedushka Pushkin', op. cit.

[122] See Isaiah Berlin, *The Hedgehog and the Fox. An Essay on Tolstoy's View of History*, London: Weidenfeld Goldbacks, Weidenfeld & Nicolson, 1967.

[123] Marina Tsvetaeva, 'You throw back your head' ('Ty zaprokidyvaesh golovu . . .') (1916), in *Selected Poems of Marina Tsvetaeva*, translated and introduced by Elaine Feinstein, op. cit., p. 5. In Russian: 'Мальчишескую боль высвистывай, И сердце зажимай в горсти . . . Мой хладнокровный, мой неистовый . . .'.

[124] Iosif Brodsky, 'Ia vsegda tverdil, chto sud'ba – igra . . .', in Brodsky, *Forma vremeni. Stikhotvoreniia, esse, piesy v 2-kh tomakh*, op. cit., vol. I, p. 254. In Russian: 'Я любил немногих, однако сильно'.

7

Rebellious Tradition: Russian Literary Laughter, between Poetry and Pain

Our soul is endowed with the ability to laugh in order for it to get relief sometimes, and not in order to relax

St. John Chrysostom (Sviatitel Ioann Zlatoust),
vol. 12, part 1, conversation 15

Profound spirit quickly discovers inner kinship between the funny and the sorrowful

Iulii Aikhenvald

Under pressure from without, humour is born from within

Mikhail Zhvanetsky

On ethical aspects of humour: Preliminary remarks

Human ability to laugh is even more astonishing and fundamentally irrational than the ability to love, enigmatic as it is. Aesthetically humour is closest to poetry, with its paradoxical and associative nature, its artistic beauty where form is inseparable from content. Just as poetry, and unlike music or painting, humour is most culturally (and – in its highest forms – linguistically) dependent. That is why perhaps the ultimate – and essentially unattainable – mastery of a foreign culture is to master its poetry and its humour.

However, these remarks are clearly exclusive to a particular strand within the vast space of what is conventionally referred to as the 'laughter culture' (смеховая культура), or, in other words, what can be broadly designated as the 'comic'. This strand encompasses what can be described as (and to what our enquiry here is limited) the culture of humour within Russian literature of the last two centuries. In other words, we aim to recreate a literary history of Russian humour of that period, with a particular focus on its irrationalist element.

This means that various types of humour – namely those that are, so to speak, evolutionary inferior in terms of their form, content and compatibility with literary context – will automatically be left overboard. A suitable model to think of this should perhaps be based on the idea of ontogenesis being a brief repetition of phylogenesis (as in the case of human foetus which progresses through multiple evolutionary stages before its ultimate birth): thus the humorous in childhood invariably starts with exploring the forbidden (as part of child's probing into the nature and extent of social boundaries), with violating the basic taboos – and hence passes initially through the bodily functions-related topics where, at the time, the subject-matter itself seems a cause for laughter. The point here is not so much a violation of taboos as such – since a rebellion against the conventional and normatively accepted often, if not always, underpins the humourous – but the primitive level of this violation and of these taboos in spiritual terms. Later on, in a normal course of personal development, the aesthetic, ethical and (especially) intellectual demands of the person, their cultural standards rise, thus changing drastically what constitutes the humorous. Likewise, the standards for our considerations here will be those set by Russian literature – for which ethical concerns traditionally are primary. Also, a major writer will never succumb to the demands of the mob, but will instead raise the mob to the level of his art. Hence, Pushkin's 'with a lyre I evoked kind feelings',[1] as well as Iskander's idea mentioned in Chapter 2 that national genius rather than reflecting his nation's most common and profound features, instead sets the ethical and cultural target for his people, thus drawing his countrymen upwards, towards the ideal.

In this connection I would like to argue, against the popular belief and at the risk of drawing fire upon myself, that the well-established line within the field of humour theories amounting to Plato's *Philebus* and Aristotle's *Poetics*, and developed further by Sidney, Hobbes and Bergson among others, which is known as 'superiority theory' (laughing at the others' expense, drawing pleasure from feeling superior to them) is out of place here, just as it is out of place in any mature humorous discourse. It is, again, to be found perhaps at an early stage of humanity's ontogenesis. What might have been the norm and the basis for the comic in antiquity, looks sad and seriously challenged in modernity, as a sign of primitivism and cultural deficiency. Even if it finds a wide enough reception, it is more of a sociological than literary phenomenon, and thus lays outside our concerns. Just as with love, whose definitions and manifestations may range from a banal physiology to the highest examples of human devotion, humour too, clearly, is very much a function of its agents. If we accept the basic theoretical premise suggested, in particular, by Bakhtin, that laughter (and humour that underlies it) reveals a fundamental human drive for liberation, a leap to freedom, then all the laughter based on superiority is directly related to what Sergei Averintsev qualifies as a leap for the opposite 'liberation' – from freedom itself.[2] It is the laughter of a Cham,

[1] Aleksandr Pushkin, 'Ia pamiatnik sebe vozdvig nerukotvornyi' (1836), in A. S. Pushkin, *Sobranie sochinenii v 10 tomakh*, op. cit., vol. 2, 1959, p. 460. In Russian: 'чувства добрые я лирой пробуждал'.
[2] Sergei Averintsev, 'Bakhtin, smekh, khristianskaia kultura', in *M.M. Bakhtin kak filosof*, Moscow: Nauka, 1992, p. 11.

which 'frees the laughing person from shame, from compassion and from conscience'.[3] A poetic line, describing human emotions at the Zoo, springs to mind: 'and the sweet feeling of superiority is only experienced here by utter fools' (И сладостное чувство превосходства здесь возникает только у тупиц . . .).[4]

In the same vein, Dostoevsky's hero, the raw youth, talks of the revealing character of human laughter: 'A man will sometimes give himself away completely by his laugh, and you suddenly know him through and through. Even an unmistakably intelligent laugh will sometimes be repulsive. What is most essential in laughter is sincerity, and where is one to find sincerity? A good laugh must be free from malice, and people are constantly laughing maliciously. A sincere laugh free from malice is gaiety, and where does one find gaiety nowadays? People don't know how to be gay. [. . .] It is only the loftiest and happiest natures whose gaiety is infectious, that is, good-hearted and irresistible. And so if you want to see into a man and to understand his soul, don't concentrate your attention on the way he talks or is silent, on his tears, or the emotion he displays over exalted ideas; you will see through him better when he laughs. If a man has a good laugh, it means that he is a good man. [. . .] laughter is the surest test of the heart.'[5]

Furthermore, as Gogol, the pillar of Russian literary humour, famously pronounced through the lips of the Governor in his 'Revizor' ('The Inspector General'): 'What are you laughing at? You are laughing at yourself!'[6] That is to say that Russian laughter is to a large extent self-reflective, and Russian irony often borders on self-irony – from Pushkin to Dovlatov its sting is directed inwards no less than outwards. By the same token, in the words of the Polish humourist Stanisław Jerzy Lec, 'when an ape burst into roaring laughter having seen itself in the mirror, a human being was born.'[7]

Nevertheless, striving upwards is relevant here, only this is not a striving towards superiority over the others with their weaknesses and misfortunes perceived as comic – such perverted pleasures are inherent only in those lacking in self-esteem, or more plainly – those lacking in human dignity. Russian literature, as for that matter any world literature and art, is ethically sound, and defence of human dignity is among its central concerns. Instead, striving upwards in this context is akin to Brodsky's: 'as a belated bird, my brain, debased by separation with you, inadvertently wants to ascend.'[8] Equally, artistic spirit as such is based on a striving to ascend, and Russian literature with its consoling pathos seeks to remind us precisely of 'our human dignity, of the highest purposes of existence.'[9] Suspension of compassion (required, say, by Bergson's understanding of humour), in Russian letters with their Pushkinian call 'for mercy to

[3] Ibid.
[4] Vladimir Livshits, 'Zoopark', in Livshits, *Izbrannye Stikhi*, Moscow: Sovetskii pisatel, 1974.
[5] Fyodor Dostoyevsky, 'A Raw Youth', transl. by Constance Garnett, London: Heineman, 1916, p. 349.
[6] Gogol, 'Revizor' ('The Inspector General'). See <http://www.online-literature.com/gogol/inspector-general/6/> [accessed 15 August 2014].
[7] Stanisław Jerzy Lec. Cited in Yurii Nikulin, *Pochti seriozno . . .*, Moscow: Vagrius, 1998 (see <http://kashlev.dyndns.org:1799/Nikulin.htm> [accessed 12 March 2013]).
[8] Brodsky, 'Penie bez muzyki', in *Forma vremeni. Stikhotvoreniia, esse, piesy v dvukh tomakh*, op. cit., vol. I, p. 236. In Russian: 'как запоздалый кочет Униженный разлукой мозг Возвыситься невольно хочет'.
[9] Chekhov, 'The Lady with the Dog', op. cit.

the fallen'[10] is intrinsically impossible, as it is in fact impossible in true art elsewhere, whose applied function is, so to speak, to be a wake-up call for humanity. It is, if you like, a fusion of religion with aesthetics, with a poetic beauty of being.

These apparently abstract considerations are, in fact, directly relevant to our discussion of Russian humour. This is because this striving upwards, which is a striving to dignity rather than superiority, is what humour has in common with art at large: it is a beautiful human effort, in essence a heroic effort given its doomed nature, to overcome the Necessity. As the champion of contemporary Russian humour Mikhail Zhvanetsky once formulated, 'under pressure from without, humour is born from within',[11] or, similarly, using Barbara Babcock's words, it is a reaction against 'the indignity of any closed system'.[12] The (main part of the) title of her article – 'Arrange me into Disorder' – brings to mind the Underground Man's revolt against rationality, or, if you like, against 'something mechanical encrusted on the living'[13] – what Bergson views as a main stimulus for humour. The dostoevskian Paradoxicalist spurns universal harmony in favour of his right to a caprice, and this, if cleansed at the roots from the egotistic element, is in fact reminiscent of the aspiration widely shared in Russian letters – towards the 'uncommonness of visage', as that of Baratynsky's muse.[14]

Thus, in philosophical terms, humour, or at any rate its ethical nucleus, is, speaking most generally, the resistance of our unique human individuality in the face of universal Necessity, it is our quixotic challenge to our tragic predicament. An instinctive joy of being, inherent in living species, is, in the human race, a manifestation of the same tendency – the more so, the more distinctly an individual is conscious of the tragic framework of life. In this sense, the type of humour predominantly demonstrated by Russian literature is, as we shall see, hard-won, achieved through suffering, 'in spite of', a result of our human resistance to fate, the other side of tears. 'The "I" has to recognize that it is confronted with a world that follows its own laws, a world whose name is Necessity. [. . .] The "I" is invaded by Necessity from the inside as well, but always feels it as an alien force. Nevertheless the "I" must accept the inevitable order of the world.'[15] Czeslaw Milosz wrote these lines in connection with the philosophical rebellion of Lev Shestov, the irrationalist thinker. However, there is a much wider rebellion, common to all mankind and conducted by means other than philosophical – this is the rebellion of art, of life itself with its highest leaps of human spirit such as courage, compassion, love, and of course – the rebellion of laughter. Pushkin's description of 'A Feast in Time of Plague' is of relevance here: 'There is joy in battle, Poised on a chasm's edge, And in

---

[10] '. . . and called for mercy to the fallen' ('и милость к падшим призывал') is a line from Pushkin's aforementioned poem of 1836 'Ia pamiatnik sebe vozdvig nerukotvornyi'.

[11] Mikhail Zhvanetsky, 'Chto takoe iumor?' <http://www.jvanetsky.ru/data/text/t8/chto_takoe_umor/> [accessed 21 January 2014].

[12] Barbara Babcock, 'Arrange me into Disorder: Fragments and Reflections on Ritual Clowning', in John J. MacAloon (ed.), *Rite, Drama, Festival, Spectacle: Rehearsals Toward a Theory of Cultural Performance*, Philadelphia, PA: Institute for the Study of Human Issues, 1984, p. 103.

[13] Henri Bergson, *Laughter: An Essay on the Meaning of the Comic*, transl. by Cloudesley Brereton and Fred Rothwell, London: MacMillan & Co., 1911, Copenhagen: Green Integer, 1999, p. 39.

[14] This is a reference to Evgenii Baratynsky's poetic lines describing his Muse, from his poem 'Muza' (1830).

[15] Milosz, 'Shestov, or the Purity of Despair', op. cit., pp. 103–4.

black ocean's rage . . .'.[16] Therefore, the leading property of real humour is its courage, for ultimately any laughter is the laughter in the face of death.

This approach, of course, essentially adheres to the other fundamental line in the existing theories of humour, which, unlike the 'superiority theory', sees humour as a relief mechanism, as a cleansing and protective valve and as a central psychological means for survival. In this light, humour is humanity's last resort. As Chekhov wrote, in his simple and witty words, to K. S. Barantsevich, 'We will all die, sooner or later, and therefore to sink into melancholy is at least improvident.'[17] Fazil Iskander expressed essentially the same sentiments in a higher register, when defining what deserves to be called a proper humour: 'In order to master good quality humour, one has to be reduced to utter pessimism, to peer into a grim abyss, become convinced that there is nothing there either, and start slowly coming back. The trail left by this backward movement is what constitutes real humour.'[18] The following famous fable also resonates with the above. An oriental monarch kept sending his tax-man around to collect taxes, and every time he asked about the people's reaction to the tax collection. 'They were weeping, saying they have nothing left' was invariably the tax-man's response, when he kept bringing back less and less money. But the cruel ruler kept sending him back for more. Eventually the tax-man said, 'This time they were laughing, saying they had nothing left.' 'Oh! Now I do believe they have nothing left indeed', the monarch uttered. In other words, when everything is lost, laughter remains. A way of resurrection from the ashes, it is also the acknowledgement of life's tragi-comic nature.

Russian laughter culture in historical perspective

We distinguished, above all, the ethical dimension of Russian literary humour and its protective function, its being among central human strategies for survival, resistance and dissidence. As a reaction against tragic necessity, laughter is thus a response to the overpowering irrationality of existence (which includes, in particular, excessive rationality, a mechanistic, soulless component). Hence the more irrational and merciless, the more unjust the reality is – imposed by whatever external forces – the more powerful and necessary humour becomes in the cultural consciousness of a nation, no matter how limited (narrow or underground) the channels are, to which it is reduced.

---

[16] Aleksandr Pushkin, 'A Feast in Time of Plague' (1830). The full song reads as follows: 'There is joy in battle, Poised on a chasm's edge, And in black ocean's rage – That whirl of darkening wind and wave – In an Arabian sandstorm, And in a breath of plague. Within each breath of death Lives joy, lives secret joy For mortal hearts, a pledge, Perhaps, of immortality, And blessed is he who, storm-tossed, Can see and seize this joy', transl. by Robert Chandler; see <http://www.stosvet.net/12/chandler/index5.html> [accessed 30 January 2014].

[17] Anton Chekhov, from his letter to K. S. Barantsevich of 15 April 1890, in Chekhov, *PSSP v 30 tomakh*, op. cit., vol. 4, 1975, p. 61.

[18] Interestingly, a similar perception of humour as conditioned by despair can be found in the camp of existentialists – thus in Albert Camus's words, 'go to the very bottom of the pit of despair, and if you try to dig even deeper, you will find humour there'.

This side of humour, responsible for our spiritual resistance to necessity, is clearly combative in character and can be associated with a 'mocking laughter', if we use Propp's classification.[19] It involves such comic genres as satire, irony, sarcasm, grotesque and so on. However, the important point is that the object of mocking here is not another person as such, but necessity itself, that is, one's fate and the oppressive order of the world more generally. This laughing rebellion is clearly resonant with the Romantic tradition, although it emerged much earlier than Romanticism. Thus Russian *skomorokhi* – street clowns, wandering actors, jesters and musicians – combined a provocative challenge to the official culture with laughing entertainment. Lotman and Uspensky, as we shall see, distinguished a defiance of the sacred, inherent in ancient Russian culture.

In historical perspective we can talk of an archaic ritual laughter, based mainly on human physicality, and characteristic for Slavic pagan times, but equally common to practically all ancient tribes worldwide. Russian Orthodoxy has transformed these bodily pre-Christian traditions by introducing spiritual aspirations, but pagan sensibility proved resilient and resistant to the encroachment of Christian culture. It had subsumed new religious canons of life giving rise to a spiritual fusion of sorts in terms of rituals and beliefs. The archaic laughter, which grew from the sheer joy of life, typical for folk festivals and rituals, from physical and spiritual health, boldness and sweep of will, became for the church a manifestation of sin and vice. This pre-civilized laughter reveals to us another – simplistic and joyful, if you like pre-ethical – aspect of humour.

These ancient sources were also absorbed by the developing laughter culture, and left an imprint on modern humour, even though they were regarded as sinful by Russian Orthodoxy and opposed by the ascetic tradition. The church, viewing humour and laughter as subversive and hostile, had launched an increasingly fierce campaign against them which reached its apogee in the seventeenth century. Laughter, associated with paganism, was regarded as having originated from the Devil, as can be traced in particular in the history of language. Thus a jester (*shut*) in Russian used to designate a demon, and hence a joke (*shutka*) is also of a demonic nature. As Averintsev remarked, 'In general an Orthodox spirituality is even more suspicious of laughter than Western, while a specifically Russian Orthodoxy is particularly distrustful of it. Apparently this is a reaction of ascetics to the Russian national features, such as being unrestrained, elemental, etc.'[20] As a result, Russian humour is, as it were, pressed between these two extremes – of quiet humility and rebellious boldness, just as Russian character is pressed between a sweeping unrestrained will and humble quietude, between shameful and shameless, between ascetic self-denigration and heroic defiance, quiet joy and disquieting contempt towards death. The strain between the two poles – of funny and sad, of laughter and tears is imprinted deeply in the literary tradition of Russian humour of modernity and mirrors the tragicomic genre of life itself.

Moreover, it is precisely that type of laughter which is united with tears, which is born out of them, inseparable from them, that was permitted and recognized by

[19] Vladimir Propp, *Problemy komizma i smekha. Ritualnyi smekh v folklore (po povodu skazki o Nesmeiane)*, Moscow: Labirint, 1999, pp. 17–20.
[20] Sergei Averintsev, 'Bakhtin, smekh, khristianskaia kultura', op. cit., pp. 7–19.

Russian Patristic tradition as divine, and which this tradition distinguished from the other type of laughter, described earlier: arising from devil and associated with sin. Thus, in the eyes of the Fathers there were 'the laughter as such and spiritual laughter. The former the Fathers called *smekhotvorstvo* (literally: "laughter-creation"), the latter – using the terms such as laughter of the soul, joy and merriment. The two are opposed to each other first of all by their moral underpinning. *Smekhotvorstvo* is in line with such indisputable sins as lying, swearing, drunkenness, adultery, etc. At the same time, spiritual laughter, on the contrary, is a sign of liberation from sin. Secondly, they come from different sources: *smekhotvorstvo* (смехотворство) is introduced to human life by the devil and his servants, while spiritual laughter is a divine gift.'[21]

In historical terms, the task of analysing Russian literary tradition of humour in the new times is complicated further by the fact that its sources, which are concealed in the laughter culture of ancient Rus' and substantially determine the comic in modern Russian literature, are being debated to this day. Indeed, there has been no consensus among the leading Russian scholars regarding the theme of laughter in ancient Russian culture. It was Bakhtin's work on Francois Rabelais,[22] written in Soviet times and not surprisingly having broad connotations concerning the concept of humour in general terms, that paved the way to the research in Russian laughter culture. However, even long before Bakhtin's seminal contribution which distinguished laughter culture as a separate object for research, various scholars, especially V. E. Zabelin in the nineteenth century and V. P. Adrianova-Perets in the first half of the twentieth century, addressed ancient Russian humour and its literary representations, and placed laughter in a broad cultural framework, considering it as a form of protest against oppression of all kinds.[23]

In the same vein, Bakhtin saw laughter, in all its ambivalence, as a universal liberating force, outside the religious and as an opposition to the officialdom. Sergei Averintsev, while sharing the general idea of laughter as liberation, later argued decisively against Bakhtin's premise of the positive nature of the carnivalesque, having discerned different types of laughter with respect to freedom, and disavowed the cruel and egotistically manipulative aspects of the carnival culture. Bakhtin's work was continued by Dmitrii Likhachev's and Aleksandr Panchenko's study *'Smekhovoi mir Drevnei Rusi'* (1976) where the question of laughter in Ancient Rus' became the central object of analysis.[24] For them, Russian ancient laughter was a tragic anti-world that opposes the ideal one. Importantly for our purposes, they distinguished a self-mocking component from

---

[21] Arkadii Goldenberg, 'Smekh i slezy v metapoetike Gogolia', in Elena Manaenkova (ed.), *Kategorii ratsionalnogo i emotsionalnogo v khudozhestvennoi slovesnosti*, Volgograd: Izd-vo VGSPU 'Peremena', 2013, p. 57.

[22] Mikhail Bakhtin, *Tvorchestvo Fransua Rable i narodnaia kultura Srednevekovia i Renessansa*, Moscow, Khudozhestvennaia literatura, 1990.

[23] For more details, see Lev Trakhtenberg, 'K istorii izucheniia russkoi smekhovoi kultury', in Aleksei Kholikov (ed.), *Russkoe literaturovedenie XX veka: imena, shkoly, kontseptsii*, Moscow–St Petersburg: Nestor-Istoriia, 2012, pp. 163–71, where a very useful overview of the history of research into Russian laughter culture is given.

[24] See Dmitrii Likhachev and Aleksandr Panchenko, *Smekhovoi mir Drevnei Rusi*, Leningrad: Nauka, 1976.

Bakhtin's universal conception of laughter as most essential – as, for example, in the humour of *shuty* (jesters), which places such laughter within the Christian tradition of humility. Along the same lines, years later, Natalia Ponyrko, shifting focus from literary sources to Russian ancient rituals involving laughter, argued for their religious subtext and Christian sensibility.[25]

By contrast, Yurii Lotman and Boris Uspensky, who were among those developing the discussion, offered an alternative vision, also based on the study of Russian rituals. According to their findings, what Bakhtin labelled as Russian laughter culture (and what they refused to classify as comic) opposed the sacred, as pagan opposed the Christian.[26] Instead they saw it as a conscious defiance of the religious values, that is, a deliberate sin committed without losing piety. As L. A. Trakhtenberg writes, 'this is a conscious sacrilege which does not disavow the sacred, but instead only confirms its immutability.'[27] This means that ancient Russian laughter affirmed and validated religious sphere through the defiance of it. Although, as Panchenko subsequently argued, the sacred and profane in Russian ancient laughter culture were compatible and initially not considered as subversive by the church, already from the fourteenth century the clerical began – with a culmination in the seventeenth century – a growing attack against laughter culture.[28] However, this attack was then cut short by Peter the Great's secular policies. Nevertheless, the ambivalence of laughter in ancient Rus' remained an issue, and a long history of its perception as a sinful anti-religious element is imprinted still in a linguistic pun that rhymes '*smekh*' with '*grekh*' ('laughter' with 'sin').

Thus one can venture to say that Russian humour was traditionally based on a dialectical struggle of subversion, violation and sin, and as if continuing the ancient defiance, has inherited a strong 'in spite of' component. Thus Averintsev, arguing with Bakhtin's theory of laughter rooted in Western cultural paradigms, stresses a typically Russian attitude to laughter as a forbidden area of life: 'Russian attitude to laughter as being an uncontrollable and hence dangerous "element", as Aleksandr Blok put it, is expressed in a charming way by another Russian poet – young Marina Tsvetaeva: "A passer-by, I too loved to laugh when it is forbidden!"'.[29] He contrasts this Russian striving to transcend the borders of the permitted with the Western European carnivalesque culture, discussed by Bakhtin, where laughter is inscribed into a fully permitted, regulated social space. '"To laugh when it is forbidden" is an emotional experience much more powerful, even orgiastic, than that of laughing when it is "permitted",

[25] See Natalia Ponyrko, 'Russkie sviatki XVII veka', in *TODRL*, Leningrad, 1977, vol. XXXII as well as '"Sviatochnyi i maslenichnyi smekh" i proizvedeniia "smekhovoi literatury"', in Dmitrii Likhachev, Aleksand Panchenko and Natalia Ponyrko, *Smekh v Drevnei Rusi*, Leningrad: Nauka, 1984.

[26] Yurii Lotman and Boris Uspensky, 'Novye aspekty izucheniia kultury Drevnei Rusi', in *Voprosy literatury*, 1977, p. 156.

[27] Lev Trakhtenberg, 'K istorii izucheniia russkoi smekhovoi kultury', op. cit., p. 168.

[28] See Aleksandr Panchenko, *Russkaia kultura v kanun petrovskikh reform*, Leningrad: Nauka, 1984.

[29] Sergei Averintsev, 'Bakhtin i russkoe otnoshenie k smekhu', in Sergei Nekliudov and Elena Novik (eds), *Ot mifa k literature. Sbornik v chest 75-letiia E.M. Meletinskogo*, Moscow: Rossiiskii universitet, 1993, pp. 341–345. See also <http://www.gumer.info/bibliotek_Buks/Linguist/Article/av_bah.php> [accessed 3 February 2014].

knowing that it is "permitted"', Averintsev remarks.[30] He notices that in Russia, by contrast, 'one laughed [. . .] always a lot, but there laughing was always more or less "forbidden" – not only due to some external prohibition on the part of authorities of whatever kind, or because of public opinion, but above all due to what the one who laughs really feels. Any permission, any "you may", pertaining to laughter, remains for Russian consciousness not quite convincing. It is actually forbidden to laugh; but it is really impossible not to laugh.'[31] This situation, Averintsev concludes, 'generates a wistful glance in the direction of the place where laughter is certainly allowed and necessary – that is, in the direction of the West'.[32]

Yet, some scholars, having placed Russian laughter in the context of world culture, have found similarities and continuities rather than distinctions. Thus Eleazar Meletinsky (1978) argued for the universal nature of laughter rituals which underpins the specificity demonstrated by Likhachev.[33] Equally, Aron Gurevich (1981) insisted that laughter and fear coexisted in Russian laughter culture, and sacrilege, committed through laughter as a certain reaffirmation of faith, is a universal cultural feature.[34]

Russian folk-tales, Ivan-The-Fool and philosophy of 'foolishness', Folkloric roots of Shukshin and Vysotsky

Even those cultural elements which are shared world-wide are not homogeneously distributed, that is, they normally occur in different proportions depending on national cultures. Thus Andrei Siniavsky comments that although Russian folk-hero Ivan-Durak (Ivan-The-Fool) is in fact an international phenomenon, it is only in Russian culture that he became so overwhelmingly popular: 'In fairy-tales of very different peoples there are such heroes-fools, who behave in an approximately similar fashion. (Compare, for instance, the German tale "The Golden Goose" by the brothers Grimm: "Once upon a time there lived a man. He had three sons, and the youngest was called a Fool. He was despised, mocked and his feelings were always hurt"). And even the perpetual laying on a stove is not a prerogative of the Russian Fool. A different matter is that the fairy-tales' fool perhaps found in Russian culture a congenial and fertile ground, so he flourished to such an extent and enjoyed wide fame.'[35] Ivan-The-Fool is an outcast, and his main feature is a total intellectual innocence, or in other words, ignorance and stupidity, which initially cause a lot of damage to his family. Not only is he clueless, but also idle and lazy, and sometimes even capable of crime (normally, stealing). At the same time Ivan-The-Fool demonstrates a purity of soul, in many ways caused by his lack of reason. Despite his foolishness, Ivan always comes on top of his

---

[30] Ibid.
[31] Ibid.
[32] Ibid.
[33] Eleazar Meletinsky, Review of Likhachev and Panchenko, *Smekhovoi mir Drevnei Rusi*, op. cit., in *Sovetskaia etnografiia*, 1978, No. 2.
[34] Aron Gurevich, *Problemy srednevekovoi narodnoi kultury*, Moscow: Iskusstvo, 1981.
[35] Andrei Siniavsky, *Ivan-durak: Ocherk russkoi narodnoi very*, Moscow: Agraf, 2001, p. 42.

clever and able brothers, and even overpowers the monarch himself – because the supernatural, divine forces are always on his side.

Clearly, the meaning of such folk tales is dependent on the ethical and moral values of a given historical context, and on a huge variety of different sources as well as general methodological difficulties of dealing with folklore, which make it impossible to draw a single conception regarding the cultural semantics of this folk hero. However, this material undoubtedly reflects in the broadest sense all the aspirations, dreams and beliefs of the nation, from noble to criminal. In particular, the premise of Dostoevsky's hero – 'human nature is diverse, too diverse, I'd narrow it down'[36] (traditionally attributed specifically to a Russian) – is fully applicable in this context. Thus the ideas behind Ivan-The-Fool's character range from the Christian axiology of 'the last one here becoming the first one There', and earthly wit and common sense being meaningless against divine wisdom, to a common apologetics of stealing.

Evgenii Trubetskoy bitterly discerns in these archetypes various negative national characteristics, such as laziness, irresponsibility, weak personal will, idleness as an ideal and so on. 'This is the same shortcoming which manifests itself also in Russian religiosity, in the habit of a Russian to shift all the responsibility onto the broad shoulders of *Nikola-Ugodnik* (St Nicholas the Wonderworker).'[37] Such interpretation is decisively contested by an opposite view, where Ivan-The-Fool is compared to a Holy Fool and 'turns out to be that very "weak one in whom Divine power is happening".'[38] Adherents of this vision insist, on the contrary, that 'Interpreting [. . .] the figure of Ivan-the-Fool outside its religious meaning sometimes leads to a primitive and false understanding of this fairy-tale character as a symbol of Russian laziness and stupidity'.[39]

What matters though are those versions and interpretations which remain in the cultural consciousness of the nation and determine the vector of its development. In this sense, it is not so much the idea of fatalism, of trust in the Divine will, as it is the force of innocence, naïveté of soul, purity of intentions and generally an anti-pragmatic mind set which are of most importance. Those values which are traditionally required for business success – a self-serving, energetic mind and psychological conformism, down-to-earth pragmatic aspirations – all have, historically, negative connotations in Russian cultural imagination. Most resourceful and cunning characters in Russian literary tradition are evil and often end up as having unhappily outwitted themselves. By contrast, those who least think of succeeding, come on top, helped by higher forces. This anti-pragmatic mind set appears so resilient to change that despite many economic and political shifts have, in some form at least, survived to this day. Thus the contemporary sociologist Natalia Vinokurova speaks of a problematic nature of adapting by Russian mentality, with its traditional (hidden or explicit) disdain for the idea of obsessively gaining of material wealth, the concept of Homo Economicus,

---

[36] See Fedor Dostoevsky, *The Brothers Karamazov*, Part I, Book 3.

[37] Evgenii Trubetskoy, *Inoe tsarstvo i ego iskateli v russkoi narodnoi skazke*, Moscow: Izdanie G.A. Lemana, 1922, p. 46.

[38] Elena Volkova, Lecture notes 'Russkii iurodivyi, Ivan-durak i Idiot' (MGU), <http://rudocs.exdat.com/docs/index-353259.html> [accessed 15 February 2014].

[39] Ibid.

whose behaviour is calculated, based on rational choices and driven by the striving to maximize his profits.[40]

The anti-pragmatic pathos of the folk-tales (always embellished with humour) about the idle and hopeless character Ivan-The-Fool being the ultimate victor, found its way into classical Russian literature. The famous Oblomov, epitomizing some profound Russianness, looks on the outside as an idler and looser, but from the inside of the Russian tradition, as depicted most forcefully in Nikita Mikhalkov's screen adaptation of 1979 ('*Neskolko dnei iz zhizni I.I. Oblomova*'), he comes across as a moving, pure and gentle soul, against the dry and unappealing rationalism of successful Shtolts, who represents Western values and mentality. If Ivan-The-Fool, traditionally laying on the stove, knows nothing and demonstrates an instinctive non-resistance to evil through his laziness and passivity, Oblomov's laying on his coach is underpinned by a fully conscious moral philosophy. For him, life merits active involvement only as long as it is meaningful, whereas the existence of people around him is devoid of true meaning in Oblomov's eyes. 'Where here is man? [. . .] Where did he vanish, how did he get exchanged into such trifle?'[41] he exclaims bitterly, looking at his visitors and his milieu more generally, at their vain and petty life motivations.

Similar continuity can be observed in Dostoevsky's 'Idiot' where the writer attempted to create a decisively positive hero, an imitation of Christ, which proved unviable. This hero, Prince Myshkin, is perceived by the others as another Russian Fool – an idiot, a person with a weak mind – not because of his mental illness (epilepsy), but because he is 'incapable of logically processing his own interests', using Iskander's words.[42] Here, once again, we can see contempt for 'low truth', for pragmatic, calculating reason and its egotistic rationality, which are opposed by divine wisdom disguised as foolishness in earthly terms.

By the same token, as Siniavsky writes, 'The Fool's philosophy in part overlaps with the statements by some great ancient sages ("The only thing that I do know is that I know nothing" – Socrates; "the clever ones are not educated; the educated ones are not clever" – Lao-Tzu), as well as with mystical practices of various religious kinds. The essence of these views is in spurning the activity of a controlling mind that hinders an attainment of the ultimate truth. Such a truth (or reality) comes and reveals itself to a person by itself, at that happy moment when consciousness seems to be switched off, and the soul is in a special state – of susceptible passivity.'[43] This passivity resonates with the (rather peculiar, but persistent) ideas discussed in Chapter 2, of the intrinsic 'void' of Russian cultural self and its high susceptibility to the outside influence; it also points to the Russian striving towards the higher truth which, however, is not located in the realm of logical reasoning.

---

[40] See Natalia Vinokurova, 'Russian semiotics of behaviour, Or Can a Russian person be regarded as Homo Economicus?' in Olga Tabachnikova (ed.), *Mystery inside Enigma: Facets of Russian Irrationalism between Art and Life*, op. cit.

[41] Ivan Goncharov, *Oblomov*, <http://az.lib.ru/g/goncharow_I_a/text_0020.shtml> [accessed 20 February 2014].

[42] Fazil Iskander, 'Ponemnogu o mnogom', op. cit.

[43] Siniavsky, *Ivan-durak: Ocherk russkoi narodnoi very*, op. cit. Part of this quotation was already cited in Chapter 3 where this range of ideas was discussed in relation to Russian propensity for dreaming.

The same passivity, echoing the 'silent' tradition of Russian hesychasm, is praised by Gogol in his 'Vybrannye mesta iz perepiski s druziami' ('Selected Passages from Correspondence with Friends'). Thus Gogol criticizes Western Catholicism, opposing to it as a positive example the passivity of the Russian Orthodox clergy (which, by contrast, was seen as negative by Russian Westernizers):[44] 'Let the Western Catholic missionary beat his chest, wave his arms and with eloquent speech and sobbing spew forth soon drying tears. A preacher of Eastern Catholicism, on the other hand, must perform in such a way in front of the people that even from his humble demeanour, faded eyes and the quiet, astounding voice exuding from his soul, in which have died all his human desires, everything would have shifted even before he had explained the matter, and would have spoken to him in unison: Do not say words, we can hear without them the divine truth of your church!'[45] Ekaterina Dmitrieva notes that the same passivity as a religious ideal was chosen at the end of the eighteenth-century by F. Schlegel for his 'renovated religion', shortly before he entered Catholicism. He argued that 'Only in a holy silence of true passivity can man gather together his entire "I" and encompass with his inner sight "the ultimate depths of the world and of life".'[46] In Dmitrieva's opinion, 'both Gogol and Schlegel relied in this regard – and totally independently at that – on the tradition of patristic literature.'[47]

Thus Russian traditional fascination with stupidity turns out to be, at least to some extent, an exaltation of different values – first of all of a humble lack of self-interest, from which then grows compassion and philosophical depth, spurning a primitive rationalism of the conventional, its prudence and calculation. The latter qualities are particularly hateful for the Russian cultural imagination, and migrate from folk-tales to classical literature and beyond. However, a calculating and rational approach, or at any rate a striving towards it, is not at all alien to Russian mentality, especially to that of a peasant, who was forced by the hardship of life to become resourceful and pawky, but whose rationality was turned on its head by the irrational external forces. Thus, as the famous Russian historian Vasilii Kliuchevsky noted, the unpredictable Russian climate 'often laughs at the most careful calculations of the Russian: caprice of climate and soil fools his most modest expectations, and, eventually accustomed to these deceptions, the calculating Russian loves sometimes to make, headlong, the most hopeless and wasteful decision, opposing to the caprice of nature the caprice of his own audacity. This tendency to tease happiness, to play the game of luck is what is known as the Russian "авось" – relying on chance.'[48] Pushkin, with his life-affirming

[44] See on this Ekaterina Dmitrieva, 'N.V. Gogol: palimpsest stilei/palimpsest tolkovanii', NLO, 2010, No. 104 (<http://magazines.russ.ru/nlo/2010/104/dm9.html> [accessed 10 January 2014]) as well as 'Obrashcheniia v katolichestvo v Rossii v XIX v.: Istorikokulturnyi kontekst', in *Arbor mundi*, Moscow, 1996, Issue 4, pp. 84–110.

[45] Nikolai Gogol, *PSS v 14 tomakh*, op. cit., vol. 8, p. 246. Cited in Ekaterina Dmitrieva, 'N.V. Gogol: palimpsest stilei/palimpsest tolkovanii', op. cit.

[46] See Hans J. Münk, 'Die deutsche Romantik in Religion und Theologie', in Romantik-Handbuch, Herausgegeben von Helmut Schanze. Stuttgart: Alfred Kröner Verlag, 2003, pp. 557–560. Cited in Dmitrieva, op. cit.

[47] Dmitrieva, op. cit., Footnote no. 110.

[48] Vasilii Kliuchevsky, *Russkaia istoriia. Polnyi kurs lektsii v 2-kh knigakh*, vol. 1, Moscow: OLMA-Press, 2002, p. 251.

and pacifying tendency, avoids the epithet 'calculating' in his description of a Russian character, saying instead that: 'a distinguishing feature of our mores is a certain cheerful cunningness of mind, mocking wit and a picturesque way of expression.'[49] However, Kliuchevsky's lines earlier can be easily extended to Russian life as a whole, ruled by unpredictability not only of natural, but also of socio-political forces as well. And the hardship of the individual existence, as well as an irrational – simultaneously capricious and courageous – response to it, has surely contributed to the bitter spice and philosophical depth of Russian humour.

Apart from magic fairy-tales, Russian folklore included epic songs on heroic themes (*byliny*) that described the life of Russian mighty men (*bogatyri*) – defenders of the country and mythological creatures at the same time. This epic genre, fully formed around the twelfth century and akin to the Western-European knight legends, shared a lot with the Scandinavian tradition (which then influenced the rest of Europe), of a ritual singing of praise to one's own national military successes. In ancient Rus', while this heroic epos revolved around its two main cultural centres – Kiev in the south and Novgorod Velikii in the north – it is in the latter that it acquired satirical rather than purely heroic features, being in some way a precursor of the modern Russian anecdote – a rather unique humorous genre.

It is also interesting to observe a certain kinship as well as a crucial distinction between the principal mighty man Ilya Muromets and Ivan-The-Fool in that both spent a long time laying on a stove, but Ilya, unlike Ivan, was confined to it not by his unwillingness to act, but by his physical deficiency. When the time had come, Ilya stood up and became a hero of supernatural strength, performing numerous heroic deeds, whose socially oriented noble nature can be opposed to the personal stories of Ivan which are often morally dubious, at least on the outside. However, importantly, Ilya's motivation is concerned with the country's well-being, and his function is heroic and protective, while Ivan's is a private story of a private man. At the same time, as mentioned earlier, Ivan-The-Fool can be understood as a representative of the Holy Fools tradition which, just as the image of the foolish character, is not exclusive to Russia, but was inherent in European culture more generally. Yet, just as the fool playing the main role in folk-tales evidently struck some vital national chord in Russia and enjoyed huge popularity, the Holy Foolishness also developed profound roots precisely on the Russian soil. And the portrait of Russian humour would be crucially incomplete without these Holy Fools who draw their roots from laughter culture, and combine both comic and tragic elements.

Holy Foolishness has been very wide-spread in Russia and much more at home in Russian religiousity than in any other (e.g. than in the Greek Church). As indicated in Chapter 2, the nucleus of this phenomenon is in the striving to the heavenly and sacrificing the earthly for the divine truth. It rejects common sense and takes on the image of pure madness, behind which, however, is a disdain for the earthly temptations and petty comfort, be it material or mental. 'Holy Foolishness is longing for the truth

---

[49] Pushkin, 'O predislovii gospodina Lemonte k perevodu basen I.A. Krylova', in *Sobranie sochinenii v 10 tomakh*, op. cit., vol. 6, p. 15.

and love, and therefore ends up castigating any injustice and deception in human life.'[50] Siniavsky draws a parallel between Russian Holy Fools and Ivans-The-Fools, arguing for their synonimicity.[51] Thus he draws on Dmitrii Likhachev's idea that Russian folk tales about fools present an invaluable source for understanding the phenomenon of Russian Holy Foolishness.[52] In Siniavsky's eyes, 'Ivan-the-Fool is akin to a Holy Fool in that he is the cleverest of the fairy-tales heroes, and also in that his wisdom is concealed. If at the beginning of the tale his opposition to the world looks like a conflict of stupidity with common sense, then as the plot progresses, it becomes clear that this stupidity is feigned or illusory, whereas the common sense is akin to platitude or meanness. In culturological works it has been noted that Ivan-the-Fool is a secular analogue of a Holy Fool, just as Ivan-Tsarevich (Ivan-The-Prince) is analogous to a holy prince.'[53] However, Sergei Ivanov essentially takes issue with this interpretation by stressing that Ivan-The-Fool is passive and lazy, all he wants is to be left alone, whereas a Holy Fool, on the contrary, is active, even aggressive, and his task is to awaken mankind, to keep it away from stupefying slumber of the everyday.[54] This lack of consensus points us once again to an undying contemporality, a persistent relevance of both Holy Foolishness and national folklore to Russian culture. As we shall see, the Holy Fools tradition had a wide following in Russian letters, and is distinctly audible in Dostoevsky's oeuvre,[55] as well as in the unique style of narrative created by Venedikt Erofeev a century later.

Ivanov's stance as mentioned earlier does not seem to take into account the multidimensional character of Ivan-The-Fool, which (the debated Holy Fool's features aside) combines a stupid side with the heroic aspects of the mighty men. The result of such a fusion can be observed in another magic Russian Ivan: Ivan-Tsarevich (Ivan-The-Prince), whose cultural meaning is somewhat ambivalent, as brilliantly expressed by Andrei Usachev's verse: 'Два Ивана ходят вместе – и на подвиг, и к невесте. Не поймет она никак – кто Царевич, кто Дурак?' ('Two Ivans are always together – when they go to perform their tour-de-force and when they go to see their fiancée. She cannot understand which one is the Prince and which one is the Fool').[56] This combination of foolish and noble has profound semantics, not least echoed in Pushkin's phrase 'поэзия, Господи прости, должна быть глуповата' ('Poetry, Lord forgive me, ought to be a bit silly'),[57] which reminds us in particular that purity, innocence and sincerity often border on simplicity, easily mistaken for foolishness, whereas cleverness in the form of a complex and cunning construction of mind is often self-serving and effortlessly merges with a lie. However, one can distinguish here two different cultural lines which originate from the duality of this image of Ivan-The-Fool come Ivan-The-Prince.

---

50   Vasilii Zenkovsky, *Istoriia russkoi filosofii*, op. cit., vol. 1, p. 47.
51   See Siniavsky, *Ivan-durak: Ocherk russkoi narodnoi very*, op. cit.
52   See ibid.
53   Ibid.
54   See, for example, an interview with Sergei Ivanov at <http://www.youtube.com/watch?v=Pjp_0d1rZiI> [accessed 30 November 2013].
55   See on this, for instance, Harriet Murav's book *Holy Foolishness: Dostoevsky's Novels & the Poetics of Cultural Critique*, Stanford, CA: Stanford University Press, 1992.
56   Andrei Usachev, *Azbuka Baby-Iagi*, <http://lib.rus.ec/b/338824/read> [accessed 23 January 2014].
57   Aleksandr Pushkin, from his letter to P. A. Viazemsky of May 1826. See A. S. Pushkin, *Sobranie sochinenii v 10 tomakh*, op. cit., vol. 9, p. 232.

One of these lines is associated with the gulf, historically present in Russian culture, between the vast majority of uneducated peasantry and a tiny minority of educated nobility. Despite major socio-political shifts of the twentieth-century Russia, the gap between the uneducated and educated remained, and the same smart peasant mentality as before, a rather provincial practical intelligence and cunning wit, proved resilient and ineradicable in their opposition to the exaltation of an academic mind and intellectual tradition of Soviet intelligentsia. The perpetual guilt of nineteenth-century Russian intelligentsia with respect to the Russian people was transformed to the uneasy feeling and acute divide that separated the headworkers and manual workers in Soviet times, with their proclaimed hegemony of the proletariat, of the low social strata. Despite their social privileges, the gap between the latter and the former remained painful. The resulting situation, in my view, psychologically resonates with that portrayed in the fairy-tales under discussion, which reflect the national folk aspirations where Ivan-The-Fool is a hero who, despite his total ignorance and implied stupidity, despite, moreover, his low origin, comes out a winner against various wizards representing devilry, even though his own moral stance is often ambiguous, and even dubious. Thus Ivan-The-Fool 'promoted' into Ivan-The-Prince by being corrupted first by the famous 'going to the people movement' of the 1860s and then by the Bolsheviks's promises that 'a kitchen maid will rule the state', on the one hand, acquires impudence and cheeky self-assurance, and, on the other, lives with a chip on his shoulders with respect to the educated, to those who in reality and in close proximity to him live indeed the life of the mind. Vasilii Shukshin's masterpiece, already mentioned in Chapter 5 – the short story 'Srezal' (1970) – is a brilliant tale of an interaction between such two men, originally from the same village, one of whom became an academic, educated in town. The story demonstrates how an adequate communication between them is impossible, and yet, the local man, who loves such 'debates' with brainy visitors and picks mental fights with them, is utterly convinced (as are his fellow villagers who enjoy the 'show') that it is him who won the argument.

The other line concerns Ivan-The-Fool's role as a positive hero, equipped with the noble features of Ivan-The-Prince. Shukshin's other work, a satirical novella 'Do tret'ikh petukhov' (published in 1975), can serve as an example. It involves Ivan-The-Fool directly, acting among other Russian literary characters, but in the ideologically oppressive Soviet conditions. Here Ivan is trying to maintain his dignity in the corrupt environment which suppresses human freedom and mirrors the everyday life under the Soviet regime. The cast of literary characters epitomizes what the totalitarian ideology turned Russia and its literary heritage into, and what Andrei Bitov aptly labelled 'cast-iron Politbureau of Russian literature'.[58] A monopoly of state control reaches not only to the private life of an individual and to the field of artistic production, but also to humour itself. The wizard here is a prototype of a communist party boss, a self-serving functionary who, in particular, is in charge of the funny and passes bureaucratic resolutions that parody the reality of Soviet artistic councils (quality assurance

---

[58] See Andrei Bitov, a shortened version of his essay *My Grandfather Chekhov and Great-Grandfather Pushkin*, Novaia Gazeta, 12 July 2004, No. 49.

committees of sorts): 'Given humour [. . .] is declared stupid! [. . .] in which connection it is stripped of the right to express the quality in the sequel named laughter'.[59] In line with the Russian folk tradition, Ivan outwits the devilry, including the Wizard, but his dignity is made to suffer and his deeds have catastrophic consequences. He cannot stay morally pure in the undignified, corrupt conditions of Soviet reality.

A similar striving for freedom and dignity as well as the motif of inner corruption is present in Vladimir Vysotsky's poetry about Ivan-The-Fool, which reflects both totalitarian Soviet reality and human condition more generally. His Ivan from the 'Song about miserable forest inhabitants' ('*Skazka o neschastnykh lesnykh zhiteliakh*', 1967) is also victorious, but equally sallied by becoming indistinguishable from the life around him, where victims and perpetrators resemble each other and are subjects to the same sad and inhuman rules. Depicted with sad irony and gentle compassion, all of the characters are equally unhappy, and the epic triumphant deeds, inherent in the original folk genre, are turned upside down and infused with contemporary associations, thus acquiring a comic dimension. 'He is all the time on the alert: whatever happens – he is already there; he was in his own way a miserable fool! [. . .] His futile exploits began, his pointless struggle against Baba-Yagas [Russian witch] . . . Of course, these forest paupers and devilry – they are also miserable in their own way'.[60] The poet's warm smile hovering over this song, which in a way recreates a metaphysical canvas of life in all its ridiculousness, is reminiscent of another author of that time, Sergei Dovlatov, to whom we shall turn later.

A likeness of Ivan-The-Prince is also to be found in Vysotsky's oeuvre – in the inescapable theme of the hero versus the tsar portrayed in another humorous song – 'Pro dikogo vepria (V korolevstve, gde vsio tikho i skladno . . ', 1966).[61] Here a 'formerly best, but now ostracised bowman' rescues the kingdom on tsar's request by defeating a wild monster. In his attempts to entice the hero, the tsar offers him, in the tradition of such fairy-tales, to marry a young princess, tsar's daughter, in the case of his victory. But the bowman contemptuously spurns the noble beauty and asks instead for a barrel of alcohol, thus humiliating the tsar. In his total and cheerful inner freedom and independence, in his tantalizing self-will and mischievous incorruptibility together with his outcast position and low status, the hero combines, once again, Ivan-The-Fool with Ivan-The-Prince and the mighty man Ilya-Muromets. His disdain for tsar's desires and commands, as well as for tsar's benefactions echo the famous tale of Emelia-The-Fool endowed with superpowers, who, even though he does not spurn the princess, initially also refuses to go to the royal palace and violently resists the royal guard.

[59] Vasilii Shukshin, 'Do tretiikh petukhov', <http://lib.ru/SHUKSHIN/do3pet.txt> [accessed 10 December 2013].
[60] Vladimir Vysotsky, 'Pesnia o neschastnykh lesnykh zhiteliakh', <http://vysotskiy.lit-info.ru/ vysotskiy/stihi/190.htm> [accessed 16 December 2013]. In Russian: 'Он всё время: где чего – так сразу шасть туда, Он по-своему несчастный был – дурак! [. . .] Началися его подвиги напрасные, С баб-ягами никчемушная борьба . . . Тоже ведь она по-своему несчастная, Эта самая лесная голытьба'.
[61] Vysotsky, 'Pro dikogo vepria' ('V korolevstve, gde vsio tikho I skladno . . '), <http://vysotskiy.lit-info. ru/vysotskiy/stihi/152.htm> [accessed 17 December 2013].

Thus most talented writers of the late twentieth century demonstrated a profound continuity with the national folk tradition, sustaining in particular its comic element, so vital in the conditions of political tyranny.

It is also folklore, and especially the folktales, which gave rise to the Russian anecdote culture – a vital branch of Russian humour, especially prominent during the Soviet times. In some sense Russian anecdote came to occupy a niche in the oral folk culture between a (compressed) fairy-tale and a proverb, equipped also with a topical sting. In it one can discern all sorts of influences, including a distinct echo of the Russian *skomorokhi* tradition as well as a sharp-cut wit of Pushkin's epigrams. Both structurally and aesthetically it is again anecdote that makes us recall poetry in the context of humour, by its neat, laconic architectonics, compressed intensity, taught composition and a brisk exhale of the denouement, a relief of tension by a final dramatic chord. Both represent a beautiful spring of human spirit that unwinds in seconds, giving an immediate catharsis – comic or lyrical.

Seth Graham in his study of anecdote in Russia classifies it as a 'marker of a lack – the severe paucity of ingenuous public discourse in Soviet culture'.[62] At the same time, given the general subversive nature of Russian laughter, as discussed earlier, the apocryphal character of the authentic Russian anecdote and a perpetual incongruence between the ruled and the rulers in Russia will always leave the room for this genre of collective wisdom, which stands next to proverbs and idioms, that is, to the evolution of the language itself. Rising or fading, depending on the historical phase, Russian anecdote is unlikely to die out, always ready, just as the language is, to react to cultural change, to a disharmony and falsity, whether social or personal, and to redeem and sustain the inner freedom of the nation.

Russian literary humour, setting the scene, Fonvizin, Griboedov and Krylov: Creative appropriation

A similar kindred with folklore, with the national tradition, the same proximity to proverbs and idioms distinguishes also the famous comedies 'Nedorosl'' ('The Minor') (1782) by Denis Fonvizin and 'Gore ot uma' ('Woe from Wit') (1822–4) by Aleksandr Griboedov. Among their principal features are their humanness, vivacity, which breaks the old strictures of classicism, and lush, juicy language with abundance of aphorisms which entered everyday speech, thus becoming part of the national cultural baggage. That is to say, a single authorship work attained, in these two cases, the heights of folk-wisdom – a sign of a rare and special quality that not many later authors can boast. Pushkin's Decembrist friend, Aleksandr Bestuzhev-Marlinsky, who was himself a well-known literary critic of the time, rightly placed these two works in the same

---

[62] Seth Benedict Graham, 'A cultural analysis of the Russo-Soviet *anekdot*', PhD Dissertation, Pittsburg, PA: University of Pittsburg, 2003, p. 243. See <http://d-scholarship.pitt.edu/9560/1/grahamsethb_Etd2003.pdf> [accessed 24 November 2013] and Graham's subsequent book *Resonant Dissonance: The Russian Joke in Cultural Context*, Evanston, IL: Northwestern University Press, 2009.

line: 'Mr Griboedov's comedy "Gore ot uma" is a phenomenon which we have not seen since "Nedorosl"'. A crowd of characters, painted bravely and sharply; a living portrait of Moscow mores; depth of soul concealed in the emotions; intelligence and wit in conversations; unprecedented fluency and the nature of spoken Russian in verse.'[63] Discussing the specifics of humour of Griboedov's comedy, he stresses its innovative features that go against the existing rational conventions of form, and prophesizes an eternal life to this truly classical work: 'Man with a heart will be unable to read it without laughing, without being moved to tears. People used to entertain themselves according to French system or insulted by the specular scenes, are saying that it does not have a proper introduction, that its author gets to be liked against the rules; but let them talk as they please: prejudice will evaporate, and posterity will see all the worth of this comedy, and will place it next to the best national creations.'[64]

These authors, just as, most notably, Pushkin himself, creatively appropriated European literary heritage, and adjusted it to Russian cultural context, having poured specifically Russian blood into foreign veins, vitalizing the existing Western-European literary patterns, full of the Enlightenment spirit, with the energy and vitality of the Russian folk tradition, irrational by comparison. Another exceptional example of this kind, who substantially contributed to Russian literary humour, is Ivan Krylov, the writer of poetic fables. In the apt characteristic given to his oeuvre by A. Arkhangelsky and A. Nemzer, they remark on 'a common sense of Krylov's fables' calling it 'a philosophy of a person who became disenchanted with the delusions of the Enlightenment and favoured instead a cheerful scepticism of the folk worldview.'[65] The same idea is elaborated at length by Averintsev who provides a detailed analysis of the opposition between Krylov's essentially irrationalist artistic stance, expressed in his fables, and rationalism of the Western-European paradigm of this genre, reflected in La Fontaine's and Lessing's work in particular, as well as in their various Russian followers: 'The new-European fable was the genre above all pertaining to the Enlightenment. La Fontaine played the part of the Enlightenment's precursor, forging future weapon for the battles of that epoch – the poetics of rational clarity. His numerous successors are typical representatives of the Enlightenment. The most brilliant and original of them was the great Lessing whose polemics with La Fontaine was no more than a family tiff. By contrast, Krylov, born 10 years later than Lessing's fables, came after the Enlightenment, and moreover – as its conscious opponent, who opposed the wisdom of a proverb to the wisdom of ideologues.'[66]

Among the features which differentiate Krylov's irrationalist approach from the rationalism of La Fontaine, Averintsev signals out Krylov's breaking the rational balance between the didactical intent and the task of colourful entertaining. If for La

[63]   Aleksandr Bestuzhev (Marlinsky), *Sochineniia v 2-kh tomakh*, vol. 2, Moscow: Goslitizdat, 1958, pp. 547–558. See <http://az.lib.ru/b/bestuzhewmarlins_a_a/text_0170.shtml> [accessed 16 February 2014] for the online version.

[64]   Ibid.

[65]   Aleksandr Arkhangelsky and Andrei Nemzer (eds), *Russkaia poeziia 1801–1812*, Moscow: Khudozhestvennaia literatura, 1989, pp. 369–70.

[66]   Averintsev, *Sviaz vremen*, op. cit.

Fontaine the moral is a soul of a fable which he tries to free from banality, Krylov, on the contrary, makes fun of the very banality of the moral. Verisimilitude as well as the rational co-ordination between the animalistic and human (i.e. social) dimension of the characters are of primary concern to La Fontaine and are often neglected by Krylov. Instead, he develops 'the irrational sensory aspect' which is more important to him 'than an abstract game of thought'.[67] Thus Krylov brightly decorates his verse, both rhythmically and phonetically, and regularly imitates animals' sounds, using 'very specific capabilities of the Russian phonics and Russian poetry'.[68] To Lessing's corrective continuation of La Fontaine's principles of fable formation, which exalted a strict minimalism of narration, and which was developed by various Russian contemporaries of Krylov, such as Dmitriev and Zhukovsky, Krylov opposed a diametrically opposite – amplifying – approach. 'La Fontaine's elegance demands laconism, Krylov's picturesque style requires concretization of the plot, mounting of details and expressivity of intonations.' Thus, 'Krylov overcomes not only La Fontaine's rationalism, but a rational logic of the global cultural development as such.'[69]

In his analysis, Averintsev is not concerned with the humour of Krylov's fables, with their comic aspect. However, interestingly, in his irrationalist approach, Krylov is much funnier than La Fontaine, who keeps serious in his adherence to his rationalist paradigm. Elegant intellectual exercises of La Fontaine and dryness of Lessing are opposed here to a playful, laughing game of Krylov. The playfulness and richness of colours and sounds are more vital for Krylov than the moral, the resulting idea, and the focus is therefore shifted from the domain of moralization and didactics (almost mocked by Krylov himself in his fables!) to the domain of the humourous. His fable art is built on the specifically Russian laughter culture, akin to the folk tradition of religious festivals, to the maskarade of mummers (ряженые), which return us to the pagan roots of the latter preserved in the devilry, in all those pagan gods come little demons in Russia under Christianity. This spirit of life, with which the whole universe is invested, is very much present in Krylov's art. His animals are always fully alive combining both distinctly animalistic, colourful features and full human personalities. Their vivacity, the bright personal nature of their individualities is more important to the writer than the idea which they embody and the moral for whose sake they were supposedly created. That is to say that we encounter here the same idea of the 'living life' which was later formulated and maintained by Dostoevsky. It is also reflected in Russian philosophy with its imperative never to separate ideas from reality, never to abstract them too much (and it is precisely the notorious abstraction for which Russian thought blamed Western-European tradition). More subtly (as was already quoted in the Introduction), in the words of Oliver Smith, when qualifying too broad a generalization by Vladimir Ern who described the Russian tradition as defined by 'ontologism and personalism',[70] – 'the spirit that lives in much Russian thought is not a fixed pattern (an "ethos" that is passed on through a given canon) but a pathos that

---

[67] See ibid.
[68] Ibid.
[69] Ibid.
[70] V. Ern, *Grigorii Savich Skovoroda: Zhizn' i uchenie*, Moscow, 1912, p. 22.

perpetually treads water between the unordered irrationality of individual experience and the concordant rationality of absolute comprehension.'[71]

Pushkin, Gogol and continuity of the tradition, Mozartian irony and mischievous pranks, laughter through tears

If Krylov in his art essentially opposed the rationalism of the Enlightenment and, just like Fonvisin, Griboedov and others of the kind, creatively appropriated Western-European heritage breathing into it a truly Russian spirit, Pushkin accomplished even more. Rather than opposing Russian irrationalism to Western-European enlightened rationalist aspirations, he demonstrated the limitations of the latter through redeeming (rather than disavowing) reason and rehabilitating the true – cheerful, supple and profound – nature of human mind, destroyed by the Enlightenment's rather one-dimensional approach. Olga Sedakova refers to Pushkin as having a 'cheerful mind' and talks, following Averintsev, of the proximity between wisdom and gaiety, of artistism and playfulness of mind being a common feature of the Greek and Biblical traditions, of Athens and Jerusalem.[72] She distinguishes Pushkin and Averintsev as almost only representatives of this mind set in the Russian tradition, adding to them also Father Alexandr Shmeman.[73] However, I would argue that examples of this sensibility are more numerous and are to be found *invariably* at the heights of human spirit, both in Russia and abroad, as can be seen in major artists and major scientists alike, in whom human reason and human heart join hands, that is, are indistinguishable from each other, represent a creative fusion, one generic whole. In these instances, we are facing reason brewed on conscience, reason which is creative, inspirational, intuitive as well as analytical, and not the narrow and shallow kind of mind against which various anti-rationalists worldwide have been forever launching an attack. The most obvious examples of this fusion, of this wise, artistic, cheerful mind which never abandons its analytical abilities, but on the contrary uses them to the utmost, in unison with 'the heart', with the emotional and subconscious, and rejoices in this fusion, are in Russian letters not only Pushkin, but also Chekhov and Iskander, Dombrovsky and Dovlatov, Vysotsky and Shukshin, to name but a few.

Fazil Iskander, in particular, emphasized the force of Pushkin's cheerful mind, claiming that 'Such a cluster of great talents in one person cannot be accidental, it can only be a guiding star – in the same way as human intelligence in general, and Pushkin's in particular, cannot be accidental.'[74] Iskander stresses above all the warmth, harmony and lightness of Pushkin's genius: 'To Pushkin's very name we respond with

---

[71] See Oliver Smith, 'Ethos versus Pathos. The Ontologization of Knowledge in Russian Philosophy', in Olga Tabachnikova (ed.), *Mystery inside Enigma: Facets of Russian Irrationalism between Art and Life*, op. cit.

[72] See Sedakova, 'Sergei Sergeevich Averintsev. Apologiia ratsionalnogo', op. cit.

[73] Ibid.

[74] Iskander, *Lastochkino gnezdo. Proza. Poeziia. Publitsistika*, op. cit., p. 428.

an inadvertent exhale of relief, a smile. What a light name has ascended above the heavy and cumbersome Russian empire! For all the readers in Russia, Pushkin, as it were, warmed the climate through his sunny verse. Up to this day we are warming ourselves by Pushkin's cheerful hearth, because in Russian culture, not to mention Russian history, there has never been anything warmer than Pushkin.'[75] Iskander also makes some useful remarks – a literary discovery of sorts – on the aspects of comic in Pushkin. Thus he calls rebellious a devotion to his master on the part of the serf Savel'ich, a character from Pushkin's 'The Captain's Daughter', who looks after the main hero Petr Grinev in the way, one could venture to say, as Sancho Pansa looks after Don Quixote. 'Savel'ich's devotion rebelled for the right to be even more devoted. His devotion got to the point when, in the most comic way, it was pushing aside the very object of this devotion, and the nobleman Petrusha could not do anything about it, because it was a rebellion of love, a rebellion inside out. Thus "The Captain's Daughter" contains two rebellions: that of hatred and that of love.'[76]

The same appreciation of Pushkin's light and blissful touch, of his perfect ease and joi de vivre, is present in Vasilii Rozanov's article 'Pushkin and Gogol' where the author, on the one hand, distinguished two main traditions in Russian literature, if not in Russian culture more generally – a healthy one, arising from Pushkin, and a diseased one, arising from Gogol. 'From Gogol', Rozanov claims, 'our society began to develop *a loss of the feeling of reality* and moreover *started to be disgusted by it*', Gogol's imagination corrupted our souls and filled them with the deepest suffering.[77] On the other hand, Pushkin represents a healthy attitude to life, his poetry is the ideal of a 'normal, healthy development'.[78] Rozanov describes Pushkin as a founder of the natural school, always faithful to human nature and human destiny.

This controversial classification, which nevertheless (as is often the case with Rozanov) captures some fundamental, as it were metaphysical, differences of two sensibilities, implicitly echoes the two types of humour inherent in these writers – Pushkin's weightless, Mozartian irony and witty mischievous pranks, and Gogol's lyrical satire, famously known as 'laughter through tears'. Furthermore, it is possible to discern accordingly, even if crudely, the two components of Russian literary humour – a darker one, amounting to Gogol and accompanied by sadness and pain, being humour's twin sisters, and the other inherited from Pushkin, which can be called, by contrast, a 'laughter through (weightless) irony' and which is full of light. Indeed, Pushkin celebrates life and rejoices in its primordial delights, inherited in particular from the ancient Slavic laughter culture, but remembering at the same time about life's tragic underpinning, steeped in Christian cultural heritage. His humour effortlessly unites two hypostases – the sublime side which retains human dignity against existential horrors, always staying at the border of sadness, and the childish and cheerful side, filled with joy of existence. However, proportionately it is Gogolean

---

[75] Ibid., p. 423.
[76] Ibid.
[77] Vasilii Rozanov, 'Pushkin i Gogol', in *Nesovmestimye kontrasty zhitiia. Literaturno-esteticheskie raboty raznykh let*, Moscow: Iskusstvo, 1990, p. 233.
[78] Ibid., p. 227.

heritage which dominates in Russian literary humour, although, as we shall see, there are some distinctly Pushkinian cases in the subsequent Russian literature. At the same time both strands represent a type of 'laughter through ideas', which mixes tears with smile, grotesque with irony, and grows from serious philosophical roots, from genuine religious-ethical striving and compassion for the weak, while being highly poetic. This is what characterizes the resulting humour at the peaks of Russian literature of the last two centuries. Yet, the ideas inhabit Gogol's and Pushkin's humour in different ways. Pushkin's laconic musicality and apparent simplicity conceal the profundity of his thought, sometimes carried by a single word used with astonishing semantic precision (e.g. an epithet as in 'ungrateful day-dreaming').[79] Gogol's form is moulded to fit the idea which then results from the very shape and intricacy of the novel form. Thus, as always in true poetry, style itself constitutes the idea.

For Pushkin, no theme was frightening or untouchable, and any theme could give rise to sparkling humour. Single-handedly, he could take on a treacherous task of writing openly and lyrically on sexual matters ('Net, ia ne dorozhu miatezhnym naslazhdeniem', 1831) in the puritanist literary environment of his day, and come out victorious. Equally, he was able to create a teasing, prankish fairy-tale (сказка) 'Tsar' Nikita i sorok ego docherei' (1822) openly laughing at the pharisaism of his censors and adversaries, or, by the same token, produce a stream of dazzling, but deadly epigrams, often too strong for the ethics of contemporary reader. Semen Frank discerned in Pushkin's pranks 'a purely Russian fervour of cynicism, a typically Russian form of pudicity and spiritual modesty, which conceals the purest and most profound feelings under the mask of a put-on mischief'.[80] Frank agrees with Pushkin's biographer Bartenev that this was the poet's personal 'Holy Foolishness': 'Not only did Pushkin [. . .] not care about eliminating the contradiction between the lowest and the highest principles of his soul, but "on the contrary, he pretended to be a brawler, libertine, some violent freethinker"'.[81] Frank finds Pushkin's formula of 'Byron's feigned mask of depravity' doubtlessly autobiographical and stresses that 'numerous Pushkin's sacrileges are manifestations of precisely this holy foolishness (this applies only to the epoch approximately until 1825, as afterwards it had stopped).'[82]

Another factor to be taken into account is that the mores of Pushkin's time and milieu differed considerably from those of the Russian sophisticated audiences of our day, thus creating a drastically different backdrop against which such prankish humour should be judged. At the same time, Belinsky's rapturous words largely repeat those of Bartenev and Frank, 'For Pushkin there was no so called low nature; that is why no comparison, no object were too difficult for him – he would take anything that came his way and turn it into poetry, thus rendering it beautiful and noble.'[83] As Pushkin

---

[79] This meaningful example was touched upon earlier: in Chapter 3.
[80] Semen Frank, *Etiudy o Pushkine*, Paris: YMCA-Press, 1987, p. 12.
[81] Ibid.
[82] Ibid.
[83] Vissarion Belinsky, 'Sochineniia Aleksandra Pushkina. Sanktpeterburg. Odinnadtsat tomov MDCCCXXXVIII-MDCCCXLI'. Statiia Piataia, in Vissarion Belinsky, *Sobranie sochinenii v triokh tomakh*, Moscow: OGIZ, GIKhL, 1948, vol. 3. See <http://az.lib.ru/b/belinskij_w_g/text_0160. shtml> [accessed 2 March 2014].

himself commented on the interplay between humour and morality, when fighting off the hypocrisy of his critics – of gloomy fools (угрюмых дураков), as he labelled them – 'a joke inspired by a hearty gaiety and a spontaneous game of imagination can appear immoral only to those whose idea of morality is childish or unenlightened, as though it is preaching, and who see literature as an exclusively pedagogic endeavour.'[84]

A mischief inherent in Pushkin's spirit and the gaiety of his cheerful mind lay at the foundation of the same tradition which more than a hundred years later revealed itself in the memorable lines of the cinematic character from a Russian version of Baron Munchausen (the script written by Grigorii Gorin): 'I have realised what your trouble is: you are too serious. A clever-looking face is not in itself a sign of intelligence, ladies and gentlemen. All the stupidities on earth are accomplished precisely with this facial expression. Smile, ladies and gentlemen, smile!'[85] In the same key, in my view, Pushkin's much discussed words from his letter to Viazemsky that 'poetry ought to be a bit silly' should be understood, as already discussed earlier. It is precisely because of his intelligence that he cleanses art from snobbery (whose name is banality) and defends the right of poetry to include light and humorous elements: in the letter to Ryleev, Pushkin says, 'Bestuzhev writes me a lot about *Onegin* – tell him he is wrong: Does he really want to banish everything light and merry from the province of poetry? What would then become of satires and comedies? [. . .] Pictures of society life enter into the realm of poetry, too . . .'.[86]

Pushkin's oeuvre thus fully reflects his outlook, echoing the aforementioned Russian fusion of the two Ivans, as if demonstrating the intrinsic inseparability of Ivan-The-Fool and Ivan-The-Prince, of the low and high, of the merry and serious. (Moreover, it demonstrates in a sense that without the one, the other not only is incomplete, but also cannot attain the depth of his own nature).

This profound and effortless understanding of life's antinomial nucleus is, as it seems, what underpins Pushkin's mischievous soul, his lyrically bridled liberty – the features which, in my view, he shares with Vladimir Vysotsky and, to an extent, with Sergei Esenin (and it is not surprising that these three poets enjoy special popularity nation-wide). As Sergei Dovlatov once remarked, it is a tragedy for a writer to have no sense of humour, but it is an equal tragedy to have no sense of drama, of the tragic.[87] An imbalance of this kind proves deadly in artistic terms, and, more generally, as Pushkin noted, an adherence to one and the same pattern in art 'proves a one-sidedness of the mind, which may be otherwise profound.'[88] Both Pushkin and Vysotsky demonstrate an outstanding diversity of themes and genres, with an intricate balance attained between the tragic and the comic, serious and jocular, for, as one of the epigraphs to this chapter

---

[84] A. S. Pushkin, 'Oproverzhenie na kritiki', in *Polnoe sobranie sochinenii v 16 tomakh*, Moscow-Leningrad: Izd-vo AN SSSR, 1937–1959, vol. 11, 1949, p. 157.

[85] The reference is to the film 'Tot samyi Munhauzen', dir. Mark Zakharov, MosFilm, 1979.

[86] From Pushkin's letter to K. F. Ryleev of 25 January 1825, in *The Letters of Alexander Pushkin. Three volumes in one*, op. cit., p. 197.

[87] Dovlatov, 'Zapisnye knizhki', in *Sobranie prozy v 3 tomakh*, op. cit., vol. 3, p. 308.

[88] Pushkin, 'Otryvki iz pisem, mysli i zamechaniia', in *Polnoe sobranie sochinenii v 16 tomakh*, op. cit., vol. 11, 1949, p. 52.

eloquently sums up, 'profound spirit quickly discovers inner kinship between the funny and the sorrowful'.[89] This is a balance which is, likely, a prerequisite for creative harmony and which reflects the inseparable nature of the above sides of life and art alike, their mutual reversibility akin to that between the rational and the irrational.

If Pushkin, whose cheerful mind can 'so wisely and archly joke about everything',[90] gives us a perfect balance between rational and irrational, Gogol, an opposing genius in Rozanov's eyes, gives us a different kind of laughter – that which resolves in tears. 'With Karamzin we were dreaming. Pushkin gave us consolation. But Gogol gave us an inconsolable picture of ourselves, and wept, and sobbed over it. And burning tears went through the heart of Russia. And maybe Russia did not become better, but that concrete image which he hated in it, Russia shook off, and very quickly.'[91] As Arkadii Goldenberg argues, the understanding of the nature of laughter drawn from the Russian Patristics, which differentiated between the devilish laughter, akin to lies, foul language and other sins, and the divine laughter, closely related to purgatorian and redeeming tears, as explained earlier, was not only known, but also kindred to Gogol.[92] This can be seen from Gogol's explicit metapoetic text, describing different types of laughter in his 'Teatralnyi raziezd' of 1842: 'No, laughter is more meaningful and profound than is thought. Not the laughter that is born of occasional frustration, bilious tendencies of character; and not the equally light laughter, serving the celebratory entertainment and amusement of people – but that laughter, which soars out of the goodness of human character, soars out of it because in its core there is locked its ever-beating source [. . .] No, only a deeply kind soul could laugh a kind, bright laughter [. . .] And who knows, maybe later on it will be accepted by all, that due to the same rules which dictate why a proud strong person is petty and weak in misery, but a weak one grows, like a titan, in misfortune, due to those same rules, that he who often weeps earnest, meaningful tears, it seems, laughs more than anyone else in the world!'[93]

What is remarkable though, as Goldenberg explains, is that in the patristic tradition purifying tears are conducive of the (divine) laughter, whereas in Gogol's oeuvre, on the contrary, it is laughter which precedes tears, leads us to tears. 'This is laughter "born out of love for a human being", "which is created in order to laugh at everything that disgraces man's true beauty . . .".'[94] This laughter 'includes all the range of artistic means of Russian homiletics.'[95] Thus Gogol's metapoetic texts demonstrate that for him

---

[89]   Yulii Aikhenvald, 'Chekhov', in *Siluety russkikh pisatelei*, Moscow, 1906–1910. See <http://az.lib. ru/a/ajhenwalxd_j_i/text_0110.shtml> [accessed 5 March 2014].

[90]   Anna Akhmatova, 'Pushkin' (1943), <http://rupoem.ru/axmatova/all.aspx#kto-znaet-chto> [accessed 5 March 2014].

[91]   Vasilii Rozanov, 'Gogol', <http://www.bibliotekar.ru/rus-Rozanov/14.htm> [accessed 4 March 2014].

[92]   Arkadii Goldenberg, 'Smekh i slezy v metapoetike Gogolia', in E. F. Manaenkova (ed.), *Kategorii ratsionalnogo I emotsionalnogo v khudozhestvennoi slovesnosti*, Volgograd: Peremena, 2013, pp. 54–61.

[93]   Nikolai Gogol, 'Teatralnyi raziezd', in *PSS v 14 tomakh*, op. cit., vol. 5, pp. 169–71. Cited in Goldenberg, op. cit., pp. 57–8.

[94]   Goldenberg, op. cit., p. 60. Quotations are taken from Gogol, *PSS v 14 tomakh*, op. cit., vol. 4, p. 132.

[95]   Ibid., p. 60.

'laughter and tears do not oppose each other, but act as mutually reciprocal aesthetic categories.'[96]

This observation can be inscribed into a more general pattern of Gogol's writing, which 'especially in recent years has been often interpreted as baroque, and hence, as built on a game of antitheses which are not mutually exclusive'.[97] This explains in particular a variety of opposite interpretations of Gogol's oeuvre. One of such oppositions exists between laughter and irrationalism in Gogol's fiction. It took a change of eras, the coming of Symbolism, Ekaterina Dmitrieva remarks looking at the reception of Gogol's 'Vechera na khutore bliz Dikan'ki' ('Evenings on a Farm Near Dikanka') – first understood as a purely cheerful, witty work – in order to 'make one see in the early Gogol's oeuvre too, irrationalism, mysticism, an interest to the subconscious, concealed demonism, opposed to materialism and utilitarianism of the democratic ideology'.[98] In the literary scholarship of the twentieth century, this work continued to be assessed ambiguously – either 'as a literary version of the folk laughter consciousness, or, on the contrary, as deliberately moving away from the element of the folk laughter'.[99] Thus its humour was defined on the one hand as 'a portrayal of the nation-wide festive laughter'[100] (L. Pumpiansky), and on the other hand as a 'purely people's festive laughter'[101] (M. Bakhtin), or, as 'moving away from the communal character of performance towards an individualisation and mechanical imitation of life, thus anticipating all the range of motifs of the "Dead Souls'",[102] as '"the cheerful" is replaced in "Vechera . . ." not merely by the "sad", but by "something uncanny and alien"'[103] (Yurii Mann).

This mystery of the alien and uncanny arises to a large extent, it seems, from the evident layers of pagan heritage with its absorbance, in particular, of the pre-Christian laughter culture, which are superimposed with the Christian in Gogol. This contributes to Averintsev's remark that Gogol was tormented by his attempts to 'combine within himself a comic genius and a religious man' in a 'typical Russian manner'.[104] Merezhkovsky appears to be right in tracing the roots of Gogol's laughter to the 'imbalance of two primordial principles – pagan and Christian, physical and spiritual, real and mystical'.[105] Thus to Pushkin's perfect balance Gogol opposed an imbalance of the rational and irrational, a perpetual struggle of basic elements.

[96] Ibid.
[97] Dmitrieva, 'N.V. Gogol: palimpsest stilei/palimpsest tolkovanii', op. cit.
[98] N. V. Gogol, *PSSP*, vol. 1, pp. 632–642. Cited in Dmitrieva, op. cit.
[99] Dmitrieva, 'N.V. Gogol: palimpsest stilei/palimpsest tolkovanii', op. cit.
[100] Lev Pumpiansky, 'Vechera na khutore bliz Dikan'ki', in *Prepodavanie literaturnogo chteniia v estonskoi shkole: Metodicheskie razrabotki*, Tallinn, 1986, pp. 100–10. Cited in Dmitrieva, op. cit.
[101] Mikhail Bakhtin, *Sobranie sochinenii v 7 tomakh*, Moscow, 1996, vol. 5, pp. 45–7. Cited in Dmitrieva, op. cit.
[102] Dmitrieva, 'N.V. Gogol: palimpsest stilei/palimpsest tolkovanii', op. cit.
[103] Yurii Mann, *Poetika Gogolia*, Moscow, 1988, pp. 12–14. See on this also Yurii Lotman, 'Gogol i sootnesenie "smekhovoi kultury" s komicheskim i seriioznym v russkoi natsionalnoi traditsii', in *Materialy I Vsesoiuznogo simpoziuma po vtorichnym modeliruiushchim sistemam*, Tartu, 1974, pp. 131–133. Cited in Dmitrieva, op. cit.
[104] Averintsev, 'Bakhtin, smekh, khristianskaia kultura', op. cit., p. 19.
[105] Dmitrii Merezhkovsky, 'Gogol. Tvorchestvo, zhizn i religiia', <http://www.vehi.net/merezhkovsky/gogol/02.html> [accessed 28 February 2014].

Nevertheless, in his inner struggle and in his despair, Gogol was led by his Christian and patristical striving to humility. His humour, his tearful laughter, although involves grotesque and sarcasm, grows from a constructive root. It is far from a bitter sardonic grin inherent in the Romantic tradition with its refusal to reconcile to necessity. Romanticism, with its rebellion against the world-order and its challenging of God, places its hero in the centre of the universe, ending up, more often than not, in egotistic solipsism and isolation. Moreover, it does not respect the distance between the author and the protagonist, while a tragedy of the Romantic hero, and hence of its author, is that he is too serious in his attitude to himself, and thus too vulnerable. A liberating valve of humour is essentially unavailable to him, or more precisely, his laughter is poisoned with angst and disdain, his smile is bitter.

Lermontov: Is there a place for humour in Russian Romanticism? Turgenev and Tolstoy: Gloomy writers?

This is to a large extent the case with Lermontov, with his proud mind and resentful vanity, and despite his increasing longing to peace and harmony, which included his perceptive and piercing depictions of nature, full of profound admiration for its indifferent beauty, for its utmost and inspiring independence. It is this independence and apparent dispassion, a 'sober ironic contemplation of life' that Innokentii Annensky strangely refers to as Lermontov's humour.[106] Yet, Lermontov's irony is caustic and his dispassion – deceptive, as it is born out of passion burning too excessively to be sustainable and thus turning into its opposite; it is dispassion growing from despair as a defensive mechanism against it. Extending Iskander's metaphoric definition of true humour being the trace left by backtracking after the peeping into a morbid bottomless pit, one could say that Lermontov had chosen a no-return, and jumped. His dominant emotion expressed in his poetry is sadness mixed with ennui, a sustained motif of disenchantment at the ridiculous absurdity of life, indicative precisely of the Romantic deficiency of a cheerful, spacious humour, of the full-lungs liberated laughter. Existence, deprived of the salvatory rail of humour, cannot be redeemed. The famous line 'All this would have been even funny, if only it were not so sad' ('To A. O. Smirnova', 1840)[107] is a light and elegant, almost inadvertent, formula of the sad overpowering the comic, but sounds as a fully conscious ideological declaration in the poem of the same year: 'Such emptiness, heartache, and no one to stretch out their hands // In comfort when storm overtake us . . .', which ends in total despondency: 'And life – if you care to look round with cool-headed attention – // Is simply an empty

---

106   Innokentii Annensky, 'Iumor Lermontova', in *Knigi otrazhenii*, Moscow: Nauka, 1979, pp. 136–40.
107   Mikhail Lermontov, 'To A.O. Smirnova' ('V prostoserdechii nadezhdy . . .'), in *Polnoe sobranie stikhotvorenii v 2 tomakh*, Leningrad: Sovetski pisatel, 1989, vol. 2, p. 55. In Russian: 'Всё это было бы смешно, Когда бы не было так грустно'.

and rather a second-rate joke . . .'.[108] The same sentiments, only expressed from the external, authorial rather than lyrical hero's stance, are objectified and summarized philosophically in the striking poem 'Duma' which is essentially 'The Hero of Our Time' *in nuce*, that is, its laconic poetic equivalent. Another motif – of the rebellious angst of a Romantic – interweaves with this despondency, but does not alleviate it: 'And yet for storm it begs, the rebel, // As if in storm lurked calm and peace! . . .'[109]

Thus in his rebellion, anger, resentment, melancholy, or in his rare, but powerful peaceful longings to harmony ('When comes a gentle breeze and sways the yellowing meadow . . .' ('*Kogda volnuetsa zhelteiushaia niva . . .*'); 'Lone's the mist-cloaked road before me lying . . .' ('*Vyhozhu odin ia na dorogu . . .*')),[110] Lermontov walks on the shadowy side of life, shackled by his Romantic stance, distant from an open unburdened laughter. Yet, with his brilliant mastery, he is also capable of a gentle caricature, as, for instance, in the character of Maxim Maximych, which, rather curiously, a literary historian of the turn of the nineteenth-century Vasilii Cheshikhin (Ch. Vetrinsky) regards as a high example of humour.[111]

However, Cheshikhin finds almost no humour in the writings of the other major Russian classics – Turgenev, Tolstoy and Dostoevsky: 'humour is less characteristic of Turgenev, and plays almost no role in Tolstoy and Dostoevsky.'[112] While one may take issue with this claim on a small scale,[113] as a general big picture it is more true than not, although various qualifications are due, especially the fact that the twentieth-century literary scholarship produced ample material on the comedy in Dostoevsky. Still, continuing the above metaphor, these literary giants, most likely, did not jump into the bleak abyss, but simply froze over it, staring down intensely and unable to move away and leave real humour as their trace. This is not to say that there are no comic elements in their writings (in fact, Dostoevsky's texts indeed give plenty of grounds for a discussion of humour, including parody, satire, irony and grotesque), or to say that these authors are unsusceptible to the comic (which would be bluntly wrong), but largely that their concerns and literary talents lay elsewhere, and that the

---

[108] Mikhail Lermontov, 'Such emptiness, heartache . . .' ('I skuchno, i grustno . . .'), in *Selected Works*, transl. by Avril Pymen, Moscow: Progress Publishers, 1976, pp. 42–3. In Russian: 'И скучно и грустно, и некому руку подать В минуту душевной невзгоды . . .'; 'И жизнь, как посмотришь с холодным вниманьем вокруг, – Такая пустая и глупая шутка . . .'.

[109] Mikhail Lermontov, 'The Sail' ('Beleet parus odinokii . . .'), in *Selected Works*, transl. by Irina Zheleznova, op. cit., p. 26. In Russian: 'А он мятежный просит бури, Как будто в бурях есть покой . . .'.

[110] See Mikhail Lermontov, *Selected Works*, op. cit., pp. 32, 47.

[111] V. Cheshikhin-Vetrinsky, 'Iumor', in *Literaturnaia entsiklopedia: Slovar literaturnykh terminov v 2 tomakh*, Moscow-Leningrad: Izd-vo L. D. Frenkel, 1925, vol. 2, pp. 1159–62.

[112] Ibid.

[113] See, for example, Jeoffrey Brooks's article on the humour in Tolstoy's 'War and Peace': 'Lev i medved: iumor v "Voine i mire"' (<http://magazines.russ.ru/nlo/2011/109/br14.html> [accessed 16 November 2013]), whose argument does not seem convincing. Various parodies and caricatures of which Brooks talks are related to the reception of 'War and Peace' rather than to the work itself. There is nothing in Tolstoy's style brought to the surface by the scholar that would suggest any humourous intent or any hidden comism implied by the novelist. The existence of 'potentially humorous' plots does not by itself prove Tolstoy's ability to write humorously, quite on the contrary: even despite the story-line humorous potential, he was still incapable of humorous discourse.

humourous, when it occurs in their oeuvre, forms a second layer hidden underground, a by-product of sorts.

Thus Turgenev, despite his gentle irony and undeniable wit, despite even his numerous epigrams written single-handedly or jointly with others,[114] remains somewhat despondent and sad in his fiction. 'Untameable outbursts of thought of Tolstoy and Dostoevsky in his eyes were harmful atavism', writes Lev Shestov on Turgenev, and sees in all his oeuvre an 'imprint of secret sadness', discerning in it 'as an exhale of a tightened chest, an eternal refrain: Resigne-toi mon coeur, dors ton sommeil de brute'.[115] After all, humour presupposes certain daring and overcoming, an ability to see the other side of life, to find the comic behind the serious. Or, if you like, it requires certain playfulness of spirit, a willingness and ability to enter life, whether real or textual, as a game or performance – something akin to the way Semen Frank, as we saw, characterized Russian spirit exemplified by Pushkin – a 'fervour of cynicism' and a 'put-on mischief'.[116] Perhaps, while the Romantic Lermontov lacked Turgenev's humble and soft touch, the realist Turgenev on the contrary lacked Lermontov's wild rebellion (as well as Pushkin's mischief). Although he could take risks in life, his spirit remained restrained, if not altogether subdued (speaking in Freudian terms, perhaps broken by the two powerful women around him, first by his mother and then by Pauline Viardo, the love of his life). 'His personal life had been so very unfortunate and stopped him from complete satisfaction: it seems as if he never breathed deeply.'[117] Also, this second vision, able to discern and celebrate the humorous, is also, as was said, an almost poetic vision, the vision which, following Pushkin, ought to be 'a bit silly' – something that Turgenev, with all the gentle poetry of his being, seems incapable of. In this sense, Chekhov's ironic advice to Merezhkovsky, whom he calls a 'pure soul', to exchange his 'quasi-Hoethean regime, spouse and the truth' to a 'bottle of good wine, hunter's rifle and a pretty girl'[118] are applicable to Turgenev, even if figuratively (since in his case a hunter's rifle, on the contrary, was present, while a spouse – absent). By the same token, Turgenev's 'Poems in Prose' of his later years are more declaratory and didactic than poetic. Notwithstanding, Shestov views Turgenev as a writer covertly irrational, who concealed under a smooth European coating a 'savage' and superstitious Russian soul.[119]

---

[114] The epigrams differ in quality, both in terms of form and in terms of semantics, but Turgenev's wit, his ability to make and appreciate a good joke is undeniable, as can be seen from the following epigram he created after Afanasii Fet, an illegitimate child of an aristocratic father, had finally managed to change his surname to that of his father: 'This man had a name, but exchanged it for a surname!' See <http://turgenev.org.ru/e-book/epigrammy/13.htm> [accessed 2 October 2013].

[115] Lev Shestov, *Turgenev*, op. cit., p. 21 (Notwithstanding, in a much more controversial way, the same despondency Shestov discerned in Chekhov!).

[116] See Semen Frank, *Etiudy o Pushkine*, op. cit.

[117] Shestov, *Turgenev*, op. cit., p. 23.

[118] Anton Chekhov, Letter to A. S. Suvorin of 01.03.1892, in *PSSP v 30 tomakh*, op. cit., vol. 5, 1977, p. 8.

[119] Shestov, 'Turgenev', op. cit., in particular, pp. 21–2.

Even less humorous is Tolstoy, with his enormous pride, which he was ultimately powerless to defeat, with his strong tendency to didacticism, his 'general-like despotism' of a 'great wizard'[120] and a considerable distance between his convoluted heavily-built stylistics and poetry. Using the words of George Nivat, who compared the two thematically close works, Tolstoy's 'Family Happiness' and Molière's 'The School For Wives', 'Tolstoy does not have even a grain of humour.'[121] It is not surprising that Tolstoy's attempts at humour when he had produced a satirical play 'The Infected Family' ('Zarazhennoe semeistvo', 1863) failed and the play was unequivocally turned down by the Malyi Theatre. Although his later comedy 'The Fruits of Enlightenment' ('Plody Prosveshcheniia', 1890), conceived as a home-play and revolving around the questions of land ownership, morality and peasantry, was highly successful, Tolstoy's own words are rather telling: 'In my opinion they [the actors who played the peasants] are acting unnaturally. If one does not look at the stage, but merely listens, then one will be often baffled: what is the public laughing at? Indeed, in peasants' words there is often a complaint, and sometimes even an attempt at a protest. In my opinion their words should rather evoke compassion with respect to their desperate situation, and certainly not laughter.'[122]

In brief, these were not humorous writers; their seriousness (in particular, their serious attitude to themselves and hence to the world) or their sadness far exceeded their ability to highlight the comism of life; the tragic for them clearly outwieghted and overshadowed the comic. Among them it is only Dostoevsky, the evident heir of Gogol, who gives us grounds for a discussion of humour, in particular because of the Holy Fools tradition which his writings artistically inherited. This tradition, as was implied earlier, lies at the crossroads of the laughter culture and the sacred sphere. Therefore, its relevance to humorous discourse is rather debated. Thus, Averintsev distinguishes specifically Russian Holy Fools as by no means funny and disagrees with Panchenko who relates them to the tradition of Russian laughter. 'If certain actions and words of Saint Francis of Assisi, and of early Franciscans, or of Abraham a Sancta Clara were specifically designed to evoke laughter (i.e. laughter was an appropriate reaction on the part of those present), then the entire line of behaviour of a Russian Orthodox holy fool is such that only out of our grievous misapprehension and sinful folly, to the extent of aberration of our mind, we can dare to laugh at it. We laugh, when in fact we should be sighing, weeping and trembling.'[123]

---

[120] These are citations from Anton Chekhov's critical remarks concerning Tolstoy: 'Devil take the philosophy of the great ones of this earth! All great sages are as despotic as generals, and as rude and indelicate as generals, because they feel certain of their impunity' (see Chekhov's letter to Suvorin of 08.09.1891, in *Letters of Anton Chekhov*, edited by Avraham Yarmolinsky, New York: The Viking Press, p. 191).

[121] Nivat, G., 'La poétique de Léon Tolstoï', in Efim Etkind, Georges Nivat, Ilya Serman and Vittorio Strada (eds), *Histoire de la littérature russe. T. 3: Le XIXe siècle. Le temps du roman*, Paris: Fayard, 2005, p. 1235. Cited in J. Brooks, op. cit.

[122] See Pavel Pchelnikov, 'Iz dnevnika', in *Mezhdunarodnyi tolstovskii almanakh: O Tolstom*, Moscow, 1909, p. 274.

[123] Averintsev, *Sviaz vremen*, op. cit.

Dostoevsky: Holy Foolishness, parody and black humour

In his battle against the growing atheism and shallow rationalism of his day, and more generally in his metaphysical searchings, Dostoevsky deployed Holy Foolishness at a variety of levels, including an adoption of it to his literary technique itself, where scandal, including scandalizing the reader, serves a purifying and redeeming purpose.[124] In Lena Scilard's view, some of his novels can be treated as battlefields between Holy Fools and buffoons, with the writer's sympathy being rather on the side of the former.[125] Ivan Esaulov, who analyses these two traditions as two types of deviation from the cultural norm, takes an even more general approach looking at Russian literature, and Dostoevsky's writings in particular, through the prism of these two cultural fields: Holy Foolishness and buffonary.[126] The Holy Fools, that allied with the Schism, were ultimately rejected by the Patriarch Nikon and then by Peter the Great, who promoted buffoonery instead. As a result of this unequal treatment, we have 'two types of parodying and two versions of unofficial behaviour permeating all the strata of Russian culture of New Time'.[127] In Dostoevsky's *Brothers Karamazov*, Esaulov thus distinguishes the 'concealed authorial linkages', a correspondence 'within the limits of the same cultural system', between the two extreme characters – the almost saintly elder Zosima whose corps stinks, and the repellent Smerdiakov (born, significantly, to a Holy Fool) whose soul stinks.[128] At the same time, Fedor Karamazov distorts the system of Holy Foolishness as a buffoon and 'becomes a cause of its fluctuation'.[129] More explicitly, 'in *The Devils*, devilry simultaneously turns out to be also buffoonery, while in *The Idiot* [. . .] the central character is defined as a holy fool.'[130]

Perhaps more significant is the Holy Foolish narrative technique which can be found in many more Russian writings than Dostoevsky's oeuvre alone, whereby 'the enactment of holy foolishness' takes place 'in the area of *grammatical space*'.[131] It appears that this Holy Foolish discourse as a stylistic device has gained in the contemporary

---

124 Further on this theme, see Hariet Murav's significant study *Holy Foolishness: Dostoevsky's Novels & the Poetics of Cultural Critique*, op. cit. See also Vasilii Ivanov, *Bezobrazie krasoty: Dostoevsky i russkoe iurodstvo*, Petrozavodsk, 1993; Børtnes Jostein, 'Dostoevskian Fools – Holy and Unholy', in *The Holy Fool in Byzantium and Russia*, Bergen, 1995, pp. 18–34.

125 Lena Szilard, 'Ot "Besov" k "Peterburgu": mezhdu poliusami iurodstva i shutovstva (nabrosok temy)', in *Studies in 20th Century Russian Prose*, Stockholm, 1982, pp. 82–4.

126 See Ivan Esaulov, 'Two facets of comedic space in Russian literature of the modern period. Holy foolishness and buffoonery', in Lesley Milns (ed.), *Reflective Laughter. Aspects of Humour in Russian Culture*, London: Anthem Press, 2004, pp. 73–84.

127 Ivan Esaulov, 'Iurodstvo i shutocstvo v russkoi literature', in Esaulov, *Paskhalnost russkoi slovesnosti*, Moscow: Krug, 2004, p. 165. Lesley Milne suggests yet another coordinate system, with three rather than two traditions as the basis: those of the innocent, the rogue and the joker as 'categorising three different types of comic hero and three correspondingly different authorial standpoints' (see Lesley Milns, op. cit., p. 8 and pp. 85–96).

128 Esaulov, 'Two facets of comedic space in Russian literature of the modern period. Holy foolishness and buffoonery', op. cit., p. 76.

129 Ibid.

130 Ibid.

131 L. Szilard, 'Ot *Besov* k *Peterburgu*: mezhdu poliusami iurodstva i shutovstva (nabrosok temy)', *Studies in Twentieth-century Russian Prose* (Stockholm, 1982), 95. Cited in I. Esaulov, op. cit., 79.

era an extensive life of its own, having transgressed the borders of literary domain and having spilled into the space of human communications at large. This 'iurodivyi' (юродивый) style nowadays often serves as a shield behind which one hides from others and from oneself alike, being unable to face one's own true emotions. This type of the Holy Foolish discourse can be viewed as a form of degeneration from an ascetic tour de force to a cowardly way out from the burdens of existence, and can be easily observed in the internet blogs, social networks and so on.

Away from the discussions of the relevance of Holy Foolishness to Dostoevsky's writings, Yurii Tynianov famously reveals how Dostoevsky follows Gogol by wrestling with him and parodying him.[132] This came at the time as a literary discovery, and is complemented, if you like, by Yurii Mann's observations of Gogol himself being engaged in parody. Indeed, in tracing Gogol's artistic evolution, Mann assesses the writer's deployment of fantastic elements, and shows how, having started with reforming essentially Gofmann's tradition, Gogol came to revolutionize it, producing 'a subtlest parody of the romantic mystery, romantic form of rumours and of unreliable, random judgements, a parody of a wonderful dream [. . .]; and more generally, the whole system, and moreover, the technique of the romantic fantastic was taken by Gogol to the most sophisticated ironic artistism, to the form *reductio ad absurdum*'.[133] Similarly, Averintsev insightfully comments on Pushkin's subtlest irony and concealed parody, on the poet's superb and unequalled technique which measures everything so precisely that no slightest diversion from the authorial intention is available to the reader and interpreter: 'Pushkin reserves the freedom to take one at a minimum distance, fixed with minimal linguistic means, towards this or that, be it the tone of the idyll, or parodying of the idyll, and much more; and in every case not too much is allowed.'[134] Idyll, that Pushkin portrays, for instance, in 'Eugene Onegin', can easily coexist with parody, Averintsev argues, and is always accompanied by laughter. But it is incompatible with any kind of ideology – either with satire or with an ideological designing of its own idyllical essence.[135]

This is closely connected, Averintsev writes, to the trickiest question pertaining to 'classical harmony' – the question of boundaries between the serious and non-serious discourses.[136] Thus Horatius, a famous Roman oracle, thoroughly mixed 'serious' with 'light-hearted', significantly confusing his audience.[137] In the same vein, Gogol is characterized as operating at both planes – a lofty, serious (or even tragic) one and a low, comic one, which is also described, notably, as irrational.[138] In Russian literature of

132 Yurii Tynianov, 'Dostoevsky i Gogol (K teorii parodii)', in *Poetika. Istoriia literatury. Kino*, Moscow: Nauka, 1977. See <http://az.lib.ru/t/tynjanow_j_n/text_01015.shtml> [accessed 2 March 2014].

133 Yurii Mann, 'Gogol', in *Istoriia vsemirnoi literatury v 9 tomakh*, Moscow: Nauka, 1983, vol. 6, 1989, p. 375.

134 Averintsev, *Sviaz vremen*, op. cit.

135 Ibid.

136 Ibid.

137 Ibid.

138 More precisely, Tynianov distinguishes the specific features of both discourses: 'high – amplification, tautology, isocolon, neologisms, archaisms, etc.; low – irrationalism, barbarisms, dialectical features, etc. Both discourses differ above all by their vocabulary, as they amount to different linguistics elements: high – to the Old Church Slavonic, low – to dialectical. Literary types, to which both

the nineteenth century, and for that matter beyond too, because of its openly didactical or ideological character, these boundaries were delineated more often than not. Keis Verheil, as we saw, noticed the Russian tradition of overstatement, of verbal excess. Those writers who differed, and are famous for their elusiveness and understatement, for keeping a perfect control over their word and authorial intention, are relatively scarce. Among them are Pushkin, Chekhov and Akhmatova. No wonder then that Chekhov's irony is, just as Pushkin's, subtle and perfectly measured.

The subtlety of Chekhovian irony: More on kinship of humour and poetry

Crowning the classical tradition, Chekhov is thus compared to Pushkin in many respects, and yet his early stories with distinctive grotesque archetypes ('Tolstyi i Tonkii', 'Smert chinovnika', 'Khameleon' and others) show direct continuity with Gogol's 'Dead souls'. Furthermore, Chekhov's humour, with its subtle irony kindred to Pushkin's, can at the same time be perceived as 'laughter through tears'.

Thus Yulii Aikhenvald, who essentially continues the Russian Orthodox tradition of identifying laughter with sin, distinguishes an invariable layer of sadness under any comic coating in Chekhov's writings. 'Chekhov's sorrow is characterized by the fact that at first it sounded in his oeuvre only as a timid note of wistful sadness, and began to dominate following his previous sparkling humour, *which, by the way, did not leave him afterwards either*.[139] Chekhov wrote in "Oskolki" and "Strekoza". He began with a joke and finished with anguish. The man who at first laughed so much and amused others so much, afterwards enveloped his life with a mourning veil'.[140] Aikhenvald inscribes this into the nature of human laughter more generally. In his observation, as the epigraph to this chapter states, 'Profound spirit quickly discovers inner kinship between the funny and the sorrowful', and thus 'Chekhov merely obeyed his elemental depth'.[141] For Aikhenvald, 'In the human world the subject and object of the funny coincide. Thus we earn the comic bitterly, at high price. [. . .] Laughter cleanses, and is therefore regarded as a desirable and positive moment of the spirit. However, a funny phenomenon which is negative, is a sorrowful one. There is just one step from the great to the comic, and hence the comic is sad. The fact that a physiological laughter at its height turns into weeping is so instructive'.[142] And following this logic, this dialectics of sadness and happiness, everything becomes poetisized, is resolved into an 'elegiac melody'.[143] This union of the aesthetic and the ethical is also noticed by Kornei Chukovsky, who wrote

---

of the above pertain, amount to different traditions: the tradition of Gogol's comedies and the tradition of his letters that evolved from the 18 century sermons' (see Tynianov, 'Dostoevsky i Gogol (K teorii parodii)', op. cit.).

[139] Highlighting is mine (O.T.).
[140] Yulii Aikhenvald, 'Chekhov', op. cit.
[141] Ibid.
[142] Ibid.
[143] Ibid.

about Chekhov, calling him unequivocally a poet: 'Chekhov's genius could not bless
with his tender poetry that hard, confident, purposeful principle of life – Lopakhin's.
[. . .] In order to reconcile with a confident and purposeful strength, the poet gave
it some degree of uncertainty, aimlessness, ignorance. He could only get to love the
strength at the moment of its weakness'.[144] Such an interpretation places Chekhovian
'gentle poetry' very close to the poetic vision of Gogol who, as the Polish writer Michał
Grabowski put it, 'was able to breathe poetry into the most ordinary thing'.[145]

This poetic nucleus of humour (observed in the opening paragraph of this chapter),
which unites Pushkin with Gogol and Chekhov – and the list, as we shall see further,
can be endlessly extended – is not accidental and can be regarded as a necessary
condition of most profound literary humour. Indeed, the following description by
Lotman of poetic structure can be applied with equal force to describe humourous
discourse:

> In the language itself there is a pool of artistic meanings – natural synonymy in
> the vocabulary and parallel forms at all the other levels. Giving one a choice, they
> constitute a source of stylistic meanings. An essence of a poetic structure is in the
> fact that it uses those units which are certainly non-synonymic and non-equivalent
> as synonyms and adequates.[146]

This description of poetic discourse to a large extent reiterates the incongruity line
in humour theories, which claims that the comic is born out of an incompatibility of
simultaneously present systems, logical, ideological, aesthetic and so on.[147]

Furthermore, Lotman speaks also of other modelling systems – such as common
sense born out of the everyday experience and spatial-temporal picture of the world –
which, together with a natural language, shapes human consciousness. Art, and poetry
in particular (and this is where humour coincides with it), 'introduces freedom into
the automated nature of these worlds, by destroying unambiguity of their dominant
connections and thus expanding the boundaries of knowledge'.[148] And it is only logical
that Lotman illustrates his point here with Gogol's novella: 'When Gogol tells us that the
nose of a clerk deserted his owner, he destroys both the system of familiar connections
and the relations within our visual perceptions (nose in relation to a human height).
However, it is precisely the destruction of the automatism of the familiar connections
which renders them the object of cognition'.[149] Thus Henri Bergson's premise of the
humourous breaking the mechanisticity of the world is fully relevant here.

---

[144] Kornei Chukovsky, 'A. Chekhov', in Igor Sukhikh and Andrei Stepanov (eds), *A.P. Chekhov: Pro et Contra*, op. cit., p. 845.
[145] Michał Grabowski's quotation is given by Yurii Mann in 'Gogol', op. cit., p. 374.
[146] Yurii Lotman, 'Analiz poeticheskogo teksta: Struktura stikha', in Yurii Lotman, *O poetakh i poezii*, St Petersburg: Iskusstvo-SPb, 1996, p. 132.
[147] See on this, for example, John Morreall (ed.), *The Philosophy of Laughter and Humor*, Albany, NY: State University of New York Press, 1987, as well as Henri Bergson, Arthur Koestler and various others, including earlier thinkers.
[148] Lotman, 'Analiz poeticheskogo teksta: Struktura stikha', op. cit., p. 132.
[149] Ibid.

Any poetic individuality, any distinct poetic voice always presents us with a new style born out of a new perception of the world. A poet is determined by his unique poetic vision. In the same way, a humourous writer has his own, unique, vision which spots, or distils, the comic behind the everyday. Thus we are dealing here with a certain type of Shkolvsky's 'astrangement' – the concept which he intended to derive from the Russian word 'strannyi' (strange, weird) – *ostrannenie* (остраннение) – but which came to be spelled with one 'n' because of a typographical error: *ostranenie* (остранение) – which is also one letter away from the concept of 'alienation' (*otstranenie*) (отстранение). All this points us into the same direction – of taking a step back and looking at the world with a fresh eye, with a new vision, poetic and comedic alike, discovering new semantics behind the old form; the two Russian Ivans which always go together, the two styles – sublime and comic; the tragicomedy of life. It is no surprise that to illustrate his concept Shkolvsky gives an example of Natasha Rostova's 'alienated, estranged' perception of opera[150] – notably, one of the very few places of *War and Peace* which can be taken as comic.

Interestingly, irrationalism, as discussed earlier, is also characterized by a specific vision, usually attained by a shift of our coordinate system. What appears rational from one vantage point seems totally irrational from another. A breach of norms and standard proportions, all sorts of semantic and syntactic discrepancies and paradoxes are intrinsic features of the irrational – which is the nerve of both poetry and humour, interlinked as they are.

Kozma Prutkov: Parody and poetry

The same coincidence of structural principles in poetry and humour – in this case, parody – we encounter in the legacy of Kozma Prutkov, a literary mystification, an imaginary author, immortalized by his hilarious oeuvre. Invented by a group of litterateurs, Aleksei Tolstoi and his cousins: Aleksandr, Aleksei and Vladimir Zhemchuzhnikov, the fictional persona of Prutkov was used to produce a highly satirical account of the bureaucratic and authoritarian Russian regime of the 1850s and 1860s. However, its continuing universal appeal and undying relevance to Russian reality of subsequent generations are hugely telling not only of the cyclic character and rigid kernel of Russian socio-political life, but also of the deeper, existential nature of this satire. The unbridgeable intrinsic discrepancy – a flagrant contrast between the servile and philistine essence of Prutkov's enormously self-satisfied character and his status of Director of the Assay office in the Ministry of Finance on the one hand, and his pretentions at being nothing less than a romantic poet on the other – creates a profoundly comic effect.

His pompous extravagance combined with extreme conformism, his pretence of a romantic irrationalist stance and his utterly rationalist agenda make this unforgettable

---

[150] See Viktor Shklovsky's celebrated article 'Iskusstvo kak priem', in *Sborniki po teorii poeticheskogo iazyka*, Issue 2, Petrograd, 1917.

character kindred to the blindly servile heroes, invented by the genius of Mikhail Zoshchenko almost three generations later. Indeed, if Prutkov, using Ivanov-Razumnik's words, in particular 'most vividly characterizes all this era' – 'the era of official philistinism'[151] of the second half of the nineteenth century, Zoshchenko's characters epitomize the philistinism and hypocrisy of the early Soviet era. When his narrator describes a friend – a young Soviet poet, who 'travelled across Italy and Germany to familiarise himself with the capitalist culture and to replenish his incomplete wardrobe',[152] it resonates strongly with Kozma Prutkov's equally innocent utterances which reveal the speaker's true nature, of the type 'to keep on the side of the people's party is both modern and remunerative'.[153] More broadly, and quite amazingly, not only did Prutkov with his Project 'Towards Creating Unanimity of Opinion in Russia' anticipate and capture in a nutshell the spirit of Soviet times and totalitarian order, but also he equally foresaw the doomed character of any attempt at genuinely reforming the Russian state and the chameleonic behaviour of the old *nomenklatura*, unequalled in their trimming the sails to the wind. They first resisted the collapse of the communist regime, but then faced with its inevitability, perfectly adjusted to the new slogans in the old conformist fashion, proving the unconquerable resilience of slave mentality and a purely cosmetic character of any reforms. 'First he felt as if the ground is shifting from under his feet, and he started to repine, ranting at every corner about the premature nature of any reforms and that he was an "enemy of all the so called questions!" However, later, when the imminence of reforms became doubtless, he started himself striving to become distinguished by suggesting reformist projects, and was extremely indignant when these projects were spurned because of their obvious insolvency. [. . .] Soon, however, he calmed down, having sensed around him the familiar atmosphere and familiar ground under his feet'.[154]

The reign of the banal and mediocre in all areas of life, including art, is embodied in Prutkov's 'romantic poetry', which, as was said, being a parody, exemplifies once again the commonality of structural principles between poetry and humour. Indeed, the very texture of poetry, as Lotman argues, has to be informative and non-automatic. 'This is achieved because each poetic level [. . .] is "two-layered" – it obeys simultaneously at least two non-identical systems of rules, whereby fulfilment of the rules of one system necessarily means breaking the rules of the other. To write poetry well, means to write it at the same time correctly and incorrectly'.[155] Therefore, 'bad poems are poems which carry no information or which carry it to an insufficient degree. But information occurs

---

[151] Razumnik Vasilievich Ivanov-Razumnik, 'Istoria russkoi obshchestvennoi mysli', in *Ivanov-Razumnik v 3-kh tomakh*, Moscow: Respublika; TERRA, 1997, p. 203.

[152] Mikhail Zoshchenko, 'Zapadnia' (1933), <http://lib.ru/RUSSLIT/ZOSHENKO/r_raznye.txt_with-big-pictures.html> [accessed 7 March 2014].

[153] Kozma Prutkov, 'Voennye aforizmy', <http://ru.wikiquote.org/wiki/%D0%92%D0%BE%D0%B5%D0%BD%D0%BD%D1%8B%D0%B5_%D0%B0%D1%84%D0%BE%D1%80%D0%B8%D0%B7%D0%BC%D1%8B> [accessed 7 March 2014].

[154] 'Iz biograficheskikh svedenii o Kozme Prutkove', <http://ru.wikipedia.org/wiki/%D0%9A%D0%BE%D0%B7%D1%8C%D0%BC%D0%B0_%D0%9F%D1%80%D1%83%D1%82%D0%BA%D0%BE%D0%B2> [accessed 7 March 2014].

[155] Yurii Lotman, 'Analiz poeticheskogo teksta: Struktura stikha', op. cit., p. 128.

only if the text cannot be guessed in advance. Hence a poet must not play a "give-away" game with the reader: the relationship "poet-reader" is always a strain and struggle.'[156] Thus, Lotman concludes, 'good poems are poems which carry poetic information – where all their elements are simultaneously expected and unexpected. Breaking the former principle renders the text meaningless, while breaking the latter renders it trivial.'[157] He uses Prutkov's verse 'To My Portrait (which is to appear shortly in the forthcoming edition of my complete works)' to illustrate the second point – of how a poem that fulfils all the readers' expectations turns into a set of clichés. It is 'compiled from the common for that era stock-phrases of Romantic poetry and imitates a falsely meaningful system which can be guessed all the way through. [. . .] This is completed with a ritualistic set of cliché at the level of phraseology, strophe and meter. Inertia is set, and is not broken anywhere: the text (as an original artistic creation) is devoid of information.'[158]

However, as a parody the poem is highly informative, for 'parodic information is achieved by indicating the relation of the text to an extra-textual reality. A textual "insane poet" turns out to be a prudent civil servant in reality. Such an indication comprises two versions of the same verse. The text reads "who is naked," while in a footnote it says: "who is wearing a tailcoat." The more hackneyed the text, the more meaningful is a pointer to its real life meaning.'[159] At the same time, the discrepancy between the two planes of existence, characteristic of parody as a genre that 'lives a double-life'[160] – the real one and the one expressed in the verse – provides the non-automatic element, necessary for both poetic and humorous structure. Thus, bad poetry makes a good parody, and simultaneously the same general principle of the author's wrestling with the audience, of the dialectical balance between the meaningful semantics and unexpected resolutions, applies to both humorous and poetic texts. Another argument to support the claim of this kinship, in semantic more than in structural terms, is that a total lack of poetic sensibility and attempts to go down with aesthetics altogether, typical for the Russian radical men of letters, the revolutionary democrats of the second half of the nineteenth century, were not conducive of humour.

Irrationalism of Russian life as sarcastic cosmos and lyrical epos: Saltykov-Shchedrin, Leskov and their resonance in the twentieth century

While the spirit behind Prutkov's legacy shares the prankish style of literary gatherings of the start of the nineteenth century, of 'Arzamas' literary brotherhood with its rather Pushkinian ethos, and at the same time Prutkov's persona evokes

---

[156] Ibid.
[157] Ibid., p. 128.
[158] Ibid., p. 130.
[159] Ibid.
[160] See Tynianov, 'Dostoevsky i Gogol (K teorii parodii)', op. cit.

strong connotations with the archetypes of Gogol's *Dead souls*, another major satirist of the second half of the century, Saltykov-Shchedrin, associates more with Gogol's poetry of the fantastic, present also in his satirical depictions. Although, undoubtedly, Saltykov-Shchedrin came as a creative genius in his own right, standing aside from any imitation, it is precisely Gogol's fantasies, his irrational element and existential concerns, which underpin the depth of Saltykov-Shchedrin's oeuvre, elevating it far above the level of just political satire. It is also Gogol's dead souls, conceived for the sake of moral redemption, as a way of castigating human 'emptiness and impotent idleness' at large, and his irrational architectonics of a dream – which gave rise, as it were methodologically and aesthetically, in terms of poetics, to Dostoevsky's fantastic realism,[161] and equally to the satirical fantastics of Saltykov-Shchedrin, featuring as a matter of course not the nose (as in Gogol's novella), but the 'stuffed head' of one character, and at once concise and inexhaustible poetic description of another (still relevant to Russia today), who 'rode into Glupov on a white horse, burnt down the high school and abolished learning'.[162]

It is because Saltykov-Shchedrin's writings conceal deep existential message under both realist and fantastic veneer, his oeuvre is compared to that by Hoffmann, Dostoevsky and Kafka. Similarly Turgenev, who admiringly called Saltykov-Shchedrin's humour 'spiteful', compared him to Jonathan Swift,[163] and Boris Eikhenbaum continued these broad literary parallels: 'By its type "The History of a Town" by Shchedrin is of the same rank as the old classic satires by Rabelais ("Gargantua and Pantagruel") and by Swift ("Gulliver's Travels"), which are caustic social and political pamphlets.'[164] At the same time, it is above all the artistic merit of these texts that ensures their universal and supra-temporal appeal. A distinctive feature of Saltykov-Shchedrin's at once poetic and courageous laughter is that he as if unites laughter through tears with laughter through thought. And it is therefore hard to agree with the qualification of his satire as 'laughter that does not laugh', that is 'in essence [. . .] serious and didactic (and hence equated with whip or rod)',[165] precisely because this caustic satire never loses

---

[161] At the same time, ideologically Dostoevsky is a heir of Pushkin as well – indeed, his main Christian idea of the worthiness of a child's tear came out not just from under Gogol's 'Overcoat', but also from Pushkin's 'Mednyi vsadnik' (see more on this, for instance, in Iskander, *Lastochkino gnezdo. Proza. Poeziia. Publitsistika*, op. cit., pp. 424–425).

[162] Mikhail Saltykov-Shchedrin, *The History of a Town*, transl. by Paul Foote, Oxford: Willem A. Meeuws Publisher, p. 22.

[163] Ivan Turgenev, *PSSP*, vol. 8, Moscow-Leningrad: Nauka, 1964, p. 315. Cited in Eikhenbaum, '"Istoriia odnogo goroda" Saltykova-Shchedrina' (see the next footnote for the precise reference), p. 461.

[164] Boris Eikhenbaum, '"Istoriia odnogo goroda" Saltykova-Shchedrina', in Eikhenbaum, *O proze: Sbornik statei*, Leningrad: Khudozhestvennaia literatura, 1969, p. 460.

[165] See Lesley Milne (ed.), Introduction to *Reflective Laughter. Aspects of Humour in Russian Culture*, p. 7, where Bakhtin's phrase (from his work *Rabelais and His World*: <http://www.gumer.info/bibliotek_Buks/Culture/Baht/intro.php> [accessed 30 January 2014]) of 'laughter that does not laugh' is applied to Saltykov-Shchedrin. Bakhtin used it to describe a 'negative, rhetorical, non-laughing laughter of the 19 century satire' in order to debate its relevance to Rabelais. While Saltykov-Shchedrin indeed belongs to the nineteenth-century satire, his writings are comparable, as was mentioned, to those of Rableas, whose laughter, as Bakhtin argues, cannot be qualified as that which 'does not laugh'. Equally, Saltykov-Shchedrin's humour is significantly deeper than this limiting description.

its profound poetic dimension and artistic–philosophical subtext. It is instructive in this context to recall that one of the most poetic and irrationalist prose writers of the twentieth-century Russian literature, Venedikt Erofeev, regarded both Gogol and Saltykov-Shchedrin as his literary teachers.[166] Notably, all three are characterized by the rare organic fusion of lyricism and epos.

Another nineteenth-century Russian writer able to unite epic and lyrical, as well as tragic and comic was Nikolai Leskov with his famous novella 'Levsha' ('The Tale of the Crosseyed Lefthander from Tula and the Steel Flea') written in 1881 in the style of *skaz*, or folk-tale. Its hero, a left-handed craftsman, outperformed his English colleagues who produced a clockwork steel flea, while Levsha and his comrades managed to do an even more intricate job by making horseshoes for the flea. However, traditionally mistreated by his own country, to which he is fully dedicated, the Russian craftsman dies tragically. As Panchenko observes, 'The Lefty managed – and a long time ago – to become a national favourite and national symbol. [...] The reader relates him to an epic and religious archetype of "the last here will be the first there"', and associates him with a version of Ivan-The-Fool who 'in the end of the day turns out to be the wittiest'.[167] At the same time, Panchenko argues that Levsha epitomizes Russia's essential defeat. What is important for our purposes, though, is that Leskov produced a perfect tragic-comic stylization, received as a genuine folk tale, and full of unforgettable neologisms, whose linguistical structure is semantically loaded.

The same manner of telling a story by a narrator who brings – through his own particular style – his personal, yet archetypical, sensibility and viewpoint, and, in an unwitting fashion, presents it to the audience, 'unaware' of the created clash of perspectives, appears to be used in the twentieth-century Russian literature most notably by Mikhail Zoshchenko and Aleksandr Galich ('Klim Petrovich Kolomiitsev' cycle). However, this parallel is rather formal, and ends with the form. Indeed, although a tragic-comic effect in these twentieth-century works stems, as in 'Levsha', from the undisturbed innocence ('openness') as well as dialectical autonomy of such self-exposure by the narrator, but, unlike Levsha's storyteller, these narrators have such a corrupt, conformist vision of the world, that it makes the value system behind this vision seems ever more ridiculous. Thus the poetics of these works, centred around a narrow-minded and servile personality, is kindred structurally to the comic principles underpinning the oeuvre of Kozma Prutkov (even though he is considerably more self-assured), rather than Leskov's 'Levsha', where the hero is selfless and self-sacrificially loyal. Those heroes' world-views distort and contract the world, while Levsha's vision, conveyed by the sympathetic narrator of, clearly, the same social stratum, expands it, in the manner, rather, of the narrator of Andrei Platonov's major novels. This happens in particular because of the sincerity and ingenuity of perspective introduced by both

---

[166] See, for instance, Natalia Shmelkova, 'Vo chreve machekhi, ili Zhizn – diktatura krasnogo', St Petersburg: Limbus Press, 1999. <http://aptechka.agava.ru/statyi/memuary/shmelkova/shmelE1.html> [accessed 10 March 2014].

[167] Aleksandr Panchenko, 'Leskovskii Levsha kak natsionalnaia problema', in *Vozrozhdenie kultury Rossii: istoki i sovremennost*, St Petersburg: St Petesburg State University Publishers, 1993, Issue 1, p. 18.

writers through their intricately distorted and entangled language, expressing a whole new sensibility, which in Platonov is revealed through new rearrangements of old words, a new syntactical order, and in Leskov – through a new lexical order as well: new words – if you like, new rearrangements of old lexical roots (meaningful syllables), whereby, as a result, the world opens up along many more previously undiscovered semantic dimensions. This stylistic (and hence semantic) continuity was spotted, in particular, by Joseph Brodsky, who wrote that 'to get into excavating the genealogy of Platonov's style, one has inevitably to mention the "plaiting of words" of centuries of Russian hagiography, Nikolai Leskov with his tendency to highly individualized narrative (so-called skaz – sort of "yearning"), [. . .] Dostoevsky with his snowballing, feverishly choking conglomeration of dictions', although Brodsky did not view it as part of a tradition.[168]

Proximity is so strong that if we list excerpts from both authors in a row, it will be difficult to distinguish between them:

There the rules of all sorts for life, science and food supply are different, and everybody there has all the absolute circumstances open to him, and because of that he has a completely different meaning . . . (. . . совсем на всё другие правила жизни, науки и продовольствия, и каждый человек у них себе все абсолютные обстоятельства перед собою имеет, и через то в нем совсем другой смысл . . .)[169]

In labour every person outdoes himself – makes creations better and longer-lasting than his daily meaning . . . (. . . в труде каждый человек превышает себя – делает изделия лучше и долговечней своего житейского значения . . .)[170]

machines have served to even out inequalities in talents and gifts, and genius does not strive to battle against industriousness and accuracy (. . . машины сравняли неравенство талантов и дарований, и гений не рвется в борьбе против прилежания и аккуратности . . .)[171]

Encouraging an increase in profit, machines do not encourage artistic daring, which sometimes used to exceed its boundaries, inspiring the people's imagination . . . (. . . Благоприятствуя возвышению заработка, машины не благоприятствуют артистической удали, которая иногда превосходила меру, вдохновляя народную фантазию . . .)[172]

The animal and the tree did not evoke compassion towards their lives, because no man took part in their creation – there was no conscious strike or precision of craftsmanship in them . . . (. . . Зверь и дерево не возбуждали в них сочувствия

[168] Joseph Brodsky, 'Catastrophies in the Air', op. cit., p. 288.
[169] Nikolai Leskov, 'Levsha (Skaz o tulskom kosom Levshe i o stalnoi blokhe)', in Leskov, *Sobranie sochinenii v 5 tomakh*, vol. 3, Moscow: Pravda, 1981. See <http://az.lib.ru/l/leskow_n_s/text_0246.shtml> [accessed 2 March 2014].
[170] Andrei Platonov, 'Chevengur', in Platonov, *Izbrannoe*, Moscow: Moskovskii rabochii, 1988, p. 56.
[171] Leskov, 'Levsha', op. cit.
[172] Ibid.

своей жизни, потому что никакой человек не принимал участия в их изготовлении, – в них не было ни одного сознательного удара и точности мастерства . . .)[173]

It will leap in any surroundings and veer in all directions . . . (. . . она будет скакать в каком угодно пространстве и в стороны вероятии делать . . .)[174]

Man is the beginning for any mechanism, whereas birds are the end in themselves . . . (. . . Человек – начало для всякого механизма, а птицы – сами себе конец . . .)[175]

Despite the fact that the author's and narrator's points of view in 'Levsha' 'not only do not coincide, but the very view-point of the narrator becomes an object of the author's reflection as a form of manifestation of the common consciousness disfigured by the centuries of slavery', and thus 'Leskov's verdict is [. . .] harsh: in the country where slavery exists, everybody is a slave'[176] – despite this, the strength of Levsha's noble dedication to a higher cause, within the given world order, no matter how cruel and unjust it is to him personally, the purity of his patriotic love, light up his unenlightened, yet ingenious, and sorrowful path. A further sad irony here is also in the similarity of Platonov's personal fate to the destiny of Leskov's Levsha, given Platonov's essentially tragic life, the genius of his (literary) craftsmanship and purity of his faith in his country, where he was made to perish in torment. This, however, is a tragic and irrational archetype of Russianness, so brilliantly epitomized by Leskov, which can be traced from medieval times (depicted in particular in Andrei Tarkovsky's 'Andrei Rublev', with deliberately blinded craftsmen) to our day.

Poetry of the absurd: From structure to ethics: Daniil Kharms and Andrei Platonov

There is, in my view, yet another line of continuity – stemming from the sphere of the humourous – with Platonov's literary universe, despite its distinct uniqueness.[177] It is its connection with the absurd world of Daniil Kharms. What is of interest here is not the actual 'deformation of language' which, as scholars suggested, Platonov shares with several avangardists who throve at the time,[178] but rather a semantic link behind some common artistic features. In fact, once uncovered, this concealed link will demonstrate

---

[173]   Platonov, 'Chevengur', op. cit., p. 55.

[174]   Leskov, 'Levsha', op. cit.

[175]   Platonov, 'Chevengur', op. cit., p. 55.

[176]   Eduard Beznosov, '"Skaz o tulskom Levshe" kak narodnyi epos', in Beznosov, *Literatura* (Appendix to the newpaper *Pervoe sentiabria*), 2004, 1–7 January, p. 28.

[177]   The question of Platonov's literary genealogy and immediate neighbourhood has been explored and debated in substantial scholarly material. See Ben W. Dhooge, 'Priem iazykovoi deformatsii. Platonov, Kharms, Khlebnikov', in *Wiener Slawistischer Almanach*, 63 (2009), pp. 283–325, for a detailed list of such works.

[178]   See Ben W. Dhooge, 'Priem iazykovoi deformatsii. Platonov, Kharms, Khlebnikov', op. cit.

to us, if you like, a miracle of creation – the way in which a rationally constructed game of logical absurd and cheerful nonsense, close in spirit to light-hearted mischief and tomfoolery, turns into a palpitating masterpiece, when infused with poetry of ethical–religious impulse.

Indeed, with his kinship to Louis Carroll whom Kharms held in very high regard, he derived from the Englishman some fundamental structural principles of a mathematical game laying at the basis of humour. Operating with philosophical and linguistic material, Carroll laid bare the poetry within mathematics, itself dissolved in the texture of existence, as well as the interplay of art and logic within language. He produced a game of words and ideas, at once absurdist and logical, liberated from didactics and dictate of hierarchies. At the same time, his 'absurdities are seen to be quite rational once the basic point (usually the dramatization of classical problems in logic) has been grasped.'[179] This game with formal logic can often (although not always) be found in Kharms too. A clear example is Kharms's tale of 'The Red-Haired Man', based entirely on negation:

> There was a red-haired man who had no eyes or ears.
> Neither did he have any hair, so he was called red-haired theoretically.
> He couldn't speak, since he didn't have a mouth. Neither did he have a nose.
> He didn't even have any arms or legs. He had no stomach and he had no back
> and he had no spine and he had no innards whatsoever. He had nothing at all!
> Therefore there's no knowing whom we are even talking about.
> In fact it's better that we don't say any more about him.[180]

Sure enough, one can derive from it a high philosophical meaning, seen here in the medieval philosophical tradition of 'Negative Theology', the apophatic school of thought. This as well as other disambiguations are presented in Neil Cornwell's book on 'The Absurd in literature'.[181] Cornwell also mentions in this context Carroll's exploitation of the Cheshire Cat (as well as Gogol's 'The Nose'). However, as Martin Gardner aptly notes, Carroll's Alice books 'lend themselves readily to any type of symbolic interpretation – political, metaphysical, or Freudian. Some learned commentaries of this sort are hilarious'; these books 'are much too rich in symbols. The symbols have too many explanations'.[182] The same is true, of course, more generally, and is clearly applicable to Kharms. The extreme case which exemplifies Gardner's point that excessive symbolism is wide open to interpretation would be 'The Black Square' by Malevich, where symbolism easily nests anywhere between nothing and anything. However, the game of formal logic which, applied to real life, creates a comic effect, can stop at just that, or, alternatively, this general style can be developed further

---

[179] Edmund Little, *The Fantasts*, Amersham: Avebury, 1984, p. 89. Cited in Neil Cornwell, *Absurd in literature*, Manchester and New York: Manchester University Press, 2006, p. 56.
[180] See Neil Cornwell, *Daniil Kharms: Incidences*, London: Serpent's Tail, 1993, p. 49.
[181] See Neil Cornwell, *The Absurd in Literature*, op. cit., p. 170.
[182] Martin Gardner, 'Introduction' to *The Annotated Alice*, New York: Bramhall House Clarkson Potter, 1960.

along seemingly the same line, when suddenly, in the manner of Pygmalion's Galatea, it comes to life and transgresses the borders of the genre. This happens in the story 'Skrepki' ('Paper-clips') by a contemporary Russian writer Dmitrii Gorchev (1963–2010), which lies, both in form and content, as if in between Kharms and Platonov, that is, it is half-way on the route from the former to the latter, and thus shows their connectedness. The trick is, as was promised earlier, in that movement of the soul which alone, according to Fazil Iskander, merits to be verbalized,[183] and the presence of which moves this story away from Daniil Kharms's formal play of 'The Redhaired Man', towards Andrei Platonov's in many ways religious ethos.

Here are some lines from the opening and from the closure of Gorchev's very short story, which should demonstrate how, enriched with real feeling, it has come very close to Platonov's discourse:

> In a distant country once lived one man. This man loved one woman very much. Only he saw her very seldom; once in fourteen years; and only once. One day this man needed something rather badly; paper-clips maybe; or possibly vermicelli, who knows.
>
> In this country there was a rule: everything was free, because no one had any money anyway. Say, you need a brush, well, you get a brush. But first you have to write a request to a special committee. You must state it clearly, for example – I have a great need in a brush. The members of the committee will visit, check everything, ask the neighbours, and in a month you can go and get your brush. The main thing is that it's free.
>
> [. . .] Suddenly the doors open and a woman enters; that very woman whom the man loved. He even got a fright, overwhelmed by joy. [. . .] Good Lord, the man thinks, will I really begrudge her glazier's putty. So he got up, and scratched off all the glazier's putty. And the window glass which was supported by it he took out and put carefully in the corner. Then he lay on the floor again and began to wait for the woman to come again. [. . .] When the members of the committee arrived to find out more about the paper-clips, it turned out that the man was already dead. He was lying on the floor, all covered in snow, and when the committee raked the snow, they saw that the man was smiling. And he was smiling so nicely that the committee quickly took off his boots and buried him in the garden.
>
> And no one asked – who is it you are burying?
>
> This is because he was one man.[184]

What we encounter here is a combination of Kharms's structural principles and Platonov's stylistic chords, particularly audible in the meeting of a helpless living being with the soulless force of mass unconscious, in the piercing notes of hopeless human love, in the smiling of the dead, and especially in the very last phrase, 'Because he was

[183]   The precise quotation reads 'Only a movement of the soul is worthy of words, only that deserves to be expressed by the means of art'. See <http://www.sergeydovlatov.ru/?cnt=1> [accessed 11 March 2014].

[184]   Dmitrii Gorchev, 'Skrepki', in Gorchev, *Delenie na nol*, St Petersburg: ACT/Astrel, 2011.

one man', a phrase simultaneously absurdist and almost religious. This example of an 'evolutional road' (obviously, in artistic rather than chronological terms) from Kharms to Platonov through Gorchev demonstrates, in particular, a drastic transformation of a 'rational' absurd into irrational, akin to a transition from a naked form to a living soul inside it. It also shows a multifaceted nature of the literary absurd, which, just as the irrational (and in many ways as an intrinsic part of it), depends crucially on the coordinate system of its subjects, on their vantage points. Thus, while Kharms's universe is indeed absurdist, and quite deliberately so, Platonov's is not – it is on the contrary highly meaningful, but only if looked at through a primordial prism, not corrupted by civilizational conventions, as was mentioned earlier, but permeated with a truly religious consciousness that recognizes a higher beginning of things. It is, if you like, a vision of Adam, the first person on earth, despite the fact that he is not in the paradisical Edem gardens, but in a hell of the early soviet system, which nevertheless is perceived as part of a given world, invested as it is with good and evil, beauty and sorrow.

What is striking – and important in our context, as it informs us of the nature of humour – is that in this newly discovered world, x-rayed by Platonov's vision, the border between the sad and the funny is erased. We do not know whether to weep or to laugh at this world.

If the conventional causal links may seem broken in Platonov, they are broken meaningfully, in order to reveal to us the ridiculous character of our perceptions and our deeds. That is why, in particular, Hans Günther was able to map Platonov's literary world between Holy Foolishness and intellect.[185] In Kharms's tales akin to the one earlier, these links are broken not so much arbitrarily, but following some formal logic rather than the logic of the 'unpolluted' human heart.[186] In other words, we have here an opposition of an artificially constructed, logical absurd, even if rooted in reality, and an absurd which manifests itself in the light of a moral perspective. This latter kind is present to a great extent in Russian literature (and not necessarily humorous only) of the last century – the century which threw into sharp relief the nonsensical nature of existence. And Gogol once again, and with even greater force, came to the centre stage – both in terms of his literary influence, and as a measuring unit for the scale of the absurd in Russian reality.[187] Both his serious attitude to laughter and his extraordinary artistic means, which transcended the boundaries of the romantic and

---

[185] See Hans Günther, 'Iurodstvo i "um" kak protivopolozhnye tochki zreniia u Andreia Platonova', in Robert Hodel and Jan Peter Locher (eds), *Sprache und Erzhlhaltung bei Andrej Platonov* (*Slavica Helvetica*), vol. 58, Bern–Berlin–Frankfurt-a-M.–New York–Paris–Wien: Peter Lang, 1998, pp. 117–31.

[186] Of course, this story does not exhaust and fully characterize Kharms's oeuvre. For a discussion of the absurd in Kharms, see Neil Cornwell, *The Absurd in Literature*, op. cit., pp. 158–83, where a variety of interpretations is offered, including those with religious, moral, ethical and other connotations rather than those based on the games of formal logic alone.

[187] Dostoevsky also has featured prominently in these comparisons which showed his prophecies having come to life, and with a greater force than he anticipated. However, the humorous and satirical are conventionally measured against Gogol, who was endowed, unlike Dostoevsky, first of all with a gift for the comedic, and whose legacy includes a greater variety of genres.

the fantastic, turned out to be most fit for Russia of the times of great political upheavals and existential crisis. Those 'diseased' depictions of life, of which Rozanov spoke with bitterness, came to be most useful to the twentieth-century Russian authors, as they found themselves struggling precisely on that no-man's territory between faith and despair which Reinhold Niebuhr called laughter.[188]

In the same vein, due to some cyclic patterns in the modern Russian history (where Chaadaev's ideas of Russia providing a non-example to the world had come true in political terms, when the country turned into a huge existential laboratory of extreme brutality), nineteenth-century satire supplied a suitable foundation for the twentieth-century dystopia and apocalyptic premonitions, being a continuation of the prophesies of classical Russian writers. From modernism to post-modernism, despite the strictures of Soviet ideology, major Russian authors drew on Gogol and Saltykov-Shchedrin, on Chekhov and Leskov, on the burning and tragic irony of Dostoevsky and the subtlest of Pushkin – in brief, on the laughter through tears and ideas, on the tragicomic genre. Russian literary humour of the twentieth century thus continued with most serious anthropological questions: ethical, religious and moral – the 'cursed' metaphysical questions which have always been at the core of Russian literature with its tradition of compassion to the fallen, of feeling pain for the 'small' person.

Ironic start to the cruel century: Laughter of pain, relevance of Gogol's irrationalism to Russian dystopian literature, Evgenii Zamiatin

For instance, both early and late in the twentieth century, we can see a direct turning to Gogol, with the same sentiment – to juxtapose the modernity with Gogol's hyperbole and grotesque in order to emphasize how his most wild fantasies and most exaggerated caricatures still fell short of what new Russian life had actually brought. Thus Vysotsky wrote in 1965, 'If only we could tell Gogol about our miserable life, honestly, Gogol would never believe us!',[189] whereas Sasha Chernyi produced a poem in 1909 for Gogol's centenary, pointedly entitled 'Laughter through tears', with the following lines:

> Oh, our dearest Nikolai Vasilievich Gogol!
> It's a blessing that you cannot get up . . .
> But we carry on living! And I fear that it's too much,
> What we have to hear, see and yet remain silent? Isn't it?

---

[188] Quoted in Martin Gardner, op.cit.
[189] Vladimir Vysotsky, 'Pesnia o sumasshedshem dome', <http://vysotskiy.lit-info.ru/vysotskiy/stihi/113.htm> [accessed 11 March 2014]. In Russian: 'И рассказать бы Гоголю Про нашу жизнь убогую, – Ей-богу, этот Гоголь бы Нам не поверил бы'.

which ends with the aphoristic and meaningful 'There are no more tears; and no laughter.'[190] And even the balanced, shrewd and intelligent Nadezhda Teffi, who became a leading humourous writer of the Russian emigration, commented thus on her gift for the comedic genre: 'my soul is drenched with unshed tears, they all remain inside. Outside of me there is laugher, "great drought", as was written on old barometers, but within there is a continuous swamp; not a soul, but one big swamp.'[191] Gogol was one of Teffi's favourite writers, and her friend and 'Satirikon' colleague Arkadii Averchenko directly used excerpts from Gogol for his own political satire, successfully imposing Gogol's grotesque onto his own time and his struggle against Bolshevism.[192]

In his feuilleton 'Otryvki iz gogolevskoi "Zhenitby"' (Exerpts from Gogol's "Marriage")' (1919), Averchenko uses the figure of Lenin to replace Podkolesin from Gogol's 'Marriage' in the scene of escaping the ultimate responsibility and fleeing through the window (in Averchenko's fable, the escape of Lenin–Podkolesin is committed for the sake of taking a safe refuge in Switzerland). A similar usage of real historical figures, only from the past rather than present times and without a narrowly defined satirical purpose, can also be found in Kharms, who makes a buffoonery and extravaganza with classical Russian writers as protagonists. In doing so, Kharms breaks the pomposity and rigidity of established hierarchies, and implicitly mocks any tendentious attempt – be it political, philistine or banal – to appropriate literature, whereas Averchenko in his political pamphlets pursues much more concrete aims, in accordance with his genre. While Kharms's mocking does not diminish the role of the literary giants featuring in his miniatures, but destroys in passing a dangerous cult of uncritical, deadening adoration and uniformity of opinion (and is, ironically, rather akin in spirit to pranks of Pushkin, a very frequent hero of Kharms's tales), Averchenko in his post-revolutionary texts purposefully castigates the new regime and its perpetrators. But in their very different genres and styles – absurd metaphysics of Kharms's short literary tales and caustic satire on the topic of the day of Averchenko's political lampoons and feuilletons– both deploy an intertextual device using a particular variety of Russian anecdotes which involve a playful adopting of famous historical figures. This device

---

[190] Sasha Chernyi, 'Smekh skvoz slezy', <http://rupoem.ru/chernyj/all.aspx#ax-milyj-nikolaj> [accessed 9 March 2014]. In Russian: 'Ах, милый Николай Васильич Гоголь! // Как хорошо, что ты не можешь встать . . . // Но мы живем! Боюсь – не слишком много ль // Нам надо слышать, видеть и молчать?'; 'Слез более не стало, И смеха нет'.

[191] See Irina Odoevtseva, *Na beregakh Seny*, Moscow: Khudozhestvennaia literatura, 1989. See <http://noskoff.lib.ru/aodoe010.html> [accessed 23 February 2014].

[192] See, for example, A. Averchenko, Feuilleton 'Otryvki iz gogolevskoi "Zhenitby"' which opens with the passage from Gogol's 'Marriage' describing the deceitful nature of a previous suitor (before Podkolesin). This passage, however, is preceded by Averchenko's 're-directing' remark: 'On the Bolshevik's official organ "Izvestiia"', so that Gogol's words are used as if applying to the Bolshevik newspaper: 'Such a strange character he had: whatever he utters – it's a lie; despite him looking so presentable. Maybe he was himself upset about it, but he couldn't do without his little lies – that must be God's will then' ('Iug', Sebastopol, 08.09.1919; see also *Ogonek*, November 1919, No. 1: http://odessitclub.org/publications/almanac/alm_35/alm_35_271–284.pdf). In 1919–1920, Averchenko wrote four feuilletons directly based on Gogol's texts. Further on the theme of Averchenko echoing Gogol, see Denis Pronichev, 'Perepevy Gogolia v felietonakh Arkadiia Averchenko', in *Kultura Narodov Prichernomoriia*, vol. 5, <http://elib.crimea.edu/index.php?option=com_content&task=view&id=75> [accessed 10 March 2014].

of inserting authentic historical names and/or narratives for humorous purposes was quite widely used in the nineteenth century – in particular, in Prutkov's heritage[193] or in Leskov's 'Levsha'. But if Leskov made reference to past Russian monarchs, Kharms involved classical writers rather than political figures, as times were becoming more and more intolerant of any political dissent or even light-heartedness with respect to ideology. Laughter was steadily appropriated by the Soviet state in a more severe fashion than during tsarizm, and the 'cast-iron politburo of Russian literature'[194] was being moulded fast.

Any new artistic voices resonated too dangerously in the thickening air of the new regime, and any writers of talent would inevitably come into conflict with the state, if only by the virtue of their new poetics that could not be squeezed into the procrustean bed of the uniform discourse of the state ideology, even despite the fact that in the 1920s there was still a sufficient leeway and no clear-cut definition of what constitutes anti-Soviet, as long as no direct attacks against the new political system were present. Indeed, 'possessing its own genealogy, dynamics, logic, and future, art is not synonymous with, but at best parallel to, history; and the manner by which it exists is by continually generating a new aesthetic reality. That is why it is often found "ahead of progress", ahead of history', and is feared and disliked by 'champions of the common good, masters of the masses, heralds of historical necessity. For there, where art has stepped, where a poem has been read, they discover, in place of the anticipated consent and unanimity, indifference and polyphony; in place of the resolve to act, inattention and fastidiousness'.[195] Humour thus, being intrinsically subversive even more than poetry, was becoming in post-revolutionary Russia a highly explosive territory.

Evgenii Zamiatin, the author, in particular, of the dystopia 'My' (1920), of which George Orwell's famous novel seems derivative, was one of these new talents with the language of their own. Ironically, criticized at the time by some literary figures for 'excessive intelligence', for writing in a 'too dry and cold fashion',[196] he was regarded at the end of the twentieth century as an openly irrationalist writer, one of those who invariably tried 'to venture towards the limits of human experience' in line with Dostoyevskian tradition that subverts a restricted rationalist vision of the world.[197] In the same vein, critic Yakov Braun, Zamiatin's contemporary, in his article 'Vzyskuiushchii cheloveka' called Zamiatin 'the most cunning writer in Russian literature', who, 'at every stage of his development [. . .] deceives us by the limitations, finiteness and horizon;

---

[193] See 'Gistoricheskie materialy Fedora Kuzmicha Prutkova (deda)' ('Historical materials of Fedor Kuzmich Prutkov, the elder' (1854–1860) discussed in connection to the usage of historical discourse for constructing a parody: <http://az.lib.ru/p/prutkow_k_p/text_0170.shtml> [accessed 20 November 2013].

[194] A phrase (already used earlier in the chapter) invented by Andrei Bitov to describe the appropriation of Russian classical literature by the Soviet ideology. See Andrei Bitov, a shortened version of his essay *My Grandfather Chekhov and Great-Grandfather Pushkin*, Novaia Gazeta,12 July 2004, No. 49.

[195] Joseph Brodsky, 'Ucommon Visage' (the Nobel Lecture), op. cit., pp. 48; 46–7.

[196] See, for example, M. Gorky, *Sobranie Sochinenii v 30 tomakh*, Moscow, 1956, p. 126.

[197] See T. R. N. Edwards, *Three Russian Writers and the Irrational: Zamyatin, Pil'nyak, and Bulgakov*, Cambridge: Cambridge University Press, 1982.

grinds and rounds off these seemingly found ends of the earth, limits of the limits, but only in order – at the last moment – to transcend them and to call us to new horizons. [. . .] Zamiatin is a new type of artist, an artist-boomerang, whose path is from himself to the world, and back'.[198] Such an artist, having come the full circle, will return at the more profound level to the question 'of the ultimate human mystery'.[199]

Instructively, Kornei Chukovsky recognized Zamiatin as a 'new Gogol',[200] and Yurii Tynianov, who wrote of Gogol's unusual perception of inanimate objects, of his ability to sense the comic in them, which is sustained by the discrepancy between two images, the inanimate and the animate (like the overcoat being Bashmachkin's life companion), also commented on the object-based metaphor in Zamiatin. 'The principles of his style include an economical image of an object instead of the object itself, and the latter is given not by its principal feature, but by a secondary one. From this secondary feature, from this point, a line is drawn which encircles the object, thus breaking it into linear squares'.[201] As a result, 'the world is turned into little tiles of a parquet floor, from which there is no escape'.[202] However, Zamiatin himself saw a way out, as he believed that 'there are two ways of overcoming the tragedy of life: religion or irony'.[203] He opted for irony of the neo-realists, considering 'humour, laughter and irony to be hallmarks of the new literary trend of "neo-realism"', the kind of irony which is, in Anatole France's words, 'not cruel; it laughs neither at love, nor at beauty; it teaches us to laugh at the evil and the stupid, whom without it we would hate in our weakness'.[204] This attitude, as Vladimir Tunimanov notes, stood in sharp opposition to the stance of Aleksandr Blok, that is, to a generally Symbolist attitude to humour – suspicious and even hostile.[205] For Zamiatin, who admired the epic irony of Swift and Anatole France, 'Blok and Russia chose the tragic' solution to life 'with both hatred and love, which stop at nothing, whereas France, chose the ironic solution, with relativism and scepticism, which also stop at nothing'.[206]

Blok's position, expressed in his essay 'Irony' of 1908, and republished twice in 1918 and 1919 – the fact Tunimanov rightly emphasizes as significant – which regarded laughter as 'an illness, related to spiritual diseases', as 'destructive' and 'devastating',[207] returns us again to the dilemma of the Russian ambiguous attitude to laughter, the dilemma which tormented Gogol and which, not surprisingly, resurged with a new force during the Silver Age and continued to the early Soviet era. Indeed, the Silver Age came as the time of anticipating – and nearly of desiring – chaos as a threshold

[198]   Ya. Braun, 'Vzyskuiushchii cheloveka', in *Sibirskie ogni*, 1923, Nos 5–6, pp. 237–9.
[199]   Ibid.
[200]   See on this N. Otsup, 'Evgenii Zamiatin', in *Okean vremeni. Stikhotvoreniia. Dnevnik v stikhakh. Stat'i i vospominaniia o pisateliakh*, St Petersburg, 1994, p. 541.
[201]   Yurii Tynianov, 'Literaturnoe segodnia', in *Russkii sovremennik*, 1924, No. 1.
[202]   Ibid.
[203]   Quoted in Vladimir Tunimanov, 'Evgeny Zamiatin: The Art of Irony', in Lesley Milne (ed.), *Reflective Laughter. Aspects of Humour in Russian Culture*, op. cit., p. 110.
[204]   Ibid.
[205]   Ibid.
[206]   Ibid.
[207]   A. Blok, *Sobranie sochinenii v 8 tomakh*, Moscow-Leningrad: GIKhL, 1960–1963, vol. 5, p. 345. Cited in Tunimanov, op. cit., p. 109.

to a new beginning; the time of a Dionysian spirit, of unruly self-will, which replaced the restrictive and crude, aesthetically narrow advance of radical intelligentsia with their idea of art based on utilitarian principles. Blok, with his super-sensitive poetic genius and acute feeling of history, and despite his clearly being an integral part of that striving for destruction and for grand re-birth which was in the air, warned against what he perceived as a mass scale drowning of his contemporaries' joy and despair, of their own selves and 'their loved ones, their works, their lives and finally their death' in laughter 'as in vodka'.[208] As Tunimanov writes, for Blok 'the age was marked by a universal epidemic of destructive irony', the irony which is 'the bite of a vampire'.[209]

Thus Blok sensed in his times that apocalyptic flavour which Akhmatova described as a 'frightful party of dead leaves'.[210] She too complained, according to Chukovskaia, about the all-pervasive ironic discourse, the attitude of avoiding at all costs being serious, perhaps an escapist attitude that prevailed in her surroundings at the time.[211] However, it seems that in some sense the situation with humour was similar to the situation with love (both being rooted in the religious), when sacred paradigms began to crumble down at the brink of the twentieth century, and suddenly, in this spiritual mayhem, 'all was permitted', using the words born of Ivan Karamazov. This caused an instinctive fear first of all in poetic minds, despite their own involvement in the 'frightful party' of the disintegration of the authentic – which in Russian poetry is almost synonymous with the tragic – in literary consciousness.

But the issue seems to go yet deeper under the surface, for there are, in fact, more similarities than divergencies in Blok's and Zamiatin's positions. The most fundamental similarity is that for both the driving force of laughter is pain – in Blok's words, 'Do not listen to our laughter, listen to the pain behind it'.[212] The same pain is looming behind Zamiatin's anti-utopian 'My'. It is the traditional compassion of Russian literature towards Bashmachkins of all sorts and creeds, towards small numbers in the anthill of a totalitarian state, towards a person, an individual, the compassion which stands, in particular, behind Russian literary humour and drives the pen of such great satirists as Gogol and Saltykov-Shchedrin (with whom Zamiatin felt a special affinity), and which gives this humour its ultimate value; which makes poetry poetic in the proper sense of the word.

Zamiatin opts for irony and scepticism as opposed to tragedy and religion,[213] but in his irony and in his scepticism there is plenty of tragedy and plenty of truly religious, as in Dostoevsky whose 'deep and tragic irony'[214] Zamiatin admired. He is accused of

[208] Ibid.

[209] Tunimanov, op. cit., p. 110.

[210] Anna Akhmatova, 'Poema bez geroia', <http://www.ruthenia.ru/60s/ahmatova/poema1_1.htm> [accessed 12 March 2014]. In Russian: 'страшный праздник мертвой листвы'.

[211] See Lidia Chukovskaia, *Zapiski ob Anne Akhmatovoi*, St. Petersburg: Zhurnal 'Neva', 1996.

[212] See Aleksandr Blok, 'Ironiia', in A. Blok, *Sobranie sochinenii v 8 tomakh*, op. cit., vol. 5, 1962, p. 349.

[213] See Tunimanov, op. cit., pp. 109–110, for the quotations from Zamiatin that the neo-realists 'believe neither in God, nor in man . . .' and that out of the 'two ways of overcoming the tragedy of life: religion or irony' they 'chose the second method'.

[214] See Tunimanov, op. cit., p. 110.

rationally constructing his texts, yet his depiction of the world is based on the irrational nature of man, on very Dostoevskyan rebellion against vulgar rationalism. The parallel with Dostoevsky is particularly transparent in 'My', where the hero is striving to impose on 'unknown planetary readers' a 'divinely rational and precise order'[215] – the type of life akin to Dostoevsky's 'Chrystal Palace', against which the revolt and disdain of his Underground Man are directed. While Dostoevsky, through his Paradoxicalist, rebels against 'mathematics' and laws of nature, essentially against any attempts of technical progress to solve the 'cursed questions', and through Dmitrii Karamazov, is appalled by the latest scientific attempts to reduce human spirituality to mere physiology,[216] Zamiatin's 'philosopher of mathematics' D-503 demands an answer from a great physicist (a prototype of Einstein),[217] who discovered that the universe is finite – what is beyond that end? By the same token, the Underground Man is bracing to run away from any final solution of human happiness for the sake of his own, individual, destructive caprice ('I am standing for [. . .] my caprice, and for its being guaranteed to me when necessary'; 'one's own caprice, however wild it may be [. . .] – is that very "most advantageous advantage" which we have overlooked, [. . .] against which all systems and theories are continually being shattered to atoms'),[218] while Zamiatin sarcastically warns in his letter to Yurii Annenkov that after the 'most delightful, sweetest-smelling public conveniences' are provided, 'everyone will run from these most delightful public conveniences into disorganised and inexpedient bushes.'[219]

Thus Zamiatin, in his revolt against a shallow rationalism behind any monological and all-equating earthly paradise, distinctly follows Dostoevsky. For Zamiatin's confused hero, 'even mathematics has disclosed all its irrational properties and has "betrayed" him'.[220] Zamiatin stands up for a living being, for an individuality of the 'I' against a cruel necessity of the 'We'. In a similar way, Blok turns against the crude rationalism which is encroaching into the domain of the individual, destroying the human in man. Thus Blok characterizes the passed nineteenth century with Briusov's words – 'flameless fire' and describes it as a 'brilliant and burial age, which threw over a living person's face a brocade cover of mechanics, positivism and economic materialism, and which buried the human voice in the din of machines; an iron age, when the "iron box" – a railway train – overtook the "*unovertakable troika*" in which "Gogol embodied the whole of Russia", as Gleb Uspensky put it'.[221] Blok's intuitive disgust in the face of a blind machinery, all things mechanical and inanimate that are pushing back the fragile inner

215 Ibid., p. 111.
216 Thus Mitia Karamazov emphatically tells Alesha about the real discovery of a contemporary of Dostoevsky's, the physiologist Claude Bernard, that little tails of nerves in the brain are the cause of his ability to think, and not his living soul and the fact that he is created in the divine image and likeness.
217 See Tunimanov, op. cit., p. 114, where he cites an excerpt from Zamiatin's sketch 'White Love' which proves this point.
218 Fyodor Dostoevsky, 'Notes from the Underground', in *White Nights and Other Stories*, transl. by Constance Garnett, New York: The MacMillan Company, 1918, pp. 76, 69.
219 Cited in Tunimanov, op. cit., p. 114.
220 Tunimanov, op. cit., 112.
221 Blok, 'Ironiia', op. cit., p. 346 (Blok quotes respectively Valerii Briusov's poem 'Fonariki' and Gleb Uspensky's work 'Krestianin i krestianskii trud' ('A peasant and peasant's labour').

world of man, is akin to Tolstoy's instinctive repulsion of the blind and deadening force of a steam-engine. Zamiatin, a naval engineer by education, who admired the beauty of ice-breaking ships, is closer to Chekhov who famously wrote that 'there is more love for mankind in electricity and steam than there is in chastity and abstaining from meat.'[222] Nevertheless, both Zamiatin and Blok (not to mention Chekhov and Tolstoy) recognized a horror exuded by the indifferent, soulless force, which arises immediately as soon as the individual humanity is suppressed, as soon as human reason is separated from its compassionate sources.

This shows that in most basic terms there is no contradiction between Blok's and Zamiatin's, or Symbolist's and Neo-Realist's, positions – both stand up for a human right to individuality, to non-uniformity, to personal freedom to be different (where Russian Orthodox self-renunciation 'is not the renunciation of one's personality, but a person's renunciation of his or her egoism'),[223] and the laughter of both is laughter that covers up a great pain, in line with the classical Russian tradition. And with a sad irony, a 'conscious agnostic' Zamiatin,[224] who admired European relativism and scepticism, was rejected as a writer by European culture as being 'too Russian'[225] for it. When hounded in his own country, he could not find his place abroad, being torn away from the elements of his language. Just as Blok suffocated in the stifling air of the new Russia, 'Zamiatin felt suffocated in Europe.'[226] And, as Aaron Shteinberg, who met up with Zamiatin in Berlin in 1931, insinuates, Zamiatin's premature death was inevitable, as if welcomed by the writer himself as the only way out of the deadlock.[227] Shteinberg, who wrote his memoirs without access to the relevant biographical information, was, as it has turned out, formally speaking wrong in his guesses. Zamiatin died of his old angina, not of suicide. But to what extent was the crisis of his heart disease a consequence of his emotional state, one can only speculate. In any case, 'Zamiatin died from angina pectoris, the death of Akakii Akakievich Bashmachkin . . . hunted down, looking around in fear, with a sealed heart and sealed lips . . .'.[228] Just as Blok, he 'died from the lack of air';[229] and with a very Gogolean sentiment at heart – 'Do not listen to our laughter, listen to the pain behind it . . .'.[230]

[222] From Chekhov's letter to Aleksei Suvorin, of 27 March 1894. See Anton Chekhov, *A Life in Letters*, Rosamund Bartlett (ed.), transl. by Rosamund Bartlett and Antony Phillips, Harmondsworth, Middlesex, England: Penguin Books, 2004, p. 324.

[223] Vladimir Solov'ev, 'Natsionalnyi vopros v Rossii', in Solov'ev, *Sobranie Sochinenii*, vol. 5, St Petersburg, 1902, pp. 42–3. Cited in A. Blok, 'Ironia', op. cit.

[224] See Tunimanov, op. cit., 110.

[225] See Aaron Shteinberg's memoirs *Druziia moikh rannikh let*, Syntaxis: France, 1991, p. 162.

[226] Ibid.

[227] See Ibid., p. 163.

[228] The words of Aleksei Remizov from his article of 1937 'Stoiat – negasimuiu svechu' ('Stand still – and bring an inextinguishable candle') in memorium of Zamiatin, <http://az.lib.ru/z/zamjatin_E_i/text_0450.shtml> [accessed 16 February 2014].

[229] The words from Blok's 'Pushkin speech': 'O naznachenii poeta' ('On the poet's vocation') (see Aleksandr Blok, *O naznachenii poeta*, Moscow: Sovetskaia Rossiia, 1971). It was written for the eighty-fourth anniversary of Pushkin's death and read out at the meeting in the House of Litteratures in February 1921. These words were subsequently used to describe Blok's own death which followed shortly after.

[230] Already quoted earlier.

Zamiatin's 'We' (1920) had to wait for nearly 70 years to be published in his homeland. A similar fate awaited Mikhail Bulgakov's 'The Heart of Dog' written in the same period (1924) – also a political satire with profound metaphysical underpinning. However, his 'main' novel, 'Master and Margarita', which Bulgakov had been writing for more than 10 years and completed shortly before his death in 1940, had to wait slightly less – it came out in 1966, during the first, rather than the second, Thaw.

It was written (and, to a large extent, set) against the background so distinctly envisaged by both writers, which Zamiatin predicted to a literal similarity. 'Yesterday we celebrated Unanimity Day, which everyone has long awaited with impatience. For the forty-eighth time, the Benefactor, who has demonstrated his steadfast wisdom on so many past occasions, was elected by a unanimous vote'[231] is a quotation from his fictional 'My'. It sounds strikingly similar in both style and content to an excerpt from the minutes of a Congress of the Communist Party of the USSR.

Carnival, colour and poetics of chance: Bulgakov, Babel, Ilf and Petrov

The irrational reality of the bloody carnival of Stalin's Russia (as well as of Palestine under the Roman rule) was thus the non-fictional drop against which Bulgakov created his fictional menippea – the term frequently used to describe the genre of this novel. Sergei Averintsev voices directly a close connection between a carnival and authoritarianism, stating that 'Stalin's regime would have simply not been able to function without its own "carnival" – without the game with ambivalent figures of the people's imagination, without the Grobianism-type "enthusiasm" of the mass media, without the precise psychological calculation underlying the effect of endless and unpredictable turns of the wheel of fortune, crownings–discrownings, ascensions and overthrowings, so that everyone is under a threat of persecution, but at the same time there is – reserved for everyone – a crazy gambling chance. [. . .] And even earlier – in the 1920s – was it not a carnival of sorts – putting God on trial at the comsomol meetings? [. . .] All in all, there had been an abundance of carnival atmosphere'.[232] Bulgakov managed simultaneously to portray the mystic horror of such a carnival and to deploy a cathartic laughter in the face of ugliness and death, be it spiritual or physical. Just as Gogol, he engaged two levels of discourse – the comic and the lyrical, interweaving them into an organic whole.

Although Bulgakov's genre in the novel is customarily defined as having elements of menippean satire, and is compared to Dostoyevsky's novels in this respect, Bulgakov's 'fantastic realism' is different from the 'fantastic realism' of Dostoevsky. Indeed, in Dostoevsky's novels the accent is above all on the inner life of the heroes, sore and

---

[231] Yevgeny Zamyatin, *We*, transl. by Mirra Ginsburg,<http://leecworkshops.wikispaces.com/file/view/yevgeny-zamyatin-we.pdf> [accessed 15 August 2014].

[232] Averintsev, 'Bakhtin, smekh, khristianskaia kultura', op. cit., pp. 7–19.

distorted; and their passionate voices, that we hear, come from the depths of individual consciousness, as if from the depth of the wells (creating, in their interplay, Bakhtinian polyphonic effect). The action thus is unfolding as if in a dream – the mundane reality with its everyday tangible detail and concrete authenticity, become secondary and blurred, while the hard core is comprised of the internal experience. By capturing it, Dostoevsky, to some extent, satisfies a definition of a true poet, given by Joseph Brodsky a hundred years later: 'A good poem, in a sense, is like a photograph that puts its objects' metaphysical features into sharp focus. Accordingly, a good poet is one who does this sort of thing in a camera-like fashion: quite unwittingly, almost in spite of himself.'[233] Interestingly, Lev Tolstoy, in many ways Dostoevsky's opposite, in fact comes close to Dostoevsky's fantastic realism, to a dream-like description from within an inflamed, almost delirious consciousness – in the episode from 'Anna Karenina', when the heroine is on her last train journey, very short distance from her suicidal deed: 'the bright evening sunshine shone through the window, and a breeze moved the blind. Anna forgot her fellow-travellers; softly rocked by the motion of the carriage and inhaling the fresh air, she again began to think. [. . .] "Yes, it troubles me very much, and reason was given us to enable us to escape; therefore I must escape! Why not put out the candle, if there is nothing more to look at? If everything is repulsive to look at? But how? Why did the guard run past holding the handrail? Why are those young men in the next carriage shouting? Why are they talking and laughing? It's all untrue, all lies, all deception, all evil! . . .".'[234]

Bulgakov's fantastic realism is quite different. He inherits Gogol's rather than Dostoevsky's tradition, even though it is the same genealogical line in literary history. Both Gogol and Bulgakov are closer to theatricality and drama, towards buffoonery rather than Holy Foolishness, and it is not surprising that both were gravitating towards writing theatre plays. However, the main point is that Bulgakov, just as Gogol, introduces the fantastic to the space of the real, offers the reader to enter his game, but at the same time touches the most profound aspects of being. Moreover, the laughter of both engages with the mythological, and itself acquires mythological dimensions. Lotman, when discussing structural principles of the narrative organization of 'Master and Margarita', talks of the device of 'story within story' which Bulgakov widely deployed in the novel, constructed at two narrative levels – Moscow one and Jerusalem one. Lotman notes that 'in the ideological and philosophical sense this descending into a "story within a story" seems to Bulgakov to be not the distancing from reality to the world of word games [. . .], but rather the ascending from a grimacing appearance of a pseudo-real world to the authentic essence of the world Mysterium. Between the two texts there is a mirror-principle, but what seems a real object is only a distorted reflection of that which itself seemed a reflection.'[235]

[233] Brodsky, 'Foreword' to *An Age Ago, A Selection of Nineteenth-Century Russian Poetry*, op. cit., p. xvi.

[234] Leo Tolstoy, *Anna Karenina*, transl. by Louise and Alymer Maude, Oxford: Oxford University Press, 1995, pp. 758–9.

[235] Yurii Lotman, 'Tekst kak semioticheskaia problema', in Lotman, *Statii po semiotike i topologii kultury*, <http://www.gumer.info/bibliotek_Buks/Culture/Lotm/15.php> [accessed 11 March 2014].

This ascent to the true essence of the universal mystery-play is undoubtedly among the elements which Bulgakov shares with Gogol, who transcends the very boundaries of the fantastic. At the same time, in a sense akin to Gogol's combining of the pagan and Christian elements, one can find in Bulgakov too a presence of potentially conflicting lines: a fairy-tale like, simplified and direct restoration of justice in a self-willed way, on the diabolic territory, and a Christian mythology which involves an earthly victory of injustice and divine expiation of human sins for the sake of mankind's moral redemption. The revenge portrayed within the former line is, however, *skomoroshii*, that is, pertaining to buffoonery, and does not aspire to contrast with the non-revenge of Christ in the latter line; these are of different order of magnitude, but both are in a certain sense therapeutic – as it were causing a psychological and spiritual exhale, respectively. Thus the two lines of 'Master and Margarita' do not conflict, but complement and deepen each other instead. Furthermore, the carnivalesque element, buffoonery and absurd re-create a context of a human life more generally, and in this context the mysterious sacred chords of existence, arising to their religious origins, sound ever more resonantly.

However, the most fundamental aspect of both writers, Gogol and Bulgakov, is a striving towards what Mann, following Hoffmann, described as 'living in poetry',[236] and this is embodied first of all in the language, in the poetics of their respective styles, which unite harmoniously the comic with the holy. In this light, Nabokov's statement that 'all the great literature is a phenomenon of language rather than of ideas'[237] is certainly true in its first half. As to the second, there seems to be no need for an opposition there, simply because in literature (and for that matter in art more generally) ideas themselves are generated by the language (by the form). Or stronger yet (as was mentioned earlier in relation to Gogol's prose) – form in art is itself an idea.

In this sense, close to Bulgakov by the highly poetic quality of his prose, although of very different variety, was his contemporary – Isaak Babel, another tragicomedian of Soviet-Russian literature, who spoke new and very distinctive voice. Babel, the writer of complex destiny, entangled with revolutionary murder, Jewish roots, Russian language and French literary affinity, perished in Stalin's terror in 1940 at the age of 45, leaving behind the works written 'as if not in ink, but in the very essence of the literary craft'.[238] Belonging to the whole pleyada of Odessa writers, Babel remains, just as Bulgakov, one of the most distinguished Russian prose writers of the twentieth century. Odessa, the legendary city, a multi-cultural international Black sea port, regarded as a cradle of humour, also produced such major literary figures in the humorous genre as Ilf and Petrov (and, later on, Mikhail Zhvanetsky), to name but a few. Fazil Iskander refers to Odessa as the town, 'invented by Babel's mighty merriment'.[239] Indeed, in his 'Odesskie rasskazy' ('The tales of Odessa') Babel re-invents this mythical town, with its

---

[236]   See Yurii Mann, 'Gogol', op. cit. A more extensive quotation was given earlier.
[237]   Vladimir Nabokov, *Lektsii po russkoi literature*, Moscow, 1999, p. 131.
[238]   Sergei Gandlevsky, 'Gibel s muzykoi (o Babele)', in *Znamia*, 2009, No. 9, <http://magazines.russ.ru/znamia/2009/9/ga15.html> [accessed 7 December 2014].
[239]   See Fazil Iskander, 'Nachalo', in Iskander, *Siuzhet sushchestvovaniia*, Moscow: Podkova Publishing House, 1999, p. 23.

picturesque Jewry – Babel's own hearth – but his Jews are 'inhabitants of a non-existent planet, ruled not by history, Bible or Talmud, but by Word, by a literary fervour alien to morality. Thus Babel does not merely aesthetisise Jewish existence, as was done by Mikhoels and Peretz, but replaces it with a completely different one, his own'.[240]

Traditionally studied in Western, especially American, scholarship as predominantly a Jewish writer, Babel is regarded in his native country, just as many other Jews who became part of Russian letters, as above all a Russian cultural figure. On this issue, Marat Grinberg disagrees with Shimon Markish who introduced the concept of binocularity – an ideal authorial belonging simultaneously to both worlds, Russian and Jewish – and believes that in Babel's case there was a crisis instead – a dilemma between 'Jewishness' and 'creativity', necessarily followed by a choice, where Babel opted for literature (i.e. literature in Russian).[241] Nevertheless, it is indeed tempting to see Babel's oeuvre as heavily influenced by the Old Testament, with its themes of violence, cruelty, power and passion. At the same time, Sergei Gandlevsky talks of the imprints of Hasidism in Babel's unyielding joi de vivre, his ineradicable cheerfulness and persistent tuning to the major tonality (as opposed to the minor melody of the 'sour dough of Russian novellas',[242] as Babel himself referred to Russian literature): 'Joviality, cheerfulness, understood by Babel as a prerequisite of wisdom became his symbols of faith: "clever people are intrinsically cheerful", "a cheerful person is always right" he tirelessly convinces himself and his readers. In this his personal convictions merge with the experience of Hasidism which is very serious about cheerfulness, regarding it as a way of understanding divine wisdom'.[243] In this light, Gandlevsky discerns in Babel's artistic credo the following, apparently non-Christian and irrational hierarchy: 'passion is above morality, joi de vivre is above reason, and cheerfulness is above all'.[244]

In this vein, as various artists at the time, carried away by the revolution with its renovating spirit and promises of a new life, Babel wanted to become a singer of the Sun. Mayakovsky wrote his famous 'Shine all the time, // for ever shine, // the last days' depths to plumb, // to shine – ! // spite every hell combined! // So runs my slogan – // and the sun's!',[245] and Gorky, in Babel's words, 'loves the sun, because Russian reality is rotten and meandering'; but not sufficiently, as 'in Gorky's affection for the sun there is something from reason'.[246] Thus Babel himself consciously strove to transcend a reason-based approach, and to entrust himself to the elements, to the power and passion of

[240] Marat Grinberg, 'V drugom izmerenii: Gorenshtein i Babel', in *«Слово\Word»* 2005, No. 45, <http://magazines.russ.ru/slovo/2005/45/gr10.html> [accessed 7 December 2014].

[241] Grinberg, 'V drugom izmerenii: Gorenshtein i Babel', op. cit.

[242] Isaak Babel, 'Vecher', <http://www.bibliotekar.ru/rus-Babel/66.htm> [accessed 25 November 2013].

[243] Gandlevsky, 'Gibel s muzykoi (o Babele)', op. cit.

[244] Ibid.

[245] Vladimir Mayakovsky, 'An Extraordinary Adventure Which Happened To Me, Vladimir Mayakovsky, One Summer in The Country', in *Mayakovsky*, transl. by Herbert Marshall, London: Dennis Dobson, 1965, p. 137. In Russian: 'Светить всегда, светить везде, до дней последних донца, светить – и никаких гвоздей! Вот лозунг мой – и солнца!'

[246] Isaak Babel, essay 'Odessa', <http://emsu.ru/lm/cc/babel.htm> [accessed 12 December 2013].

life, 'in the manner of Mopassan'.[247] As Marat Grinberg argues, 'Babel's project was incredibly complex and daring: to demoralise Russian language with the French turn of phrase, having interbred a sacred piety of Russian literature with the idolized lust, of Maupassant's heroes'.[248] Hence, 'cruelty and sensuality' of his prose, whose main drive is 'passion rather than love'.[249] However, isn't nostalgia which permeates his 'Tales of Odessa', a part of love? And does not a breath-taking – as it were symphonic – poetic beauty of his texts transcend cruelty even in his 'Red Cavalry' – a description of the military campaign of 1920, with its brutal realities?

Trying to sing praises to the Sun, to inject joy into literature and existence, Babel was turning any little petty thing, any object or anecdote into high art: 'I take a trifle – an anecdote, a market story – and make of it a thing from which I cannot break away myself'.[250] This is precisely the aforementioned skill of Gogol (which the latter regarded a prerequisite for any serious writer), to be able to 'breathe poetry into the most ordinary thing'.[251] This skill, it seems, is akin in spirit to Acmeism, to focusing on a concrete things of earthly life and discovering poetry in them. Yet, Russian Acmeist poets, such as Akhmatova and Gumilev, still tended to fly away into the higher empyrean, having used a particular and tangible as their runway, while Babel could stay with the object until the end, could poetise the earthly without idealizing or sanctifying it. Hence his verbal art is often called 'Rabeliasian'. Or was this because, again, the Judaic in him indeed overpowered the Christian, so that the tormenting body–soul dilemma did not exist, and flesh not only did not have any shame, but had instead a fully fledged life of its own? Indeed, with Babel, it is a celebration of the flesh rather than a tragedy of it. And, as Paustovsky commented on Babel's writings, 'his writings will evoke laughter not because he is funny, but because one always wants to rejoice faced with someone's success'.[252] In part, this sentiment can be repeated about Gogol too – the writer who, unlike Babel, laughs through tears, but who can at the same time be placed next to Babel by his dazzling fantasy and metaphoric thinking. Interestingly, in his 'Peterburgkskii Dnevnik' published in 1918 in Gorky's newspaper 'Novaia zhizn' (notably in opposition to the Bolsheviks), Babel recalls this immortal name, exclaiming about his protagonists, 'How well Gogol would describe them!'[253] Another affinity of Babel is, unexpectedly, with Platonov – in the broken language of uneducated protagonists who try to express their extreme emotions, but also more generally – in new meanings born out of a new vision (in turn, brewed on the new Russian reality), full of associations linked by poetic metaphors rather than by causality.[254]

---

[247]　Gandlevsky, 'Gibel s muzykoi (o Babele)', op. cit.

[248]　Grinberg, 'V drugom izmerenii: Gorenshtein i Babel', op. cit.

[249]　Gandlevsky, 'Gibel s muzykoi (o Babele)', op. cit.

[250]　See Konstantin Paustovsky, 'Rasskazy o Babele', <http://www.avtoram.com/paustovskiI_rasskazy_o_babele> [accessed 14 February 2014].

[251]　This quotation from Grabovsky was already given earlier in connection to Gogol himself.

[252]　Paustovsky, 'Rasskazy o Babele', op. cit.

[253]　See Isaak Babel, *Peterburgskii Dnevnik*, Moscow: Prospekt, 2013.

[254]　There is no room here to go into detail on this rather fascinating theme. For further discussions on this affinity, see, for instance, Artemii Magun (one of a number of scholars publishing on this topic), 'Otritsatelnaia revoliutsiia Andreia Platonova', in *NLO*, 2010, No. 106, <http://magazines.russ.ru/nlo/2010/106/ma7.html> [accessed 12 December 2014].

Gandlevsky contrasts Babel's 'Tales of Odessa' and their mythical hero Benia Krik, a romantic gangster and mob leader, with another legendary fictional character – the Grand Schemer Ostap Bender, created by the writing brotherhood of Ilya Ilf and Evgenii Petrov, Babel's contemporaries, in their satirical dilogy 'Dvenadtsat stuliev' ('Twelve Chairs') and 'Zolotoi telenok' ('Golden Calf'). 'The Odessa cycle had been created during a decade, and, along the line, the author as well as the characters of his heroes undergo substantial changes, therefore the reader may get the impression that it is strangers that feature under the familiar names. The protagonists of the writers from Odessa, who are also literary relatives – Benia Krik and Ostap Bender – develop in opposite directions. Bender becomes more and more humane and charismatic from chapter to chapter of the dilogy, whereas Benia Krik degenerates and stops evoking compassion.'[255]

The uniting feature of these works, however, is situated more on the artistic than philosophical–ethical plane – they are verbal masterpieces, to such a degree rooted in their literary craft, in the unique choice of words and the unique way of linking them together, that translating these works into another language, be it a human language or, say, a language of cinema is a highly problematic and ultimately unfulfilable task. Thus Babel's poetics unites, probably in equal parts, other art forms such as music and painting. His texts are designed with the same musical metric size as 'poetry proper' and require analogous breathing rhythm when read out loud. Equally, his colours are tangibly rich, almost protuberant in their glare. Therefore in screening Babel's writings, the camera-man job, and possibly that of a composer, are highly important for approximating the ethos of the original, even though in this case no non-verbal means can equal the verbal intricacy of the original. By the same token, in Ilf and Petrov, the text is so densely rich and unique in its own right that it is lost in translation into cinematography. For example, the following 'exchange of smiles' between Bender and Koreiko compared in the text with a musical score of Franz Liszt is so tightly dependent on the verbal art that it is intrinsically impossible to act it out even by the most genius of actors:

'Citizen Koreiko?', Ostap asked, beaming. 'It's me', said Alexander Ivanovich, also showing joy at meeting with a representative of the authorities. 'Alexander Ivanovich?', Ostap enquired, smiling even more radiantly. 'Exactly so', confirmed Koreiko, as much as possible fueling his joy. After that, the great schemer could only sit on the bentwood chair and inflict on his face a superhuman smile. Having done all this, he looked at Alexander Ivanovich. But the millionaire-clerk stiffened and displayed devil knows what: affection, delight, admiration, and silent adoration; and all this because of the happy encounter with a representative of the authorities. The build-up of smiles and feelings, that was taking place, was reminiscent of the score of the composer Franz Liszt, where the first page specified to play 'fast', the second – 'very fast', the third – 'much faster', the forth 'as fast as possible', and still the fifth – 'even faster'. Seeing that Koreiko reached the fifth page and further competition is impossible, Ostap got down to business.[256]

[255] Gandlevsky, 'Gibel s muzykoi (o Babele)', op. cit.
[256] Ilya Ilf and Evgenii Petrov, *Zolotoi telenok*, <http://lib.ru/ILFPETROV/telenok.txt> [accessed 12 January 2014].

That is why, in my view, screening the dilogy presents an eternal challenge, and the existing multiple attempts, although provide an entertaining cinema, are still an example of a failure, as at worst they are doomed to drop several levels down from their literary source to end up with a simplified vaudeville of sorts, or at best they are high examples of comedy, but of little resemblance to the literary original.

As opposed to Benia Krik, Ostap Bender never uses force, just his wits. Among his literary predecessors one can, arguably, find, apart from Benia, also 'pícaro of a picaresque novel, witty crooks of O. Henry [. . .] the noble Count of Monte-Cristo, a superfluous man of Russian literature [. . .], the detective-intellectual Sherlock Holmes and demonic philosopher-provocateur Julio Jurenito'.[257] However, despite him being the Grand Schemer with '400 relatively honest ways of relieving people off their money',[258] his nucleus is not pragmatic, for his artistism easily defeats his pragmatism. Indeed, the process is, clearly, far more important to Ostap than the result, for he is by nature a gambler and a romantic; a rogue, but an irrational one. 'He is, in his own way, a poet, a philosopher and even something of an aesthete.'[259] Something similar can be said of Benia Krik, an opportunist, admired by Babel (whose own lyrical hero sees life as 'a meadow in May, walked over only by women and horses',[260] and whose poetry gets transmitted into his characters). Equally, for Ostap Bender life is a game of chance, wit and inspiration. He mirrors the scepticism, verve and wit of his creators who 'were young and merry, and their joint irreverence kept their eye clear and their tongue sharp';[261] and whose youth coincided with the youth of the revolutionized country.

Conceived as a topical novel, 'Twelve chairs', as well as its sequel, spilled far beyond the scope of immediate contemporality, and just as is the case with most immortal texts, for instance with 'Don Quixote' by Miguel de Cervantes Saavedra, turned out to gain depth and dimension that dramatically exceeded its topicality, to which it was thus tied only very tentatively. Rebelling against anything routine and down-to-earth, Ostap's spirit is close to that captured in one of the first songs of the amateur songs movement which gained momentum in the 1960s. This song was almost Bender's contemporary, written in 1937 by Pavel Kogan (with the music by Georgii Lepsky). It conveyed a distinctly romantic ethos, the philosophy which also reflects that of Ostap despite his trickster's activities: 'We are drinking to those vehement and unruly, who despise petty comfort . . . // [. . .] Filibusters and adventurers, // Brothers in blood, hot and thick'.[262] However, another song also springs to mind in Bender's context – Okudzhava's 'Kakoe nebo goluboe!' – the song of the famous rogues Fox Alisa and Cat Basilio from 'Buratino' ('Pinoccio') who exploit other people's inferior wit: 'while there are fools in this world,

[257] Aleksandr Zholkovsky, 'Iskusstvo prisposobleniia', <http://www-bcf.usc.edu/~alik/rus/ess/isk-prisp-11.htm> [accessed 21 February 2014].
[258] Ilf and Petrov, op. cit.
[259] Lesley Milne, 'Jokers, Rogues and innocents: Types of comic hero and author from Bulgakov to Pelevin', in Milne (ed.), *Reflective Laughter. Aspects of Humour in Russian Culture*, op. cit., p. 88.
[260] See Isaak Babel, 'Istoriia odnoi loshadi', <http://militera.lib.ru/prose/russian/babel/18.html> [accessed 12 March 2014].
[261] Ibid.
[262] Pavel Kogan, 'Brigantina', <http://rupoem.ru/kogan/all.aspx#nadoelo-govorit-i> [accessed 13 March 2014]. In Russian: 'Пьём за яростных, за непокорных, // За презревших грошевой уют . . . // [. . .] Флибустьеры и авантюристы, // Братья по крови горячей и густой'.

we will always profit from being tricksters.'[263] These two hypostases of Ilf's and Petrov's protagonist, taken together, place him indeed (though not without reservations) in the long line of Russian 'superfluous people', only in this case parodying a morally dubious romantic hero, a lonely peak over the dull surroundings (even though a great majority of them, in contrast to Bender, prefer – with a few exceptions – reflection to action).

At the same time, for Aleksandr Zholkovsky, what underpins Bender's world as well as that of the authors is a boundless social mimicry, a parody of the surrounding reality, the art of supermimicry as a platform for a peculiar kind of independence. 'Ostap parodies the world around him [. . .], tries on all possible masks, pushes together, uses and mocks all possible cliché, pre-revolutionary as well as Soviet, joining in this his creators. [. . .] Ostap goes through the Soviet world as a knight of the Bourgeois Countenance, who draws, like Don Quixote, his values from the idealised historical past, but who turns out to be head and shoulders above his surroundings. The point is not, as one sometimes writes, that Ostap is a charismatic conman, but that he is a charismatic individualist, in the extreme: a charismatic anti-Soviet, only his charisma is spiced with a strong pro-Soviet sauce.'[264] Thus for Zholkovsky, Ostap Bender and his authors represent a perfect case of mediation, an interplay between the subversive and ideologically loyal. Such mediators, Zholkovsky writes, 'always mixed in with the official voice some alien notes, introducing an element of polyphony into the monotonous sound of the state ideology. Thus they were loosening a totalitarian dogma, assisting the ideological and artistic re-education of the readers. Maybe Ostap Bender was the first who pushed many onto the path of emigration and dissidence?'[265] By the same token, Zholkovsky imagines Bender as a contemporary Chichikov, a trickster who is 'thrown out of real life and loses all that he strives for'.[266]

However, what is vital, in my view, is not Ostap's capitalist enterprising skills – which are secondary – but his adventurous spirit, his addiction to life as a game – which are primary. In this semantic range Chichikov's archetype is clearly out of place, as in Chichikov's personality, in contrast to Bender's, calculation suppresses feelings. The joy of risk, a search for an immediate gratification, trying to outwit the world in the game of chance – these are Bender's qualities which place him directly into Russian literary genealogy, despite his 'Oriental' origins, and make him of particular interest in our exploration of Russian irrationalism within Russian humour.

Lermontov's lines neatly describe this sensibility: 'Whatever Voltaire or Descartes might have been saying, for me the world is a deck of cards, life is the bank, fate deals, I play and apply the rules of the game to people';[267] although the connection here between Lermontov and Ilf and Petrov is akin to that between tragedy and farce. Thus

---

[263]   Bulat Okudzhava, 'Vtoraia pesnia Lisy Alisy i kota Bazilio' ('Poka zhivut na svete khvastuny . . .', ili 'Kakoe nebo goluboe! . . .'), <http://www.pseudology.org/songs/Buratino.htm> [accessed 14 March 2014]. In Russian: 'Пока живут на свете дураки, обманом жить нам стало быть с руки'.

[264]   Zholkovsky, 'Iskusstvo prisposobleniia', op. cit.

[265]   Ibid.

[266]   Ibid.

[267]   Lermontov, *Sochineniia v 6 tomakh*, op. cit., vol. 5, 1956, p. 339. In Russian: 'Что ни толкуй Вольтер или Декарт – Мир для меня – колода карт, Жизнь – банк; рок мечет, я играю И правила игры я к людям применяю'.

even closer in spirit to Bender's sensibility are Yulii Kim's lines written specially for Ostap (in the 1976 screen adaptation of 'Twelve chairs'): 'Agree with me – it's such a pleasure to get straight to the target almost without aiming' and 'Oh, what joy it is to walk the edge. Angels, stay still and look – I am playing. Leave the judgement of my sins for now, just appreciate the beauty of the game.'[268]

A very important mechanism is at play here, which explains in particular Ostap's drive – it is the mechanism of gambling as a 'model of human wrestling with Unknown Factors.'[269]

As Lotman notes in connection to Pushkin's 'Queen of Spades', Western-European plot-lines tended to explore the logical patterns, while Russian plots were preoccupied more with the accidental. 'The former concerned with the immanent nature of the money century, the latter – with the excesses that it generated.'[270] Thus, Lotman writes, 'in the plotlines pertaining to Russian reality there is one more link introduced between social causes and plot consequences. This link is fortuity, "events which may or may not occur as a result of an experiment"'.[271] That is why in Russian texts the idea of becoming rich is traditionally linked to a card game or a fraud, a con. Such a conman's game with all the beauty of its artistic performance and walking a tight-rope above the abyss of the mundane is what Ostap Bender is about.

Indeed, 'the same mechanism of the game serves different purposes as well: in the external world it serves as a manifestation of the superior rules, which are irrational only from the point of view of human ignorance; in the internal world it is predicated not only on a thirst for money, but also on a need for risk, a necessity to de-automatise life and to open up space for a game of forces suppressed by the burden of the daily routine.'[272] It is thus 'a mechanism of introducing to the everyday an element of alternative, unpredictability, and de-automatisation.'[273] In this light, Lotman suggests a division into 'alive (mobile and changeable), and dead (motionless and automated)',[274] with a possibility of these categories interchanging in certain circumstances. Thus either the everyday world is ordered, rational and opposed to the 'chaotic world of the irrational, of chance and game' which constitutes entropy; or on the contrary, it is the everyday world which represents entropy by being 're-ordered, inflexible, dead' and opposed to a Chance – a 'powerful, immediate weapon of the Providence' which intrudes into the mechanical existence, animating it.[275] These two models interact not only at the outer level of the plot, but also in the inner worlds of the heroes.

---

[268] Yulii Kim, 'Net, ia ne plachu . . .', <http://www.bards.ru/archives/part.php?id=6108> [accessed 18 January 2014]. In Russian: 'Ведь согласитесь, какая прелесть Мгновенно в яблочко попасть – почти не целясь' and 'О наслажденье – ходить по краю. Замрите, ангелы, смотрите – я играю. Разбор грехов моих оставьте до поры. Вы оцените красоту игры'.

[269] Lotman, '"Pikovaia dama" i tema kart i kartochnoi igry v russkoi literature XIX veka', op. cit., pp. 389–415.

[270] Ibid.

[271] Ibid. The quotation given by Lotman is from A. Yaglom and I. Yaglom, *Veroiatnost i informatsiia*, 3rd edition, Moscow: Nauka, 1973, pp. 21–2.

[272] Ibid.

[273] Ibid.

[274] Ibid.

[275] Ibid.

In our context, Bender clearly embodies this drive for animating the dead and mechanical aspects of existence, and yet, as in Lotman's analysis, his very game may become a deadening and mechanical factor when it comes into a conflict with the higher order of human feelings and morality. Thus when Bender rejects Zosia, the girl he had fallen in love with, he is defeated by the inertia of his own game, which makes him spurn the authentic.

What is conceptually important here is that, in the same vein, 'it is precisely the faith in a motiveless nature and suddenness of salvation that Dostoevsky regards as a typically Russian feature'.[276] In this sense, a '"terrible thirst for risk" is a typically Russian psychological feature, and a "roulette is a game predominantly Russian" based on the striving to "change one's entire destiny" "at once".[277] Dostoevsky focuses on the 'antithesis of a bourgeois money-making of Europe and Russian striving to change one's destiny "at once": "Why is a game worse than any other method of acquiring money, say, for instance a trade?"'[278] speculates Dostoevsky's hero, but, notably, views both tendencies as equally repulsive.

*   *   *

Renaissance of Russian humour during and after the Thaw: Sergei Dovlatov and Venedikt Erofeev: Sad smile and purifying sob

The official 'humour', produced and approved by the system, when totalitarian regime had firmly settled in, was confined either to a forced laughter or a toothless satire – on carefully chosen petty topics. As in the Oriental type despotism, 'on the outside everything is sparkling, beautiful and eternal; on the inside, at the same time, there are horrors'.[279] As Stalin famously commented himself, 'Life has become better, life has become merrier.' And this bloody carnival, as Averintsev described Stalin's, and, more generally, any despotic rule, was decorated by a stream of most sweet and cheerful comedy-films, portraying precisely that, non-existent, 'sparkling, beautiful and eternal' coating. The Thaw and its subsequent decline saw a steady increase of the anecdote culture, as well as of the 'Amateur Song Movement' (which, in its humorous strand, in many ways echoed the liberating character of an anecdote), as powerful valves for the sanity of national consciousness and survival of national cultural spirit.

As a natural reaction to the degree of hypocrisy and faithlessness, if you like as an antidote of sorts against political demagogy, against the false and discredited pathos, there was an upsurge of irony, including self-irony, which became dominant not only in Russia, but also generally in the cruel historical context of much of the twentieth century. In fact, self-irony became a necessary prerequisite of a noble personality. The

---

[276] Ibid.
[277] Ibid., the quotations from Dostoevsky are from Dostoevsky, *Polnoe sobranie sochinenii v 30 tomakh*, op. cit., vol. 5, 1973, pp. 294, 317 and 318, respectively.
[278] Ibid (including the quotation from Dostoevsky, op. cit., p. 216).
[279] Lev Shestov, 'Dostoevsky i Nitzshe: Filosofiia tragedii', op. cit., p. 369.

figure of an ironic individual acquired a distinct romantic aura captured by the poet Yuri Levitansky. In his famous poem 'Ironic Person', he describes the latter as essentially heroic, always ready to sacrifice himself for others while never stepping out of the shadow; the one who maintains dignity in our tragic age using irony as his shield. Yet, at both ends of the century one could find an opposition of sorts, as the Blok-Zamiatin opposition described earlier, between the irony as dignified resistance, and the irony as all-permissiveness, or as a form of despair. Nevertheless, the main ethos of the irony and laughter in the late Soviet period was a total and excruciating deconstruction of pathos, of the stifling hypocrisy and lies of the officialdom, because the need to restore the time which 'went out of joint', using Hamlet's expression, was pressing.

Also, by contrast to the beginning of the century with its social and artistic experiments, its search for new religions and new forms, the end of it felt acutely the ultimate bankruptcy of the attempts to bend art to any non-artistic aims – either political or self-promotional, of the futility of worshipping pure form, divorcing it from the ethical nucleus with its religious origins. In other words, before the next crisis – marked by post-modernism – the renaissance was strong. Thus in Vasilii Shukshin's and Vladimir Vysotsky's oeuvre the motifs from Russian history, from folk sources, from ancient and classical traditions are so distinctly audible.

Such continuity with the classical tradition, enriched with modernity, with self-irony extended to a genre in its own right, and having absorbed the anecdote culture, is to be found in the writings of Sergei Dovlatov. Not published in his homeland, effectively forced into exile, Dovlatov, with a bitter irony of fate, found recognition in the West, published in the prestigious *New-Yorker*, and then, with *perestroika*, made his way to his Russian readers, among which he is now, posthumously, has become something of a cult figure. His works exemplify precisely Aikhenvald's point earlier about a deep intrinsic proximity of the sad and the funny. Although Dovlatov always wanted, in his own words, 'to resemble Chekhov',[280] and the proximity between them in both ethical and aesthetic terms, as I argue elsewhere,[281] is indeed strongly present, there is also a clear continuity of the Gogolean 'laughter through tears' tradition, as Dovlatov's lyrical hero is akin to a sad circus clown who is telling us how funnily tragic our life is, how we make a right mess of it, and tears are going down his smiling face. 'Because of the tears I lost my vision for a moment. . . .'[282] says Dovlatov at the end of a farce about convicts staging a play on the Russian revolutionaries. In the same vein, Fazil Iskander called him 'a writer so smiling and so sad',[283] and Joseph Brodsky borrowed for the title

[280] Sergei Dovlatov, 'Zapisnye knizhki', op. cit., p. 271.
[281] See Olga Tabachnikova, '"The world is ugly and people are sad". On Chekhov's ethics and aesthetics in the works of Sergei Dovlatov', *Essays in Poetics*, vol. 31, Autumn 2006, pp. 319–54, as well as 'Ot Chekhova k Dovlatovu: Proslavlenie bestsel'nosti, Ili Poetika, okazyvaiushchaiia soprotivlenie tiranii', in Anatolii Sobennikov (ed.), *Filosofiia A. P. Chekhova*, op. cit., pp. 238–56. Here I only give a sketchy summary of some of the ideas expressed in the earlier publications.
[282] Sergei Dovlatov, 'Zona', in *Sobranie prozy v 3 tomakh*, op. cit., vol. I, p. 154.
[283] Fazil Iskander, Afterword to *Sergei Dovlatov, Rasskazy*, Renessans, Moskva, 1991, p. 331.

of his piece on Dovlatov the words of the American poet Wallace Stevens: 'The world is ugly and people are sad.'[284] By the same token, Andrei Arev summarized the nucleus of Dovlatov's prose in a neat formula – 'There is laughter, where there is weeping', and explained, 'This is not a fable about a fool who confused burial with wedding. It is the content and meaning of the prose of Sergei Dovlatov, one of the most intelligent prose writers of recent times. All his "funny stories" are told for people who know what "invisible to the world, unwitnessed tears" are.'[285]

Striving 'to look, and in general to correspond to that perception of an honourable person which have developed' in him 'under the influence of the literature of Chekhov and Zoshchenko',[286] Dovlatov created a lyrical hero who, within the autobiographism of Dovlatov's writings, reflects the author's perception of the unattainable human ideal borrowed from Chekhov's oeuvre. This ideal in many ways captures the interpretation of Chekhov as 'a writer of delicately and deeply concealed inner courage',[287] as a 'knight of dignity and knight of shame',[288] where dignity and shame 'are the working instruments of a personality',[289] and democracy of vision is a sign of real inner freedom.

Thus Chekhov's Gromov from 'Ward No. 6' despises idle preaching of general good and condescending dismissal of suffering as simply a philosophy most suitable to a 'typical lackadaisical Russian', and believes that laziness and the spineless character are true reasons for apathy, for the aspiration to 'arrange things so that nothing bothered you or budged you from the spot'.[290] In other words, Gromov's accusation implies that idealistic philosophizing in reality turns into criminal indifference. The same idea is expressed by Dovlatov with respect to general attempts at moralizing: 'The world, as we know is imperfect. [. . .] Instead of the desirable harmony, chaos and disorder reign on Earth. [. . .] What does a moralist do in this situation? He is [. . .] trying to achieve harmony; only not in life, but in his own soul instead – by the way of self-improvement. Very important in this case is to avoid confusion between harmony and indifference'.[291] This is an example not only of Dovlatov's recoil from preaching and moralizing of any kind, but also of his shrewd and ironic stance. At the same time, Dovlatov's lyrical hero continues the line of numerous unassuming Chekhov's characters in his longing for personal peace and quiet (as a sort of harmony with the world as divine creation), and in his fear to disturb something in the universe by his own existence: 'When I was a child I had a nunny, Luiza Genrikhovna' – Dovlatov

[284] Iosif Brodsky, 'O Serezhe Dovlatove: "Mir urodliv i liudi grustny"', in Sergei Dovlatov, *Sobranie prozy v 3 tomakh*, op. cit., vol. III, pp. 355–62.

[285] Andrei Arev, 'Iistoriia rasskazchika', <http://www.sergeidovlatov.com/books/ariev3.html> [accessed 13 March 2014]. The reference is to Gogol who thus characterized his authorial approach to life and writing in his poem *Dead Souls* (vol. I, chapter 7).

[286] Sergei Dovlatov, *Epistolyarnyj Roman s Igorem Yefimovym*, Zakharov, Moskva, 2001, p. 436.

[287] Fazil Iskander, 'Poet', in Iskander, *Siuzhet sushestvovanija*, op. cit., p. 130.

[288] Andrei Bitov, a shortened version of his essay 'My Grandfather Chekhov and Great-Grandfather Pushkin', *Novaia Gazeta*, 12 July 2004, No. 49.

[289] Ibid.

[290] Anton Chekhov, 'Ward No. 6', in Chekhov, *Ward No. 6 and Other Stories*, Oxford, New York: Oxford University Press, 1988, p. 49.

[291] Sergei Dovlatov, *Sobranie prozy v 3 tomakh*, op. cit., vol. I, p. 56.

writes in his collection *Chemodan* – 'She did everything absent-mindedly because she was afraid to be arrested. Once she was getting me dressed in short trousers, and placed both my legs in the space for one. As a result I walked like that all day .. . . I remember plenty of such stories. Since my childhood I would endure anything just to escape unnecessary hassle.'[292]

This is Dovlatov's self-irony at work – making oneself a target of laughter, while displaying a seriously unassuming stance, an absence of any exceptionalism as a life credo; walking a tight rope between various extremes, such as harmony and absurdity, humour and despair, while, at the same time, remarkably, 'his heroes are burning as brightly as the heroes of Dostoevsky only in a much more frivolous hell.'[293] Yet, 'it is as if he does not demand attention to himself, does not maintain his conclusions or his observations on human nature, he does not force himself on the reader,'[294] and his self-irony serves as an anti-dot against any attempts of making the author superior. For the generally didactic Russian literature, this is a rare quality which sends us once again back to Chekhov and Pushkin – to the writers who 'lived out their lives [. . .] as a private matter of no concern to anyone else. And now, this private matter turns out to be of general concern.'[295] Just as Chekhov, Dovlatov almost never openly ascends to universal topics, and yet, for him, as for Chekhov, they are all present in abundance in the daily routine, and, 'like a genius actor on the stage', Dovlatov 'saves any hopeless role.'[296]

This quality of self-ironic non-didacticism, of trying to understand in order to understand rather than in order to judge, is responsible for the distinctly therapeutic effect of Dovlatov's prose, and grows from his infinite compassion for individual existence which he sees in all its vulnerable absurdity. Thus in 'Kompromiss' ('The Compromise') when talking about human insanity he writes: 'Over time it seems increasingly normal to me, whereas the norm is becoming unnatural.'[297] Equally, in 'Zapovednik'('Pushkin Hills') we read, '. . . the world is seized with insanity. Insanity is becoming a norm. The norm evokes the sensation of a miracle'.[298] The same absurdity is present in his prison camp collection 'Zona' where the camp is conceived, in a typically Dovlatov's manner, as a portrayal of equality – in the sense of a striking similarity between 'a prison camp and the outside world'.[299]

Thus, if you like, in Dovlatov's world the irrationalism of being is accepted as the norm, and the hero succumbs to this irrationalism, allowing it to absorb him, but without losing sight of it, keeping his faculties of observation fully intact. And an almost Kharms-like absurdity is once again filled in Dovlatov's works with higher meaning by being intensely ethically charged. At the same time, Dovlatov displays the irrational

[292] Ibid., vol. II, p. 306.
[293] Adam Gussov, quoted in ibid., p. 16.
[294] Iosif Brodsky, 'O Serezhe Dovlatove: "Mir urodliv i liudi grustny"', in Sergei Dovlatov, *Sobranie prozy v 3 tomakh*, op. cit., vol. III, p. 359.
[295] Boris Pasternak, *Doctor Zhivago*, New York City: Pantheon Books, 1958.
[296] Andrei Arev, 'Nasha malenkaia zhizn', op. cit., p. 17.
[297] Sergei Dovlatov, *Sobranie prozy v 3 tomakh*, op. cit., vol. I, p. 271.
[298] Ibid., p. 410.
[299] Ibid., p. 62.

strivings of the human soul which are not grounded in any tangible underlying causes, and arise organically, almost as a 'fatal feature of organic matter'.[300]

Dovlatov's aesthetics fully corresponds to his ethics. His style is at once profoundly poetic and severely self-disciplined (e.g. one of his self-imposed rules was never to have in one sentence two words beginning with the same letter). As Brodsky put it, 'in hindsight it is clear that he was aspiring to a laconic, lapidary style inherent in poetic speech: to the extreme conciseness of expression.'[301] This is akin to the simplicity of Pushkin about which D. H. Thomas said: 'His most moving lines are often so simple that we do not know why we are moved.'[302] However, this severe self-discipline and economy of expression closed for Dovlatov a possibility of extended metaphors in the style of Gogol, or even of Chekhov. Instead his style allowed a deployment of no more than single phrases which Dovlatov often joined together into an ascending intensifying sequence. He thus wriggled out of the self-imposed restraints of his own unique genre of self-irony by using short metaphors in a multilevel or nuclear chain-like manner – when every subsequent sentence deepens and specifies the previous one building up the mockery within it. For example, in the description of the author's cousin Boris in the 'Nashi' ('Ours: A Russian Family Album') collection Dovlatov writes: 'He was reminiscent of Levin from "Anna Karenina". On the verge of his wedding Levin was tormented by the fact of his lost virginity in his youth. My brother was tortured by an analogous problem. Namely, can one become a communist having a criminal conviction? Old communists assured him that one can . . .'.[303]

Another poetic principle of Dovlatov's style is his rather Chekhovian great attention to detail, which he drew in part from his musical afflictions: 'an admirer of jazz improvisations from his youth, Dovlatov wrote his prose following internally not so much the main theme, but its variations.'[304]

Igor Sukhikh, the author of a monograph on Dovlatov, draws a parallel between him and Venedikt Erofeev,[305] the creator of 'Moskva-Petushki' and of other gems. In his view, 'in the last, already passed, literary era, there are no two writers, it seems, closer than these – with all their differences that follow from their initial profound kinship.'[306] One of the fundamental organizing principles of their prose Sukhikh sees in the 'anecdotal-like vision' of both writers, where 'an anecdote is a cell, a unit and a starting point of the narrative.'[307] Other similarities, in his view, include blurring of the boundaries between life and literature, an auto-psychological character of their writings, and a subtle and precise work with the language. At the same time, Sukhikh

---

[300] A phrase from Fazil Iskander's story 'Nachalo', op. cit., p. 26.

[301] Iosif Brodsky, 'O Serezhe Dovlatove: "Mir urodliv i liudi grustny"', in Sergei Dovlatov, *Sobranie prozy v 3 tomakh*, op. cit., vol. III, p. 358.

[302] Donald Michael Thomas (trans.), Introduction to *Pushkin, The Bronze Horseman and Other Poems*, Harmondsworth, Middlesex, England: Penguin Books, 1982, p. 27.

[303] Sergei Dovlatov, *Sobranie prozy v 3 tomakh*, op. cit., vol. II, p. 211.

[304] Andrei Arev, 'Nasha malenkaia zhizn', op. cit., p. 21.

[305] Igor Sukhikh, 'Dovlatov i Erofeev: sosedi po alfavitu', <http://www.sergeidovlatov.com/books/suhih.html> [accessed 11 March 2014].

[306] Ibid.

[307] Ibid.

stresses two major distinctions of Dovlatov and Erofeev – stylistic and ideological. The distinctions are indeed major, to the point of pushing similarities to the background, if not rendering them altogether illusory. However, this illusion, in my view, is easily created. Indeed, what Dovlatov and Erofeev undoubtedly do share is an extreme striving to anti-pathos which provides a feeling of a common ground. This striving is realized through the use of a 'descending metaphor', through the laughter at the 'broken washtub'[308] of their personal and of our common destiny – laughter through tears of the horrifying Russian history. It is also, arguably, stems from the fact that both writers exemplify the third type of irrationalism, described in the Introduction, and touched upon just now, in connection to Dovlatov – the most characteristically Russian type: a pure form of irrationalism, an illogical, unreasonable, inexplicable anguish, a seemingly groundless torment of the soul, rather than a reaction against a frontal attack of rationalism (as an opposition to the Enlightenment ideas) or the irrationalism as the other side of rationalism which exceeded any sensible boundaries. As we saw earlier, this peculiar causeless type is also inherent most visibly in the writings of two other contemporaries of Erofeev and Dovlatov – namely, Shukshin and Vysotsky.

The name of Venedikt Erofeev emerged as a major literary phenomenon that crossed the sky of Russian literature precisely in the manner of a 'lawless comet among the calculated luminaries'.[309] To Dovlatov's courageous self-irony and 'organic spitelessness',[310] to his extreme economy of expression, Erofeev juxtaposed a continuous exhale, unrestricted and boundless purifying sob. In his streaming words which unburden the soul he goes even further than irony – into Holy-Foolishness and jester-type behaviour – in order to free himself of any falsehood and to speak out his non-subdued mind. As Vladimir Murav'ev notes, '*Moskva-Petushki* is a profoundly religious book'; its religiosity is in the 'constant presence of a higher power, an attempt to live up to it, and the rejection of a legalistic manner of fulfilling this by just following the instructions'.[311] Sukhikh elaborates on these claims by observing that 'whatever the specific relationship with this power, in Erofeev's book it is present as a dominant meaningful entity. The poem's heroes are not only [. . .] occupants of the suburban train's carriage, but also angels, Satan and God, who, although He does not come to the rescue of the hero and remains silent, but is still incorporated into the picture of the world', and more generally, 'Erofeev's picture of the world is vertical, as in medieval

---

[308] This is a metaphor drawn from Pushkin's famous tale of 'The Fisherman and his golden fish' ('Skazka o rybake i rybke'), where the fisherman's greedy wife kept making increasingly more ambitious wishes until her greed was punished by returning her to her initial status – sitting by her broken washtub. Here the process of excessive demands is irrelevant, but the reference is merely to the hopelessness of the initial state which is never surpassed.

[309] A phrase from Aleksandr Pushkin's poem 'Portret' (1828) (see Pushkin, *Sobranie sochinenii v 10 tomakh*, op. cit., vol. 2, 1959, p. 216). In Russian: 'беззаконная комета В кругу расчисленном светил'.

[310] Part of the phrase 'Дар органического беззлобия' ('the gift of organic spitelessness'), which was used by the writer Viktor Erofeev as a title of the interview he conducted with Sergei Dovlatov for the literary journal *Ogonek* (published in No. 24, 1990).

[311] Quoted in Igor Sukhikh, 'Dovlatov i Erofeev: sosedi po alfavitu', op. cit.

Mysterium.'[312] Thus, Sukhikh concludes, '"Moskva-Petushki" is indeed a Mysterium on the suffering of the human soul.'[313]

As I argued,[314] Venedikt Erofeev, although different temperamentally, can be placed in the same literary row as the irrationalist philosophical writer Lev Shestov and neo-romantic poet Marina Tsvetaeva – in their philosophy of tragedy and discomfort, in their total absence of defensive mechanisms, in their almost conscious, almost intentional inability to live, to inscribe yourself into the world order (in Shestov's case – philosophically, in Tsvetaeva's case – quite literally).

In the same way as Natalia Ivanova described Dovlatov's writings and their enigma, borrowing Pasternak's lines: 'разгадке жизни равносилен' ('equal to the solution of the mystery of life itself'),[315] I. Fomenko wrote on the mystery of Erofeev's 'Moskva-Petushki', 'the poem's enigma is in the fact that *any* reading of it is convincing and does not contradict other interpretations. It overthrows familiar treatment of interpretations as versions of a certain invariant, because it does not contain a dominant (or, at any rate, it has not been found hitherto). It can be understood this way or that way, and all will be "correct", convincing, grounded and will not conflict with other readings.'[316] As Fomenko notes, 'The text easily responds to any approach: it can be read as a parody [. . .], as tragic irony dressed in a guise of the carnivalesque comedy [. . .], as a travesty text [. . .], as a unity of two autonomous principles – parodic and personal', and at the same time its 'structure-forming principle can be traced to both Gogolean [. . .] and Biblical [. . .] stratum.'[317] Moreover, 'The narrative is constructed in such a way that the boundaries between being and otherness, dream and life, visionary and reality [. . .], between the concrete meaning of the word, daily authenticity of an episode, and symbol are indistinguishable. The poem is constantly flickering, playing with its meanings. In other words (roughly speaking) it behaves as lyrical poetry.'[318]

Thus once again we face a striking proximity between humour and poetry, with all the irrationality of evasive and mutually non-exclusive poetic meanings, and also observe a continuity of Russian (and broader – European) tradition, fertilized by modernity.

---

[312] Ibid.

[313] Ibid.

[314] See Olga Tabachnikova, 'Poperiok miroporiadka: Lev Shestov, Marina Tsvetaeva i Venedikt Erofeev', *Toronto Slavic Quarterly*, vol. 26, Fall 2008.

[315] Natalia Ivanova, 'Razgadke zhizni ravnosilen', in Moskovskie novosti, 1996, 14–21 January, p. 37.

[316] Igor Fomenko, 'O fenomene "Moskvy-Petushkov": Vmesto predisloviia', in *Literaturnyi tekst: problemy i metody issledovaniia 7, Analiz odnogo proizvedeniia: 'Moskva-Petushki' Ven. Erofeeva*, Volume of conference proceedings, Tver 2001. <http://lib.rus.ec/b/161685/read> [accessed 12 March 2014].

[317] Fomenko refers to the authors of this variety of approaches, naming Anna Komaromi, Valerii Tiupa, Elena Liakhova, Ekaterina Kozitskaia, Nina Pavlova, Samson Broitman, Evgenii Egorov, Georgii Prokhorov and others – all being participants of the above conference dedicated to 'Moskva-Petushki'. See Ibid.

[318] Ibid.

Fazil Iskander: 'Laughter through thought'

A very different writer who, as it were, enlightened the Gogolean 'laughter through tears' by restoring Pushkinian irony and simultaneously enriching a genuine life-affirming humour with profound philosophical thought is Fazil Iskander, a Russian writer of Abkhazian and Persian descent, and a rare for Russian letters example of 'laughter through thought'.

Iskander's humour is born of wisdom, of 'reason brewed on conscience'.[319] In many ways, he is a heir of Pushkin – in his penetrating intelligence and poetic sensibility, in his compassion to a human being, and most of all – in his radiant acceptance of being, with all its good and evil. Perhaps most fruitful approach to understanding Iskander's world is to contrast him with Joseph Brodsky, another voice of genius in Russian literature of the late twentieth century. This has an echo of the juxtaposition of Pushkin and Gogol, suggested by Rozanov, of the 'healthy' and 'diseased' strands, although rather than Gogol, Brodsky better corresponds to Baratynsky, with his disillusioned scepticism. Both of them, Iskander and Brodsky, with their lyrical epos, are in essence philosophers, but their philosophies are, as it were, of different signs. The main feature of Iskander as a writer is his unique moral power. The writer admiring human thought and himself generating profound ideas, he at the same time understands that 'mind without morality is not intelligent, whereas morality is intelligent even without the mind'.[320] He firmly believes that 'the aim of mankind is a good person, and there is not and cannot be another aim'.[321] While Brodsky, if you like, oppresses the reader by the power of his intelligence and by his almost supernatural penetration into the nature of things (looking at our world as if from the yonder and depths of cosmos, as the Moon which equally lights the path of preditor and of prey), Iskander 'oppresses' by the power of his moral stance. It is thus not surprising that they diverge – as we saw in the previous chapter – in the question of what is primary, ethics or aesthetics. For Brodsky, 'aesthetics is the mother of ethics',[322] while for Iskander the ethical perception of the world is older than aesthetic, the good is primary and a 'later splitting of ethics and aesthetics in human consciousness is the result of man's tragic fall'.[323]

Consequently, Iskander's oeuvre is, as it were, a feast of moral strength, a pilgrimage to the unwavering profundity of spirit. This strength is in many ways a product of his upbringing of him growing from his native Abkhazian soil organically, just as a tree or a mountain, of being nourished by the spirit of his native land. His writings, it seems, have absorbed the harmony of nature and the harmony of his national culture, even though Iskander, as a Russophone writer, belongs to Russian letters. The main motif of his oeuvre, in my view, is nostalgia – for his homeland and for childhood, which in his case are one. Consequently, his mighty humour is a corollary of the spiritual health which he absorbed from his early years and from the life of his people. Thus, not by

---

[319] This is a quotation from Iskander's phrase: 'wisdom is intelligence brewed on conscience'. See Fazil Iskander, 'Stoianka cheloveka', <http://lib.ru/FISKANDER/stoyanka.txt> [accessed 14 March 2014].
[320] Iskander, 'Ponemnogu o mnogom. Sluchainye zapiski', op. cit.
[321] Fazil Iskander, 'Utraty', <http://lib.ru/FISKANDER/looses.txt> [accessed 14 March 2014].
[322] See Joseph Brodsky, 'Uncommon visage' (the Nobel Lecture), op. cit.
[323] Iskander, 'Poet', op. cit., p. 143.

content or form, but by the nucleus of his writings Iskander is folkloric, for his wisdom of heart is akin to the wisdom of proverbs, of eternal truths. His works are a celebration of life, a glow of the joy of living. One of Iskander's characters, the protagonist of his novella 'Poet', says, 'one has to try mercilessly to know everything about death that a living person can know, but at the same time one should avoid the motifs of decline. I am myself guilty of this. But in the highest sense such motifs are tactless'.[324] Brodsky clearly satisfied this requirement – he indeed mercilessly knows everything about death. But, as we saw earlier, the same poet from Iskander's novella notes, 'in Brodsky's case everything is inside death – even life itself'.[325] For Iskander, undoubtedly, it is the opposite: everything is inside life, even death. Olga Sedakova inscribed Brodsky's sensibility into the paradigm of the New time, liberated from illusion: '"modern man" [...] in his thoughts has long since outgrown the childishness of hope'.[326] This is, in her words, courage of despair. To this mental make-up Sedakova opposes that of Pushkin which disavows a 'screaming asymmetry of the sceptical view of the mind'[327] and seeks balance where illusion and disillusionment go hand in hand, co-exist peacefully in a stream of life. In this Iskander, again, is very close to Pushkin – in that both, if one can put it like this, trusted life.

Yet, the courage in the face of despair, as in Brodsky's case, underpins also Iskander's stance. After all his definition of humour involves peeping into the black abyss, realizing that it is empty and slowly going back, leaving the trace which alone deserves to be called a real humour. So Brodsky and Iskander both agree on the vision of the dark pit of nothingness, only it prompts one to sardonic scepticism of despair and the other to life-affirming humour.

One can attempt to generalize these two sensibilities and two polar approaches to life and creativity, two cases of lyrical epos which their respective oeuvre represent. In the first case the writer represents a sacred holistic world of which he feels an integral part, and which reflects the harmony of national traditions, the clarity and righteousness of the age-old way of life. In the second case (although Brodsky liked repeating, 'I do not represent anybody except myself')[328] we encounter a common to all human catastrophy – of solitude, individualism, a tragic loss of kinship and mental balance. The fact that Brodsky speaks on behalf of *bezvremen'e*, of the gap in cultural and historical development, on behalf of the 'lost generation' is merely a natural continuation of this catastrophy. Equally, Iskander's lyrical hero is forever tormented by his having moved to the city, to metropoly, by thus betraying his roots – which invariably leads to self-destruction. Brodsky, on the contrary, is a child of urbanism, and the tragic disunity of people which depresses Iskander in a big city is for Brodsky his native element. Thus we have here multiple pairs of opposites, hiddenly debating

---

[324]   Ibid.
[325]   Ibid.
[326]   Olga Sedakova, 'Mysl Aleksandra Pushkina', <http://www.pravmir.ru/mysl-aleksandra-pushkina/> [accessed 11 March 2014].
[327]   Ibid.
[328]   See Brodsky's interview ('Ia nikogo ne predstavliaiu, krome samogo sebia') given to Michael Scammell, *Journal Index on Censorship*, No. 3/4, Autumn–Winter 1972, in Polukhina (ed.), *Iosif Brodskii. Bolshaia kniga interviiu*, op. cit., pp. 7–12.

with each other: primacy of ethics versus primacy of aesthetics; full acceptance of life versus preparations for death; homeland, its nature and its ethos of togetherness versus the city, urban individualism and solitude; warm and life-assertive humour of joi de vivre versus a sardonic grin, the courage of stoicism and tragic disillusionment. To an extent it is also the polarity between humility and pride, humour and passion.

As a man of Pushkinian 'cheerful' wisdom, Iskander never rejects reason. But reason for him is indistinguishable from conscience and hence from morality. He exemplifies how intoxicating, how delicious it is to think – that thinking is as enjoyable and powerful as feeling, and, importantly, inseparable from it. Chekhov's words encapsulate this sensibility: 'If you want to become an optimist and to understand life, then stop believing in what others say and write, but instead watch and think for yourself.'[329] Iskander, it seems, did precisely that, and as a result he is showing to us how powerful and lyrical laughter is – laughter as a way of life, 'laughter as a remedy against fear';[330] and how close it is to poetry with its associative nature. In his own words, 'humour is a certain readiness of spirit to an associative jump. You know how one tries to get to the other side of a stream: one person finds rocks to step on, which are sticking out of the water, with difficulty; another – one–two–three – and he is already on the other side. Humour is something similar.'[331]

Undoubtedly, Iskander is a living classic and as such he absorbs and develops the classical tradition. Thus in his writings he unites Pushkinian outlook at life, Tolstoyan scope and striving to the ultimate honesty with oneself, Dostoevsky's preoccupation with 'eternal questions', Chekhovian quiet courage and Gogol's mighty playfulness. However, affiliating himself unequivocally with Russian culture, Iskander also brings to it an archy smile of Hodja Nasreddin, a type of Near-Eastern concealed wisdom, as if oriental folk tradition joins hands with the Russian one, and its epos is thus grafted into Russian literature.

Further on absurdity of life as a source of humour: Satirical novels of Vladimir Voinovich

Another radiant and life-affirming author of the same cohort of those who started coming to prominence from the 1960s and saw the collapse of the Soviet system in the 1980s is Vladimir Voinovich, a creator of the private Ivan Chonkin. Often seen as a Russian relation of the good soldier Shveik, Chonkin is in fact quite different in that he is passive, naïve and totally free of spite or roguery. 'The honest innocent in an absurd world of pretence, conditioned by fear of Stalin and of the secret police',[332] Chonkin

---

[329] Anton Chekhov, 'Zapisnye knizhki. Zapisnaia knizhka IV', in Chekhov, *PSSP v 30 tomakh*, op. cit., vol. 17, 1980, p. 169.

[330] A literary critic Natalia Ivanova entitled her book on Iskander as *Laughter against fear, Fazil Iskander* (Moscow: Sovetskii pisatel, 1991).

[331] Interview with Fazil Iskander, <http://gazeta.aif.ru/_/online/aif/1084/03_01> [accessed 15 February 2014].

[332] Milne, *Reflective Laughter. Aspects of Humour in Russian Culture*, op. cit., p. 92.

is simple-hearted, thorough and amiably ridiculous. He does his utmost to adhere to the rules and to display a diligent service. But since reality is more nonsensical than a caricature, and the rules contradict the hypocritical and incompetent system which nominally declared them, Chonkin finds himself in an endless stream of comic (for the reader rather than the hero) situations born out of this discrepancy, and the resulting effect is, if you like, the irrational of the real. The discrepancy itself has been widely used in Soviet (or rather anti-Soviet) humour (as, for instance, in Dovlatov's 'The Compromise')[333] where a simultaneous display of the real events and their officially intended or portrayed scenario serve as a source of comism, but almost never in the context of war. In this sense, Voinovich broke a new ground by introducing laughter culture to the sacred and intrinsically tragic territory. He caused a lot of controversy and was accused of blasphemy and treachery. His Chonkin, however, is a folkloric figure, and grows out of Russian fairy-tales, from the characters of Ivan-The-Fool and Emelia, discussed earlier, as well as Russian tales about soldiers – restless, simple-minded, but resourceful wanderers. By Voinovich's own admission, 'Chonkin is basically a folk character, and people recognised in him, especially in Soviet times, many features of Soviet existence, which I mocked, and readers also started to realise that it was funny. I did not conceive my soldier to be an idiot. It is just that he found himself in such idiotic situations, which may cause a normal person to become an idiot. And these are our standard Soviet situations.'[334] Chonkin's literal perception of the world around him is at once funny and refreshing, for it reveals the world's absurdity. 'An elementary proximity to real life (given the social–psychological absurdity of that life) guaranteed a powerful satirical effect within the parameters of would-be grotesque and supposed fantasy',[335] noted Tatiana Bek. She ascribed Voinovich's oeuvre to a 'tragic-comic hyper-realism', where the source of the comic lies in the most truthful description of reality.[336] As Iskander once wrote, 'Not everything truthful is funny, but everything funny is always truthful', and moreover 'the funny is indeed funny precisely because it is truthful.'[337] For Bek, the origins of Voinovich's humour, 'unprogrammed and gushing from all intonational gaps' should be sought not only in the poetics of the Russian folk-tale, but also in Gogol, Saltykov-Shchedrin and to an extent in Mark Twain and Yaroslav Gashek.[338]

Unpublishable in Soviet Russia in the 1960s when it was written, the novel on Chonkin was spread underground and then appeared in the West in two volumes, 'The Life and Extraordinary Adventures of Private Ivan Chonkin' (or, 'Untouchable Person') and its sequal 'Pretender to the Throne', 5 years apart (1975, 1979). As a result, in 1980 Voinovich was exiled from the Soviet Union. With the collapse of communism, the

[333] See Sergei Dovlatov, 'Kompromiss', in Dovlatov, *Sobranie prozy v 3 tomakh*, op. cit.
[334] Interview with Vladimir Voinovich (*Rossiiskaia Gazeta*, 21.06.2012), <http://www.rg.ru/2012/06/21/reg-ufo/voinovich.html> [accessed 12 March 2014].
[335] Tatiana Bek, 'Vladimir Voinovich i ego geroi', *Literatura* (Appendix to the newpaper *Pervoe sentiabria*), No. 24, 2000, <http://lit.1september.ru/article.php?ID=200002401> [accessed 10 March 2014].
[336] Ibid.
[337] Fazil Iskander, 'Stoianka cheloveka', op. cit.
[338] Tatiana Bek, 'Vladimir Voinovich i ego geroi', op. cit.

novel was finally published in the writer's homeland, to which he was able to return, once his Soviet citizenship was restored in 1990. In 2007 Voinovich produced the third book, 'Displaced Person', of what has thus become a trilogy on Chonkin, in the genre described as the 'anecdotal novel'.

Culture of the anecdote and volcanic humour of Vladimir Vysotsky

The relevance of anecdote as a genre to various types of literary humour in Russia since 1960s can be traced as well in the songs of Vladimir Vysotsky, who also adhered to the aforementioned tradition of compassion to a 'small' person and of disavowing the officialdom with its pathos and hypocrisy. Vysotsky, for many – a hero symbolizing the time and epoch, undoubtedly continued Pushkinian line – of cheerful freedom, of life-affirming humour, interwoven with the tragic, as a means of survival and resistance to Necessity. In many ways, he epitomized the whole archetype – that of a 'genuine' Russian character – what Gogol meant with respect to Pushkin: 'Pushkin is an exceptional phenomenon and, perhaps, the only phenomenon of the Russian spirit: he is a Russian developed to a point which perhaps all Russians will achieve in two hundred years. Russian nature, the Russian soul, the Russian language and the Russian character are reflected in him with such unadulterated, pure beauty as one sees in a landscape reflected in the convex surface of an optic lens.'[339] And it is not surprising that the outstanding Russian historian Natan Eidelman in his lecture of 1983, when mapping Vysotsky's place in history, in the line of comparable historic personalities in (predominantly) Russian culture, names Pushkin among them, alongside the famous Decembrist Lunin and the writer Saltykov-Shchedrin.[340] Notably, Eidelman also mentions Don Quixote, whose life credo, 'Freedom, my friend Sancho, is one of the very few things in the world which is worth dying for',[341] is so consonant with Vysotsky's sensibility. Gogol's words about Pushkin from the aforementioned note, which develop the main claim of the poet mirroring the whole Russian national spirit, can be applied to Vysotsky with the same force: 'His very lifestyle is nothing but Russian. [. . .] he was affected by that same debauchery and liberty for which Russians sometimes strive when they forget themselves. [. . .] Bold deeds are easier to understand and they animate the soul more forcibly and expansively. [. . .] No other poet in Russia had such an enviable fate as did Pushkin. No one's fame spread so quickly.'[342] [Similarly, Vysotsky's songs could be heard from every window, played out on the first – primitive – recorders].

---

[339] Nikolai Gogol, 'A few words about Pushkin', in *Arabesques*, transl. by Alexander Tulloch, Ann Arbor, MI: Ardis, 1982, p. 109.

[340] Natan Eidelman, 'Vladimir Vysotksy v kontekste istorii', <http://otblesk.com/vysotsky/i-edelm1.htm> [accessed 14 March 2014].

[341] Cited in Eidelman, op. cit., <http://otblesk.com/vysotsky/i-edelm3.htm> [accessed 14 March 2014].

[342] Nikolai Gogol, 'A few words about Pushkin', op. cit., p. 110.

'There was already something electrifying about his name. [. . .] A poet can even be nationalistic when he is describing a completely strange country, although observing it with the eyes of his own national element, the eyes of the whole nation, when he feels in such a way that his fellow countrymen think that they are feeling and saying these things themselves.'[343] [Again, very few Russian poets – and Vysotsky is among these together with Pushkin – had lines in their poetry that entered the language and were used in the everyday speech as proverbs and folk-wisdom, without even remembering the original source]. [. . .] 'his brush flies. His short play always stands like a complete poem. He is a rare poet indeed who can include in a short play [in Vysotsky's case – in a song] so much grandeur, simplicity and power as one finds in Pushkin's.'[344]

Notably, in Gogol's descriptions, Pushkin's oeuvre is in harmony with the poet's personality. The same is true of Vysotsky, although he was of different temperament and represented a sensibility which, in its strivings to the extreme, exemplifies the phenomenon of Russian irrationalism in its concentrated form. Not only did Vysotsky give voice to the suffocated nation, but he also consolidated the best features of national culture, having combined creative and passionate intensity, a romantic dream embodied in the tour-de-force of an individual self-immolation, with the utmost inner freedom. All the superlatives in the previous sentence are intentional, that is to say, justified – for this is precisely the *podvizhnichestvo* (подвижничество), identified by Averintsev as a hallmark of the peaks of Russian cultural consciousness.[345]

Interestingly Eidelman, speaking only 3 years after Vysotsky's untimely death, prophetically describes a complex path of the poet's heritage – as a function of time – that lies ahead in terms of its reception and treatment. Instructively, in this respect too he draws a parallel with Pushkin, 'When Pushkin died, there came several beautiful, spontaneous artistic impulses. [. . .] But then [. . .], well, it's not as if his popularity started to drop, but it changed. [. . .] This reflects not just a "lack of poets", but a lack of a certain public mood. [. . .] Every master experiences his first life, and then second, and then third . . . [For Vysotsky] it will be a long and complex life. In some sense it will be no less complex than that which he experienced when he was alive. Well, we were his contemporaries during his first life, and will be his contemporaries during the second, and maybe the third . . . Because we are connected with history as one whole [. . .]. And Vysotsky is a historical figure. [. . .] Whether you like it, or not. It does not matter – he is. And this says it all.'[346]

Vysotsky's style and choice of genre grow from urban romance, brewed on Soviet realia, and equally absorb balladas, folk songs, anecdotes and fairy-tales. With his perfect mastership and feel of Russian language, he endowed a crowd with speech – not through descending to the mob level as some think, but on the contrary by elevating it to a higher plane and evoking catharsis. Just as Iskander or Brodsky, Vysotsky too

---

[343] Ibid.

[344] Nikolai Gogol, 'A few words about Pushkin', op. cit., pp. 110–11.

[345] Sergei Averintsev, 'O nekotorykh konstantakh traditsionnogo russkogo soznaniia', in Sergei Averintsev, *Sviaz vremen*, op. cit.

[346] Natan Eidelman, 'Vladimir Vysotksy v kontekste istorii', op. cit., <http://otblesk.com/vysotsky/i-edelm4.htm> [accessed 12 March 2014].

worked mostly in lyrical epos; and akin to Chekhov, he created a huge canvas of characters whom he gave distinctive voices. Not only people of all sorts and social strata spoke in the poetry of his songs, but so did also the inanimate and even ideal world – mountain echo, a fighter plane, a pacing horse, herbarium insects as well as truth, lie and love themselves. His world is based on comradeship, on human dedication, on immutable, eternal values that resist all the deviance and temporality of political regimes; it looks outward, it listens to the Other with intense, attentive sensitivity and is opposite to solipsism. Vysotsky's phonics, acute and rich as musical hearing, involves what can be called his vocal discovery: lingering over consonants, rather than vowels as was traditionally done. His distinctive poetic devices are anthropomorphism and alliteration, as well as most sophisticated rhymes, reminiscent of Mayakovsky's poetics. They frame a giant universe of metaphors and allegories, and, most importantly, they lay bare infinite resources of language, layer after layer. If anthropomorphism is perhaps one of the brightest stars in this poetic universe, its oxygen is Vysotsky's volcanic humour, which always combines syntacsis with semantics and reveals the extreme potential of language. If you like, Vysotsky's humour is linguistic in character, for it grows from the nature of language itself. In a way, the same phenomenon can be observed in Saltykov-Shchedrin's oeuvre: 'linguistic discoveries, exposure of unexpected, rough, sharp combinations, and suddenly, in the collision of these combinations, some totally unexpected truth is revealed.'[347]

Intellectual wit of Mikhail Zhvanetsky: Between poetry and sociological absurd, the bankruptcy of contemporary humour

Vysotsky's is a very different (and rarer) type of humour than an intellectual wit, say, of Mikhail Zhvanetsky – another name without which the canon of Russian literary humour would certainly be incomplete. Zhvanetsky, a satirical writer, who also started his career in the 1960s, is what in the West one calls a stand-up comedian, although his humorous texts were performed by others as well – played out as theatrical performances, and later on published. Zhvanetsky's humour is of sociological and broader – of anthropological – orientation, and delivered by essentially poetic prose. Andrei Bitov contemplating the enigma of Zhvanetsky's enormous popularity compares it to that of Vysotsky, although in contrast to the latter, Bitov comments quizzically, all Zhvanetsky has to operate with is 'just prose'. However, 'this is prose just by one feature: it has no rhyme. The meaning flies between words with the speed inherent only in poetry.'[348] Zhvanetsky's prose indeed easily crosses the border into the poetic realm and becomes free verse. As Valerii Krasnopolsky comments, 'Mikhail Zhvanetsky has his own unique rhythm; his prose is distinguished by a high semantic charge of every word,

[347] Natan Eidelman, 'Vladimir Vysotksy v kontekste istorii', op. cit., <http://otblesk.com/vysotsky/i-edelm2.htm> [accessed 13 March 2014].

[348] Andrei Bitov, 'Zhvanetsky Mikhail. Pod kupolom glasnosti', in *Bagazh*, ArsisBooks: Moscow, 2012.

rhythmic completeness of every phrase, and a subtle sense of intonational periods in every line, without which a true vers-libre is impossible. Constantly balancing on the boundary of poetry and rhythmic prose, skilfully wielding form, Zhvanetsky, at critical moments, masterly escapes from banal logical and rhythmic solutions.'[349]

In a very different register than Vysotsky, Zhvanetsky too has painted the panorama of Soviet life as existential laboratory. 'Zhvanetsky is brave as silence. We do not hear him. We hear ourselves. Zhvanetsky is our silence which has suddenly, after all these years, become so expressive!'[350] This is Andrei Bitov's paradoxical formula which sums up the irrational nucleus of Zhvanetsky's humour – as a prism refracting the quintessence of the irrationalism and absurdity of life. Notably, the writer himself observes in his typical aphoristic manner, 'What is humour? It is salvation. And what are tears? They are life. Therefore laughter through tears is our main achievement during all the years of our existence.'[351] Once again, we observe a fusion of poetry, intellect and laughter through tears – a sad underpinning of the funny, a means for survival, salvation and liberation. Indeed, in Zhvanetsky's words, 'Humour is not jokes. It is not words. It is not an old lady who slipped. Humour is not even Chaplin. Humour is a rare state of a talented person and talented time, when you are merry and clever at the same time. And you cheerfully discover the laws by which people move. Humour is a prerogative of the low strata. [. . .] As for us, it helps us survive. It brings us closer. Welcome to an anecdote as to a treat.'[352] As Zhvanetsky's epigraph to this chapter stated, 'under pressure from without, humour is born from within.'[353] Furthermore, 'humour, like life, is fleeting and unique', because structurally (and semantically alike), 'only once [. . .] can one compress the truth to the size of a formula, and the formula to the size of a witty remark.'[354] This means in particular that, precisely as in art generally, cliché is impossible, it means artistic death.

However, the post-Soviet cultural space looks very differently to the Soviet one, because the evil, which used to have distinctly delineated borders in Soviet times, has become blurred and all-pervasive, and hence, scarier: 'To preserve the purity of your conscience was easier during the Soviet power than it is today.'[355] This is because, at that time, crossing the (distinctly visible) borders between good and evil was a self-conscious act – 'If you, despite the voice of conscience, crossed these boundaries, you knew what you were doing. It was a free manifestation of your personal will and therefore not too scary. [. . .] During the Soviet power there was a certainty that it cannot get any worse. Now there is no such certainty. The Soviet power, having forced

[349] Valerii Krasnopolsky, Foreword to Mikhail Zhvanetsky's 'Verlibry', *Oktiabr*, 2004, No. 3, <http://magazines.russ.ru/october/2004/3/zhvan4.html> [accessed 14 March 2014].

[350] Andrei Bitov, 'Zhvanetsky Mikhail. Pod kupolom glasnosti', op. cit.

[351] Mikhail Zhvanetsky, 'Chto takoe iumor?' <http://www.jvanetsky.ru/data/text/t8/chto_takoe_umor/> [accessed 15 March 2014]. Fazil Iskander's words are highly resonant with the above sentiments of Zhvanetsky: 'Humour is the last reality of optimism. So let's take advantage of this (I nearly said "sad") reality' (see <http://lib.rus.ec/b/132545/read#t5> [accessed 15 March 2014]).

[352] Ibid.

[353] Ibid.

[354] Ibid.

[355] Interview with Fazil Iskander (*Rossiiskaia Gazeta*, 04.03.2011), <http://www.rg.ru/2011/03/04/iskander.html> [accessed 16 March 2014]).

us into a pit, thus protected us from an abyss'.[356] These thoughts of Iskander, because of their broad scope, have bearing also on the nature of post-Soviet humour.

Sergei Averintsev's similar contemplations make the connection evident and further-reaching – applicable to the globalized world more generally, part of which Russia has in many ways become. 'There is not, and there cannot be, any humour without an opposition of inter-connected poles, without contrast between conservative values and rebellion, between rule and exception, between norm and pragmatics, between stable taboos of the inherited ethics and the mores of the particular, singular and real; moreover, it is necessary that this opposition is perceived as sharp, that it really brings one to tears – but to laughter too – otherwise what kind of humour would it be? But this means that human being is capable of humour in that case and in that measure in which he remains capable of obeying commandments and prohibitions'.[357] Hence, when this prerequisite of humour is no longer fulfilled, humour naturally comes to a halt. 'If the dialectical premise of humor and comic is uncompromising, unyielding seriousness, then, on the other hand, frivolity, so typical for the current times, ubiquitous, monotonous, widely accepted and no longer shocking for anyone, even not attracting anyone's attention, this frivolity, in the sphere of which nothing is any longer black or white, but gray only – means the end of humor. Humans have a fatal choice between an absence of humor and seriousness; and there is no middle ground'.[358]

In particular, this returns us to the eternal problems posed by classical Russian literature, most notably by Dostoevsky: a narrow rationalism is unable to solve the irrational mystery of human soul. Thus, in Averintsev's words, translating existential problems from the moral to psychological sphere and solving them in a medical way leads humanity to a dead-end: 'too comfortable and trouble-free, in a word – too anesthetized, life becomes devoid of significance, and then it is no longer worth living'.[359] Ironically though, such a life, where 'commandments' and 'prohibitions' ('заветы и запреты') have been broken, serves itself as a source of humour – but only for those, of course, who are still aware of the violated taboos. One of the writers first to capture such a life on paper with all its tragic comism is Viktor Pelevin. 'Offering playful but devastating perceptions of his contemporary society', Pelevin 'reflects the current state of confusion in Russian culture as it absorbs Western capitalist ideas, vocabulary and consumer goods'.[360] The crisis is, however, broader, as it affects Western society just as well, conditioned by the shift of values, which, as Averintsev argues, leads ultimately to a meaningless existence, where, in particular, humour has degenerated too.

Mikhail Zhvanetsky, speaking of the state of humour in Russia today, says rather bitterly, 'one has to alternate laughter and tears [. . .]. Because, if one speaks of the truth of life, then laughter always has a sad underpinning. If it is not there, but you are still

---

[356] Ibid.
[357] Sergei Averintsev, 'O dukhe vremeni i chuvstve iumora', in Sergei Averintsev, *Sviaz vremen*, op. cit.
[358] Ibid.
[359] Ibid.
[360] Milne, *Reflective Laughter. Aspects of Humour in Russian Culture*, op. cit., p. 94.

laughing – you are an idiot. But we are now laughing and laughing, while there is no sadness, no regrets, no truth of life.'[361]

That is why extreme rationalism, as seen through the Enlightenment example with its attempts to exterminate human suffering, also exterminates humour, since the comic is an inseparable companion of the serious and sad. That is why also the cultural crisis of modernity affects our (irrational) ability to laugh, and, paradoxically at the first glance, but in fact not surprisingly, it is only our return to the tragic morality and the difficult world of conscience, which had been so intensely propagated by classical Russian literature, that can redeem and preserve our humour. Thus the Russian tradition of (intrinsically poetic) humourous discourse, which sustains highly lyrical laughter through tears and self-irony as its main streams, has far more importance than it may rationally seem.

---

[361] From the interview with Mikhail Zhvanetsky (*Komsomolskaia Pravda*, 08.10.2010), <http://www.kp.ru/daily/24571/743880/> [accessed 21 February 2014].

Index